.

ECHOES

FROM THE

WELSH HILLS

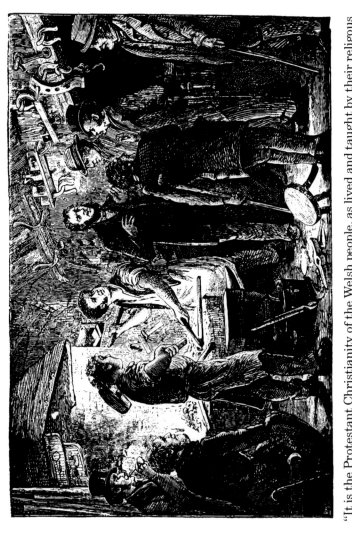

"It is the Protestant Christianity of the Welsh people, as lived and taught by their religous teachers during the last two centuries and a half, that has preserved them from ignorance, lawlessness, and irreligion, and made of them one of the most Scripturally-enlightened, loyal and religious nations on the face of the earth." —p.143.

Echoes

FROM THE

Welsh Hills;

*Or Reminiscences of the Preachers
and People of Wales.*

BY
REV. DAVID DAVIES,
WESTON-SUPER-MARE,
(Author of "The New Name and other Sermons")
ILLUSTRATED BY T. H. THOMAS, R.C.A.

Stoke-on-Trent:
Tentmaker Publications
2000

Tentmaker Publications
121 Hartshill Road, Hartshill, Stoke-on-Trent, ST4 7LU.

ISBN: 1 899003 31 2

2000

Originally published by
Alexander and Shepheard
21, Castle Street, Holburn, E.C.
1883

This edition, completely re-typeset.

THIS BOOK

IS

AFFECTIONATELY DEDICATED

TO THE MEMORY

OF

MY MOTHER

Preface

THESE are but very few of the many echoes which have reached my ears. This book has been closed, not because the old friends have given up talking in the smithy or the life of the villagers has ceased to be interesting, but because I dare not allow the work to become more bulky.

There are Welsh institutions, customs, and characteristics which have scarcely been referred to in these pages; they did not chance to come up in the conversations which took place during one winter and spring in Shadrach's workshop or David Lewis's parlour. Even the references to preachers and religious services, which are the staple of discussion in this, as in almost every other smithy throughout the Principality, on rainy days and wintry nights, have been few compared with the thousand sayings of Welsh preachers, which are repeated by enthusiastic admirers in the fields and workshops of the land. How inadequately can friends, in occasional social gatherings, extending over one year or less, reproduce the reminiscences of preachers with which every hamlet in Wales abounds! Some names which are household words have only been incidentally referred to here, while others of scarcely less note have not been mentioned at all. It will appear to every thoughtful reader that the task of reproducing in an English garb customs, sayings, and modes of thought which are essentially Welsh is one that necessarily involves many drawbacks. The charming simplicity of many a custom and incident, the force and pertinence of well-known idioms, as well as the quaintness and beauty of certain turns of expression, to say nothing of a rich variety of cadence peculiar to the Welsh voice and language, must, to some extent, be sacrificed in the transformation. It is seldom that the translation conveys the whole meaning and beauty of the original. By translation, too, the conversation between the friends in the smithy is robbed of that freshness and attractiveness with which a local dialect would invest it.

With a keen sense of these deficiencies and many others, which in better hands would have been more successfully supplied, I send the book forth in the fervent hope that in some measure it may prove worthy of its theme. My aim has been to illustrate in a popular form the religious and social life of the Welsh people, their generous hospitality, ardent loyalty and patriotism, as well as the quaint humour, the poetic fancy, and rich pathos of their religious teachers. Whatever I may have lacked in the discharge of this congenial task, I was moved to undertake it by an enthusiastic admiration of, and love for, my countrymen, and by the firm conviction that now, when so many of the disabilities formerly imposed upon them have been removed, and the English Government is beginning to show an unprecedented interest in their higher education, they are destined to play no secondary part in the commercial growth and moral advancement of the united peoples of this realm.

I gratefully acknowledge my indebtedness to my Welsh friends who have courteously supplied me with any information which I sought to obtain, as also to the three hundred subscribers who many months ago ordered copies of the book.

Should this effort receive a kindly welcome, I hope at some future time to publish a companion volume.*

DAVID DAVIES
Wentworth,
Shrubbery Walks,
Weston-super-Mare,
May 10, 1883.

---

* *John Vaughan and His Friends or More Echoes from the Welsh Hills* by Revd. David Davies, London, 1897. A reprint of this book is available from Tentmaker Publications.

Contents

NOTE.—The allusion to the sick child in page 216 was given by the Preacher on the occasion mentioned as an illustration from "Gravenhurst."—D.D.

CHAPTER I

𝔗𝔥𝔢 𝔙𝔦𝔩𝔩𝔞𝔤𝔢

THE heart of Wales there nestles among the hills a little village the name of which would be more than a match for any of my English readers to pronounce, and even when pronounced would still remain an inexplicable mystery. Such names were never intended for Saxon tongues, and the beauty of their rhythm and the richness of their melody were never adapted to that strangely sensitive construction called the "English ear". Let the name of that hamlet therefore be among those of unknown villages to which the world owes a great debt and but for which life would lack much of its simple beauty and rugged force.

The everlasting hills surround and caress in their mighty yet tender embrace this little hamlet. All round the scores of humble homesteads of which it consists, excepting at one narrow outlet, an amphitheatre of hills rises gracefully toward the sky to catch every gleam of sunshine and every changeful shade of passing clouds. In early summer the slopes are adorned with patches of ripening corn, and with rich pasture-land where sheep fleck the verdant fields and where cattle graze the fresh green herbage or browse on the tender shoots of the luxuriant hedgerows. The village reposing peacefully in the hollow seems half asleep to the busy townsman who chances to pass by. The greater part of the small population are at work in the fields, only an occasional house-wife on her way to or from the well carrying the pitcher on her head, her hands meanwhile busily engaged in knitting, or an honest peasant taking a horse to the smithy to be shod, or a knot or two of children at play, may as a rule be seen during the busy hours of the day, while only the distant low of the cattle on the neighbouring slopes, or the harmonious sounds from the village anvil, break upon the stillness which reigns around. One traces but little of the rush of life in this secluded hamlet, but finds much of its sacred hush. There is here none of the crowding and elbowing which so mar human existence in our large towns, and there is almost as little of that burning enthusiasm which expresses itself often in the more honourable activities of our commercial centres. Here, each one has his niche and is happy, ambition does not distract and as a rule does not inspire. To one wearied out of all patience with the persistent and almost cruel din of town life, there is something indescribably sweet and soothing in the whole scene. It is such a place as any one longing to go for a short time out of *man's* world into *God's,* delights to find. It is one of the many *unknown* Bethanys of earth, a fit resting-place for wearied men, and home of contented ones; where love and simplicity delight to dwell, but where few of the world's ambitions linger.

Through the hamlet there runs an old turnpike road, which long since was constructed at considerable labour and cost, excavated as it is in many places out of the solid rock, notably at the summit of the two hills which it crests, the one as it dips into the village, and the other as it emerges from the hollow on the other side. For many years this road continued to be the scene of much traffic. In addition to the stage coach and the ordinary market vehicles, long and frequent processions of wagons and carts passed along at certain seasons on their way for coal and lime, to say nothing of the well known but mysterious-looking cheese and butter hawker, who in the days of smuggling drove through on his way to "the hills"* to ply his trade, and who not unfrequently concealed in what appeared to be butter casks, many a keg of brandy and gin, called respectively by the wily trader and the initiated customers of "the hills" yellow and white cheese.

In the centre of the village is the inn, where the horses were supplied with water, and where their drivers, the honest wagoners, who suffered

---

* Merthyr Tydvil and Neighbourhood

from a chronic feeling of dryness, were refreshed with something stronger. Next to the inn, and on the corner of cross roads, whence there is a commanding view of the approaches to the village, is the old smithy, where the horses were shod, and broken-down vehicles repaired. The smithy corner, as long as men can remember, has been the centre of interest, the spot where the villagers in their leisure hours have been accustomed to congregate. There, many years ago, the forefathers of the village used to meet to the merry music of harp and violin, many of whom, according to tradition, were droll and jovial fellows, and in their day were the life of the neighbourhood, whose presence was always the signal for a good-natured laugh, who were perfect adepts at telling amusing stories and cracking innocent jokes, and whose jests and pleasant sayings still live in the memories of those who have survived them, though they themselves rest in peaceful slumber in the parish churchyard, or in the Nonconformist burying-places close by.

Many years have passed, too, since the stage coach, the long train of lime and coal wagons, and the suspicious-looking butter vendor have disappeared, for within a few miles a new turnpike road in a more direct line has been constructed, and that in turn has been superseded by a railway running through one of the many valleys which in that district separate the hills. In addition to these reasons, the fact that very few, if any, of what the old butterman was pleased to call "yellow and white cheeses," are now washed up on the Cardigan shore has made his journey, and those of a kindred nature, things of the past. The world jogs on in another way now, while the old butter-vendor for many years has laid him down in deep slumber in some obscure village burying-ground where trickery is unknown, and all falsities are for ever silenced.

No longer is there a constant cross-firing between the village wits on the smithy corner and the droll fellows from the adjacent county who used to pass through. Even the disparaging epithets which the sons of each county exchanged in good spirit are now all but forgotten.

In general, the advance of commerce has shut this little hamlet more than ever out of the world. It is one of those places which suffer in that massacre of the innocents which must to some extent accompany all progress. A few of its speculative and ambitious sons, impelled by news of prosperity in other districts and other lands, have left the hamlet in which they were born, and which is still dear to them, and are engaged in many instances in the sterner battle of life as fought in large centres of activity, but the majority continue to adorn the same callings as their fathers, and on the spot made sacred to them by a thousand traditions.

Most of the old institutions of the village remain. The smithy, the shoemaker's, and tailor's shops continue as they were. The inn, however, has undergone a change for the worse. Indeed, in the halcyon days of the stage coach, there was a second inn in the village which prospered moderately well, but that suffered extinction so many years ago, that it has well nigh been forgotten. The sign-board, which has so long since been taken down, has been preserved and fixed upon four legs by the village carpenter, and, thus transformed into a table, it still remains in the family of the former proprietors as a curious relic of past prosperity. The old "Greyhound," who from his exalted position in former days looked down with graceful pride upon every passer by, now peeps dimly through the faded paint with grim astonishment at the vanity of all earthly things. Even *the* inn, which still exists and is known as "The Village Inn," has ill-survived the changes which time and progress have wrought. If the last rumour be true, the Temperance Movement has almost completed the havoc which the construction of a local railway began. On one wintry night, we are told, the sign-board fell down with a melancholy thud. Since then, the exchequer has not been sufficiently flourishing to justify the struggling landlord in replacing it. It is, therefore, through the charity of our amiable artist that the old "sign" is still represented as swinging upon its hinges at the bidding of every summer breeze, as well as creaking forth its sad tale of better days to the accompaniment of the dolorous moan of the wintry wind.

Other houses remain; a few in more modern garb, but others as they were from the beginning, with scarcely an improvement save the periodical thatch, and the annual white-washing within and without. The two chapels of the village, the one belonging to the Baptists, and the other to the Calvinistic Methodists—the Independent Chapel chances to be about a mile distant—are the buildings which appear to be in the best condition, having been more than once enlarged, or rebuilt, and undergone many other important improvements since they were first erected. These sanctuaries represent an important change which has taken place in the life of the villagers. The older of the two has only a history of a little over a century and a half and compared with that of most of the Free Churches in Wales, it is an exceptionally long one. In the graveyards surrounding these village chapels lie the ashes of the past four generations; the dust of earlier ancestors rests about three miles distant in the Parish Churchyard, situated in one of the many quiet and fruitful valleys which hide themselves among the majestic hills of ancient Cambria.

CHAPTER II

𝔗𝔥𝔢 𝔓𝔞𝔯𝔦𝔰𝔥 𝔆𝔥𝔲𝔯𝔠𝔥

HE Parish Church is an ancient structure, grey and damp with the mildew of centuries. Concealed among the stately trees which surround it in that romantic glen, and disfigured by the deep scars which Time, that merciless destroyer, has inflicted upon it, and which modern art has not tried to hide or soften with its charitable and transforming touch, the old church looks as if it belonged to another age, and not to this. The church-yard, too, has the same desolate appearance. Broken slabs and frag-ments of tomb-stones of different shapes and dimensions lie about in every conceivable position, as if long ages ago they had marked the graves of the antediluvians, but the Deluge, in visiting those stony tablets, had rudely shaken them, and in some instances had cruelly swept them from their places to lie in inglorious confusion as the shattered records of a dead and forgotten past. Thus in this secluded spot even graves, which as a rule are but too freshly dug in this our mortal world, have become sadly old, and but for a very occasional grave that is opened, or tombstone erected, it would seem as if Death himself had died, and thus there were no more to follow. But "thereby hangs a tale." The humble peasantry have gradually severed themselves from the temples and resting places of their fathers, choosing in their life to worship God in humbler edifices erected by their own toil and maintained by their own self-denial, and in their death preferring to sleep in those little plots which surround the sanctuaries where they first met their God, and where since then they have often conversed with Him.

Near the Church, on the opposite side of the road, is the public house. For generations the closest relationship continued to exist between these two institutions. The declaration of Charles the First, further confirmed by the cordial assent and blessing of so pious and distinguished a dignitary as Archbishop Laud, concerning lawful sports to be used upon Sundays and upon holy days, was most religiously observed for very many years in this parish by all who attended church, from the parson downward. Thus, as the house of God closed, the other house opposite opened to receive the bulk of the congregation, who by common consent looked upon what was to follow as by far the most interesting part of the day's proceedings. To them, tortured as they had been by having to listen to an English clergyman who knew next to nothing of the Welsh language, reading a sermon about which he knew still less, a convivial glass and a spirited game of football were a welcome relief. A good kick was the same in both languages, and few could beat the parson at that. There was one clergyman in particular of whom the oldest people speak frequently. He was a novice at preaching, especially in Welsh, but he had excelled in football ever since he was a boy at Eton, and that was his forte when in the University. The clerk at the time to which they specially refer was too old for the sports; he did his part in drinking the health of the parson and the success of the game, and that we are told he did right well. In those days the church was well attended, especially as the hour for football drew near. There were a few who, notwithstanding they sometimes failed to come to the church service, never failed to be in time for the other engagement, and thus made up for lost opportunities.

Since then things have greatly changed. Some of the reformers of the last century visited this parish on their journeys through Wales. They spoke to men in their own tongue, and the words they uttered were struck off at white heat. They denounced the evils of Sunday sports with irresistible eloquence, and in less than half a century after the first revival the Welsh people had turned their backs upon the Established Church and the games associated with its services. The church in this parish, in common with almost every other parish in Wales, is not in *any* sense the church of the people. There is still a pew reserved in it for "the squire," and two or three for neighbouring farmers, who are supposed to attend the services, but the whole country has deserted the old church, and the honest peasantry on Sundays and other stated times stream to their little Bethels or Bethanys on hill and dale, forgetful of the hoary sanctuary, whose associations, though ancient, have no sacredness for them save that they link them to the sepulchres of their fathers.

The last clergyman, or rather the one who until within a few years ago officiated at this ancient church, had been there for fifty years, and thus, from long residence on his living had, like his pulpit, become a kind of sacred fixture He was a jovial, good-natured man, without his equal in the neighbourhood on the hunting field, and was generally acknowledged to be the best judge of a good bottle of port in the whole county. As a preacher, however, he dealt largely in what the people significantly called "cawl dw'r," or water broth, a concoction to which the poorest of the peasantry are forced to resort in exceptionally hard times, and which has not even the most distant savour of meat about it, but consists of water, a little of the hereditary leek cut up, a sprig of parsley minced, a pinch of oatmeal, and salt to taste. Hence they apply the words "cawl dw'r" to a species of spiritual food which is not too rich, but which is rather profitable for banting, and in that sense they used the phrase in referring to this clergyman's sermons. His voice, possessing as it did a marvellous compass, had enough of thunder in it, but unfortunately it lacked the lightning. It contrasted strangely, too, if not comically, with that of the clerk, a little tailor, whose voice always produced the impression that he gave the responses through a pipe-stem—so celestially thin was it. Some of the unsympathizing people, struck by this strange contrast in the responses at the very occasional funeral services which they attended at church, irreverently designated it bubble and squeak," the name by which it was henceforth known, a phrase, too, strangely enough applied to a savoury preparation of bacon and cabbage fried together, the words "bubble and squeak" being expressive of the conflicting noises in the frying-pan as the cooking went on. Whether or not the one exercise was in any way associated with the other in the mind of the wag who first applied the phrase to parson and clerk it is impossible to divine, and how far the comparison held good none but those who witnessed both performances and heard their discordant sounds could judge. Would that these had been the only failings of the two who thus ministered in holy things in this ancient sanctuary. Would that their natural unfitness had not been supplemented and aggravated by far more serious defects in character and life; but enough, their part is played, the curtain is dropped for ever, and the good old villagers have long since commended them and their irregularities to those "uncovenanted mercies" which are far more tender than our covenanted ones. The story of the sporting parson and his clerk happily belongs to a state of things which is fast becoming obsolete even in the Established Church in Wales, a consummation as devoutly wished by the hundreds of thousands who are without its pale as by the smaller number who still cling to it and mourn sadly over its sullied history and its dishonoured name.

The present clergyman is of a very different type from any of his predecessors. Had they resembled him more the Established Church in Wales would have had another aspect now. Fervent speech and a holy life on the part of those who were the recognised religious guides of others would have then won a highly sensitive and enthusiastic people into that Church's embrace, but the opportunity has gone by, and gone, it would seem, for ever.

Thus the ecclesiastical policy of appointing English clergymen to Welsh livings, who, for various reasons into which it were better not to inquire, were unfit for similar spheres in England, men who neither knew the Welsh language nor sympathized with the people, and who in the majority of instances were never qualified by gifts or grace for the ministry of love to which they were nominally devoted—a state of things which continued for centuries—has emptied the churches of the Establishment throughout Wales, and there seems to be no prospect of their being ever filled again. The deep conviction of one of the noblest sons of the Church in Wales, who died without its fold because in the dark times in which he lived he dared to preach beyond his own parish, a conviction which on his lips assumed the solemnity if not the authority of an inspired prophecy, that "the bees would return again to the old hive" ("Fe ddychwel y gwenyn ir hên gwch etto") seems to be as far from realization to-day as when first uttered by his dying lips. The old hive, we are glad to know and grateful to testify, has been cleansed from most of its former impurities, but since that "son of thunder" uttered his solemn prediction the bees have found other hives, and are no longer shelterless seeking a home. The church of which we speak—like most others from Holyhead to Cardiff—is a deserted hive; but who will blame the bees? And if they never return, what wonder?

CHAPTER III

𝕿𝔥𝔢 𝖁𝔦𝔩𝔩𝔞𝔤𝔢 𝕾𝔠𝔥𝔬𝔬𝔩

OUT half a mile distant from the village the old school-house still stands, although in a dilapidated condition and no longer fit for use. It is a building of a very primitive type, and has a chequered history reaching far into the past. Even fifty years ago various portions of the walls threatened to dissolve partner-ship, but the friendly ivy came to the rescue, bound in its loving embrace the disunited parts, and, like charity, covered many a glaring defect and gaping cranny in the frail structure. The building consisted of four plain walls sadly out of square, with openings in them which passed for windows, but which were quite as convenient for ventilation as for the admission of light, a door about four feet high, and crowning all an ancient thatch, which for many years and while yet in use produced a crop of grass that would have done credit to any plot of pasture-land of the same size, and which no hungry horse could see without being moved with strange yearnings for a longer neck.

The pedagogue, to whom for many years the instruction of the rising race was entrusted, had in his earlier days been a soldier, and after various services in foreign fields had returned to his native land *minus* important parts of his frame, which he had left in the trenches as a testimony of his fidelity to his country and his loyalty to his king. As described on one occasion by an "old boy"—the tender recollection of those early days of discipline meanwhile giving a strange quivering modulation to the voice, which might either express the comic or the pathetic according to the disposition of the one who listened—"He was a battered fragment of a fine specimen of humanity, a tempest-tossed brother, the greater part of whom consisted of timber, put together and repaired gratuitously by a patriotic carpenter of the neighbourhood. At school the first lesson, as a rule, which he gave to a new boy in mental and moral philosophy was a box in the ears, and if a boy happened to be rather more earthly than the rest he was made to stand upon as little of earth as possible—on one leg—thus affording a better opportunity for the upper region to reflect and consider."

He was the scribe of the whole neighbourhood, and was an adept at writing love-letters for the young swains and their blushing damsels, in which sweet exercise it fell to his lot not uncommonly to answer his own epistles, a task which he rendered easier by anticipation. Many a palpitating heart unbosomed its secrets into his ear, and as the sentiments of all hearts are much alike at such seasons the old soldier had a set of phrases at hand expressive of every shade of sentiment, which he called into requisition with great promptitude and ease, and gauged skilfully according to the temperature of his client. His terms withal were exceedingly moderate, for he would cram a genuine sheet of the old-fashioned quarto note paper brimful of the sweetest sentiments and fondest hopes for the nominal consideration of threepence. And who that could not write would not gladly pay that, when in love, for the privilege of having the soul's emotions and upheavings represented in black and white!

During his long service in the army he had mastered the rudiments of learning—reading, writing, and arithmetic—and had learnt to speak English fluently and correctly. He turned these attainments to good account on his return to his native village. In those days he made no little impression on the villagers. This he judiciously maintained by his military bearing, an occasional pet quotation from the poets, which he had learnt from a book of extracts, and a frequent repetition of the magic words, "When I was on the field of Waterloo."

In the school he was looked upon by the boys as a prodigy of military prowess and courage. Notwithstanding the fact already alluded to that there was a deal of timber about him, telling of serious damage sustained, yet *what* timber! It was the same kind as that of which the men-of-war were made. That leg, they knew, was made by Cadwaladr Jones, the village carpenter, out of the very *heart* of oak, and only to think of its thickness and weight! It took a strong man to carry such a leg as that! And then only to look at him! He was a soldier every inch, as erect as his wooden leg was straight. But never did he appear to such advantage in their estimation as when teaching them to throw expression into their recitations; he used to stand erect in the middle of the schoolroom, his head all but touching the rafters, and suiting the action to the word, repeated his favourite couplet from "The Lady of the Lake,"

> "Come one, come all! this rock shall fly
> From its firm base as soon as I."

The boys were lost in admiration. How he brandished his cane and planted his wooden leg upon the stone floor! They were not at all surprised that Napoleon the Great was beaten on the field of Waterloo by their master and the Duke of Wellington!

The school was ruled by military law, specially adapted to the condition of the pupils. Flogging at that time prevailed largely in the army, it was also extensively practised in the old soldier's school. He was an enthusiastic believer in its efficacy, and indulged in it freely when opportunity presented itself. Another favourite method of punishment was to put a fool's cap upon the culprit's head and, placing him upon a form, to make him stand in that exalted position on one leg with his face turned toward the wall and his hands tied behind in order to bring the shoulders well back—as the old pensioner used to say. Should the boy put down for a moment the uplifted foot, or cast a furtive glance at his companions, a ruler would be hurled toward him like a shot out of a cannon, and woe betide the unlucky wight if the aim were true.

The old worthy taught the younger children the alphabet by adapting it to "The March of the Men of Harlech," a song which never failed to arouse within him slumbering memories, or to fan into white heat his patriotic zeal. In closing the school he would at a specified time call "attention" with the authority of a commander on the field of battle, then "stand at ease," then having offered a brief and characteristic prayer would add, "right about face," "quick march"— and the school was dismissed.

Many and amusing are the stories told of the adventures of the wooden leg, and the tricks played upon its owner by the boys. Specially amusing is the story of one humiliating episode which occurred when he was entertaining his admiring pupils with one of those dramatic recitations to which we have referred; how, when his wooden leg stuck fast between the roughly-laid slabs of the schoolroom floor, the hero of Waterloo, impatient of such trivial inconveniences, gave a desperate jerk, which broke the leather strap; how the leg was taken to the shoemaker's by two of the older boys who performed strange exploits with it on the way; how at last, attempting to stop a mill-wheel with it, it sustained, to their surprise and horror, a compound fracture; how the patient old master waited weary hours in vain for his leg, and when at length the sequel was made known it grieved him more than the losing of his first leg on the field of Waterloo. But these and many others are among the things of the past, and with the present generation will be forgotten.

The "Welsh note," or a notched stick, which was given to a boy or girl as a penalty for talking in Welsh, was a favourite device which the old schoolmaster had for discouraging the indulgence on the part of the children in the free exercise of their mother tongue during school hours. The "Welsh note" was called in at stated times, and the unfortunate one who was the bearer of it was submitted to the discipline of the cane. The natural result of all this was that the possessor of the notched stick was very busy during playtime, anxious to confer the privilege upon an unwary companion, and for that purpose would not uncommonly act as a decoy, and, sending out an occasional "feeler" in the form of a Welsh word, would at length catch in an unguarded moment some youthful Briton whose Welsh enthusiasm had been kindled to the point of utterance; and so the game would proceed and the stick would in turn fall to the lot of a large number of children, but it mattered little if they were not the unhappy possessors of it when the schoolmaster called it in, and subjected its owner to a caning.

All this was of course primitive and crude, but it answered its purpose in its day, and prepared the way for another dispensation under Llewellyn Pugh, who accepted the position of schoolmaster when the old pensioned soldier entered into his well-earned rest. He was a man of considerable culture and extensive information, but withal somewhat eccentric. When a young man he had been educated for "holy orders," but in some way or other he had departed from the prescribed course, and had become estranged in sympathy from the Church at whose altar he was appointed by his parents to serve. He used to say that when he went to the University he was piously inclined, but that ever since he had looked upon it as a miracle of grace that they had not made an atheist of him. "Thank God," he used to add, "I am a Christian still."

When asked what induced him after all his advantages to come back to his native hamlet and live the obscure life of a village schoolmaster, he used to say, and his eyes moistened as he proceeded:— "Ah, it takes a long time—longer than my short life—to snap the bonds which early scenes and associations bind round our heart. They hold a hallowed place in the recollections of later days. How sacred to memory and dear to heart are the homes of our childhood and the land of our birth—the rich green meadows—the rugged hills and hoary mountains—the wild stream rushing down the hill-side, leaping impetuously from crag to crag, until at length it pours its playful and sparkling life into the quiet majestic river in the valley beneath—the sturdy oaks and the stately elms with whose every branch we were once familiar—the narrow glens with the same old paths here and there as when we were children—the fields and the woods where we made garlands for the brows of our little sisters, for brows which wear other garlands now, woven and placed there by a divine and loving hand. Well, all is over; a thousand tendrils have since then been broken and have sorely bled; and *yet, yet,* life can never be so sweet as where it gathered its first impressions and sipped its earliest joys, however humble the sphere and obscure the lot. Grander scenes may open before our view and more exalted occupations engage our attention, but none so sacred and none so lovely as those which link us to our birth-place and to our Fatherland."

For some time Llewellyn Pugh continued to teach the children of the village in the old school-house. At length another building more worthy of the teacher was provided, and there for over thirty years, with an intermission of only a fortnight a year, he imparted instruction to those under his charge, which, taking into account the difficulties of language and of place with which he had to contend, would compare favourably with the elementary education given at that time in any part of the land.

In such a humble calling most of his attainments were not in any way called into requisition. The boys knew he could do magnificent flourishes—not, like the old school-master, with the cane in imitation of Fitzjames, but—with his quill. The swans he drew with one flourish of the hand are still shown in old copy-books, and curiosity wonders how many of our schoolmasters could do that to-day.

One feature of Llewellyn Pugh's instruction, which had a great charm over the boys, was his aptness in teaching what very frequently is the driest study—the memory of which many years after has a strange fustiness about it,—viz., mathematics. In his hand it became quite fascinating. He indulged very freely in experiments. He would, for instance, take a birch broom and ask the older scholars, "Boys, how many cubic inches of wood are there in this broom?" Naturally enough they would suggest that as there were so many twigs tied together no one could find the solid measure. To which he would say in a tone of strange misgiving, "Oh, indeed!" and having told one of their number to fetch the schoolroom bucket, place it on the doorstep, and fill it with water, he would quietly dip the top of the broom into the water, and as quietly taking it up again, would bid them measure the number of cubic inches of water which had been displaced. When this was done, he would add with a nod of triumph, *"That* then is the number of cubic inches in the top of the broom; you see, boys, that you must *think* in mathematics."

It will be readily seen from this one instance how, with such an apt method of teaching, even mathematics in his hand became an interesting study.

But we have not seen the last of Llewellyn Pugh.

CHAPTER IV

The Smithy

ORNING, noon, and evening the curling smoke from the smithy and the merry sounds from the anvil tell that Shadrach Morgan, the smith, and his son Jenkin are busy at work. The smithy and the adjoining house were built by Shadrach's father about seventy years ago, and during the period which has intervened have undergone but few changes. In the dwelling-house the old-fashioned, bonnet-shaped chimney, through which one might with ease study astronomy, is precisely the same as when Shadrach's father and his youthful friends sat beneath it to smoke the social pipe and to tell ghost stories in olden times. Beneath the broad chimney, on each side of the fire, are two settles, made of oak and dark with age. At the end of one of these, just at the corner of the large hearth, which extends far into the room, is the long-cased clock, still occupying the same place as that in which it was first placed long before Shadrach's birth, and ticking forth the moments with a deliberation and authority which it seems to have gained with increasing experience and growing age. Like a venerable chronicler with pensive look and quivering hand it records each moment as it flies, and like an eager herald with speedy steps and clear tones it announces the advent of each hour as it comes. It is the only moving, speaking presence which connects the present with the earliest past of that home. Near the clock, and adorned with richly coloured jugs and with the orthodox willow-pattern plates, is the dresser, which Mary, Shadrach's better half, bees-waxes with much energy and perseverance every Saturday. On the opposite side of the room, and immediately beneath the front window, is the table, also of oak, and so substantially made as to promise to be of service to the family for many generations. A mysterious oak cupboard, a massive chest in which the parchments of the smithy are kept, half a dozen chairs and one or two stools, made out of the same infallible wood—to which the Welsh peasantry swear as faithful an allegiance as to their flannel—make up the furniture of the room where Shadrach and his family live. Adjoining this room, in the back part of the house, is the little dairy, just large enough for an establishment which has only one cow. This is a cool room, in which, besides the necessary dairy utensils, Mary Morgan keeps the rack in which are placed very carefully the wooden basins, platters, and spoons. A number of smaller things are also stored there, such as the flour and oatmeal bags, and a large jar containing the remnant of last year's honey. At the end of the house near the smithy is the "parlour." The walls have been partly papered by the busy house-wife, at different times as occasion demanded, and have been decorated by illustrated almanacks of all colours and dimensions, obtained from the tradesmen of the market town about four miles distant. Professional paper-hangers have never touched these walls with their unscrupulous hands, and as long as Mary lives they never will. On different parts hang the likenesses of Daniel Rowlands, Llangeitho, Christmas Evans, W. Williams, of Wern, John Elias, T. Charles, of Bala, and other worthies of the Welsh pulpit. This little room, which is used only when an intimate friend calls, has been the scene of many a little gossipy talk over a cheerful cup of tea. The round table upon which the tea is served on such occasions is as bright as a mirror, and the chest of drawers close by is as glossy as when Mary received it as one of the wedding gifts from her father almost forty years ago.

Always busy from morning till night, when her pattens are not heard clattering on the cemented floors of the kitchen or dairy, or her quieter footsteps about other parts of the house, the whirr of the spinning wheel tells that she is still at work; and, when no sound is heard, she not unfrequently is seated near the window busily converting the skeins of yarn into balls, or knitting stockings for her husband or her son Jenkin.

The same healthy activity prevails in the smithy, for although on rainy days and wintry nights, when the farmers and neighbours have little or nothing to do, they resort to the smithy, as their fathers did before them, for a chat and an occasional discussion; yet all has to be carried on amid flying sparks from forge and anvil. Seldom is Shadrach's arm at rest, and then only when a lively discussion engages his attention for a moment, after which he proceeds with more enthusiasm than ever, driving a remark home with special force of muscle as he deals a mightier blow than usual to the glowing iron upon the ringing anvil.

On one wintry day in particular Shadrach had been specially busy. During the preceding night there had been a hard frost, and the farmers of the neighbourhood had sent their horses to be rough-shod during the day in such numbers that he had not had a moment's leisure until dusk. The evening crept on unawares, and as it darkened brought out into glorious relief the pillar of fire in the smithy. Shadrach chanced to be alone. He shut the window through which the dark night peeped sullenly and the freshening breeze rushed coldly, and left only the upper half of the door open, through which a shaft of light shot across the road, casting its warm glow at a little distance upon the opposite hedgerow, and, thrusting its way through the bushes into the field beyond, made the frosted dewdrops upon a thousand blades glisten like diamonds in the dark. It was a beautiful sight, such as only a special compromise between darkness, light, and frost could produce. But withal the night was ominous. A storm was rapidly gathering; already Shadrach could hear the plaintive moaning of the wind growing louder and louder as it swept through the leafless branches of the trees close by, but it seemed to him to become more furious and less sad, and at any moment it might burst into a terrible hurricane mad with rage. Everything promised an angry night that would frown in darkness and snarl in storms. There seemed to be but little prospect of company at the smithy that night.

So Shadrach thought when suddenly in one of the brief pauses of the boisterous wind he heard outside familiar footsteps on the crisp earth, and then a voice, which he well knew, saluting him.

"This is a rough night," exclaimed John Vaughan, the village shoemaker, as he hurriedly entered the smithy.

"It is indeed," replied Shadrach, "and I fear we haven't seen the worst of it yet; I didn't expect to see any of you here to-night."

"It isn't likely you'll see another," said the shoemaker, with a significant nod, "I shouldn't have come myself hadn't I wanted a dozen nails or so with which to finish a pair of boots for Hugh Roberts, of Pentre-mawr. I promised to take them home, too, without fail to-night, and you know the old proverb that he sometimes repeats, 'A promise made is a debt to be paid.'*

"Yes, and that's a good proverb too," responded Shadrach, as his eye twinkled merrily, "but my good fellow, the dear old man will think the millennium has come if he sees you with the boots at Pentre-mawr to-night."

"Because of the storm!" inquired John, in a tone of strange surprise.

"No, not because of the storm," said the blacksmith, "but"—and here his tones became confidential—"because he will have lived long enough to see a shoemaker true to his promise; the good old soul won't want to see any more on earth, that'll be the last pledge he'll want to have about the world's future, he may confidently expect anything after that."

"Come, make haste with the nails, my boy," replied John, somewhat patronizingly, "You *can* make them with any man in the county, it's when you forget your trade, and try to be clever and a bit sarcastic, that you make a mess of it. Aim, Shadrach, at making your *own* 'calling and election sure' and never try your hand at anybody else's. A man who may be good at making nails and things like that is often a very poor hand at preaching."

Shadrach smiled good-naturedly, and placing aside what he had in hand he swept the anvil carelessly with his apron by way of preparation for the next job, meanwhile remarking that the last things even good men wished to be reminded of were their faults. "They are very much," he continued, "like Sampson Lloyd in the society the other night. He gave his experience, so I understand, and told them what a dreadful man he had been before his conversion, bad beyond description, and yet when Evan Pantbach,† innocently got up and said that he could endorse all that the brother had said, that he knew him well at the time he had referred to, when he was the worst man in the whole neighbour-hood, poor Sampson got up evidently with a little of the

---

* "Dyled ar bawb ei addewid".

† The name of a man's house, or trade, is frequently used among the peasantry instead of his surname, as being more distinctive. Here "Pantbach" (or "The little hollow") is the name of the house.

old Adam still in him, and said, "Will the man confess his *own* sins?
He is indulging in a good many falsehoods about me.'"

"It was rather ridiculous, no doubt," said John, "for Sampson to
have acted in that strange fashion, but Evan Pantbach, was not a whit
wiser in enlarging upon Sampson's sins instead of his own. There are
some good men who have a special gift for confessing other people's
sins. I am disposed to think, Shadrach, judging from your feeble
attempts to-night, that you covet that gift. Make haste, my boy, with
the nails, you can do *that* well."

Shadrach and John were cousins, and had played, gone to school,
and slept together for many years when boys. The old love still united
them very closely together, and often the old playfulness returned,
and they would banter a little, as on this occasion. It used to make
them feel young again. There was no bitterness in the banter, only
playful humour and friendly home-thrusts. There was nothing that
Shadrach would not put aside in order to make a few hob nails for his
cousin John.

"I do hope we shall have good Anniversary Services to-morrow,"
said Shadrach, as he blew the bellows with one hand and with the
other held a thin short bar of iron in the fire. "I hear that the stranger
who's coming is a wonderful preacher."

"So he is," said John, with an emphatic nod. "He is not very
theological; I never heard him use many doctrinal phrases such as
you will find in 'Bodies of Divinity,' or for the matter of that even in
the Epistles of Paul, but for all that he gives the theology of the Gospel
in every sermon. He speaks more in the style of Jesus Christ Himself
than of His great Apostle, and I like him none the less for that. For
instance, instead of saying, 'A man is justified by faith,' he says, 'Believe
in the Lord Jesus Christ, and thou shalt be saved,' and to my mind
there is quite as much theology in the one as in the other. He makes
the Gospel appear to you such a tender, melting message, and brings
the Lord Jesus so near to you that you no longer think of Him as
living on earth eighteen hundred years ago, but as being with the
preacher in the pulpit, yes, and as being with you in the pew; and I
am sure He is there whenever that good man speaks about Him."

"Ah, that's the sort of preaching I like," said Shadrach, as he drew
the bar, white with heat, out of the fire and began to strike it on the
anvil. "I like something struck off at white heat, with plenty of sparks
flying about.

There is not much done without that. I wouldn't give thanks for a sermon that didn't melt me. I can't do anything with this iron until I soften it with heat, and there's nothing done with the poor sinner worth reckoning unless he is softened by the Divine flame. I hope the stranger doesn't use paper, John; I believe in what John Elias said, that paper is a very poor thing for carrying fire in, and I never saw any fire carried that way in my life except it be in the form of 'tinder and flint' we used to carry when boys, but, bless you, what knocking, and blowing, and wasting of time before you could get a spark out of that. We were almost frozen with cold before we succeeded in getting a flame. Ah, that was poor work, John. I never like to see that experiment tried in chapel."

"But, there's fire often in a read sermon," said John Vaughan, with an evident desire to put Shadrach right.

"Perhaps so," replied the impetuous blacksmith, "and they tell me there's fire in everything if you can only get it out—but then, that's the difficulty. It's small consolation for poor mortals starving with cold to-night that in the very stones on which they lie, and the very ice outside, there's fire in some form or other. They want to *see* it and *feel* it, as we do this blazing forge. I seldom, if ever, feel it, John, when ministers hang their heads like weeping willows over a written sermon. I have no doubt there's fire there 'in some form or other' if I were but clever enough to see it, but then I am not clever, and I must have a Gospel that is not intended only for long-headed people."

"Ah, there's a vast amount of nonsense talked sometimes about 'fire,'" said John. "A great deal of bad temper passes for 'fire,' and it is fire of a certain sort—the fire that James speaks of in his Epistle (James iii. 5 and 6). When John and James were younger and besought Christ to call fire from heaven upon the Samaritans, they no doubt attributed their warmth very complacently to a heavenly source, but I have a keen suspicion that they got their kindlings from another quarter just then. They 'knew not of what spirit they were,' they claimed kinship with the wrong fire, and the Master was not long in undeceiving them. Fire, Shadrach, is sometimes a *very cheap* article, and may be had in any quantity, while forbearance may be very costly and exceedingly scarce. We want patience and charity as well as the so-called 'fire,' depend upon it."

"So we do, John," replied Shadrach, "and both of us are rather short of those commodities, I'm afraid."

"Very likely," responded John, "anyhow, you will not have your patience tried to-morrow by any paper-sermon.

"I'm thankful for that," said Shadrach.

He soon finished the two dozen nails that John wanted, and having taken them up in his horny hand, which did not seem to feel the slightest inconvenience from the fact that some of them were almost red hot—so thoroughly in love with fire was this son of Vulcan—he placed them in his cousin's leathern apron and with a "Good night" the two friends parted, John going forth into the darkness and the storm, and Shadrach remaining in the ruddy glow of the blazing forge.

CHAPTER V

Anniversary Services at "Horeb"

EFORE John Vaughan had returned home from Pentremawr on Saturday night the storm had burst into a hurricane, and, until Sunday dawn-ed, it raged with scarcely a lull. Throughout the night the wind shrieked furiously through the chinks of the doors, and howled wildly in the large chimneys of the humble homesteads in the village and neighbourhood. The moon which had risen early in the evening tinged everything with its silvery hue, and thus gave a weird appearance to the whole scene. In its clear light the storm, raging in its fury, could almost be *seen,* as well as felt and heard. Far into the night it reached its highest pitch. To the fanciful listener, half asleep and half awake, it would seem as if Æolus had been moon-struck and was roving at will, stark mad through creation. Few could sleep. The night was as terrible as it was light, and altogether was a very poor preparation for the Sunday.

There was one man, however—a fond child of Nature, who gloried in her sublimities, and revelled in her wild play—who seemed to catch an inspiration from the sweeping hurricane. He was to be the first preacher for the morning service on the following day at "Horeb Chapel." As he listened in the dead of night, he possibly remembered that in the long ago God had spoken much in the same manner at another Horeb, when, as He passed by, "a great and strong wind rent the mountains, and brake in pieces the rocks before the Lord" (I. Kings, xix. 11). It was quite true that on that occasion He did not seem to Elijah to be in the wind, but rather in "the still small voice," which hitherto the old prophet had been too prone to ignore, yet the wakeful preacher was sure that on *this* night "the Lord was in the wind." It flashed upon him like a revelation that that storm was a new illustration of a text from which he had once preached, "Was the Lord displeased against the rivers? *was* Thine anger against the rivers? *was* Thy wrath against the sea, that Thou didst ride upon Thine horses and Thy chariots of salvation?" (Hab. iii. 8). He thought he could hear on that very night the rumbling of the royal chariots, and the neighing of the imperial steeds—and were they not all engaged as of old in the service of salvation and not of destruction? Did not God save His people in ancient time at the Red Sea in one of the fiercest storms and wildest nights the world had ever seen? Why should not storms be chariots for the great God on His redemptive journeys still?

The storm had given him a text, and he would preach from it on the morrow. To a preacher whose heart was sensitive to every touch of mystery, and ever throbbed with intense sympathy with all that was grand and thrilling in Nature, having to preach withal in Welsh—a language majestically strong and rugged, yet sweet and rhythmical, whose cadences seem to sweep the whole gamut of human thought and emotion, which has in it the terrible might of the tempest, as well as the soothing calmness of the summer breeze—this text was as congenial to his own mood as it was fitted to the temper of the occasion.

With the dawn of the Christian Sabbath the angry storm subsided as suddenly as did another in olden days, when, on the Sea of Galilee, the Lord of the Sabbath breathed forth His "peace" into the troubled elements. The light of God's holy day touched the raging tempest, and it became a calm, illuminated with its kindly smile the cold, cheerless earth with its battered trees and shrubs, and melted with its warm kiss the frosted dewdrops which the chill blast of the preceding night, save where it had shattered them, had crystallized into still denser and colder forms. It was a bright and sacred morning, typical of another that shall yet dawn, which shall succeed all the storms of time and usher in eternal sunshine.

From all directions, for many miles distant, companies of worshippers—some on foot, others on horseback, or in conveyances more or less primitive—wended their way to the sanctuary on this high day. An occasional hymn, sweetly and plaintively sung in the broad valleys and narrow glens, ascended on the morning air, and was echoed and re-echoed by the rocky buttresses of the everlasting hills.

The morning prayer-meeting at seven o'clock had been well attended by the villagers and those who lived in the immediate neighbourhood. Shadrach Morgan, at the close of the meeting, predicted a glorious day, as he had never found heaven so near as he did on that morning; "and," he significantly continued, "I have never known the Lord's days to be 'foxy days,' bright in the morning, and wet and cold all the rest of the day; when He gives us heaven in the morning He gives it, too, in the afternoon and evening. He does nothing by halves. 'My voice shalt thou hear in the morning, O Lord: in the morning will I direct my prayer unto Thee '—*now we have done that;* 'and will look up '—*ah, brethren, that's what we have to do all the day long,* LOOK UP! LOOK UP!" John Vaughan nodded his head in cordial assent, and said, "You've struck the key-note to-day, Shadrach;" and all left for their homes, saying that they had never in their lives seen Shadrach look so much like a prophet; and feeling convinced that what he had said must prove true.

At ten o'clock the chapel was filled with worshippers. The devotional part of the service was conducted with much fervour and pathos by the pastor of the church, after which the younger minister* of the two appointed to preach that morning—who, as we have seen, had spent most of the preceding night in reverie amid the wild tumult of the raging storm—ascended the pulpit, and read his text, "Thou didst ride upon Thine horses and Thy chariots of salvation." The strangeness of the text, the commanding presence of the preacher, the people's previous knowledge of him, as well as their pre-disposition to listen, secured at once eager attention.

It was quite apparent that—like some of the ancient prophets, who were trained by God for their work amid the wild solitudes and conflicting elements of nature, and who derived much of their inspiration from such surroundings—the present preacher had caught much of the wildness of the storm, and the weirdness of that terrible

---

* Rev. B. Thomas ("Myfyr Emlyn") of Narbeth. The invariable custom is that at services where more than one minister preaches the younger minister preaches first, the position of honour being the last in the service.

moonlit night, through which he had passed. There was a wild play about his countenance, and his whole sermon bore traces of his "vision in the night."

"Various," he said, "are the representations we have of the great God, and of His movements in His vast creation. Sometimes He is represented as *'sitting'.* Thus Daniel and John saw Him in their visions as sitting upon the throne of His glory. Sometimes He is represented as *'walking,'* walking between the seven candlesticks, walking upon the wings of the wind, and as having His 'way in the sea' and His 'paths in the great waters.' Sometimes He is represented as *'riding,'* riding upon the cherub—upon the cloud—upon the heaven of heavens—and in the text He is described as 'riding upon His horses and upon His chariots of salvation.'

"Thus Scripture language is highly figurative with regard to the Almighty and His movements. How could it be otherwise? *The Almighty is ever active in His universe.* He has, to use the words of Habakkuk, 'his chariots and horses.' In Himself He is immovable and unchangeable. He is 'the same yesterday, to-day and for ever,' 'without variableness or shadow of turning,' but in the development of His plans, and the revelation of His attributes, He is ever moving onward, riding upon His horses and chariots, and making sweeping strides on the kingly highway of His vast empire.

"In the theology of some men, God is merely an inactive, unconcerned, and passive observer in His own universe, a *mere looker-on.* They attribute to Him the work of creation, they believe that He made the machine and wound it up, but that since then He has left it to itself or to what they are pleased to call 'the laws of nature.' But in our theology He is a living and ever-active God, moving in ceaseless and divine activity in His vast creation; is a constant visitor of all parts of His great empire, His frequent visitations giving life, order, beauty, and happiness to everything, from the tiny blade to the mighty cedar, from the humble lily to the tree of life, whose branches embrace both sides of the river. He is, to use the phraseology of Ezekiel, 'the spirit of life in the wheels' of the great machinery, the life and sustainer of the universe.

Here John Vaughan, the village shoemaker, who was also the leader of the men's Bible class at "Horeb Chapel," and the oracle of the whole neighbourhood in all abstruse points in theology, got up from his favourite corner in the "large pew,"* stood erect, and, with a countenance beaming with joy, looked intently upon the preacher. It was at once evident that the preacher's doctrine was wholesome, or John would have retained his seat, closed his eyes, and hung his head like a bulrush.

The preacher proceeded—

"Creation is full of activity. The rivers flow to the ocean, and the ocean ever rolls restlessly upon its rugged bed. The sun, like a giant, daily runs his race and the gentle moon month by month pursues her rounds of nightly service. The planets move in their orbits, the stars glide on at infinite distances, and the comets ever sweep in their erratic courses through the sky. Mind is active and matter is ever at work. Angels are ever on the wing, and seraphim are constantly engaged in their service of holy adoration before the throne. The whole universe is full of activity, from the smallest atom to the sweeping planet, from the little babe to the princely archangel in the presence of God.

"But all the activities displayed in creation are but a faint symbol of the unlimited and ceaseless movements of the Creator. They are but bubbles on the rushing torrent of His onward sweep, sprays from the august cataracts of His operations, wavelets upon the fathomless ocean of His activity."

John Vaughan had by this time become almost motionless. He seemed to be transfixed. This was the *second* stage of John's hwyl†— that of *wonder.* He only occasionally reached the third—the *rapturous.* Unlike his cousin Shadrach, he did not respond much until he had fairly lost himself. Meanwhile he would only *look* at the preacher, but what a look! The glance of his full and luminous eyes on this and similar occasions was piercing. His whole soul looked through in intense wonder and adoration.

The preacher continued—his voice meanwhile gaining in force, and variety of modulation—

---

* The large pew or "Y sêt fawr," is the pew in which the recognized leaders of the church generally sit.

† "Hwyl" primarily means "sail," hence "to be in *'llawn hwyl!'* " means "to be in full sail"—"llawn" meaning "full." "Awel," the Welsh word for "breeze," the plural of which is "awelon," is frequently used in connection with the word "hwyl." Often in prayer and in song it is earnestly asked that God may send the refreshing "breeze" or "breezes", the one condition of a happy and profitable service.

"Again, God moves and works in His vast creation by *instrumentalities.* He has His horses and chariots. Thus He announces His being, and reveals His existence. Worlds are but signs of His presence, systems are but His initials in bold type, and the universe but His flaming superscription.

"'God is a spirit,' therefore unseen and mysterious. We cannot see God, but we can see His horses step majestically on the highways of creation. We cannot see the august Majesty of Heaven, but we can see His glittering chariots as they pass along, and this is as much as we can at present sustain, and more than we can thoroughly appreciate.

"To the atheist, the laws and forces of nature are but horses without riders, and the universe is a chariot without a charioteer. What a revolting sight! what a dismal and distressing idea!

"To the Christian, God seems to move through all His creation. Amid the chequered scenes of life, and the mighty changes of time, God appears as riding 'upon His horses and chariots.' The mighty thunders are but the noise of His wheels, the earthquakes but the world's vibrations under their ponderous weight, the whistling storm but the bugle of His charioteer, and the forked lightnings but the quivering strokes of His lash, urging His steeds on with greater speed and spirit.

"It is by instrumentalities that He fulfils His grand and benevolent purposes in the material, mental and moral worlds. By natural laws He governs worlds and systems, by instinct He governs the animal kingdom, by mind He governs His thinking creatures, and by His Son and Spirit and Word He governs the heart of humanity.

"God has innumerable chariots which pass through all parts of His vast empire, 'for the chariots of God are seventy thousand, even thousands of angels.' Were His horses to stumble, or His chariots delayed, the whole creation would be paralyzed. Should His *royal mails* lose time for a single moment oceans would become dry, suns dark and cold, and stars dim. The earth would perish for want of supply, heaven would become tame and silent for want of inspiration, and the universe sink for want of support. His horses, however, never stumble, and His chariots are never delayed in their coming.

"But our text teaches us that God comes to *this* world *on a message of salvation.* Chariots of old were associated with destruction and bloodshed, but these are the chariots of *salvation.* It is to this *world alone that these chariots seem to come.* Methinks when they were first brought forth to the front of Jehovah's palace that I hear one of the oldest servants talk with the other, "Where is our divine Master going today? What can now be on foot? Something of special and infinite importance is to be done, because there are in front of the royal palace horses and chariots innumerable, more beautiful and glorious than anything I have seen before. That was a grand day when Saturn was ringed, when the moons of Jupiter were set going, and the earth was received as a member of the family of worlds, when 'the morning stars sang together and the sons of God shouted for joy,' but all fade into oblivion before the glory and grandeur of this equipage. Some great campaign is about to be opened, some powerful enemy is about to be conquered, some valuable province is about to be saved from destruction, for 'SALVATION' is written on the chariots, and 'HOLINESS UNTO THE LORD' upon the bells and bridles of the horses."

Shadrach Morgan was by this time all aglow. For some time he nodded his head, and jerked out an occasional *"Ie!" "Ie!"* (yes! yes!) by way of hearty assent; but during the last two or three minutes, Shadrach had been rapidly running up the scale of emotion, and now had reached quite an octave higher, when he shouted out *"Bendigedig"("Blessed").* * Another brother joined in with his peculiar ejaculation, for which he was known throughout the whole neighbourhood, "Oh—*oh!*" "oh—*oh,*" while John Vaughan still *looked,* lost in wonder, and might at any moment break forth into the rapturous. There was a general movement, too, through the congregation, which cannot be defined, but which could be felt by all present, and which gave a fair promise that Shadrach's prediction at the morning prayer meeting would be fulfilled that day.

The preacher continued—

"As the Prince of Life entered methinks I hear him say to the Charioteer, 'Proceed to that speck you see far away on the confines of creation, which is the world at whose opening services you sang so melodiously the other day.'

"The procession advanced, passing systems and worlds, until the sweet music of heaven died away on their ears. Adam heard their approach in the cool of the day. He thought he could hear the tramp of the steeds of Justice, on the errand of retribution for transgression and disobedience. But let heaven wonder and earth adore, they were God's 'horses and chariots of *salvation,*' laden with the gladsome news of a

---

* This response is synonymous with the English phrase "Bless the Lord."

Redeemer. They proceeded along the highways of the Old Dispensation, and, as they went, nature paid them homage. The sea heard and turned aside; the waters saw and were afraid, the depths were troubled, and the Jordan retreated; the sun stood on Gibeon, and the moon in the valley of Ajalon, while the horses and chariots of God passed by. The 'hills melted like wax,' and the everlasting 'mountains flowed down,' the 'earth shook and trembled,' 'the heavens dropped,' and even 'Sinai itself was moved at the presence of God—the God of Israel.'

"The Prince of Life alighted often on the way to talk with patriarchs, psalmists, prophets, and priests. Isaiah exclaimed as he saw the august procession advancing, 'Prepare ye the way of the Lord, make straight in the desert a highway for our God.' The word 'prepare' echoed and re-echoed from age to age. At length the great Forerunner took up the prophetic message and shouted it in the desert until the wilderness of Judæa rang with its music."

Here the preacher dwelt with special emphasis and fondness on the Lord alighting in the incarnation—His going about doing good, healing men by touching them—entering the house of mourning and filling it with joy—bearing on *foot* His heavy cross for us—taking the "handwriting" which was against us, and with the nails which penetrated His hands and feet "nailing it to the cross," and with the spear which pierced His side writing "settled" upon it, as He exclaimed triumphantly in the hearing of Heaven and earth, "It is finished"— His entering the grave—rising again, and after a period of forty days, during which He had frequent interviews with His humble followers, entering His chariot, which bore Him to the skies.

"But," the preacher added, "He has not passed away for ever. 'I will come again,' and 'I am with you alway' were among the last of His promises. He ever comes, not in the humble garb of His incarnation, but in 'His chariots of salvation,' scattering blessings where'er He goes, and taking up those who, weary on life's highway, pause for rest. 'Come unto me all ye that labour, and are heavy laden, and I will give you rest' are the words of the great King as He passes by. He is passing by to-day, He passed by last night in the storm, this bright morning He passes by in the sunshine and in 'the still small voice.' There may be some one waiting this joyous morning after a night of tempest to be caught up with Him. Oh glorious prospect when He will take us to His palace! Poverty hinders our visiting various parts of *this* world. I confess that were my means more ample, and opportunities more frequent, I should certainly see more of the beautiful world in which I have the honour of being born and bred. I should like to visit Italy—the land of music and song—so rich in refined associations and classic lore. I should dearly like to visit America— the new world—the land of freedom and plenty—the stronghold of liberty, and the dread of tyranny. How I would gaze upon her towering mountains, her fruitful plains and valleys, her princely rivers, her broad and extensive savannahs and prairies, and especially her terrific and matchless cataracts thundering in their solitude, and imitating the very voice of God. Above all, how I should like to visit Palestine, to Christian faith the most blessed and hallowed spot under God's heaven! The land of the fathers—the land of Abraham, Isaac, and Jacob—the land of the patriarchs and prophets, of poets and seers— the land of the Temple and the Shechinah—the Land of Promise, and the earthly shadow and prototype of heaven itself. Yes, the land of our dear Saviour's birth! How I should like to visit Bethlehem where He was born, Nazareth, where He was nursed and bred, and trace even in imagination the walks trodden once by His blessed feet, look upon the mountains sanctified by His prayers, the grass consecrated with His tears, the garden made for ever sacred with His sweat, the whole neighbour-hood hallowed with His divine life, and the little spot immortalized by His death! I would gladly spend a night on the slopes of Olivet, and should almost expect to hear in the sacred stillness the tread of those feet which trod it eighteen hundred years ago, and the sweet strains of that voice which once filled the air with heavenly music. I could scarcely believe that He had gone away.

"Those are feelings common to most of us at times, but I have slender hope of visiting any of those places. But those self-same chariots which bring God down to man will bear us, if we trust in His salvation, up to God. The prophet Elisha saw some of His horses and chariots covering the mountain above Dothan, and were our eyes opened we too should see Mount Zion covered with fiery horses and chariots ever on the watch as the 'life guard' of the Lamb's bride. It was in one of these chariots of fire that Elijah was conveyed home. These are they which in all ages have borne the martyrs and saints of God to the skies. One of them was sent to take to the realms of light the seraphic Christmas Evans, who was heard to exclaim to the charioteer as they entered the dark valley of the shadow of death, 'Drive on,' 'Drive on,' as if in haste to reach the palace of his King, and the home of his God.

Oh what joy to hear there the golden harps and the outburst of Heaven's own harmonies, to hear 'The Messiah'as performed in the concerts of the skies, to hear the 'Sweet Home' sung in Heaven, and the grand 'National Anthem' of the blest as rendered by the choristers of the King of Kings."

The whole congregation was now greatly moved, the preacher's variety of intonation adding special force to what otherwise was telling. Shadrach and one or two others shouted "*Gogoniant*" ("Glory.")

"Yes, brethren," said the preacher, "Shout '*Gogoniant'* as loud as you may! Take your key-note from the angels' song over the fields of Bethlehem. We shall sing a nobler song than *theirs* yonder, but it is only very rarely that we can surpass it here. 'Gogoniant!' Let the first words on angelic lips, as they announced the advent of the Saviour of the world, be our last ere I sit down; and may my brother be enabled to lead you to the level of a yet sweeter song, and a more rapturous strain. Meanwhile we will shout 'Gogoniant'—'Glory to God in the highest, and on earth peace, goodwill toward men.'" (Luke ii. 14.)

The preacher sat down; the sermon was over just when the people wanted to hear more. A short hymn was sung, during which the preacher descended into the large pew, and another,* well-known by name throughout the Principality, but who had never preached in that neighbourhood before, ascended the pulpit. He was the "wonderful preacher," who came from a distance, of whom Shadrach and his cousin John had spoken in the smithy the preceding night.

He presented a startling contrast to the preceding preacher, being short in stature, with a meek and childlike countenance, but withal excessively nervous—every line in his features telling of intense anxiety, and his hand twitching convulsively as he opened the Bible. The storm of the previous night had unnerved rather than inspired him. He could not have preached the sermon he had heard for all the world, but he could preach *another.*

When the hymn was sung he read his text.

"'And behold, two blind men sitting by the wayside, when they heard that Jesus passed by, cried out, saying, Have mercy on us, O Lord, Thou Son of David, &c." (Matt. xx. 3-5). The preacher read his text with a tremulousness of tone and diffidence of manner, which would lead any one *who did not know him,* or who had not heard of

---

* Rev. R. Hughes, of Maesteg.

him, to conclude that it was his first effort in public. To those who
knew him, however, who had previously seen him almost break down
in reading his *text,* but who had instead seen the sturdiest of their
number break down completely before the *sermon* was closed, knew
that this was but "the hiding of his power." He paused after the reading
as if to gather strength. The tension was overpowering, the
congregation in a few seconds were held helplessly in breathless
suspense, and were made to feel what an infinitude of meaning there
may be in the *silences* of some men. They had seen the lightning flash
in that eye, and the preacher's whole frame quiver beneath the shock,
but as yet they had heard no sound. It was the suspense which spans
the distance between the lightning's *glance* and its *voice.* Would it
ever be heard, and if so would it not after such a pause be feeble?
When at length it was heard it *was* feeble. It had the sound of distance
about it, as if it came from far off skies. It had lost power, but gained
softness on its way. It came to the congregation in broken murmurs.

The preacher, leaning over the pulpit, and pausing briefly every
three or four words, said:—"My dear friends—you have been
reminded—that our God—is sometimes represented in Scripture—as
sitting—at other times—as *walking*-and, at other times—as *riding.*
We felt a strange thrill—as we listened to the descriptions given of
Him—as *riding* in His royal chariots through His vast empire. We were
impressed very deeply with a sense of His majesty and greatness—
even when engaged in the work of saving men. My text represents
God—not as 'riding' in 'His chariots,' or 'sitting' upon 'the wings of
the wind'—but as *walking* not in the sea or the deep waters—but on
the dusty and probably rugged highway near Jericho—which many
other wayfarers trod and which He walked as one of their number—
one who like them knew what it was to be often wearied by the way
and one who was often without a place to lay His head. Thus, as we
have been reminded, our God is not always in His chariot—but often
on foot, and in humble garb, treading our rough way—blessing us as
we walk, or even when, for want of strength, or sight, or heart, we
halt and sit down helplessly by the wayside."

By this time the preacher had all but ceased to pause; at least the
audience had ceased to notice his pauses. The tremulousness of voice
still continued, but it became all the more charming for the clear
silveriness of tone, which now imparted to it exceptional richness and
force. Every passing shade of thought modulated the voice, and every

touch of feeling throbbed in the utterance. One was inclined to think that with a voice *so clear,* and *so sensitive,* no height of thought, or depth of feeling, *need* be unexpressed.

There was a strange contrast between the congregation now and fifteen minutes before. Then they seemed to be riding with their God on the wings of the rushing tempest, now they realized that they were back again in their dear old "Horeb" but, like Moses of old, they took their shoes from off their feet, since the place upon which they stood seemed to be "holy ground." God had come down and had touched with His sacred feet the earth upon which they stood. Wondrous condescension to have alighted thus! The first preacher had reminded them of this, still more did the one who now spoke.

Continuing, he said, "This is one of the many incidents recorded of Jesus as 'going about doing good.' In comparing the Gospels, it would seem to us that Our Lord opened the eyes of the blind, in going out of Jericho as well as in going into that city. It is a great thing to be able to go out of a wicked place as we enter it. All are not able to do this. The disciples on one occasion failed to come out of Samaria as they went there, for though they entered it in a tranquil spirit they came out of it ablaze with revengeful passion."

John Vaughan nodded significantly, as if remembering what he had told Shadrach the preceding night.

"Jesus came not to stay in Jericho, but only to *pass* through it. It was a greater blessing to that city that Jesus even *passed through* than that all others should remain in it. The history of Our Lord's life is the story of a *passing* by, and even that is so important that its effects are felt in eternity. Flowers of virtue grow to-day in the footprints of the Saviour, and their perfume purifies and sweetens the world's moral atmosphere. His progress through this world was like that of a majestic river which gives fruitfulness *as it passes by* to the land it laves. There were sick ones who had been healed, lame ones who could now walk, and dead ones who had been revived, who might be seen in Palestine by the waysides, and who were living proofs that some *One* had 'passed by.' So still it is in vain for sceptics to affirm that the Saviour has not been in Wales, since in every town, neighbourhood, and village there are traces of his having *passed by.*"

"*Diolch byth,*" * exclaimed Shadrach. This allusion to the Saviour

---

* "Praise for ever."

in relation to Wales had touched the tenderest chord in his nature, and, true as the needle to the pole, he responded to that touch.

The preacher proceeded to divide his text very simply, calling attention, first, to the blind men, then to the multitude, and finally to Christ.

Speaking of THE TWO BLIND MEN ON THE WAYSIDE, he said—

"*We are reminded here of one thing which is exceptional in nature,* namely, *blindness*—'Behold two blind men.' It would have been exceedingly sad if there had been the necessity of saying, 'Behold *two who could see,'* thus intimating that seeing was the exception and blindness the rule. The order, however, is that men *see,* and this order brings to light many important attributes of the great Creator.

"See how *good* He is in making blindness and other infirmities rare *exceptions* and not the rule!

"How boundless His *power,* too, in maintaining this original order unchanged throughout the ages! At the outset He did not go beyond the scope of His power in establishing an order of things which He could not maintain, in creating beings whose wants He could not satisfy to the end of time. In the presence of the fulness of Divine provisions for man's needs, the Psalmist exclaimed, 'The earth is full of Thy riches' (Ps. civ. 24). It is a mercy to have a *small* place full of riches, but the earth is vast, yet the *earth* is full of riches. If the capacity of creatures to enjoy be great, here is enough for all—*the earth full.*

"How great is His *mercy,* too, in maintaining this beneficent order. How often have men, by the misuse of God's most precious gifts of sight, speech, hearing, &c., deserved that He should change His plans, by turning the rule into the exception and the exception into the rule, and yet the blind, the deaf, the dumb are rare exceptions still, some one or two among many hundreds or thousands.

"Again, *we are reminded by these blind men of the position generally occupied by the infirm*—Sitting by the wayside.'

"This was a *very narrow place* to occupy. It is on the margin, the edge, or outskirts of things that the infirm are accustomed to be. As a rule there is no room for them on the highways of life, but unless *all* their rights are to be ignored we should at least be willing for them to have full possession of the wayside since they have held that as a possession from time immemorial. Houses and lands become acquired property if occupied for twenty-one years without any acknowledgment of claim. On that principle the wayside has become the acquired possession of the blind, as they have sat there since the time of Our Saviour, and probably long before, and they have made no acknowledgment to anyone for it. It is imposition of the worst kind to deprive the blind of their lawful property. Yet the hard world aims constantly at narrowing the wayside and usurping the landed property of the blind."

"Yes, indeed!" murmured Betty Ddall, or *Blind Betty,* to herself, but those in the next pew heard.

"This, too, was a convenient position in which *they could be seen.* Few of us are able to keep in mind the infirm unless they are by our paths and are easily seen, but as they are ever by the *wayside* they are easier seen than not. We cannot even read the daily and weekly papers without seeing them, as they are there by the wayside represented by Deaf and Dumb Institutions—Asylums for the Blind—Hospitals—Orphanages—Explosion Funds, &c. Thus the helpless, though their position in the world is narrow—just a strip on the wayside—have yet a large place in the hearts of many, since *they are so easily seen.*

"This, too, was a convenient position in which to *extend aid.* No one need have much difficulty in finding an opportunity to bless suffering ones, as they ever sit by the wayside. This is a very convenient world for the exercise of sympathy, since the infirm and needy are so near to us, and so much in sight. We need *not go out of our way* to bless them—*no further than the wayside.* It is some comfort to the infirm to know they are not far from the strong.

"Again, *we are reminded of God's care even for the blind men spoken of.* They were blind, but they could *hear* and *speak.* All the ills that flesh is heir to are far too disagreeable to be put together as neighbours, hence they are mercifully distributed by the great God."

"Thou stayest thy rough wind in the day of the east wind," whispered Betty to herself.

"Again, *our attention is called to the wise use which these blind men made of the powers thy had.* They could not see, but they *listened,* and *'cried out.'* By a merciful provision with which we are happily familiar these blind men could *hear* all the more quickly for having lost their sight. Though they were blind it would have been difficult for Jesus to pass without their knowing it—and knowing that the Opener of the eyes of the blind was so near, they were bound to cry out.

"They asked for *mercy* of Him. It would have been enough if these blind men had only asked *justice* of some that passed, and *sympathy* of others, but they could ask for nothing less than *mercy* from Jesus, the Son of David."

"Bless Him, and He'll give nothing less," said Shadrach in an undertone to his cousin John.

"They *'cried'* for it. They could do nothing else; they had no language but a cry; but that was enough, as a cry is a confession of weakness, and in weakness the strength of the supplicator is made perfect. The cry of the feeblest can reach the ear of God—'This poor man cried and the LORD heard *him,* and saved him out of all his troubles.'"

The preacher in the next place called attention to

THE MULTITUDE.

"They desired that the blind men should hold their peace—or be silent. Generally speaking, the multitude are neither wearied nor pleased by anything save sound. Good principles as a rule are not the things which please a multitude, and bad principles are not the things which grieve them. It is not often that they rise higher than sound, and it is not often that they will go below it.

"The multitude sought to force them to be silent—'Rebuked them that they should hold their peace.' What an insight into the *chief aim of persecution* in every age! Stephen died beneath a shower of stones, that he 'should hold his peace;' Saul persecuted the Christians in every city 'that they should hold their peace;' Paul stood in chains before Caesar that he 'should hold his peace;' Bunyan was for twelve years in Bedford gaol 'that he should hold his peace;' and Penry, our beloved reformer, was executed in London 'that he should hold his peace.'"

*"Felly'n wir"** exclaimed Shadrach Morgan, with much emotion. The reference to the young Welsh martyr had quite melted him.

"This, too, gives us an insight into the secret of the *power of persecutions.* It was the voice of a multitude that rebuked. The doors of prisons would not have been shut so firmly upon the excellent of the earth, apart from the influence of the multitude. There is great power for good or ill in the multitude. Religious persecutions have all but ceased in our land because the multitude to some extent have changed their creed and feeling, and have set their face against persecution and for liberty.

"But observe, great as is the power of the multitude, they failed to

---

* "Thus indeed!" or "Truly so!"

silence these blind men. While they rebuked them that they should hold their peace they only cried *'the more.'"*

Blind Betty nodded approval in her quiet corner, while a triumphant smile lit up her aged countenance.

"It mattered little to them that the multitude rebuked them. They knew what value to attach to a popular rebuke. There are some men and women who do precisely what the multitude expect of them. Though the very Christ pass by they will not cry to Him, until the multitude say they may. Thus there are voices which the multitude can silence, but they are not the voices of those who have realized their need of, or who exult in the joy of being blessed by, the great Saviour, and who know withal that He is passing by. Opposition only adds force to such voices. These blind men never knew that they could cry so loudly until Christ was near and the multitude tried to silence them. It is ever thus. There is a strength which needs resistance to develop it, and to give it full play. The Church of to-day does not know the energy of its life, and the power of its voice, since the multitude no longer rebuke it, that it should hold its peace. The Church never speaks so loudly and so well, never throws so much of irresistible might into its cry, so that heaven and earth shall hear, as when the whole multitude exclaim *'Hush!* HUSH!' These blind men had caught the inspiration of the Master's presence—for He was passing by—and there was no power on earth, or in hell, that could suppress their voices. They challenged the rebuke of the multitude with a *cry,* which grew louder and yet louder:—'They cried THE MORE!' Yes, and despite the multitude, Jesus heard, and, hearing, *stood."*

"Diolch byth!" shouted blind Betty and Shadrach Morgan simultaneously. John Vaughan, who had been sitting down since the singing of the last hymn, and had been listening intently to all that the preacher had said, once more stood up and *looked* as he only could.

The preacher paused, looked at the Bible, and, with a rich modulation of voice, as well as with exquisite pathos, he read the rest of his text—"And Jesus stood still, and called them, and said, What will ye that I shall do unto you? They say unto him, Lord that our eyes may be opened. So Jesus had compassion *on them,* and touched their eyes: and immediately their eyes received sight, and they followed him." After another brief pause, he said—"Jesus stood. The multitude were advancing, but He *stood.* The multitude stand when they see an opportunity of *receiving,* but Jesus stands when He finds an opportunity of *giving.* The multitude stand to gaze at the great and wonderful, but Jesus stands to look with pity upon the poor blind."

Here poor blind Betty was quite overcome, and the eyes which could not see shed tears at the thought that the Lord Jesus did indeed stand to cast a kindly look upon the neglected blind, who sat on the waysides of this busy, earthly life. Shadrach Morgan shouted *"Bendigedig,"* and John Vaughan, who had hitherto only reached the second stage of his "hwyl"—that of *silent wonder*—now shouted *"Bendigedig"* too. John had forgotten himself, and had reached the third stage—the *rapturous.* Shadrach Morgan soon reached the rapturous, not so John, as we have seen. In the gradations of his *"hwyl"* he seemed to observe the Divine order, as given by the prophet, for at the outset he "rejoiced," but was satisfied with expressing his joy in an approving smile; then as other thoughts and emotions crowded upon him—the smile being no longer an adequate expression of his hidden but increasing joy—he became "silent in his love;" and finally, when silence was no longer possible, as he was swayed by a master passion, which he could neither govern nor resist, he "joyed with singing." Thus he passed through the three stages—the *approving,* the *silent,* the *rapturous.* When John reached the last stage, which was comparatively seldom, *"Bendigedig,"* *"Gogoniant,"* and *"Hallelujah"* were all called into requisition to express those feelings which were too big for ordinary words.

The preacher proceeded—

"He also *'called* them.' The multitude wanted to keep the blind at a distance from the Saviour, but He called them. It was a new thing for these blind men to be called by anyone; they had doubtless been accustomed to be driven. Behold the tender Saviour *calls* them! One of the things that makes the Gospel so dear to us is the fact that it is the voice of Jesus calling upon us, and acknowledging us as those whom He longs to bless. He also intimated His readiness to bless them:— 'What will ye that I should do unto you? He was not afraid that they would ask for more than He could do for them. Who could have asked this question save Jesus? The wants and wishes of the blind are so great that none except Jesus can fulfil them. But His power to bless is as great as the need of suffering humanity, yea, greater, for He is still the mighty One who 'is able to do *exceeding* abundantly above all that we can ask or think.' *'Exceeding!'* Man's need has never yet been greater than the Saviour's power to bless."

"Never!" exclaimed John Vaughan. *"Never!"* echoed Shadrach Morgan.

"The world has had abundant opportunities of testing His credentials as the infallible Healer of all its infirm and helpless ones, and now He repeats the challenge. Who of you will test His power? The Saviour expected these men to tell Him *what* they wanted, not because He did not know, but because He knew, and because He loved to hear them ask for such a large blessing—'*that our eyes be opened.*' Their words to all others were, 'We will receive whatever you will please to give us, and we shall be grateful for the smallest gift;' but they would ask for nothing less of Jesus than that their eyes be opened!"

"Bless them, no," murmured Betty, tremulously, "and I don't blame them, poor souls." It was clear throughout that Betty was having a little *hwyl* for herself. She evidently thought that she understood *this* question, and that this sermon was more for her than it could be for anyone else there. She walked two miles each way to every service, and that only by the aid of her God and her stick, and it was a pity if now and then she could not monopolize a sermon.

"This asking for so great a blessing shewed great faith in the Saviour. There are some who ask so little of Him, that their request is barely worth the words that convey it, or worth the Saviour's notice, as it has not in it the true ring of faith. These men asked more of Him than they would ask of anyone else. Our desires expand, our expectations are enlarged, and our petitions assume nobler proportions when Jesus Christ draws near to us in our needy moments. Alexander the Great commended one for asking of him a great gift, as the very request shewed confidence in his large resources; and, in granting the request, the question was not so much whether the receiver was worthy of the gift as whether the gift was worthy of the giver. Was it a gift that Alexander was not ashamed to acknowledge as his? Ask great things all of you of God, tell Him what you need—the opening of blind eyes—the forgiveness of sins—holiness—or anything that you need and Omnipotence can give. 'Covet earnestly the best gifts'—gifts which will not only greatly enrich you, but which will afford the greatest pleasure to your God to acknowledge. 'What will ye that I shall do unto you?' There is the sound of Omnipotence in the question; let not our request fall below the level of this encouragement. Take the Saviour at His best. May He forgive you that you ask for toys when He is anxious to give you sight!"

"*Amen!*" exclaimed John Vaughan, "*Lord forgive us all,*" murmured poor Betty in her corner. Shadrach wept, he knew not why, save that he felt very happy!

"Jesus gave them what they desired—'He touched their eyes, and immediately their eyes received sight.' A touch is a small thing, but the least things of Jesus Christ are far greater than man's greatest things. It was His touch that healed the sick and raised the dead in ancient Palestine, and that touch is almighty still. His touch is the secret of all healing virtue in the world. He 'touches' men and they are healed. 'O, thou Christ, touch these that they may live and rejoice in Thee!'

"He opened their eyes immediately. Healing has its tedious journey to take as a rule along the links of secondary causes, by mineral and vegetable means, and through the channels of medical and surgical skill and practice, but, in the opening of the eyes of these blind men, healing called nowhere on the way, but came direct from the source of all life into living contact with the two sufferers. There is, too, one instance at least of spiritual healing as suddenly and directly as this:— 'This day thou shalt be with me in Paradise.' Oh, thou great Healer, heal now, as in the ancient days!"

"AMEN!" came from the large audience suddenly, like a loud crash of thunder. The emotions of the whole congregation had been for some time pent up like an electric charge in a thunder-cloud. It only awaited a divine touch—at that touch it burst into a burning, quivering, startling exclamation.

The preacher's gentle voice as he proceeded contrasted strikingly with this outburst.

"'He opened their eyes.' It would appear that through this miracle they received their sight in body and in soul. 'They followed Him'— Here the miracle reached its highest point. It would indeed have been a vain thing for the multitude to have sought to hinder these two to follow Christ once they had received their sight. If the eyes of the blind were but opened in our services today we should see people begin to follow the Master. It would be a difficult task for anyone to hinder them; as difficult as to prevent the river from flowing, the thunder from roaring, the wind from blowing, and the sun from shining. As certainly as planets revolve round the sun, will the numberless throng of redeemed ones who have been kindled into life by the healing rays of the Sun of Righteousness revolve round that centre to all eternity."

A very powerful feeling had for some time swept over the whole congregation. The responses at one time came from all parts of the chapel with suddenness and irregularity like stray shots in a bivouac, at another like the loud clang of arms when the battle is raging, and finally like the shout of triumph when the citadel is won, and the enemy defeated. The position was at length gained, and all knew it. Even old David William, Ty-mawr,* the senior deacon, who generally gave out the notices—a man of exceptional bulk and substance, who, too, was a great stickler for personal and unconditional election, had a very keen scent for detecting the least savour of Arminian heresy, claimed an intimate familiarity with the eternal decrees, and acquaintance with the few who in common with himself had been chosen, and who, as the result, had been hanging his head ominously during the sermon, as it made the love of God a deal too cheap—was now all astir. He had fondly cherished the thought that the last sentence the preacher uttered favoured the doctrine of the final perseverance of the saints, and that in the circumstances covered a multitude of sins. He was quite moved, and forgetting all the incipient heresies which in calmer moments he thought he had detected, he now responded with the others. Shadrach Morgan and John Vaughan were enraptured, while poor blind Betty looked as if she had received her sight that very morning, and, like the blind men of old, was determined to praise her Saviour come what might.

Meanwhile the preacher had finished his sermon, and closed his eyes for the usual brief prayer in a Welsh service immediately after the sermon. The prayer having been offered, and the orthodox collection and announcements having been made, a hymn was sung, and thus one of the happiest services ever held in "Horeb" Chapel was brought to a close.

Those who had come from a distance accepted the hospitality for the day which the villagers on such occasions generously extended.

The morning service was the theme of conversation in every group on the way home, and round many a hearth during the dinner hour, and many hopeful predictions were made with regard to the afternoon and evening services.

John Vaughan and Shadrach went down through the little village together toward their homes. They soon reached the smithy corner, and there they stood. They had been charmed by the sermons. The first had carried them in rapture to the skies, the second had brought them into close and tender contact with the great Friend of suffering humanity on earth. In both cases they had felt the same gracious presence.

---

* "The big house."

"I never before," said Shadrach, "realized that God was so glorious, and yet so very near to me, so exalted in Heaven, John, and yet so homely with us here on life's dusty way. We needed both sermons to-day, and the last sermon was a beautiful finish to the first. It looked as if the preachers had agreed. The stranger was very touching at the close, John. I couldn't stand it. Nothing melts a man like the love of the blessed Saviour."

"No, nothing," said John, with an emphatic nod, "and that preacher delights to dwell upon the love of God. I shall never forget a sermon I once heard him preach from the words, 'But * Zion said, The LORD hath forsaken me, and my Lord hath forgotten me.' He said the *world* had said that many a time, but the Lord pays no heed when the *world* says it, if *Zion* does not say it:—'*Zion* said.' But He is surprised at Zion coming to that conclusion after all His mercies toward her. Did I not, says the Lord, deliver her from Egypt, divide the Red Sea before her so that she might pass through on dry land; did I not lead her through the wilderness with a pillar of cloud by day, and with a pillar of fire by night for forty years! Did I not divide the rocks in the desert causing rivers to flow from them to quench her thirst on her weary journey; and did I not give her manna from heaven! Did I not lead her safely through the Jordan, bringing her to the mountain of my holiness, conquering her enemies for her! Yes—Yet Zion said, The Lord hath forsaken me, and my Lord hath forgotten me. What persistency is in this *'yet'* of Zion, and how firmly it withstands the miracles of God's mercy! But there is also a *'yet'* in Divine mercy that is mightier than Zion's—'*Yet* will I not forget thee.'"

"Oh, that's glorious," exclaimed Shadrach, and, taking his cousin's arm, continued, "Go on, John."

"Then he went on to explain the Lord's reply to Zion's complaint—'I have graven thee upon the palms of my hands.' 'What a wonderful thing,' he said, 'that all the while Zion was saying, "The Lord hath forgotten me," her likeness was graven upon the palms of His blessed hands! Both His hands were Zion's, and engaged in her interests. When the Lord lifted up His *finger* against Pharaoh He changed the rod into a serpent, and the water into blood, and the families of the Egyptians were filled with mourning; but Zion has the protection of *both His hands*—her likeness is graven on them. When God would

---

* "Yet" in Welsh.

make an image of Himself He made it of clay in human form, but when the Lord would take a portrait of Zion, the Lamb's bride, it was not in clay that He made the likeness, but on the palms of His own hands. When we see the image of God in clay, the likeness is of infinitely greater worth than the tablet; but when we think of Zion's likeness on the palms of the Lord's hands, the tablet or canvas is of infinitely greater value than the picture.'"

"Oh that's sweet! Go on John," said Shadrach.

"Then he went on to say—I almost forget, but I know he said this:— 'Zion's likeness will be *safe* on the palms of the Lord's hands, as long as those hands themselves are safe. The great Lord never saw any place sufficiently consecrated for that portrait save His hands. The likeness will come to sight every time He opens His hand to supply the wants of every living thing.'"

"Grand! Grand!" exclaimed Shadrach.

"Then let me see, what did he say next? There are five years since I heard it, Shadrach. Ah, then, he went on to speak from the words, 'Can a woman forget her sucking child, that she shall not have compassion on the son of her womb? Yea, they may forget, yet will I not forget thee.' 'The Lord's love toward Zion,' he said, 'is stronger than a mother's love to her sucking child. Of all the fond affections in creation, nothing comes up to that of a mother towards her child. A father's love toward his children is strong; and the love of God toward Zion is brought to light to some extent when it is said, "As a father pitieth his children, so the Lord pitieth them that fear Him." We must have a father's feeling to understand the *"as"* of that text. The secret is in that word. Although it was from the father that the mother was first taken, yet there is much of the mother's tenderness still left in him. As a rule, however, it is easier for a father not to pity his children than it is for a mother to forget her sucking child.

"'The most glorious passages in the Bible are parts of Divine nursery songs over Zion, the infant child. For instance, "I have loved thee with an everlasting love;" again, "The mountains shall depart, and the hills be removed; but my kindness shall not depart from thee, neither shall the covenant of my peace be removed, saith the Lord, that hath mercy on thee." We have the affectionate mother here, singing her nursing song over Zion, her "sucking child." If perchance a maimed child is seen in its mother's arms, let nothing be said about it in her hearing, or she will feel it keenly. Is there a blemish on Zion, the sucking child?

Yes, yet let not much be said lest the tender parent feel it. Let the child alone for the sake of the loving One who cares for it.'

"Then, coming to the close of his sermon he said:—'Though a mother's affection be so strong yet she *may* forget her sucking child. Not easily, she must forget herself first; but she sometimes *does* forget herself. "Yet I," says the Lord to Zion, "will not forget thee." Oh my brethren, while He remembers His word, His love, His sacrifice, Himself, He will remember the child. Before He can forget Zion the mediatorial work must collapse, the Heaven of heavens must become empty, every harp he silenced, the songs of the redeemed be hushed, and the very ear of God become deaf.'"

"That's the sort of preaching to touch a man's heart, John, and to teach him to trust in the infinite love of our blessed Lord," said Shadrach. "Oh, it's grand! Grand! John. It reminds me somewhat of what I heard one say. It was the Rev. E. Williams, late of Aberystwith, but now of Heaven. He was preaching from the words, 'Who shall lay anything to the charge of God's elect?' For some time he explained the meaning of the text and its surroundings. He dwelt upon the impossibility of any charge being sustained to the hurt of God's own people, and, warming with his subject, he repeated the words of the text in a loud and triumphant tone,

'"Who shall lay anything to the charge of God's elect?" "I will," says Satan. "Yes, I daresay thou art ready enough to say anything, but will thy evidence carry much weight with it, dost thou think?" I remember a trial in North Wales some time ago. A respectable man, honoured by all who knew him, was brought up on the charge of perjury. There was only one witness against him, but his evidence seemed to be conclusive, until the counsel for the defence got up, and asked

"What is your name?"

"Joseph Thomas."

"Yes, but by what name are you generally known?"

"Joe the Fiddler."

"So it seems. Where do you live?"

"Well, I don't live anywhere; I go about."

"Playing your fiddle?"

"Yes, Sir."

"Where do you generally exercise your profession?"

"Well—"

"Speak up, Sir! In the public-houses and on the corners of the streets, I suppose?"

"Yes, Sir."

"So it appears. Now listen! Is this the first time you have occupied a prominent position in a court of law?"

"No, Sir."

"But the first time you have stood in the witness-box?"

"Yes, Sir?"

"So it seems. Have you ever appeared at the prisoner's bar?"

"Well—"

"Speak out, Sir. You have, I believe?"

"Yes, Sir."

"And more than once?"

"Yes, Sir."

"Now, come, have you been at the prisoner's bar thrice?"

"Yes, Sir, I have."

"So it appears. Now let us hear what you were charged with in the first case?"

"Well—"

"Speak up, Sir. Don't be bashful!"

"Stealing, Sir."

"Ah! so it seems. Found guilty?"

"Yes, Sir."

"And sent to Denbigh Prison, I think?"

"Yes, Sir."

"So it seems! In the second case you were committed for forgery, I think, and sent to Beaumaris Gaol?"

"Yes, Sir."

"Yes, so it appears. And, to be brief, you were found guilty, in the third case, of perjury, and sent on a second and more extended visit to Denbigh Prison?"

"Yes, Sir."

"So it seems. Now, Sir, tell me on your oath, have you any ill-feeling towards the prisoner?"

"Well, I might as well confess I have."

"That's my case, my lord," said the counsel, in a confident tone, as he sat down. The prisoner was *acquitted*. Why? Because all the evidence against him was given by an old fiddler with a broken character, who, withal, bore an old grudge against the accused.'

"Then the preacher repeated the question in a shout of triumph, "'Who shall lay anything to the charge of God's elect?'" The devil will try, but will he succeed? Methinks that at the Last Assize of the world the great Judge of all will ask the question, and methinks I can see Satan come forward to give his evidence against them, which at the outset appears strong and overwhelming. But I see the great Advocate for the defence, whose name is "Wonderful, *Counsellor,* the Mighty God," begin to cross-examine him.

'"What is your name?"

"Satan."

"Yes, but you have a few *aliases,* have you not?"

"Yes."

"What are they?"

"The Serpent."

"Again?"

"Devil."

"Again?"

"Accuser of the brethren,"

"So it seems. Where do you dwell?"

"Hell is the centre of my operations."

"And what is your occupation?"

"Well—"

"Speak out, that heaven and earth may hear."

"Walking about in the earth seeking whom I may devour."

"So it appears. Were you ever in Heaven?"

"Yes, there I commenced my existence."

"Yes; and were you ever driven out for pride, ambition, and rebellion against the Supreme authority, for lying, and other evils?"

"Well, those were the charges against me."

"Yes, and *proved,* I believe?"

"Yes, I suppose."

"So it seems. Have you not done all you can against God's elect, and do you not bear them the greatest animosity on account of their allegiance to Him who has bought them?"

"Well, I cannot deny that."

"That is my case, my Lord," says the great Advocate.

"Justified," exclaim the jury, "Justified," exclaims the great Judge. "Who shall lay anything to the charge of God's elect?" The devil will try, but will he succeed? NEVER! He is an old fiddler with a broken character, and is withal a biased witness, whose word has no weight in the Court of Heaven.'"

"Ah, that's excellent!" said John. "It describes Satan in his true character—'He is a liar and the father of it.' He is always insinuating evil things about God's children; but the Lord knows him well. Sometimes when I am assailed by the Tempter I like to read the Book of Job. Some say it is the oldest book in the Bible, and in the world, and all agree that it refers to very, very early times. Yet one of the first things you read in that book is that when the sons of God—the angels, you know—came to present themselves before the Lord, Satan came among them—the old hypocrite! One might have thought that he would have been ashamed to show his face again after having disgraced himself, and suggested the base insinuations to our first parents in Eden concerning the good Lord. But it would take more than that to shame him; there he stood among those who were his compeers before he fell, but no longer one of them, a Judas in an angelic circle! The great God soon unmasked him, and said to him, 'Whence camest *thou?* I did not expect to see *thee* here.' He was not in the least disconcerted by that, but answered, 'From going to and fro in the earth, and from walking up and down in it.'—A restless life enough; like the old fiddler, he seemed to live nowhere. But he did not speak the whole truth even in the Lord's presence. One might have thought from all he said that he was an angel of light still very busily engaged in his Lord's service, and not like 'a roaring lion seeking whom he may devour.' The Lord said, 'Hast thou considered my servant Job that there is none like him in the earth, a perfect and an upright man, one that feareth God and escheweth evil.' It does one good to read those words, and to think that the great God prides Himself so much on His poor children on earth; just as we, Shadrach, used to like people to look upon our little ones and notice anything worth noticing in them. God is exactly the same. 'Hast thou considered my servant Job,' said He to Satan as He would to an angel of light, in order that the old hypocrite might expose himself. Now listen to what he says. Ah, he's so pious! So anxious that the Lord shouldn't be imposed upon! He's as disinterested as he was in Eden! Listen to him—'Doth Job fear God for nought?' That question has the venom of the old Serpent in it. Angels do not speak in such terms of good men. They are too kind and good, Shadrach. Such insinuations as this come from hell; they never could come from anywhere else. It was Satan, who had become a kind of spiritual detective on his own account—*Satan*—that asked, 'Doth Job fear God for nought?'"

"Shame on him," said Shadrach.

"Yes," said John, "let God Himself, or one of His pure unfallen angels, find fault, if it is to be found; it ill becomes the devil to rebuke sin. He, indeed, breathes out suspicions about the saints of God, *he* who has been found out himself plotting against the very God he professed to serve! How such insolence must surprise the angels, and make even God impatient! I thank God that no unfallen angel who has kept his first estate has ever tried to find fault with His poor children on earth."

"Bless them, no," said Shadrach.

"No, it's not like them to do that, they come to minister to those who shall be heirs of salvation—that means to *serve* us. Oh, that's wonderful, those pure beings come to serve *us!* Yes, and in serving us they spread their white wings like charity over our sins, and what a large number of sins those wings cover! It is this old 'Accuser of the brethren' that comes to spy out inconsistencies, and to conjure up falsehoods against us. He is exactly like a man who came the other day to Carmarthen. He went about saying that there wasn't a single tinman worthy of the name in the whole town; he had looked round, and it was a shame, he said, that the public were saddled with inferior goods by men who had never learnt the trade, and who only consulted their own interests. He was going to settle down there, and he would see that the public should have their money's worth. A great philanthropist he was! And hadn't he a smile! You might have thought he was all sweetness, and born, as old Fortunatus Jones the astrologer would say, under the sweet influences of the fairest planet that ever shone in the sky. Well, the people began to open their eyes. What a pity they hadn't known him before; and one old fellow, who had always known how to reckon the pence, calculated what he would have saved in pots and kettles the last twenty years if he had only known this wonderful man. Well, there was some inquiry made as to where he had been living all those years, and how it was that they had not heard of him before, but he, modest man, was anxious to remain in humble obscurity. *He* would not have his left hand know what his right hand had done! There were some who thought he must be a wealthy man, who from pure goodwill towards the general public settled down among them; but there were a few who thought his professions were too good to be true, and who fancied they saw the play of the serpent in his smile. But one market day all doubts were set at rest when a policeman in disguise walked up to him, and, patting him patronizingly on the shoulder, said, 'Tom, you're wanted, lad;' and sure enough he was wanted, for he was a broken-down tinker, who had disappeared suddenly from his home, leaving his wife and family to the mercy of his creditors and the parish; and so the man who had settled down in the new place simply to protect the innocent people from designing men, had to return to his native town, and there in the county gaol to pass through a process of penance for neglecting his family, and forgetting his creditors, in his enthusiastic desire to expose rogues. Ah, Shadrach, there's a deal of the old broken-down tinker about Satan; and more than that, whenever you see a man turn up the whites of his eyes, shake his head and sigh, and hear him ask in sanctimonious tones whether 'Job fears God for nought,' and whether there are 'a few names even in Sardis who have not defiled their garments,' adding that what with the lethargy and unspirituality of the Church, and the wickedness of the children of wrath, he feels like Elijah under the juniper tree *alone—alone*—you may conclude that he and the old Tempter are close friends. It's Satan's old calling to suggest evil about the good, and he's never so dangerous as when he appears as an angel of light."

"Ah, that's exactly it," said Shadrach, "it's the wolf in sheep's clothing that we are to beware of."

"Yes, Shadrach," said John, "and yet if we were but prayerful and watchful we should not be deceived even then, for the wolf is a longer animal than the sheep, so that when he tries to pass off as a sheep the sheep-skin doesn't cover him; the knave must show either his teeth or his tail."

"Old Hugh Roberts, of Pentre-mawr, once told me that," said Shadrach, "and I am quite sure it's true, spiritually. I've seen the wolf's teeth a few times in my life, and felt them, too, when he has had a sheep's-skin on, and he would have had me but for the tender Shepherd's care. I well remember, too, how, after a narrow escape, I've stood as closely as I could by the Shepherd's side, and how, when the enemy has sneaked away, I've seen the wolf's tail plainly enough."

"Yes, the secret of safety is in being near Him, Shadrach; in having our great Lord between us and the old Tempter. I remember hearing the Rev. Evan Harris, of Merthyr, preach from the words 'Forasmuch then as the children are partakers of flesh and blood, he also himself likewise took part of the same; that through death he might destroy him that had the power of death, that is, the devil.' In his own way he divided it into three divisions:—First—'The children;' second—'He also;' third—'The devil.' And then he said, 'I hear some timid disciple say: "Ah! I see, the *devil* lurks in that text." Yes, he does, but remember that "HE ALSO" is there too. Fear not, timid one, for it cannot fare badly with "the children" if "HE ALSO HIMSELF" is between them and the "devil."'"

"That's exactly it, John. 'None shall pluck them out of my hands,' said the blessed Lord. If it hadn't been for those words, and words like them, I should have given up long ago, and the old Tempter would soon do for me if I were left to myself."

"Yes, Shadrach, that's just what my little boy felt the other day. He came to me almost out of breath, and, looking very much in earnest, asked, 'Father, is Satan bigger than I am?' 'Yes my boy,' said I, 'and I thought what a little he knew of his devices yet. Then he asked, 'Is he bigger than *you,* father?' I thought, Ah, my boy, you think a great deal of your father that he is a very wonderful man, but he is nothing in the old Tempter's hands, and I said, 'Yes, my boy, he is bigger than your father?' He looked surprised, but thought again, and then asked, 'Is he bigger than Jesus?' 'No, my boy,' said I, quick as lightning, 'Jesus is bigger than he is.' As he turned away, he said with a smile, 'Then I am not afraid of him.' I thought to myself—and I couldn't help shedding a tear, Shadrach—what a beautiful illustration that was of the verse, 'Little children... greater is he that is in you than he that is in the world.'"

Shadrach was touched by this simple story, and his eyes glistened as he said, "That's beautiful, John, I shan't easily forget that."

The two friends shook hands and parted for their homes.

The services in the afternoon and evening, as well as those held on the following day, more than maintained the character of the morning service. But enough; we will listen to what Shadrach and his friends have to say about them in the smithy, and that shall suffice.

CHAPTER VI

After-meeting at the Smithy

URGENT work had kept Shadrach, much to his regret, away from the service on Monday morning; but in the afternoon and evening he was in his place at Horeb. John Vaughan had brought a week's operations to a close on Saturday night when he took home the boots as a trophy to Hugh Roberts of Pentre-mawr. He and his workmen had cast hammer and lapstone, awl and stirrup, knife and polishing irons, all aside. The temple of Janus was closed, and universal peace proclaimed throughout the dominion of the workshop until Tuesday. It would, indeed, have required something very urgent, something far more pressing than is generally associated with leather, to disturb that peaceful tranquillity.

Two well-known ministers, in addition to those who officiated on Sunday, were announced to preach on Monday, and thus there was a very special interest felt in the services. Although the church at "Horeb" was a Baptist. Church, and the ministers who preached were Baptist ministers, yet, as is customary on such occasions, members of all denominations attended in large numbers on Sunday afternoon and during Monday. The farmers and their servants not being busily employed at that season of the year were able to attend in large numbers, and, it being about full moon, they were able to return home at night along narrow roads and devious by-paths without any serious inconvenience. Many a quiet glen and secluded nook were awakened out of their slumbers by the songs the pilgrim bands as they wended their way homeward on that bright, calm, moonlit night. The whole country for many miles round was astir with the music of the sanctuary.

On the following night, Shadrach was busy at work in the smithy, when John Vaughan entered. John was anxious to know how his cousin had been getting on since the services. Shadrach, who from his youth had been a member of the church at "Horeb," was a man of a volcanic nature, ever throbbing with a hidden fire, which at any time might leap forth into a livid flame. Throughout Sunday and Monday he had been ablaze, and whenever that occurred in Shadrach's experience the flame did not soon subside, but burned brightly for many weeks together. Thus John, although he had been hard at work, had been thinking of him all the day, and could stay away no longer.

John Vaughan had been brought up carefully in the Methodist persuasion. His mother was a Calvinistic Methodist of the most rigid type, and, according to a custom very prevalent among that body in those times, used to cut John's hair evenly all round, very much after the same fashion as the thatch on the humble homestead in which they lived, with the exception that the latter had one pleasing variety, for at each gable end a white wall shot boldly up, while John's thatch came down to the same dead level all round, concealing a good forehead, even as far as his two large luminous eyes, through which his whole soul seemed to look out in wonder. Early in life John departed from the course prescribed for him by his mother, was baptized by immersion, and joined the Baptist Church in the village. When John joined the Baptists, and especially when he began to court the blushing maid who afterwards became his faithful and loving wife, he discarded the then Methodistic style of hair, and tried to originate a parting; but as strangely illustrative of the influence of early training, it may be said that, notwithstanding the fact that John's young wife insisted upon the vigorous and frequent application of the brush on each side of the extemporized parting, John's hair never took kindly to the new-fangled style, for even now in damp weather, and at the least possible neglect on the part of John, some of the most stubborn of his Methodistic locks show their original tendency, and despising the idea of a parting, collapse in sweet confusion on his brow. For many years

John has been the leader of the men's large Bible class at "Horeb," and is considered to be one of the most enlightened men in Scripture in the whole neighbourhood.

"How are you to-night, Shadrach?" said John.

"All the better for having had the Anniversary Services," said Shadrach. "I've been thinking a great deal about them when at work to-day, and specially about the 'chariots,' John. I felt like going up to heaven in a whirlwind on Sunday morning when Mr. Thomas spoke about God's chariots taking the old saints home. Bless you, the air is full of them if we could but see them. I'm sure one came to this place when my father passed away. Why, he passed away like a prince! Poor fellow, he never had any kind of chariot here. It must have seemed strange to him to have stepped into such a glorious one all at once! I've been thinking, John—he died on the same day as Christmas Evans, and only about an hour later. He used to be a great admirer of Christmas Evans. Who knows, perhaps he was taken in the same chariot, at least he entered heaven very soon after him, and shouted 'Hallelujah' almost as soon."

"Yes," said John, "there is no doubt about their having gone to the same place—the Father's house—and you may depend upon it they got into the *'hwyl'* as soon as they got there, each anxious to shout 'Hallelujah' first. That seems to be the favourite word in heaven. You know John says that he 'heard as it were the voice of a great multitude, and as the voice of many waters, and as the voice of mighty thunderings, saying Alleluia.' That's something like *'hwyl'* Shadrach!"

"It is, indeed," exclaimed Shadrach, "if we could only hear it our best *'hwyl'* here would sound very tame ever after."

"It's a good thing we haven't heard it, Shadrach, and a very good thing that we don't see as much of heaven as we sometimes want to. It would spoil us for this world, and we should have no patience with the praises of earth. It is wonderful how a good *'hwyl'* spoils us for a poor one. Why, the best praises on earth must appear very tame to the angels, a thousand times more so than the English words 'Glory be to God' appeared to Francis Hiley, of Llanwenarth, when compared with *'Gogoniant.'* He was preaching very powerfully on one occasion, when an Englishman came to hear him who knew just enough Welsh to understand the sermon. He caught the fire, and while others shouted *'Gogoniant'* he shouted as loudly as any of them, 'Glory be to God' over and over again. The confusion of tongues seemed to disturb the people very much as it did at Babel in olden days. They looked round, and wondered where that strange sound came from. At last old Mr. Hiley noticed it, and sang as only he could with his rich silvery voice, 'Yes, "Glory be to God;" let our English friend praise Him as best he can with those thin English words—you can drive a hundred of them through the hole of a brad-awl—thank God for a word with a soul in it wherewith to sing His praises—GOGONIANT.' Those who heard him shout *'Gogoniant'* on that occasion say they will never forget it. It might have been a voice from heaven for its compass and tenderness. They used to call Mr. Hiley the 'silver trumpet,' as you know, but that 'silver trumpet' never sounded so powerfully in the hearing of men as it did then."

"Ah! we only get a few good responses here, John," said Shadrach. "The world seems to chill us, doesn't it? And the fire burns low very often, and when a brother is warmer than the others, and feels himself near Heaven, and shouts 'Hallelujah' much in the same way as they do up yonder, the others look so surprised."

"There's a very good story told of Mr. Hughes, who preached yesterday and on Sunday," said John. "There was a member of his church named Henry Davies, who now and then shouted *'Hallelujah'* when he forgot himself in the *'hwyl.'* Henry Davies died, and Mr. Hughes, speaking at the grave, said:—'Dear Friends—Henry was allowed to say 'Hallelujah' hundreds of times by himself here, but he will not be permitted to say 'Hallelujah' by *himself* any more. There are others yonder who can shout the word as well as he."

"Here they are, like David and Jonathan," said Caleb Rhys to his old friend, Hugh Roberts, as both leaned upon the lower half of the smithy door, and looked in.

"Don't they look exactly like Peter and John—when a little on in life, you know, before Peter went home and John went to Patmos?" said John Vaughan to his cousin by way of response.

Caleb Rhys and Hugh Roberts had just been at the society, which was held weekly in the Calvinistic Methodist Chapel barely a hundred yards distant, but as usual called at the smithy on their way home. They had a special interest in calling on this night, as they had attended the services at "Horeb" on Sunday afternoon and on Monday. It was only just eight o'clock, and they could have a good half-hour's chat about the services with Shadrach, and with his cousin, who they felt sure would be there.

Caleb Rhys, like his old friend, Hugh Roberts, had for many years been a prominent member of the Methodist Church. He was a weaver by trade; who when he had with the aid of one or two workmen furnished a large stock of flannel during the winter months, used to go in the summer on a journey through different parts of Wales to dispose of it. He had thus at various periods of his life been in almost every part of the country, and being so intensely interested in religious services, and having such an unconquerable craving for sermons, that he would, rather miss a good transaction than a discourse, he had heard almost every preacher in Wales worth hearing; and thus, by long experience, could readily discriminate between a good and an inferior sermon.

"Well, my friends," said Caleb, "you had 'a feast of fat things' yesterday and on Sunday; you won't want anything now for some time to come."

"Bless you, it has only sharpened our appetites for more," said Shadrach. "When Mr. Hughes was preaching yesterday about the Transfiguration* I felt ready to say with dear old Peter, 'Lord, it is good for us to be here; let us build three tabernacles.' The smithy looked more tame and dusty than ever this morning after the Mount of Transfiguration, where we were yesterday, I can tell you. I don't know how the leather looked to you, John, or the flannel to you, Caleb, or the old plough to you, Hugh Roberts; but there, we can bring the glory of the Mount down with us, as the preacher said, can't we; and just as when this blazing fire throws a kind of warm light on these old walls and on the very dust, and makes one feel that Shadrach Morgan's smithy is a dear old place after all on a cold winter's night, so that glory, it seems to me, brightens up this old world, Caleb, that wouldn't be much of it if the light of heaven didn't stream down to touch it up a bit, and give it life."

"That was a beautiful sermon," said Hugh Roberts. "I liked that part where he spoke about the disciples fearing as they entered the cloud—the cloud from which the Father's voice came so soon after— and, when addressing us, he said, 'Timid ones, are you afraid to enter the cloud? Remember *the Father is in the cloud*—for it was from the cloud that the voice came—and if *He* is there *you* need not fear to enter.' I thought of Moses entering the cloud on Sinai. It was all dark and terrible outside, and he never saw the glory until he got right into the cloud, but what glory there! What wonder that his face was

---

* See Appendix. Page 331.

all aglow when he came out. Oh! we are silly creatures to be afraid of the cloud. I remember. well when I had to enter a very dark one. It was when I lost my dear wife. When our best friends disappear it is a cloud that takes them out of sight, just as in the case of Moses and Elias on the Mount, and when our Lord Himself left His disciples. Well, I went with her right into the cloud. It was dreadfully damp and chilly at first, it made me shudder, but it grew warmer and brighter as I went in; and right in the centre of it I heard the Father's voice. It's true I lost sight of my dear one, but I saw One still more dear— Jesus—and Jesus *only.*"

Hugh Roberts could say no more. The earthly house of his tabernacle had become frail with age, and any extra movement on the part of the tenant made the old dwelling quiver to its very foundations.

Shadrach brushed away a tear with his right hand, while he blew the bellows with his left. He thought of the many hours his father and Hugh Roberts spent together in that smithy when they were young men, before they knew very much about clouds; and, thinking of what had taken place since, he wondered how soon Hugh would go still further into the cloud, and so far into the glory within that he would never wish to return to this dim sphere again.

"Yes," said Caleb Rhys, "and I liked very much what he said about Jesus in prayer rending the cloud of glory that was above the mountain, so that it descended in cataracts of light upon its summit."

"Yes," said John Vaughan, "and what he said about its not being at all likely that the disciples would have known Moses and Elias in any other light than the light of the Transfiguration, and that we don't know who we mightn't see—how many heroes of faith—did the light of the Mount stream down upon us."

"And then," said Shadrach, as he woke up from his reverie, "wasn't that good when he was speaking from the words 'His face did shine as the sun,' and 'his raiment became shining, exceeding white as snow,' and when he said, 'What a compliment to the sun and to the snow!'— adding that if the sun could but hear it he would show his face a little more even in this humid climate, and that the snow, if it could but hear, would never again be quite so cold as it is now."

"He spoke very beautifully, too," said Caleb Rhys, "about Love* Sunday afternoon, especially when he spoke of Love not rejoicing in

---

* I Cor. xiv. i. "Follow after charity," ("Love," Welsh.)

iniquity, but rejoicing in the truth, and said:—'When God in the beginning founded the earth, it was the voice of love that was heard in the chant of the morning stars, and in the song of the sons of God; and when the birth of the Saviour of men was announced it was the voice of love that the shepherds heard in the angelic song. *Love* in the Son of Man all but rebuked the disciples for *rejoicing* in the subjection of even evil spirits, bidding them rejoice because their own names were written in heaven. "Love rejoiceth not in iniquity, but rejoiceth in the truth."''

"And didn't you like," said John Vaughan, "what he said about love suffering long, and bearing all things?—'The love of God, like a bridge, spans the gulf of time. It has held up under the heaviest pressure. At different times, such has been the weight of human sins that the best of men have feared that the bridge would give way beneath the burden. But it has borne all things, and "suffered long," even until now. In the time of Noah the Bridge of Love suffered such depression under the weight of the world's iniquity, that for a brief season it disappeared beneath the Flood, but still it stood unbroken in the rushing torrent; and ever since that time it has been reflected in the heavens in the "bow of the covenant," the pledge and promise of the abiding character of that which it mirrors forth.' Then when speaking about Love as thinking no evil, hoping all things, and enduring all things, he said that selfishness delights to publish the weaknesses and failings of others, but Love delights to hide them. It never lacks graves wherein to bury offences, and what has cost Love most of all is a burying-place in which to place the world's sins out of sight."

"Yes," rejoined Shadrach, "and that reminded me of what I once heard Mr. Jones,* of Fishguard, say at 'Horeb' when preaching from the words, 'Let him know that he which converteth the sinner from the error of his way shall save a soul from death, and shall hide a multitude of sins.' He said that one of the Puritans, I forget his name, affirms that there is a reference in the verse to the burial of Moses; the preacher didn't agree with that, but, speaking about that burial before he went on, he said it was very exceptional. In that burial not only was the body buried, but also the grave and graveyard. 'This is an illustration,' he said, 'of the way in which God's mercy buries sins. No one is in the funeral with Mercy, and if any should meet her on returning from the burial and ask her, "Mercy, where didst thou bury

---

* Rev. W. Jones, Baptist Minister.

our sins?" her answer would be, *"I do not remember."* When the merciful God forgives the sin He *forgets* it:—"For I will forgive their iniquity, and *I will remember their sin no more.""*

"I heard Mr. Jones,* Carmarthen, say in a sermon," said John Vaughan, "something like that when preaching from the words:—'To wit that God was in Christ reconciling the world unto himself, not reckoning† unto them their trespasses.' 'God buried Moses, and though men sought for his grave there was not a bit of fresh soil to mark it out; yet even Moses will rise at the sound of the trump on the last day, but God has opened a grave in which to bury your sins and mine, from which they will never rise, not even when the dead of all time shall rise again.' Ah, Mr. Jones was a very wonderful preacher, one of the best on the 'stage' in an association I ever heard; he had such a wonderful voice, and he there found full scope for it as he could in no building; how he used to like to have his heavenly Father's roof above him when he preached the everlasting Gospel to men. Though in his later years the asthma troubled him very much, yet there was a charm even about his asthma when he preached. He made *that* musical. On one occasion a member of a neighbouring church was speaking to one of his members. Each began to praise her own minister. At last the first said to the other, 'But Mr. Jones has such a cough.' 'Yes,' said his faithful disciple, quick as lightning, 'But there is more in Mr. Jones's cough than in your minister's whole sermon.' Well, I heard him on another occasion preach from the text, 'Thou wilt bury† all their sins in the depths of the sea.' He said, 'God buried Pharaoh and his hosts, his horses and his chariots in the depths of the Red Sea, so that not the hoof of a single steed could be found ever after. That is the kind of burial which the gracious Lord gives to your sin and mine, oh, penitent sinner, wherever thou art.'"

"I remember hearing Mr. Kilsby Jones‡ once preach," said Caleb Rhys, "from the verses, 'Thou hast cast all my sins behind thy back,' and 'My sin is ever before me—God's treatment of forgiven sin—and the penitent sinner's treatment of forgiven sin. He said that the penitent sinner had his sin ever before him; first, in order to keep alive a sense of the sweetness of forgiveness—to appreciate *restored*

---

* Rev. Hugh Jones, Baptist Minister.

† Welsh Version

‡ Rev. J. R. Kilsby Jones, Congregational Minister, Llanwrtyd Wells.

health, it is good to remember sickness; again, in order to teach him to be merciful to others; and, lastly, to lead him to watchfulness and prayer. But speaking about God's treatment of forgiven sin—casting it behind His back—he said it not only meant that sin was *out of sight,* but it also conveyed the idea of *unreachable distance,* then asked— 'Where is God's back? And where the regions behind that? Who can find them? Let the Accuser of the brethren set out in search of this unknown and untrodden land. If he reach it he *may* find the sin, but not till then.'"

"That's the kind of preaching that touches me," said Shadrach, "and that is what I can best remember. It reminds me of what I heard once from the words, 'As far as the east is from the west, so far hath He removed our transgression from us.' The east will never come to the west, nor the west to the east. God is represented as putting the sin in the east and the sinner in the west, or the sinner in the east and the sin in the west. The devil even though he find *one* cannot find both together. When he finds the sin in the west the sinner is away in the far east, and so the old enemy has one eternal round in trying to bring both together. He'll never succeed! God has separated them; and who can bring together what He separates? Nothing, Caleb, should be too much for us to do which He asks in return for this, and yet how we stint our services, and calculate our little sacrifices. You, John, referred to Hugh Jones, Carmarthen, preaching from the words, 'God was in Christ, reconciling the world unto himself, not reckoning unto them their trespasses.' You have all heard of Richard Jones, the Calvinistic Methodist leader"—here all assented—"he thought once that he would keep an account in order to see what his office in the church would cost him each year. He bought a book for the purpose, and was determined to put down all the money he gave—the time he lost—and the food he provided for preachers who stayed at his house on their visits. He sat down to consider what he should enter first in the book, when the words came to his mind, *'Not reckoning* unto them their trespasses.' 'Well, well,' said he to himself, 'if that is it I shan't reckon either,' and so it turned out, he never put an entry into his book, though he had bought it for the purpose. How could he! *We* keep our little account against Him when we know all the while that He doesn't reckon against us that awful debt which would make us bankrupts in an instant if He only claimed it! The good Lord forgive us for putting down peppercorns to His account, when at the greatest sacrifice He strikes out for ever a debt against us which would crush the world if He but called it in."

"Bless Him," said Hugh Roberts.

"Yes, bless Him, Hugh," said Shadrach. "Why I heard one of your ministers—Ishmael Jones* speak in your chapel years ago about an old man and his wife in Flintshire. Their neighbour's cattle used to go over the fences into their wheat and grass, causing great loss to the poor old people. David, the old man, got impatient at last, and one day, entering the house, he said to his wife:—'Our neighbour's cattle have been again in our wheat. I'll make him pay the damage *this* time!' 'Don't talk about *paying,* David. "I will repay, saith the Lord."' 'No, indeed, he won't,' said David, He's too ready to forgive a great deal to do that.' We smiled at David's saying, but Mr. Jones said—'You may smile, but it was David that knew Him best. "Thou Lord art good and ready to forgive." It would be easier for me, my friends, to ask God to forgive all my sins, though they were as great as mountains, than ask the best of men for the loan of sixpence.' Ah! and so would I, John. He doesn't *reckon* what I owe Him. He knows I can never pay him, and therefore doesn't expect payment, and never asks for it. He *'waits* that He may be gracious'—wants the opportunity, and *waits* till he gets it. Oh, it's wonderful! *He* claim His own! *Never!"*

"That's very true, Shadrach," said Hugh Roberts, "and I very much liked that part of the sermon on Sunday afternoon in which the preacher spoke of Love seeking not her own, and when he said:— 'It is not the sole aim of Love, or indeed any part of her aim, to seek "her own". Love chooses to give to others more than is their due rather than insist upon having "her own" rights. She has a right to all that is good and great on earth and in heaven; they are all "her own," and if she but put in her claim, and withdraw "her own" at any moment, all nature would become bankrupt; but Love, so that this poor world may stand on its feet and have a chance for its life, "seeketh not her own."' I thought those words were as true as they were beautiful. Ah! Love—the love of God; and all human love that is worthy the name springs from that—has never yet had 'her own,' and has never yet demanded it. She delights to give herself away, as well as all that she has, so that some poor one may be the better, and happier. That's my experience, and I have lived long enough in God's world to know something about the matter. And, better still,

* Calvinistic Methodist Minister, Rhos, near Ruabon.

Love never fails; just as the preacher said, she does not fall away amid the changes of time and passing seasons. 'Other things,' he said, 'crumble away with age—rocks, hills, and mountains—and we, too, though we should live to become old, only live to fail more and more. We have to pay dearly for the privilege of living many years. "The hoary head is a crown of glory if it be found in the way of righteousness," but that crown, like every other, has its cost.' Yes, silvery hairs are very beautiful—so I used to think when I was young, and so I think still, now that I am old and have them—yet these silvery hairs are not bought with silver but at a much dearer price; at the cost of failing strength, failing mind, and failing desire. The other day the 'Squire showed me a very beautiful gold watch. It's a wonderful watch; it keeps time to a minute all the year round. He opened the watch and explained the principle to me. One of the wheels has two rims, the first of steel and the other of brass; as one expands the other contracts, so that in heat or cold the wheel is perfectly balanced. I thought to myself, Yes, there is a 'compensation balance' in the timepiece of life, so that if by a favourable Providence our days, by reason of strength, are lengthened to fourscore years, there is at the same time a contraction of buoyancy and joy. 'If by reason of strength they be fourscore years, *yet is their strength labour and sorrow.*' The 'yet' in that verse is the compensation balance. God's compensation balance makes everything right—come what may, hot or cold, winter or summer, short life or long life. Young people desire life, and love many days; well, those blessings have their price, and it must be paid every farthing. Many days mean failing energy and many other drawbacks. But, as the preacher said, 'this love will never fail through the decay of age, but will become stronger with increasing years—stronger in God and stronger in us. "Thou lovedst me," said our blessed Lord to His heavenly Father, "before the foundation of the world."' It was on the old love that He delighted to rest, and we, too, can trust in that. There is nothing that can make us feel so young as that old love; 'Even the youths shall faint and be weary, and the young men shall utterly fall'—ah, yes, I know it—'but they that wait upon the Lord shall renew their strength'—yes, and I know that, too—'*shall renew their strength,* they shall mount up with wings as eagles, they shall run and not be weary, and they shall walk and not faint.' Well, I'm getting old, and my voice begins to fail—this asthma has been very bad of late—I'm not what I was when your father knew me, Shadrach, fifty years ago; but though I'm old my spirit is young and rejoices in God its Saviour, and though my voice is failing my theme isn't exhausted—'Love never faileth'—*Never!* It has in it the life of God Himself, from whom it springs; there's no failing in that spring, come what may, and there's no faltering in my hope:—'My heart and my flesh faileth, but God is the strength of my heart and my portion for ever.' I never knew how sweet those words were until I was old. Shadrach, my boy, you will not know half the sweet things God has for you even in this life till you have lived long enough to need them."

Here his voice faltered, and there was a general pause; each felt a kind of choking sensation in the throat, and knew not how to break the silence, when at a most opportune moment Jenkin, who had been out on a message, and David Lewis, the village grocer, entered. It was at David Lewis's house that the different ministers who preached at "Horeb" Chapel generally stayed; and it was in his parlour that they delighted to meet after Anniversary or Association Services for a fraternal chat. He was a great admirer of ministers, was always brimful of the reminiscences of those gatherings, and as a rule loved "to point a moral and adorn a tale" with what he had heard some minister say in his parlour.

On their entering the ordinary greetings were exchanged, after which John Vaughan said:—"Do you, Shadrach, remember a powerful sermon which Mr. Richards,* then of Fishguard, but afterwards of Pontypridd, preached at 'Horeb' about thirty-five years ago? When speaking from the closing words of his text—'For thou lovedst me before the foundation of the world'—he spoke of the old love to which Hugh Roberts has referred, and said:—'There are some learned men who profess to know a great deal about the earth, and the different dates which every layer in its firm foundations bears, until you reach the lowest layer of all, which the great Master Builder laid. There is considerable difference between them in their statements and calculations. Their measuring lines are not all according to the same standard; but take the longest reckoning of geologists, and with them fix the period of laying the first layer of earth's firm foundation back a million years or more, even then—I'll give the preacher's exact words—this love of which my text speaks out—distances all in the receding depths beyond—'*before* the foundation of the world.' It is on this old love, older and firmer than the foundations of the earth upon

---

* Rev. James Richards, Baptist Minister.

which the great Saviour fixes his plea. Oh, powerful plea! oh, firm resting-place! This is the rock upon which Jesus stood under the burden of His petition, and this is the ground upon which we can stand beneath the burden of our heaviest sin.'"

"Remember that!" said Shadrach, with a look of strange surprise. "Do you forget, John, that it was my turning-point? Remember *that*— *if* I forget it let my right hand forget her cunning." Here Shadrach's hammer dropped on the anvil, as he placed his left foot upon the block beneath, and proceeded:—"Remember, indeed! I should think no one who heard that sermon could ever forget it; and it was then that I was converted—then I was converted, bless the Lord," repeated Shadrach. *"Remember,* John! Yes, and I can remember when he came about twelve years after that and preached, 'We love him because he first loved us,' and I said to myself, 'Bless the Lord, that text suits me now; it wouldn't have suited me when you preached here last, but there, the good Lord sends everything in the right time.' That was a sweet sermon, too, do *you* remember that, John?"

"Yes, Shadrach, I do, and I can remember now all about your conversion, too."

"Of course you can!" said Shadrach. "And that second sermon! He said that there were two loves spoken of in the text. First, the love of God and then our love. There was no mistake about the order. He said the two loves didn't bear the same dates—then I thought of the first sermon, and shouted 'Bless Him, no!' 'No,' said the preacher, 'did not the Lord Jesus say, "Thou hast loved them as thou hast loved me." *"As!"* Who can explain that word? Let the Lord Jesus Himself explain it in the words which follow—"Thou lovedst me *before the foundation of the world"*—thus the word *"as"* reaches back into eternity.' And so the preacher began where he left off before, and went on to speak about the love of God. '"God,"' he said, '"is *rich* in mercy." "Look now toward heaven," said God to Abram, "and tell the stars, if thou be able to number them. Canst thou see them, Abram?" "Yes." "Reckon them." "I cannot, good Lord." "So shall thy seed be." *So!*—a child for every star and a star for every child. God can give them a world each. God's love is a love with infinite wealth behind it.' By-and-by he went on to say how weak and poor our love to Him was, but it was a love kindled by His. Ah, I thought, there's hope for it then. If it isn't much in quantity, the quality is right if He has kindled it. 'You love Him,' said the preacher; 'well, why did you begin to love Him?'

'Because he first loved us,' shouted blind Betty, and the whole place was ablaze. 'Ah,' said the preacher, 'your experience, my sister, is the same as John's. Yes, that's why! Loving God for His own sake—His purity, and wisdom, and greatness—may suit an angel, but the poor sinner cannot see a place where he may fasten his love but God's love in the first place. "We love Him because he first loved us."' Remember it, John! I shall never forget it—*Never!* "

"I heard him preach once in his own pulpit at Pontypridd many years since," said Caleb Rhys, "on Love* the bond of perfectness; speaking of Love as the clearest proof, and the proof nearest at hand of our conversion, he referred to the verse, 'We know that we have passed from death unto life, because we love the brethren,' and said after a pause:—'Next in value to the blessing itself of having passed from death unto life is the certainty of it. Only to have this certainty is enough to outweigh all the sorrows of this mortal life. This certainty may be had—"We *know.*" Has Gabriel then been down to tell you? No. Have you ascended to the heavens and read your names in the Book of Life? No. How do you know then? *"Because we love the brethren.*"'"

"Ah, that's the secret," said Shadrach, "as one of your ministers,† Caleb, once said, 'it is not heaven that makes Christ worth following, but Christ makes heaven worth seeking. The miser loves his money-bags better than his God; his heart is as warm toward the gold as the furnace in which it was melted. Those who love the Lord have plenty of reason to give for loving Him—"because he first loved us." But He loved us—Why? Only He Himself knows why. That is a very unseemly question sometimes asked the Lord by very devout people in prayer meetings, "What didst Thou see in us more than others that Thou didst notice us?" See in thee! Depend upon it, poor uncomely thing as thou art, there was nothing in thee to see but poverty and uncleanness. Because there was boundless pity in His heart, and there was nothing in thee, thou poor worm, He pitied thee. Never ask that question again. When *we* love Him, however, it is because there is so much in Him to love that He draws us out of our miserable selves.'"

"I heard him preach once," said John Vaughan, "on the Love of God. He said the love of God to man appeared never so great as when it chose our poor nature, this house of clay, for its residence. Angels

---

* Welsh Version.

† Rev. R. Thomas, Llidiardau, Calvinistic Methodist Minister.

descended in hosts, yea, all heaven seemed to come down to earth then, and it was not surprising because there was a far greater wonder on earth than in heaven."

"Ah, yes," said Shadrach, "'which things the angels desire to look into,' and how they must have looked, and wondered, and gazed when they saw the Lord of Heaven in the lowly manger on earth. Oh, isn't it strange we don't wonder and adore more than we do?"

"This is the theme that *should* fill us with wonder, Shadrach," said David Lewis. "There are some dry souls who dwell upon all kinds of mysteries which were never intended to be revealed to men. They puzzle their heads almost to cracking point about the Eternal Decrees, the Seven Vials, the Antichrist, the Millennium, the Identity of the Ten Lost Tribes, the State of the Lost, and the Return of the Jews to Palestine, when all the while this great truth of the Love of God, the greatest of all mysteries, which is also the greatest of all certainties, is sadly overlooked. Clever people who study the decrees and the like have no time to dwell upon that. Mysteries surround us everywhere, but there is surely no mystery so glorious as the mystery of God's Love. Old Mr. Powell,* of Cardiff, went to Devonshire, I think, to collect. One gentleman, who thought Christianity was merely a heap of puzzling problems, said to him—'That is a very strange verse in the Ninth Chapter of the Epistle to the Romans, "Jacob have I loved, but Esau have I hated."' 'Very strange,' said Mr. Powell. 'What is it, Sir, that you see most strange about it?' 'Oh, that part, of course,' said his host patronizingly and with an air of surprise—"Esau have I *hated*"—it's certainly very *strange!*' 'Dear me, Sir,' said Mr. Powell, 'how wonderfully are we made and how differently constituted. The strangest part of all to me is that he could ever have *loved* Jacob.' That's exactly how it strikes me," continued David Lewis, "the mystery we ought to dwell upon in wonder and awe is the mystery of love; not the mystery of iniquity, and all the long list of subjects that come in its train."

"Ah!" said John Vaughan, in an authoritative tone, well known to those who attended his Bible class, "if we could but see a little clearer than we do we should find that every mystery in God's dealings with us is a mystery of *Love*. As Mr Williams of Wern† once said:—'As the

---

* Rev. Lewis Powell, Congregational Minister.

† Rev. William Williams, the distinguished Congregational Minister, and contemporary with Christmas Evans (Baptist) and John Elias (Calvinistic Methodist).

ocean is one sheet of water, although it assumes various names borrowed from the different coasts washed by its waves, so the numerous attributes and perfections of the God of Love have names given them from the various aspects which He presents in His varied relationships to man, but all are only modifications of one principle, and that is Love. It is the same principle that builds a hospital and erects a prison—the good of man.'"

"That's true, John," said Shadrach. "The love of God is an ocean entering every nook and cranny of our life. It appears under different names, and often in the darkness and in the storm, as well as in the light and the calm, but in every form it's the same love, bless Him, the same in the heaving billow as in the gentle ripple. I was thinking so when near Fishguard a few months ago. It was late at night, and a storm was raging; the sea came in lounging at the cliffs, as if it meant to destroy them there and then, the sound of the boulders and pebbles was something terrible, and if I had never seen a storm before I should have thought the end of days had come. But, bless you, the following morning was one of the most beautiful I ever saw, and the sea so calm and bright reflecting the heavens. I looked for the pebbles and boulders; they were so clean and smooth, with all their sharp edges cut off. I thought, ah, it has taken the rolling of a good number of storms like last night's to make you so smooth and round; and then I thought about the trying storms of life, and that we were like so many stones of awkward shape, with any amount of sharp edges and queer corners, needing a deal of polishing, and that was just the thing the storms of life did for us. 'Bless Him,' I said, 'for storms!' They are all love—all *Love!* Ah, I wish with you, David, that people rejoiced in this more, and bothered themselves less about mysteries which belong only to God. How much better and happier they would be, if they took it for granted that God had done everything all right in the eternal decrees, and that He doesn't want them to explain what He doesn't condescend to explain Himself; and just believed the words, 'God so loved the world, that he gave his only begotten Son, that whosoever believeth in him should not perish, but have everlasting life.' I lose my patience when I hear a man who stands up in the name of God to speak to poor sinners spend precious time in trying to tell them what neither he nor anyone else knows, about the Decrees and the Millennium, when all the while there is this glorious message of Divine love to proclaim."

"Very true," said John Vaughan, "a conceited brother once preached in the hearing of the late Mr. Davies, of Tredegar,* and manifested great anxiety to know Mr. Davies's opinion. At last Mr. Davies said, 'Well, brother, you preached more election—personal, unconditional, and everlasting—in one sermon than the Son of God preached during the whole period of His ministry.'"

"That reminds me," said David Lewis, "of what I once heard Mr. Jones,† of Blaenannerch, say at our house one evening. He was asked whether he had ever heard a certain minister, who was a great hyper-Calvinist, preach. 'Oh, yes,' he answered, with a merry twinkle in his eye 'he is a dear old brother. I heard him preach once on election; he had the strangest bit of election—for it was only a very little bit in that sermon—that I ever heard. His election, dear man, would be very narrow and contracted if he had it all in his own hands. Not only was there no way to get out of it, but there was also no way to get into it. He made it like a sack with both ends sewn up. What a blessing it is that we are not dependent upon the old brother's election, or the hope of ever being in it would be very faint for the great majority of us.'"

"I don't understand those hyper-Calvinists," said Jenkin, "they are like those creatures with very long necks, with their heads up somewhere in the clouds—*giraffes,* I think they call them—there they are, a select few, priding themselves on high doctrine, stretching their necks upward and away from all others, and sniffing the upper elements as they pick a choice leaf from a favourite tree here, and another leaf there, till they are half starved, just because they are not willing like shorter and humbler souls to join the common herd, and partake of the rich and abundant pasture of free grace which God has provided, but which they tread under foot."

"Very good, Jenkin," said David Lewis.

"Good in one sense," said old Hugh Roberts gently and tremulously. "There's a great deal of truth in what you say, my boy, and I agree with it, for though I am a Calvinist I am not a hyper-Calvinist. But, Jenkin, there is danger, too, in the other direction. As you say there is danger of sniffing the upper air too much, like the giraffe, but there is also danger of having your nose too near the earth like a badger, and it is hard to know which to choose, a hyper-Calvinistic giraffe, or an Arminian badger."

---

* Rev. J. P. Davies, Baptist Minister.
† Rev. John Jones, Baptist Minister.

"Yes," said Caleb Rhys playfully, ready to improve every opportunity of giving the Arminians a home-thrust "the badger, too, is lopsided isn't he, Hugh, having his legs shorter on one side than on the other, so that he can run up a hill only in one direction, and that crosswise; it's the same 'free-will,' 'free-will' with those Arminians from beginning to end."

"I am not quite sure that your illusion to the badger has any truth in it," said Hugh, "besides that figure applies to extreme Calvinists as well as to Arminians, only they are lopsided the other way, and take the opposite path, 'predestination', 'predestination' and they can run up the hill in no other way.

"Or as I heard Mr. Jones, of Blaenannerch," rejoined David Lewis, "once say in my house one evening after service, during which we had a very good *hwyl* but a poor collection. 'There are a great many Christians who, like the badger, will run splendidly if you let them take their favourite path. They have a pet virtue, and don't they go; but send them along any other way, and they won't budge. One has as much sympathy as you like, but very little justice; another, plenty of justice but no patience; you have others who pray and praise from Sunday morning till Saturday night, and from January to December, but come to the collection they give nothing to that.' As they say, Hugh, in the North of England, where John, of Brynmelyn, has gone, 'That's up another street,' and that's the street they never take; it's the wrong slope, and, like the badger, they can't run it."

"Yes, Hugh, it's quite true," exclaimed John, "we are all too ready, whether Calvinists or Arminians, to go our own way and follow our own paths, instead of the Master's leading. When Mr. Hughes was speaking about following after Love, I was reminded of another sermon I heard him preach years ago, on the disciples going back and walking no more with Jesus. He read the words 'Went back,' paused for a moment, and then said:—'Could they have *gone forward* by leaving the Master they would have had an excuse for their conduct; but in leaving Him they were obliged to go "back." It is possible to leave others, and yet to go forward. We can leave Moses, and the prophets, and John the Baptist, and in leaving them go far in advance of them, but none have ever gone forward by leaving Jesus. There is a path leading away from others without leading back, but every path that leads from Christ leads "back."' I thought, in listening, that what was true about Him who is Love is also true of the Christian grace which

He gives, and which bears the same name as the Giver. We must follow after her if we would go forward. It is toward her that every path of progress leads. We cannot get away from her without going backward; but, if we go on to all eternity, still she—angel as she is—will beckon us on. We shall never overtake her. In heaven we shall be following after Love into new heights and joys for ever and for ever. We can go a little way on earth in loving Christ and in loving our brethren, but here we are poor scholars enough. We are only learning the first lesson in the horn-book. We shall be better scholars yonder. We shall not be tempted to skip so many lessons there. 'We shall *follow on—follow on*—to know the Lord,' as we don't here often, I'm afraid, and we shan't find it half so hard there, depend upon it."

"No we shan't, John," rejoined Hugh, with much emotion. "That's *one* difference between the 'following' there and the 'following' here. Here often it's with weeping and with fear that we follow our gracious Master up rugged steeps, or along narrow winding paths over moor and fen, while the very heavens above us weep in sleet and rain until we sometimes almost sink into marshy ground and lose sight of the blessed Leader; but there on the heights and in the sunshine we shall 'follow the Lamb whithersover he goeth, and he shall lead us unto living fountains of waters, and God shall wipe away all tears from our eyes.' But there and here it's the same following John. Even here He does not want us to go where He hasn't been before us, and why need we murmur if He never murmured?"

"Besides," said John Vaughan, "those who are partakers of His sorrows are those who shall be partakers of His joys, and those who know 'the fellowship of his sufferings' are those who shall 'know him and the power of his resurrection.' It was so with the women of whom Mr. Parry* spoke yesterday morning. They who were nearest the cross, and were the first at the grave and the longest to remain there, were the first to rejoice in a risen Lord."

"I missed that sermon," said Shadrach. "David William, of Ty-mawr, sent a plough just as I was preparing to go, and said it must be repaired at once, so that Jenkin and myself had to stay in the smithy all the morning, but it was a little against the grain I can tell you."

"Yes, and to improve matters," rejoined Jenkin, "old David William called here on the way to 'Horeb' to see if we were at his plough, and

---

* Rev. A. J. Parry, Baptist Minister, Swansea.

then when he saw everything was going on all right he went to the service looking so devout. I felt a little cross at the time, and I couldn't help thinking it was just like those hyper-Calvinists; they are very fond of their own spiritual comforts, and won't miss them on any account, but they care very little, if the elect are enjoying themselves, what the poor reprobates outside are doing—mending ploughs or anything else."

"Jenkin, my boy," replied Hugh Roberts, gently, "you'll learn to exercise a little more patience and charity as you get older. You know the old proverbs, 'Better suffer than inflict a wrong,'* and 'Better be silent than speak ill.'† They are good proverbs. Your grandfather repeated them often, and acted upon them, too. I don't think you can do better than imitate him, my boy. I am sorry, however, that you both were disappointed. The preacher spoke about the women at the grave, taking for his text the account given by Mark."‡

Just then Shadrach took down the Bible from a recess about a foot square in the wall close by the forge, and therefore within easy reach of the smith. For the last sixty years at least all those who had frequented the smithy must have been very familiar with the place in which the smith's Bible was kept. This copy had an exceptional history. It belonged to the first edition of the Welsh Bible which the Bible Society, in two years after its formation,§ that is in the year 1806, sent to Wales. The interesting part which, in the providence of God, Wales was permitted to take, through the Rev. Thomas Charles, B.A., of Bala, in the formation of the Bible Society, made this fact all the more significant. There was only one other copy belonging to that edition in the whole neighbourhood. Shadrach's Bible had in the first place been bought by his grandfather within a month of the arrival of the first consignment at Bala. At his death it became the property of Shadrach's father, who was then a young man. It was some time before he made much use of the Book, as he was an ardent admirer of the hunt, the football, the fair, and the tavern, and felt he had enough of the Bible when he went to hear the parson occasionally on Sunday morning before the sports. It was, he thought, very well in its place, in church or chapel, in the cupboard-drawer, or on the parlour table;

---

* Gwell goddef cam na'i wneuthur.
† Gwell tewi na dywedyd drwg.
‡ Mark xvi. 1-4.
§ The British and Foreign Bible Society was formed in 1804.

but who would think of reading it during the week. Besides, there were the parson and those preachers who came to the little chapels in the village, many of whom, so he had heard, could "read like a parson," and speak a deal better, whose calling it was to read the Bible and let the people know something about it on Sundays. In those times the staple talk of the smithy on rainy days and wintry nights was a highly-seasoned mixture consisting of reports of hunts, of football matches and wrestlings, as well as ghost stories and fairy tales.

At length a religious awakening took place in the village, in common with many villages throughout Wales at that time, when Shadrach's father and most of his companions, including Hugh Roberts, became disciples of Jesus Christ. The recess, which was made for very different purposes when the smithy was built, now became the place where the Word of God was kept as the Book of final appeal in the smithy on all points of doctrine and practice. Since those days the Book had been well thumbed. Even before the death of Shadrach's father the binding had given way, and only kept together loosely a heap of disconnected sheets and in some instances of severed leaves, yet the dear old man would neither have a new Bible nor have the old one rebound. He could not find the passages he wanted in any other copy, but in that Bible he knew in what part of the page, and how far from a well-known blur, to look for almost every verse he desired to find. Hence with that conservatism, which, whatever may be our politics, we are forced to respect and revere in old age, he neither wanted another copy of the Scriptures, nor the dear old copy which his father had given him, and which had been all the world to him, "done up," as he called it. *That* was the Book he knew and loved, and he was not ashamed of his old friend in a ragged garb. "It won't be the same book to me," said he to Shadrach, "'if you go and put new leather on it, and cut it down, and do it up. I shall be lost, I shan't know my own Bible. Wait till I die, my boy, wait till I die, before you touch my Bible; an old Bible suits an old man."

At his death the Book fell to Shadrach's lot. He committed the difficult task of binding it to his father-in-law, who to his half-dozen other trades and professions added this one of bookbinding. Shadrach was satisfied that he would take great care of the Book, and would not cut more out of the margin than was necessary; and then he would take great care of the blank fly-leaves next the cover, which Shadrach's grandfather and father had converted into a family register. There were other leaves, too, which had been joined to the fly-leaf, and which contained important memoranda and extracts, the most important being copies of the letters written by John Penry, the young Welsh martyr and reformer, previous to his execution at St. Thomas-a-Watering, Surrey, in 1593, which had been written in a clear round-hand by the old village schoolmaster of wooden-leg renown—the hero of Waterloo. Next to the Bible itself, Shadrach, like his father, prized these letters most.

All things considered, it is doubtful whether Shadrach would have entrusted so precious a parcel to any bookbinder in the world other than his own father-in-law, and the frequency with which he repeated to *him* the injunctions to be sure not to mislay any of the loose leaves, to beware of cutting too much off the margin, and a host of similar requests was probably more than any bookbinder save his own father-in-law would have endured. The Book was bound in the thickest calf, and in the strongest style, the object being not so much elegance as durableness. In that the binder succeeded well, for notwithstanding the dust and handling of the last thirty years in the smithy, the binding looks as if it would yet outlive another generation. In the circumstances it is not surprising that Shadrach attaches very special value to this Sacred Volume.

On this night Shadrach, having observed the preliminary process of rubbing his hands in the corner of his apron, took down the Bible from the recess, and then carefully blowing off any dust that might have been deposited on the covers he opened it carefully, and said, "Well, what did he say, Hugh?"

"Let me see," said Hugh, as he pondered briefly. "Oh, I remember; he said:—

"'Our Lord's followers may be divided into three classes, according to the degree of constancy they shewed in their attachment to Him. There were those who followed Him only so long as things went well with Him. They were fair weather followers. Others were seen to come forth identifying themselves with His cause only when that cause wore its darkest aspect. Those were not fair weather friends but His companions in the storm, and they were certainly of the nobler sort. But some there were who clung to Him both in fair and foul weather, in the calm and in the storm. Of the first-named class were the bulk of His disciples, of the second were Nicodemus and Joseph of Arimathaea. The third were represented by John and the women.'

"I thought that was very clearly put. Then he went on to say:—

"'Often have we stood on a high point above the sea when the tide was at its height. All below was calm and smooth, the waters one vast expanse of level surface without a ripple to break its placid smoothness. But presently the tide recedes, and lo, how different the view. Now huge boulders come to sight that were but a while ago concealed by the tranquil waters. So was it in the case of some of our Lord's followers. When the tide of public favour was at its height, Nicodemus and Joseph were concealed, they followed Him only in secret. But when the tide of public favour had ebbed, then like great massive boulders on the exposed beach firm and immovable they come to view. And how grandly they acted on the eventful occasions, when they revealed themselves. Why Nicodemus and Joseph remained secret disciples it is difficult to say. Some think it was from natural timidity; that may be, but for all that it was clear that there was deep robust courage in their nature. The evangelist Mark, with his usual graphic touch, describes Joseph as "going in boldly unto Pilate" to crave the body of the Lord. There was evidently boldness and fearlessness lying down deep in his nature, and it needed only the fitting occasion to draw it forth into fullest play. Some natures need powerful events to draw out their better traits and their nobler qualities.'

"Then the preacher gave us another illustration. He said:—

"'Close to Bracelet Bay, Mumbles, is a bell-buoy, marking a concealed rock. This bell rings only in the storm. It is only when the wind is high and the billows roll and beat against it that it gives forth the music that is in it. Such were the two characters in question; they gave forth the deep grand music of their souls only in the ruthless storm. But these women of the text form a class who cling and serve in all weather, foul and fair, storm and calm. There is something singularly beautiful in all the references of the Gospel narratives to these women's services to Jesus during His sojourn among men. But now, as they stood by the cross sustaining His heart by this proof of their sympathy with Him, and as they followed His body to the grave and sought it again the third morning they stood alone, and the beauty of their conduct, the tender clinging of their love came out more conspicuously from the fact of its being singular.'"

"How true that is," said John, "that some natures need great events to draw out their nobler qualities. Stirring and troublous times have always produced heroes. There's nothing so bracing as hindrances and trials. These times of peace, when almost everybody agrees about religion and liberty, and no one is called upon to suffer and die in their defence, may produce good men but not extraordinary men. The air is too soft—not bracing enough—for heroes. They are always nursed in the storm. They tell me that the best masts for ships grow on the bleak hills of Norway, where from the first day the shoot peeps above the earth the tree has to fight with tempests. It is so with the brave; they are born and bred in bleak and boisterous times. God doesn't make heroes—at least He doesn't bring them out—until they are wanted, and the difficulties they have to overcome are the very things to bring them out. I have heard Llewellyn Pugh say—and he is a great scholar and knows all about old Greek tales and fancies—that Hercules, who was, as far as I can gather, the Samson of the old heathen world, was cradled between two serpents which were sent by a jealous goddess—Juno, I think he called her—to destroy him, but the child, though not a year old, rose in his crib and strangled them one in each hand, while his twin brother—I forget *his* name, and Llewellyn said that very little was known about him—screamed so loudly as to frighten everybody in the house. That's an extraordinary tale, like many more I have heard Llewellyn repeat, about those old Greeks and Romans. I should like to see the child who could do all that before it was time for him to walk; but there is one thing that we can learn from it, supposing it to be true—and I expect there's *some* little truth in it—and that is that the strangling of those serpents had a great deal to do with making Hercules what he was afterwards, and that the helpless screaming on the part of his twin brother accounts pretty satisfactorily for the world not having heard much about him after that. Everything is promised in this life, and in the life to come, 'to him that overcometh.' If men lie on their backs and scream at dangers and difficulties they are doomed weaklings for ever, they have missed the opportunity to become strong, but if they lay hold of them and strangle them they become heroes."

"And then the preacher compared Joseph and Nicodemus to the bell which only rings in the storm, and thus sends forth the music that is in it. Quite so; and the music that throbs in the darkness of the night, or is borne upon the wings of the storm, is always the sweetest. How sweet that bell must sound to mariners amid the howl of the wild hurricane, and yet it is the very storm which terrifies them that rings the bell. It is the power which creates the discord that sends forth the music. How comforting that the fiercest tempest that sweeps across the seas can only awaken the music that in calmer times lies asleep in that bell; and so it was with those men, when the darkness thickened and the storm blew furiously—but there, I forget myself, and go on talking. Now then, Hugh, tell Shadrach what else the preacher said; I liked it all very much."

"Well, I almost forget," said Hugh, "my memory isn't what it used to be, but yet I can remember sermons pretty well, and this sermon is a very easy one to remember. Well, let me see; he said in the next place that *Love acts promptly,* for the women came to the sepulchre *'early* in the morning the first day of the week.' He spoke a great deal on that point, and then said:—

"'Another lesson suggested by this incident is *love's obliviousness to obstacles.* There was a stone on the door of the sepulchre, and Mary, at least, was aware of it, for she had seen it when, on the day of His burial, she sat over against the grave, probably had witnessed the placing of it there. Yet it would seem from her conduct here that in the eagerness of her devotion she had forgotten all about the stone. How typical of love is this! Love never takes into consideration the hindrances and the obstacles that may interfere with its plans. It forms its plans, marks its course, regards ardently its object, but in all this it takes no account of the stones, great or small, that may be in its way. And well it has been for the world that such has been the case, that love has been thus characteristically blind to the hindrances; for ninety-nine out of every hundred of the efforts made for its welfare have been the achievements of men who have been gloriously oblivious of the stones. Those cool, calculating persons, who have been so discreet and cautious as to note carefully all the possible and impossible hindrances in the way of enterprises for the world's good have not been the world's benefactors. Had Carey counted the stones in his path he would never have reached India. Had Livingstone done so he would never have succeeded in opening the vast continent of Africa to the Gospel and to commerce. And so it has been in relation to all the achievements accomplished by the apostles of progress.'"

Here Shadrach turned to the record of the women going to the grave, as given in the Gospel by John, for which Evangelist he had a special liking, and said, "How true that is that love doesn't reckon hindrances; bless you, no. Hear what Mary said, 'Tell me where thou hast laid Him, and I will take Him away.' Thou take Him away! Mary, it would take half-a-dozen of thy sort to carry His blessed body. 'I will take Him away,' says Mary—not 'perhaps,' or 'if I am strong enough'; no, nothing of the sort, 'I *wilt.'* There's nothing that love cannot do. No; the preacher was quite right when he said that Love never reckons obstacles—Never! What else did he say, Hugh?"

Hugh considered for a moment, and said—"The preacher in the next place went on to say:—

"'Another lesson suggested by this incident is that *love never retreats.* It would seem that at last the fact of the existence of the stone flashed upon the mind of Mary. They had nearly reached the end of their journey when the fact occurred to her. The sight of the grave as it came into view in dim outline in all probability revived her recollection of it. We can imagine Mary when the fact struck her, turning to her companions with a somewhat perplexed air, asking, "Who shall roll away the stone?" No answer is recorded. Did they suggest to each other the propriety, under the circumstances of their retracing their steps? Clearly not, for we find that they still kept on their way. Love is ever accompanied by faith and hope, and in their company it always dares to pursue its course, however the odds may appear against it. This is strikingly characteristic of Love's tenacity of purpose. It never retreats.'"

"It was then, Hugh," said David Lewis, "that he gave the anecdote of the drummer boy, and said:—

"'The little English drummer boy's very apt reply to Napoleon indicates the spirit of love in this respect. The story is that when the little drummer was brought prisoner before the Emperor, he was told to sound the retreat; "I never learnt it," was the prompt answer. Love has never learnt to sound the retreat, or to practice it.'"

"Yes, that was it," exclaimed Hugh, "and then he said:—

"'The last suggestion of the incident we shall point out is, *that God has angels over against the stones that may be in the pathway of love.* "And when they looked they saw that the stone was rolled away, for it was very great." An angel had been there before them. He was God's messenger, he bore his Master's livery, his countenance was like lightning, and his garment was white as snow, and, as one old Welsh preacher observed, the brightness of his face sufficed to melt the seals on the stone, and the flapping of his wing to roll it away. There was need for the removal of that stone more urgent than that involved in the purpose of the women. The fact is nevertheless significant as a lesson in the direction we have suggested; it shows that over against the stones there are angels. We are inclined to think that if the removal of the stone had not been required for a higher end, God would have honoured the women's faith by removing it for their sakes and to gratify their devoted love. God has always His angels whom He employs to remove obstacles in the pathways of His servants who are honestly seeking to honour Him. The form of the angel will depend very much upon the size of the stone to be removed. In this particular case, because the "stone was very great," God sent an angel from heaven to roll it away. There was a stone on the door of another sepulchre, but no angel from heaven was summoned to roll it away. Jesus merely commanded the men that stood by to do it. So it is always, the stones will be removed either by heavenly or by earthly agents. And men are angels, that is, God's messengers, when they throw themselves into the work of removing stones. Yes, men are never so angel-like as when engaged in removing hindrances out of the way of those who seek to serve God.'"

"That narrative is throughout very beautiful," said John Vaughan, who for the last few minutes had been looking intently at Shadrach's Bible, and nodding significantly as he generally did when in one of his expository moods. "First, you see that Mary's tears at the grave of her Lord drew the attention of the 'two angels in white, sitting the one at the head and the other at the feet where the body of Jesus had lain, and they say unto her, Woman why weepest thou?' How interested they must have been! Why this tear upon the countenance of a human being—a woman? This makes an angel inquisitive; it awakens deep and earnest inquiry. How anxious those beings who have never wept must be to solve the problem of a tear! But they are not the only ones interested in Mary's tears, there is another greater than they, though Mary does not know it at the time, in whose heart her tears awaken sympathy and love. 'Jesus saith'—yes, *'Jesus* saith, Why weepest thou? Whom seekest thou?' It's something that angels who have never wept are interested in our tears, but how much more that Jesus—for that's the human name of the Son of God—is interested in them. *He* knows what they mean."

"Bless Him," ejaculated Shadrach.

"Yes, Shadrach, He knows what they mean. Ah, it is blessed when He who knows what it is to shed a tear—the good Lord Himself—draws near to us and asks, 'Why weepest thou?' It was solicitude on the part of the angels, but it is sympathy here."

"Yes," added Shadrach, "and Jesus is interested in our tears even when we shed them unnecessarily. Mary weeping by the empty grave of her blessed Master! If He had been there in the grave she would not have been half so grieved. Poor Mary is short-sighted, like most of us when we look through our tears. When the angels asked her why she wept, she said, 'They have taken away my Lord, and I know not where they have laid Him.' 'Poor soul, thou dost not know even as much as thou dost imagine.' 'They'—who are 'they,' Mary? She doesn't know, only her fears conjure up the soldiers, a host of them, no doubt. And then the Master comes to put her right, and asks, 'Why weepest thou?—whom seekest thou?' and poor Mary is so blinded with her tears that she thinks her very Lord is the gardener who, perhaps, had taken 'Him' away. She saw everybody but her Master."

"Quite true," said John, with a nod, "You see, Shadrach, she gives too much prominence in her grief to the 'they' while she speaks of 'Him' as the helpless dead one, whom 'they' could carry easily away. She missed the relative power of the Lord and His foes, Shadrach. The other evangelists tell us that the women were afraid when they first visited the grave. Mary was not much better now when she came to the grave the second time, for she 'stood *without* at the sepulchre weeping.' Now there is nothing that hides or disguises the Lord Jesus like fear on our part. When the disciples 'were affrighted' on the Sea of Galilee they mistook Him for a demon, and now when Mary feared at the grave she thought the very Christ was the gardener, whom she fancied must have taken away her Master's sacred body. We want that love, Shadrach, which casteth out fear, and which therefore can see the Master even by the graveside and in the storm."

Here old Hugh Roberts gave an approving nod, while a sweet smile lit up his saintly countenance.

"And yet," replied Shadrach, "Mary *stood there,* though it was '*without,*' when the disciples went away, and then you see how she was all taken up with the thought of her blessed Lord. '*Him*'—Who is it that she speaks about? Llewellyn Pugh used to tell us when we were boys at school, that a pronoun must have a noun before it. I didn't learn much grammar—you could always beat me at that, John, like a good many other things—but I remember that very well. 'Tell me where thou hast laid *him.*'—'Mary, thou hast forgotten thy grammar, poor soul, at the empty grave of thy Lord, thou hast no noun before thy pronoun, and no one can be expected to tell who is in thy thoughts except thou give His name.' Ah, as she looks at that grave she expects all who are near it to know who she means. There's only one she can think about now, and she can't understand how others could think about anyone else. '*Him*'—Of course everybody knows who she means, so she thinks, and, bless Him, the One to whom she spoke *did* know. Love doesn't bind itself down to grammar, does it, Hugh, it takes a short cut at things which grammar knows nothing about."

Hugh again smiled assent.

"Exactly so, Shadrach," rejoined John, "and you see how soon Mary, with all her fears and mistakes, found Christ, or rather how soon He found her. Such love to Him as Mary had, even though at first it is mingled with fear, must triumph before very long. The great Saviour will not suffer it to abide in gloom. He will speak sooner or later to those who love Him, and they know His voice whenever He speaks, whether on sea or on land, in the darkness of the night, or at the dawn of day. When His words, 'It is I, be not afraid' sounded out of the darkness on the Sea of Galilee, the disciples knew that voice. They had heard it before on those waters, and they could never forget it. And so when Mary heard His voice she knew who it was that spoke to her. She had heard Him call her before now. No one else had thrown so much sweetness into her name as He had, and she would know Him anywhere if He would but call her by her name. When, therefore, He said 'Mary' to her, she turned herself, for she knew that voice. She had just turned *away* from her Lord even when He questioned her about the meaning of her tears, mistaking Him for someone else, but when He called her by *name* she was not long in turning to Him again and exclaiming 'Rabboni'—Master."

"Bless the Lord," responded Shadrach. "It's when the great Shepherd calls His own 'sheep by *name*' that 'they know His voice.' They can't mistake Him *then,* John. But I never saw it so clearly as I do now. May the good Lord call us 'by *name*' when we are in the darkness, or by the grave! It's dreadful to have Him so near to us and yet not know Him."

"Yes," replied John, "but He soon makes Himself known if in our sorrow we are seeking Him in right earnest: and from the very graveside He will send us, as He did the women, with a Gospel to others, to those who ought to be our teachers, but who have missed the teaching by omitting the patient waiting—'Go to my brethren and say unto them, I ascend unto my Father and your Father; and to my

God and your God.' Blessed are they who from the graveside go forth to other sorrowing ones with the Gospel of a risen Christ."

"And what a Gospel that must have been to poor Peter," said Shadrach. "You remember, John, talking in the Bible-class once from the words, 'Go... tell his disciples and Peter.' You said it was Mark that gave that account—Mark, Peter's close friend—and you said he had no doubt heard Peter often talk about it. Others could forget that the angel had said 'and Peter,' but Peter never forgot it. No, poor soul; he wasn't likely to. But why, you asked, add 'and Peter,' wasn't the word disciples enough; and you said it was because if his name had been left out, and only the word 'disciples' given, Peter would have said, 'That can't mean me—can't mean me—I denied him thrice, and with oaths, too.' And so the gracious Lord bade His angel say to the women, 'Go your way, tell his disciples and Peter.' *And Peter!'* I imagine the angel say in surprise. 'Yes, *and Peter.'* 'And *Peter;'* say the women to themselves in wonder! 'Yes, *and Peter."* 'And *Peter;'* say the disciples within themselves. 'And *Peter;'* says poor Peter himself to the women, 'Are you *sure* you heard my name.' 'Yes, sure,' say the women. 'Bless Him,' says Peter, it's just like Him, 'I thought I should never see His face again after that time He looked me through and through when I had denied Him; and yet even that look was kind, but it was its very kindness that seemed to pierce me so and make me rush out into the dark night to weep bitterly, anywhere out of His sight. But I want to see that, face once more, and have one look, if it be only one, and just tell Him how I grieve. I want to confess all to Him—yes, even if He never forgives me.' But there, Peter knew the Master too well to suppose that He could do anything else than forgive when the poor sinner confesses his sins."

"And he hadn't to wait until his Lord would meet him on a mountain in Galilee," added John. "No, the sinner hasn't to go very far to find his risen Saviour. Next in order of time to the women Jesus appeared to Simon. Thus He appeared first to those who needed Him most—Mary Magdalene and Peter. What took place in that first interview with Peter—his confessions and the Lord's answer—we don't know, Shadrach. That was too sacred even for evangelists to tell. When the good Lord meets the sinner for the first time after his sin, He meets him alone, when there is no one else to hear the confession of a broken heart."

"Bless Him," said Shadrach, "as Mr. Morris Jones, 'the old prophet,' used to say when the Lord chastens us for our sins it's not in the open streets that He does it, where all can see, but in the *jail-court* out of sight."

"And very often He doesn't punish us as we deserve even there," said John. "The other evening my second boy had done something wrong, and his mother sent him to bed early. He went to the bedroom obediently enough; but his mother followed him with the rod. When he saw it he looked up tenderly to his mother's face, and said, 'Mother, let me say my prayers first,' and down he 'went on his knees, his mother standing over him with the rod. He got up at last, but do you think she could touch him? No, her hand was paralyzed by that boy's prayer; she couldn't move the rod, so she gave him a few words of warning, and kissed him and put him to bed. She wouldn't have told me a word about it if I hadn't asked how it was she hadn't punished the boy after all. She smiled, while tears filled her eyes, told me all, and then said, 'Do you think I could wait for him to get up from his knees and beat him? No, John, he had the best of me.' Now do you think the good Lord can be more unkind than our Kitty? No."

"No, never!" exclaimed Shadrach.

"No," continued John, "He sometimes takes us aside to chasten us, but if we fall on our knees His arm is too weak to strike us hard. But even when God does punish us for our sins it is generally done out of sight."

"Yes," rejoined Hugh Roberts, "and as I heard Mr. Ishmael Jones once say, when speaking about the scapegoat, over which the high priest confessed the sins of the people. It's to the wilderness that He sends our sins, not to the city, so that no one who may bear us a grudge can say, 'I saw thy black sins pass my house yesterday on the head of the poor scapegoat.' No, not into the city, but into the wilderness, out of the sight of men, He sends forgiven sins."

"That was a powerful sermon," said John Vaughan, "which Mr. Thomas,* of Cardiff, preached last night upon confessing sins, when he spoke from those words, 'I acknowledged my sin unto thee, and mine iniquity have I not hid. I said, I will confess my transgressions unto the Lord; and thou forgavest the iniquity of my sin.' He said a great many striking things, but there was one thing that particularly struck me. He told us that the emphasis was on the words

---

* Rev. N. Thomas, Baptist Minister, Cardiff.

'acknowledged'—*'not hid'*—*'will confess'*—and went on to say:—'The natural tendency of us all is *not* to confess, but to throw the blame upon another. Adam of old blamed Eve, and Eve the Tempter. God gave an opportunity to Adam and Eve to confess, though they neglected it—"Hast thou eaten of the tree?" "What is this thou hast done?"— but He gave no such opportunity to the Tempter. He asked *him* no question which would encourage a confession, but pronounced his doom—"Because thou hast done this thou art cursed above all cattle."' Then the preacher said—'My dear friends, what a privilege it is to be permitted to *confess* our sins. I find no record of a fallen angel being permitted to do so. It is a privilege, however, extended to fallen man. The great God would not have given us the opportunity to confess if He did not mean to pardon; but now "if we confess our sins He is faithful and just to forgive us our sins, and to cleanse us from all unrighteousness." Who of you will confess anew to-day?"'

"And that appeal wasn't in vain," said Shadrach, "for a large number stayed for the society at the close."

It was now half-past nine, and Mary's familiar voice calling Shadrach and Jenkin to supper brought the after-meeting at the smithy to a close. The fire subsided, the friends parted, the smithy door was closed, and darkness settled where a few minutes before all was aglow with the light of the blazing forge.

CHAPTER VII

A Talk about Olden Times

FORTNIGHT speedily passed during which nothing specially interesting transpired at the smithy. One evening Shadrach and Jenkin were busy at work, when the familiar form of Hugh Roberts, of Pentremawr, appeared at the smithy door. His face beamed with kindliness in the ruddy glow of the smithy fire. His presence was always welcome. From his early days he had been a most intimate friend of Shadrach's father, and since the death of the latter had been specially attached to Shadrach for his father's sake. When in the mood he would repeat the reminiscences of their early life, the tricks of their boyhood, and the friendship of their manhood. Those days were gone now, and one of the prominent actors had withdrawn for ever from the scene; Hugh, who had been left behind, often felt he had outlived his age, and almost wished he had gone too, yet he loved to tell about bygone days, and he had no more willing listener in the world than Shadrach, who used to tell him that the good Lord well knew what He was doing in keeping him here. Hugh's presence, he affirmed, was as necessary for the village, and especially for the smithy, as the presence of the aged John was for the little church at Ephesus, therefore Hugh must not be impatient about going to heaven. There were plenty of good people there, and the Lord knew full well there were not too many here; it was a pity if the earth couldn't now and then keep a little longer than usual a choice spirit of its own. Then Shadrach would repeat the saying of the Rev. Daniel Rowland, of Llangeitho, "Oh, heaven, heaven, heaven, thy mansions would be empty enough had not Zion been nursing children for thee on earth."

Hugh had no sooner arrived at the smithy than the sound of Samson Lloyd's crutch, as it struck the ground outside, announced his approach. He was no sooner heard than he hoisted himself into the smithy, and in his usual self-assertive manner accosted the company.

Samson Lloyd was the village tailor. His parents were pious people. When he was born his father took the Bible to choose a name for him, and at last selected "Samson". It was evident to all who knew Samson Lloyd that his father had fondly chosen that name before he knew what manner of man the child would be, for besides being of anything but a "sunny" disposition and cheerful countenance, Samson was lame and exceedingly diminutive in size. Taking all things together it would have required a very extraordinary imagination to picture him carrying away the gates of Gaza or of any other city on his shoulders. Judging from appearance, his locks must have been cut *very* early in life. Samson, however, seems to have been scarcely conscious of his diminutiveness, for he used to say that he had when a boy grown almost visibly for three years, a statement which used to call forth from Jenkin the sarcastic remark that he must have grown *invisibly* all the other years. Samson was of an ambitious turn. He had the firm conviction that tailoring was not his calling, and that he was eminently qualified for the work of the ministry, a conviction which unfortunately no one shared with him. He had composed two sermons, the outlines of which he would occasionally repeat as a specimen of the style of preaching he would adopt if he had the opportunity of exercising his gifts. One was on Zaccheus. He divided his subject into—I. Zaccheus before he went up the tree. II. Zaccheus up the tree. III. Zaccheus after he came down the tree. Another sermon illustrative of the same lucid style was from the words, "What is man that thou art mindful of him," which he divided thus—I. What was man? II. What is man? III. What will man be? This was a style which may be termed preaching in the three tenses, and which, whatever may be said against it, had the advantage of exhausting all time.

Samson had united himself at different periods to each of the three denominations in the district—the Baptists, the Independents, and the Calvinistic Methodists—hoping, as he used to say, to find "a sphere of usefulness." He had left each church in bitter disappointment, shaking the dust from his feet at the doorstep as he departed in judgment against their blindness. and exclaiming "a prophet hath no honour in his own country." Unfortunately no one in any other country knew him. At length there was a vacancy in the parish church, for the clerk, who, like Samson, was a tailor, had to give up through increasing infirmities, which seriously affected the vocal organs. Samson was impressed with the fact that the last two clerks had belonged to his own calling, and recognizing this as a sign that the third should also be a tailor, he became a zealous Churchman. He already worked for the clergyman, and that certainly would be a recommendation. But again his talents and zeal to find a suitable sphere were overlooked, and another was chosen, an event which convinced Samson that the Established Church was rotten to the core. Thus, like his leg, he was completely out of joint with all churches, and was dreadfully disgusted with the want of appreciation of genius and true worth which he said so distinguished this age. Like most disappointed men he was a self-constituted censor and general busy-body.

Samson, who was always at home in narrating his own feats, told them that on the way to the smithy he had seen a group of people looking over the wall into the grave-yard by "Horeb" Chapel, terrified by a light that seemed to play upon one of the graves, and which they thought looked very much like a spirit, but that he soon jumped over the wall and brought the supposed spirit out in his hand, for it was nothing but a decayed piece of wood. Samson looked quite heroic as he told the story.

Jenkin suggested that the "group of people" must have been small children, as there was no grown-up person in the village now stupid enough to mistake a piece of rotten timber in the dark for a spirit. The time had gone by for corpse-candles and the like. The light of Christian truth had frightened all spirits out of the country, and as for corpse-candles there was not enough wick and tallow in all the land to manufacture one of them.

"You, Hugh, could tell us something about spirits and corpse-candles, fairies and goblins, which were supposed to flourish when you were a boy," said Shadrach.

"Yes, I could tell a great deal about those things," replied Hugh Roberts, "they are among my earliest recollections. I remember well when a boy sitting with my brothers and sisters round a blazing fire on wintry nights and listening to my father relating strange stories about ghosts, goblins, and fairies. It's seventy years ago, yet it seems like yesterday; I can almost see my father sitting on the old oak settle, and my mother by his side knitting stockings for her family, and each of us children opening our eyes wide and listening eagerly to all that was told us, until we were afraid to move from the spot, lest some mysterious being might take us by the heels clean away. I very well recollect him telling us about his grandfather ploughing on one dark, foggy day in November in that field just above the house, and that drawing near the hedge on the right hand, near the corner of the field, just where the ash tree is, he heard the sweetest music he ever heard in his life, and looking into the hedge saw a host of little beings scarcely a foot in height dancing in high glee. He stopped the horse, and stood for almost an hour watching those fairies; for he had often heard of them, but had never seen them before. At length, leaving the plough, he gradually drew near, but all at once, so my father used to say, the little tribe threw very fine dust into his eyes, which all but blinded him for the time, and while he was wiping his eyes they disappeared, and were not seen by him again. But, continued my father, the shepherd boy was not so fortunate, for one very dark morning, when on the mountain with the sheep, he and his dog, before they knew it, entered the dancing circle of the fairies, went on dancing all day, and had it not been for the shepherd who went in search of them would have danced themselves to death."

Llewellyn Pugh now entered the smithy, greeted all present very cordially, and in his usual deferential way urged upon Hugh Roberts to proceed.

"Many strange things were said about the fairies," continued Hugh. "They were of two distinct kinds—'The Fair Family'* and 'The Goblins.'† The Fair Family were gentle and kind toward all, especially young and virtuous lovers, faithful servants, loving children, and clean, industrious, and hospitable house-wives. Thus at night the careful house-wife, before retiring, made the room tidy, cleaned the hearth, and filled the pails with water, believing that the Fairies came to the neatest homes and the cleanest hearths to enjoy their harmless revel until the dawn when they were supposed to sing the well-known melody, 'The Break of Day,'‡ and then leave a piece of money, generally silver, on the clean hearth as

---

* Y Tylwyth Teg.

† Yr Ellyllon.

‡ Toriad y Dydd.

a small acknowledgment. They also gave pleasant dreams to those whom they favoured. They were generally to be seen on small hillocks, on gentle slopes, in bushes, on the banks of brooks and rivers, and in shady glens. The Goblins, on the other hand, frequented rocky and mountainous districts, and delighted in mischief. Unlucky indeed was he who was beset in a fog by those mischievous beings, for they would take him by force, and having given him the option of travelling above the wind, in the wind, or below the wind, they would take him according to his choice. If he chose the first they carried him far into the heights, right through the clouds; if the last they bore him with great speed through brambles, brakes, and hedges. The wise, therefore, chose the middle course, and thus evaded alike the clouds and the brambles.

"When I was a young man I learnt the Song of the Fairies, which ran like this:—

From grassy glades, and fenny shades,
 My happy comrades hie;
Now day declines, bright Hesper shines,
 And night invades the day.
From noonday pranks and thymy banks,
 To Dolyd's dome repair,
For our's the joy, that cannot cloy,
 And mortals cannot share.

The light-latched door, the well-swept floor,
 The hearth so trim and neat,
The blaze so clear, the water near,
 The pleasant circling seat,
With proper care your needs prepare,
 Your tuneful tabors bring;
And day shall haste to tinge the east,
 Ere we shall cease to sing.

But first I'll creep where mortals sleep,
 And form the blissful dreams;
I'll hover near the maiden dear,
 That keeps the hearth so clean:
I'll show her when that best of men,
 So rich in manly charms,
Her Einion, in vest of blue,
 Shall bless her longing arms.

Ye little sheaves or primrose leaves,
  Your acorns, berries, spread;
Let kernels sweet increase the treat,
  And flowers their fragrance shed;
And when 'tis o'er, we'll crowd the floor,
  In jocund pairs advance,
No voice be mute, and each shrill flute,
  Shall cheer the mazy dance.

When morning breaks and man awakes,
  From sleep's restoring hours,
The flocks, the field, his house we yield,
  To his more active powers.
While clad in green, unheard, unseen,
  On sunny banks we'll play,
And give to man his little span,
  His empire of the day.

"Both the fairies and the goblins indulged in recruiting their own numbers by carrying away children or young people. The fairies took only orphans of pious parents, while the goblins found great delight in snatching away unbaptized children, especially when they were the heirs of wealthy parents. Those thus snatched were allowed to appear on two different occasions to their friends, once at the end of seven years, and again at the end of fourteen years."

"It's wonderful how a superstition clings to a people," said Llewellyn Pugh, as he took an old and well worn note-book out of his pocket. "Now I'll read to you what is given by Giraldus Cambrensis as a popular belief seven hundred years ago. How similar it is to the stories we heard when boys, Hugh. Just listen:—

"'A short time before our days a circumstance worthy of note occurred in those parts (Neath, in Glamorganshire), which Elidorus, a priest, most strenuously affirmed had befallen himself. When a youth about twelve years of age, in order to avoid the severity of his preceptor, he ran away, and concealed himself under the hollow bank of a river; and after fasting in that situation for two days two little men of pigmy stature appeared to him, and said, "If you will go with us we will lead you into a country of delights and sports." Assenting, and rising up, he followed his guides, at first through a path, subterraneous and dark, into a most beautiful country, murky, however, and not illuminated with the full light of the sun. All the days were cloudy, and the nights extremely dark. The boy was brought before the king and introduced to him in the presence of his court, when, having examined him for a long time, to the great admiration of the courtiers, he delivered him to his son, who was then a boy. These people were of the smallest stature, but very well proportioned, fair-complexioned, with long hair, particularly the females, who wore it flowing over their shoulders. They had horses and hounds adapted to their size. They neither ate fish nor flesh, but lived, for the most part, on milk and saffron. As often as they returned from our hemisphere, they reprobated our ambition, infidelities, and inconstancies; and though they had no form of public worship, they were, it seems, strict lovers and reverers of truth, for no one was so utterly detested by them as a liar.

"'The boy frequently returned to our world, sometimes by the way he had gone, sometimes by others; at first in company and afterwards alone, making himself known only to his mother, to whom he described what he had seen. Being desired by her to bring her a present of gold, with which that country abounds, he stole, while at play with the king's son, a golden ball, with which he used to divert himself, and brought it in haste to his mother, but not unpursued, for, as he entered the house, he stumbled at the threshold, let his ball drop, which two pigmies seized and departed, showing the boy every mark of contempt and derision. Notwithstanding every attempt for the space of a whole year, he never again could discover the track to the subterraneous passage; but, after suffering many misfortunes, he did at length succeed in securing his intimacy with the mysterious race.'

"Now you have noticed, Hugh," continued Llewellyn Pugh, "that Welsh superstitions generally convey a good moral. There can be no doubt that this story was repeated by the old monks to discourage falsehood and theft."

"Excuse me, Mr. Pugh," said Jenkin, with an apparent diffidence which became a young man as he addressed his old schoolmaster, "but that's scarcely the story I should have expected you, Sir, to write in your note-book for reference. There's doubt that that story was written by some wicked school-boy to justify 'miching,' for it was by playing truant by the river-side instead of being at school and obeying his master that that young hopeful got into such nice company and learnt so much. I shouldn't like to read that story in the hearing of a lot of schoolboys, Mr. Pugh," added Jenkin, as a mischievous smile lurked about his countenance.

The old schoolmaster knew Jenkin well, and detecting the furtive smile he answered quietly but emphatically, "I've never read that in the hearing of school-boys, Jenkin; I forgot there was one here to-night. I am very sorry that unawares I have read it in his hearing."

"I have no doubt that the old Welsh superstitions often conveyed very wholesome truths," said Hugh, "but they also did a deal of harm in taking the place of better things in people's minds, as well as in interfering with the ordinary industries of life. Men were afraid of ghosts or evil spirits at every turn, and thus were frightened out of doing many things for their good. For instance, as long as my father lived not a grain of wheat was sown in that field below our house, though it was the best field for that kind of crop on the whole farm, because during my grandfather's time, for two years following it was said, some evil spirit untied the sheaves almost as soon as they were bound by the harvesters."

"I remember very well, too, old William Jones, of Pentrebach. He never dared to be out at night after ten o'clock, as a white horse, carrying a mysterious-looking rider, so they said, was sure to gallop after him at terrific speed, and as soon as it overtook him would walk by his side so long as he walked, and stop when he stopped, and the only way in which he could get rid of this unwelcome companion was to go home."

"What a capital cure that white horse would be," said David Lewis, "for some men who are fond of being out late at night. I wish the old nag still lived and put in an appearance occasionally in some of our towns; it would make many a man more fond of his home.

"Ah, they were strange times," continued Hugh, "I can recollect well that when I was a boy the father of David William, of Ty-mawr early one dark winter's morning put on his waistcoat inside out and wore it like that all day to prevent ill-luck."

"I should think," said Jenkin, with a wicked smile, "that that interesting event accounts for David William being a hyper-Calvinist in this enlightened age. What do you think, Hugh?"

"You seem to owe the hyper-Calvinists a grudge, Jenkin," said Hugh, playfully, "you'll be less impulsive as you grow older, and may yet be a worthy descendant of your grandfather. Well, there were many omens in those days: for instance, to be followed by a strange dog was a favourable omen, while the shriek of an owl, or a magpie crossing one's path, and making hideous noises as it passed, were unmistakable signs of ill-luck. The sudden blazing of the fire was sure token of a sweetheart or a good husband to the servent who sat nearest to it. A bright speck in the candle or in the griddle was sure to be either a letter or a stranger, but if the candle burnt blue there was a spirit in the room. The untimely blossoming of an apple tree, or the sound in the ear like the sound of a bell was a certainty of death. Then there were the corpse-candles, which are generally seen to proceed from the house, where a death was to take place, along the same road to the graveyard as the funeral would go. If a child was to die the candle was faint like a glow-worm, if a young man it blazed forth, if an older man it had a red light, if a woman it was white. The church bell, too, frequently gave warning. It gave three tolls in the depth of the night when a parishioner of influence was about to die. The church at Blaenporth, in Cardiganshire, was noted for this throughout the country, the sound of that bell being specially solemn. These and a great many other things I used to hear when I was young, but happily hear no longer; they have all vanished before the light of God's truth.

"There were very few Bibles about when my father was a young man. There was one at Ty-mawr, but it was locked up and kept there for months together in the old oak chest, where David William's grandfather—for it was he who lived there at that time—kept his parchments. He placed it there very much for the same reason as he nailed the horse-shoe on the stable door—to keep the devil away. My father used to tell of one incident which happened before he was born— that would be more than a hundred years ago—when one of the cows at Ty-mawr was taken very ill. The old man gave her medicine, but apparently with no effect. At last, thinking that she was dying, he went into the house, asked his wife for the key of the coffer, and, taking the Bible out he went and read a chapter to the poor creature."

"What was that done for, Hugh," asked Jenkin "to keep death away, or to administer consolation to the dying cow?"

"My father never told me, my boy," answered Hugh, "and at this distance of time it's better not to guess. Perhaps the old man at Ty-mawr could scarcely have told you had you asked him. My father used to tell, too, how on one occasion your great-grandfather, Samson, suffered from rheumatics, as they used to call it. He, like yourself, was a tailor; they ironed him with a tailor's goose, thinking that the heat would drive away the pains, but all was of no use. At last they were told that if he could only have a Bible under his pillow for a few nights he would be quite cured. The Bible at Ty-mawr had been already lent, so they sent to the 'Squire's. He had only an English Bible, and lent that. Some of the older people shook their heads, and said that was no good, others said that it would do, but it would take a longer time than a Welsh one. In a week the rheumatics disappeared, but that was, so some said, four days later than if they had had a Welsh Bible. When the Bible was returned the old man's wife praised 'The Good One,' as she called Him, that they had been married for thirty years, and that there had never been any need of a Bible in their house before; and should there be any need of one again—which she hoped wouldn't be for many a day—she trusted that she would be fortunate enough to have a genuine Welsh Bible, as she hadn't much faith in English, and she doubted whether 'The Good One' took much account of it. He knew Welsh, of that she was sure, but about English—well, she didn't know. It was all a risk to have an English Bible—a great risk with rheumatics—but there, it had done her husband a good turn this time; and yet Peggy Thomas, who knew a great deal about those things, had told her that the cure was a great deal longer about, and another thing it wouldn't be so thorough."

"Is the goose which you use the one with which your great-grandfather was ironed on that interesting occasion?" asked Jenkin, "because if it is I should let it be known, as it would be sure to draw trade. Only imagine having one's coat ironed by the very goose which a hundred years ago soothed the aching joints of your illustrious great-grandfather!"

Samson, who had with great difficulty listened to the interesting narrative of Hugh Roberts, now grew furious, shook his little head fiercely, and said he knew nothing about the matter.

"How did they spend their Sunday then, Hugh?" asked Shadrach, by way of calming the troubled waters, as he shook his head disapprovingly at Jenkin, who seemed immensely to enjoy the fury of the little tailor.

"The Sunday was then the worst day of the week," said Hugh. "I well remember hearing my father say that when he was a boy it was customary for young people to meet early on Saturday evenings and dance to the music of the harp and violin till the dawn of Sunday, and on the afternoon of that day to resume the singing and dancing, or when they preferred it to witness or join in the sports. In the summer months interludes were played and people would walk many miles on Sunday afternoon to see them. They were announced by the clerk at the close of the morning service. I myself heard old David Jones, the tailor, who was then clerk, publish the sports many a time, and saw the parson join in them, too; but I never heard an interlude announced. That was before my time."

"The first great Revival had made itself felt throughout Wales before your time, Hugh," said Llewellyn Pugh, "and ever since the history of our country has been one of increasing brightness. If we went back a little over three hundred years, say to the time of the Protestant Reformation in England in 1534, we should have a sad tale to tell about our country. From the Act passed in the fifth year of Queen Elizabeth—that is *twenty-nine* years after the establishment of the Protestant religion—authorizing the translation of the Scriptures into Welsh, it appears that the people of Wales were 'utterly destitute of God's holy Word,' and remained 'in the like, or *rather more* darkness and ignorance than they were in the time of Papistry.' The morality of the Welsh clergy at that time, and for a hundred years later, baffled all description, the disclosures made being simply shocking; as I heard old Mr. Robert Jones, of Llanllyfni, once say, 'They were as bad as the devil could make them, or would have them be.' In 1560 Dr. Meyrick, Bishop of Bangor, affirmed that at that time he had in all his diocese only two clergymen who preached; and that, notwithstanding the liberty of marriage granted, there were a large number of the clergy in that diocese who openly paid pension for the right of keeping concubines."

"It would seem that then the old proverb was true," said David Lewis—"'The nearer the church the further from Paradise'" ('Po agosaf i'r eglwys, pellaf o Baradwys').

"Yes," said Llewellyn Pugh emphatically, "and possibly that proverb originated then. It exactly expresses the truth about those times." Here Llewellyn Pugh took his old note-book from his pocket, and continued, "I copied this fifty years ago when a student at Oxford, from a book in the University library—'Strype's Life of Archbishop Parker.' Now just listen, I'll translate it:—'In the latter end of this year 1565,... a resolution was taken for the speedy supplying of two Welsh bishoprics, viz., that of Llandaff, and that of Bangor, the former of which had been two or three years, in effect, void, and wanted a vigilant bishop to manage that diocese; which, therefore, the Archbishop, in the year 1563, had earnestly put the secretary in mind of. But the great dilapidations had so impoverished that see that few that were honest and able would be persuaded to meddle with it. As for Bangor, that diocese was also much out of order, there being no preaching used, and pensionary concubinacy openly continued; which was allowance of concubines to the clergy by paying a pension, notwithstanding the liberty of marriage granted. And the Archbishop was at that time earnestly solicited to have such a commissioner there as kept openly three concubines, as men of good reputation offered to prove before him. Things, in fine, were in such disorder here that our Archbishop was desired by some well affected of that country to have a visitation, and to set such order there as whosoever should come to the bishopric should be forced to prosecute it. And accordingly a visitation was instituted, by the Archbishop's commission, to Dr. Yale, which did great good, as he that was afterwards Bishop there wrote him word. So that Wales, being in an evil condition as to religion, the inhabitants remaining still greatly ignorant and superstitious, the Queen left it particularly to the care of the Archbishop to recommend fit persons for those two sees now to be disposed of.'

"The majority of the Welsh people at that time were still Papists," said Llewellyn, "in so far as they were anything. Wales had only supplied three to the noble army of martyrs in the reign of Queen Mary; one was Bishop Farrar, of St. David's, who was martyred near where the old oak stands now in Priory Street, Carmarthen, another was William Nicol, of Haverfordwest, unknown except for this, and one other a Rawlins White, a fisherman, at Cardiff. The great bulk of the priests renounced their Popery or Protestantism with equal ease, according to the bias of the particular king or queen who reigned. On the accession of Mary they embraced Popery, while on the accession of Elizabeth all, save three bishops and a few other dignitaries, suddenly became enthusiastic Protestants."

"So much, then, for the Reformation so far as Wales was concerned," said Shadrach.

"The Reformation did but little for Wales for nearly a century," said Llewellyn, "for although the translation of the Bible into Welsh may be said to be the result of the Reformation, yet with the exception of Salesbury's New Testament that work was not done by the authority of Parliament or command of the Queen. Those who were appointed to do the work failed, and not until thirty-four years had passed after the Protestant religion had been established did Dr. Morgan, on his own responsibility and amid much persecution, bring out his Bible.

And even then—listen to what Dr. Thomas Llewellyn* says:—'For upwards of *seventy years* from the settlement of the Reformation by Queen Elizabeth, for near *one hundred years* from Britain's separation from the Church of Rome, there were no Bibles in Wales, but only *in the cathedrals or in the parish churches and chapels.* There was no provision made for the country or for the people in general, as if they had nothing to do with the Word of God, at least no further than they might hear it in their attendance on public worship once a week. This is astonishing!'"

"But wasn't there any translation of the Bible into Welsh before the Reformation?" asked Shadrach.

"Not of the Bible," replied Llewellyn. "Certain parts of the Scriptures had been translated, but they were all in manuscript, and some of them had been lost."

"The first, as far as can be found, to have translated any part of the Bible into the Welsh language was Taliesin, a noted bard, who flourished in the middle of the sixth century. This translation was a kind of paraphrase in verse of certain portions of the Bible, viz., The Ten Plagues, The Rod of Moses, and a few passages referring to God and to Christ.

"It is also said that in former times there was in the Library of St. Asaph Cathedral a very old translation in manuscript of the four Gospels. This translation was considered old in 1282, as in that year a letter of protection and privilege was granted by the Archbishop of Canterbury authorizing the priests to carry the manuscript about as a sacred thing, and to show it to all who desired to see it. This translation was kept at St. Asaph until the time of Bishop Goldwell, the predecessor of Bishop Davies. He was deprived of his see on the ascension of Queen Elizabeth to the throne, because he would not become a Protestant, and went to Rome and died there. It is supposed that he took the old manuscript with him to Rome, where probably it is to-day.

"Ah, indeed," said Samson, who had an inbred hatred toward the Church of Rome, which expressed itself on every available opportunity. "Then it's gone where a great many other good things have gone— never to come back again."

"Yes, Samson," replied Llewellyn, "you are right. Well, another

---

* An Historical Account of the British or Welsh Versions by Thomas Llewellyn, LL.D., London, 1768, p.36.

poetical paraphrase of certain portions of the Word of God was written about the middle of the fourteenth century by Dafydd Ddu, of Hiraddug, and consisted of a part of the Psalms, a part of the first chapter of Luke, the song of Zacharias, the angel's greeting to Mary, the song of Simeon, and the song of the three youths.

"It appears, too, from what Dr. Malkin learnt from Iolo Morganwg* that Thomas Llewellyn, a noted Welsh bard,† a distinguished Protestant, and a man of high moral character and devout spirit, translated Tyndal's English Version of the New Testament into the Welsh language about the year 1540. Having in common with some others in those days received a license from Archbishop Grindal to preach, he would often read in different houses the Church Service, which he had in his own handwriting—for as yet it had not been printed—and would preach very acceptably to the people who came to hear him. Thus he formed many small Christian communities in the country. It is also said that there is a letter in manuscript in the library of Sir Thomas Mostyn, Flintshire, from Thomas Llewellyn to Dr. Richard Davies, the second Protestant Bishop of St. David's, urging upon him to translate the Scriptures into the Welsh language, and giving a brief account of what he himself had done. It is highly probable that Llewellyn's manuscript was on William Salesbury's table when he was engaged, at the request of the Welsh bishops, in the translation of the New Testament into Welsh.

"Dr. Richard Davies, the Bishop of St. David's, refers to another old Welsh translation of a portion of the Scriptures. He says in his letter prefixed to the first Welsh version of the New Testament, which appeared in 1567—'I remember to have seen, when a lad, a translation of the five books of Moses in the British or Welsh tongue, in the possession of a learned gentleman, a near relation of our family.'

"The first book known to be *printed* in Welsh consisted of a few

---

* Iolo Morganwg, or Edward Williams, was a stone mason, also bard and antiquary, was horn at Peron, in the parish of Llancarvan, Glamorganshire, on March 10, 1746. He died December 18, 1826, and was buried in the secluded graveyard of Flemingstone, Glamorganshire. Although he was never at school, he became a distinguished writer and an acknowledged authority in Bardic and Historic Literature.

† He lived in the reign of Edward VI. at Glyn-eithinog, near Ystradyfodwg, Glamorganshire.

leaves only, and appeared in 1546. It was written by Sir John Price,* of Brecon, was entitled 'Bible,'† but contained The rudiments of the Welsh language, The Calendar, The Creed, The Lord's Prayer, The Ten Commandments, the customary games, &c. The word 'Bible' was printed in large letters at the top of the title-page, probably in the original and more general sense of 'book', or perhaps in order to secure attention, as it contained numerous extracts from the Bible, which in those days was almost entirely unknown in Wales.

"The next book was published in the following year. It was a 'Dictionary in Englyshe and Welshe by Wyllyam Salesbury,' but that may scarcely be called a Welsh book. Four years later (1551) the same author published a translation of the Psalms, the Gospels, and the Epistles, as appointed to be read in churches, at the celebration of the Communion, and on Sundays and fast days.

"Besides these I have not heard of any translation of the Scriptures or any part of them into Welsh until the version of 1567 appeared.

"Tell us something about that translation," said Shadrach, earnestly.

"Not to-night," said Llewellyn, "but I will the next time I call—let me see—this night week."

"Very well," said Shadrach, "and I'll get you a congregation."

---

* Sir John Price, LL. D., was educated at Oxford, and having taken his degrees there was called to the bar. He soon attracted the notice of Henry VIII., was a great favourite at Court during the whole of his reign and on the dissolution of monasteries was appointed one of the Commissioners for their suppression.

† Beibi. Yn y llyvyr hwn y Traethyr Gwyddor Kymraeg. Kalendyr. Y Gredo, neu bynkey yr ffydd Gatholig. Y Pader neu Weddi yr Arglwydd. Y Deng air Deddyf. Saith rinwedd yr Eglwys. Y Kampau arferadwy, a'r Gweddiau Gocheladwy ac Keingen (Llundain, 1546, 4 plyg).

CHAPTER VIII

𝔗𝔥𝔢 𝔇𝔞𝔴𝔫 𝔬𝔣 𝔱𝔥𝔢 𝔚𝔢𝔩𝔰𝔥 𝔕𝔢𝔣𝔬𝔯𝔪𝔞𝔱𝔦𝔬𝔫

SHADRACH Morgan did not fail to fulfil his promise to find a congregation for Llewellyn Pugh. All Shadrach's friends who came to the smithy during the intervening week were acquainted with the fact that the other night Llewellyn Pugh was in a good humour, and told them all manner of learned things about old Welsh translations of different parts of the Scriptures, one of which had been written more than a thousand years ago. They had never been printed, and only great scholars like Llewellyn Pugh knew anything about them. Ah, he was a very wonderful man! Shadrach could not make out how he could contain all those things in his head. Next Monday night he was going to tell them the history of the present translation, and Shadrach expected that he would tell a good many things of interest. David Lewis was going to try to draw him out on John Penry, and if he succeeded they would have a treat.

The result of this was that long before Llewellyn Pugh came most of Shadrach's immediate friends had arrived. There were Hugh Roberts, John Vaughan, Caleb Rhys, David Lewis, Samson Lloyd, and one whom we have not seen in the smithy before—Theodore Augustus Swash.

Theodore Augustus Swash was an Englishman who had some years before come over from Somerset—"the country of summer," (Gwlad yr haf) as the Welsh call it. By profession—for he was not an artisan, or even a tradesman, and nothing annoyed him so much as to be mistaken for either—by *profession* he was an insurance and commission agent. He was also a general valuer, a capacity in which a very wide and diversified prospect opened before him, for he had to bring his judgment to bear upon a great variety of objects, from a hen to a horse, and from a rake to a hay-rick. From long stay in the village, and his constant dealings with the surrounding farmers, he had a very fair knowledge of Welsh. His pronunciation, however, was execrable, being an incoherent mixture of the true "Zummerzet" and the genuine "Shirgar."*

He had all the style of a gentleman, but unfortunately his profession was not a very lucrative one in that district, hence, though he indulged in broad cloth and a tall hat, his clothes had an unctuous glossiness about the knees and elbows, and his hat a mysterious shine about it which gave evidence of the morning rub with a wet towel.

Swash, like all true men, was a great believer in his nationality, and in all pertaining to it. David Williams, of Ty-mawr, the hyper-Calvinist, had five points of doctrine, for each of which he was prepared to shed his blood. Swash had four articles in his creed, which he held as dear as life:—I. Himself. 2. The English. 3. The Established Church. 4. Commissions.

Swash had come to the smithy on this occasion, in common with the others, to hear Llewellyn Pugh's learned disquisition.

Llewellyn Pugh arrived in due time, greeted the company, and joined in the conversation.

"You see, Mr. Pugh," said Shadrach, "the congregation is waiting for the preacher. We want to know about this book"—pointing to the Bible in the recess—"and how it came to be translated for us."

"Well, I told you last time how dark Wales was for many years after the Reformation in England, and how in the year 1563 it was described as being probably darker than even 'in the time of Papistry.' In that year it was enacted† that the Bible, with the Book of Common Prayer,

---

* Colloquial for Carmarthenshire, or anything pertaining to it, a parallel word to "Zummerzet."

† "That the Bible consisting of the New Testament and the Old together with the Book of Common Prayer and the Administration of the Sacraments should be translated into the British or Welsh tongue—should be viewed

and the Administration of the Sacraments should be translated into the Welsh tongue; should 'be viewed, perused, and allowed by the Bishops of St. Asaph, Bangor, St. David, Llandaff; and Hereford,' and 'should be printed and used in the churches' by the first of March, 1586, under a penalty in case of failure of forty pounds, to be levied on each of the five Bishops. William Salesbury,* an intimate friend of the Bishop of St. David's, was engaged by the Bishops, and was partly assisted in the work by Dr. Davies† and probably by Thomas Huet,

---

perused and allowed by the Bishops of St Asaph, Bangor, St David, Llandaff and Hereford—should be printed and used in the churches by the first of March in the year 1556 under a penalty in case of failure of forty pounds to be levied on each of the above Bishops.

"That one printed copy at least of this translation should be had for and in every cathedral collegiate and parish church and chapel of ease throughout Wales to be read by the clergy in time of Divine service and at other times for the benefit and perusal of any who had a mind to go to church for that purpose.

"That till this version of the Bible and Book of Common Prayer should be completed and published the clergy of that country should read in time of public worship the Epistles and Gospels the Lord's Prayer the Articles of the Christian Faith the Litany and such other parts of the Common Prayer Book in the Welsh tongue as should be directed and appointed by the abovementioned Bishops.

"That not only during this interval but for ever after English Bibles and Common Prayer Books should be had and remain in every church and chapel throughout that country."—v. *Eliz. cap. 28.*

* William Salesbury was of an eminent family, being the son of Foulk Salesbury, Esq., of Plas-isaf, Llanrwst, Denbighshire. He was born early in the sixteenth century, and was educated at Oxford. He was master of nine languages, besides Welsh and English. During the reign of Queen Mary he resided at Caedu, in the parish of Llansanan, Denbighshire, a very secluded spot, in a mountainous and unfrequented district. Owing to his valuable services to the cause of Protestantism he was exposed to many dangers during that reign. Hence he had a small chamber so constructed that it was accessible only by climbing inside the chimney. He was residing at the same place when he undertook the task of translating the New Testament. We hear nothing of him after the dispute he had with Dr. Davies, save that he died in 1570.

† Dr. Richard Davies, son of a clergyman, born in 1501 near Conway, Carnarvon. He was educated at Oxford, and in 1550 was presented by Edward VI. to the vicarage of Burnham, and to the rectory of Maidsmorton,

then precentor of St. David's and vicar of Cefnllys and Disserth.

"In 1587, or one year after the time appointed by Parliament, for the publication of the Bible and the Book of Common Prayer, the Welsh Translation of the New Testament appeared.* It was a handsome quarto of 399 leaves, printed in black letter, was divided into books and chapters, having subjects and contents, and had marginal explanations of difficult words.†

"After the translation of the New Testament there was a long and painful pause. Salesbury was residing with the Bishop of St. David's in the Palace at Abergwili, for the purpose of carrying on the work of translation. This went on for nearly two years, when a dispute arose between them on the etymology of one word, a dispute which gathered to itself such an amount of feeling—altogether out of proportion to the gravity of the point in question—as to separate the two friends for life, and to deprive them for ever of the honour of completing a work which they had so well begun."

"A bishop—a successor of the Apostles—quarrel! Shocking!" said Jenkin, "but there's one comfort it was with a lawyer he quarrelled, and the Lord Jesus Himself got out of patience sometimes with their quibbles."

"But Salesbury was a lawyer of a very different type from those you mention, Jenkin," said John Vaughan, with an evident desire to

---

Buckinghamshire. On the accession of Queen Mary he lost his preferments and fled to Geneva, where he suffered much poverty. On the accession of Queen Elizabeth he returned, and was consecrated Bishop of St. Asaph in 1560, and in 1561 was translated to St. David's. He died at The Palace, Abergwili, Nov. 7, 1581.

* Testament Newydd ein Arglwydd Jesu Grist. Gwedy ei dynnu, yd y gadei yr ancyfiaith 'air yn ei gilydd o'r Groec a'r Llatin, gan newidio ffurf llythyren gairiae-dodi. Eb law hynny y mae pob Gair a dybiwyt y vot yn an deallus, ai o ran Llediaith y wlat, ai o ancynefinder y deunydd, wedi ei noti ai eglurhau ar ledemyl y tu dalen gydrychiol.

† From the marginal notes it also appears that the Book of Revelation was translated by T. H. C. M., supposed to be Thomas Huet, Chantor (or Preceptor), of Menew, or St. David's; and that the second epistle to Timothy, the epistle to the Hebrews, the epistle of James, and the first and second epistles of Peter were translated by D. R. D. M., that is Dr. Richard Davies, Menevensis (or Bishop of St David). All the other books bore the initials W. S., representing William Salesbury.

maintain correctness in Scriptural allusions, and in any inferences which may be derived from them. "This quarrel was very humiliating, no doubt, but we must not be too hard on this successor of the Apostles, when we remember that Paul and Barnabas had a quarrel very much like this. The fact is, there's perfection no where but in God. There's a strange mixture of wisdom and folly, of grace and impatience, of the sublime and the ridiculous, in most of the best men."

"Yes," said David Lewis, "it's in vain that we look to men—and for that matter even to women—for perfection. That's the prerogative of lovers and of the heroes of novels. There's a flaw, a weak point, somewhere, in every one else, even in bishops."

"But this was a quarrel about the etymology of a word," said Jenkin; "what a thing for two great men to quarrel about."

"It's generally the case that the less people have to dispute about the more bitter they get," said Hugh Roberts, gently. "The greatest quarrels of the world, and especially religious ones, have been about words,—*words*. If men only went deeper, and got at the spirit underlying all, they would cease quarrelling. It's this verbal hair-splitting that has been the curse of the Church in all ages, from the time of the scribes until now."

"Yes, Hugh," said Llewellyn, "and in this case, as in most other cases of the kind, it was a great calamity to others who had no part in it. Another result of this humiliating episode was that the Welsh people were for twenty years longer without a Bible. Dr. Davies seems to have been the only one of the five Bishops who took any interest, or at least any active part, in the work imposed upon them by Parliament; hence, when this unhappy quarrel took place between Dr. Davies and William Salesbury the translation of the Scriptures was at a complete standstill, so far as the bishops were concerned, for twenty years, during which time the Welsh people were without a Bible. And had it been left with those Bishops it is probable that that state of things would have continued to this day. The penalty enforced was too insignificant to ensure obedience, for the Bishops, who seem to have had to bear all the expenses of translation, would have had to pay more than the fine in order to accomplish the work.

"But the work, which those who had been authorized to perform had failed to do, was accomplished by a holy man in the quietude of an obscure country vicarage, for in 1588, after a lapse of twenty-one

years, Dr. Morgan,* vicar of Llanrhaiadr, Denbighshire, published an
edition of the whole Bible, consisting of his own translation of the
Old Testament and Apocrypha, and a revised edition of the Salesbury
version of the New. Thus the first translation of the whole Bible was
presented to Wales, not by Royal command, or Act of Parliament, or
nomination of Bishops, but from a good man's keen sense of the great
need of his country and proportionately of personal responsibility. In
his Latin dedication to Queen Elizabeth there is no reference to what
Salesbury speaks of in his dedication as 'the appointment of our most
vigilant Pastours, the Bishops of Wales.' But such a work was sure to
arouse opposition. Among other things the charge of incompetency
was laid against him before the Bishop of the diocese and the
Archbishop of Canterbury. But God overrules the wrath of man to
His praise, for by that persecution the hitherto obscure Vicar was
brought to the notice of the Archbishop, who, having satisfied himself
as to his qualifications, encouraged him to proceed with his great task.
Dr. Morgan, in the dedication, refers gratefully to the kindly interest
of the Primate,† and says that he would have sunk under his difficulties
and discouragements, and would have relinquished all, or have
published only the five books of Moses, had it not been for the
Archbishop's support and encouragement. In 1595 Dr. Morgan was
promoted to the see of Llandaff, and six years later was translated to
the see of St. Asaph. Dr. Morgan, before his death, again revised and

---

* Dr. William Morgan was born in the parish of Penmachno,
Carnarvonshire. He was educated at St. John's College, Cambridge, was
presented to the vicarage of Welshpool in 1575. In 1578 he removed to the
vicarage of Llanrhaiadr-yn-Mochnant, Denbighshire. He became Bishop of
Llandaff in 1595, was translated to the see of St Asaph in 1601. Died
September 10, 1604.

† In his dedication there is not only this grateful reference to Archbishop
Whitgift, but also most honourable mention made of all those who aided
him, some granting him free access into their libraries, others perusing and
examining his version, others revising and correcting it after him. Among
the persons mentioned are the Bishops of St. Asaph and Bangor, Dr. Gabriel
Goodman, the Dean of Westminster, at whose residence he lived while
attending the press, Dr. David Powell, Vicar of Ruabon, Archdeacon Edmund
Pryse, the well-known author of the Welsh Metrical Psalms, and the Rev.
Rd. Vaughan, rector of Lutterworth, afterwards Bishop of Bangor, of Chester,
and of London.

corrected the New Testament but that version was never printed."

"Is that the translation we have now?" asked Shadrach.

"Oh, no," replied Llewellyn, "that was used for only a short time. In sixteen years later (1620) Dr. Richard Parry, the successor of Dr. Morgan as the Bishop of St. Asaph, published a revised edition of the Welsh Bible,* and that translation is practically our present standard version. This Welsh Version was published nine years after the Authorised English Version of King James; unlike the English translation this was not under Royal patronage, but Dr. Parry†—like his predecessor—published it at his own free will and sole responsibility, from a consideration of the pressing wants and necessities of his country. The spiritual destitution of the people was still most lamentable. Listen to what he says in his dedication:—'The former impression of the Bible being exhausted, and many, or most of our churches being either without any, or having only worn out and imperfect copies; and nobody, as far as I could learn, so much as thinking of a re-publication; in these circumstances of this matter, and induced by these considerations, I set about revising our translation.'

"That there must have been a great scarcity of Bibles and Testaments even for the churches is clear from the fact that only six hundred copies of William Salesbury's Translation of the New Testament, and the same number of Dr. Morgan's Version of the Bible had been printed at all, and these had been in use fifty-three and thirty-two years respectively."

"He and Dr. Morgan," said David Lewis, "were a slight improvement on their predecessor, the Bishop of St. Asaph, I forget his name."

"Ah yes," replied Llewellyn Pugh, "you refer to Dr. William Hughes, the Bishop of St. Asaph. He was accused, in 1587, of misgovernment, and the toleration of the most disgraceful abuses within his diocese. The inquiry resulted in shocking disclosures. The Bishop himself held sixteen of the richest livings *in commendam;* most of the other rich livings were in the possession of clergy who lived out of the country, while one clergyman who had two of the largest livings boarded in an

---

* Assisted by his learned chaplain, Dr. John Davies.

† Dr. Richard Parry, born at Ruthin, Denbighshire, in 1560, was educated at Westminster School and Christchurch, Oxford. On the death of Dr. Morgan, in 1604, he was consecrated Bishop of St. Asaph. Died Sept.26, 1623.

alehouse. Only three preachers resided in their parishes—Dr. William Morgan, the translator of the Bible into Welsh, Dr. David Powell, of Ruabon, and the aged parson of Llanfechan, who by reason of strength had reached four-score years."

"It was then that John Penry,* as a young and unknown student came forth in the service of his country, wasn't it," said David Lewis.

"Yes," replied Llewellyn Pugh. "He was of a comparatively obscure parentage, and went to Cambridge as a Papist, but coming into contact there with the Puritans of his day, he became a Protestant, caught their fire, and, returning to Wales for his holiday, his whole being was aroused into righteous indignation at the immorality of the clergy, and the degradation of his countrymen.

"Thus in the same year as that in which the shameful disclosures were made in connection with Dr. William Hughes, the Bishop of St. Asaph, he published a pamphlet on the spiritual destitution of Wales,† addressed to Queen Elizabeth and Parliament." Here Llewellyn Pugh took out his old note-book, which was a kind of *Index Rerum,* and looking into it continued:—"In it Penry says—'Thousands of our people know Jesus Christ to be neither God nor man, priest nor prophet, almost never heard of Him. O desolate and forlorn condition! Preaching itself in many parts is quite unknown. In some places a sermon is read once in three months.' He attributed all this to the fact that the clergy were either non-resident, unable to preach, ignorant of the truths of the Gospel, immoral in their lives, or unacquainted with the Welsh language. Then he proposed a plan for the evangelization of his country, which was that as many devoted Welsh clergymen as could be found in England should be asked to return to their native land, and that pious laymen should be encouraged to exercise their gifts in preaching.

"A petition embodying the substance of this pamphlet was presented to Parliament, and was introduced by a powerful speech from a Welsh

---

* John Penry, the son of Meredith Penry, was born at Cefnbrith, in the parish of Llangamarch, Brecon, in 1559. When nineteen years of age he entered Cambridge University, and in 1586 became a student of St. Alban's Hall, Oxford, where he immediately distinguished himself as 'a famous preacher.' The other events of his life are briefly referred to above.

† See "A History of Protestant Nonconformity in Wales" by Thomas Rees (now Dr. Rees, of Swansea). 1861, p.20. A reprint of this work is available from Tentmaker Publications.

member. The only result, however, was an order for the immediate seizure of the pamphlet and the apprehension of its author. Penry having been kept in close confinement for a month was taken before Archbishop Whitgift, who severely condemned his plan for evangelizing Wales, characterizing it as intolerable, and denounced as an execrable heresy the statement contained in the pamphlet that no unpreaching clergyman was a true Christian minister. Our noble Penry before the Archbishop, like Caractacus, his illustrious countryman in earlier days, before the Roman Emperor, stood unmoved. In a deliberate and emphatic tone he said—and it seemed like the utterance of an Apostle—'I thank God that I ever knew such a heresy, as I will by the grace of God sooner leave my life than leave it.' The Bishop of Winchester, who was also present, said, I tell thee it is a heresy, and thou shalt recant it as a heresy.' 'Never! God willing, as long as I live,' replied the intrepid Penry. He was then remanded, and, after brief imprisonment, released.

"Unmoved by the dark threats of the frowning prelates of his day he, in the following year—the year in which the first Bible ever given to the Welsh people in their own tongue was published—at the early age of twenty-eight, published his 'Exhortation,'* in which he says:— 'Wales is said to be in a tolerable condition, for it hath many preachers of a long time. The more the shame, then, for them that it hath no more teaching. This I dare affirm and stand to, that if a view of all the registries in Wales be taken, the name of that shire, that town, or of that parish, cannot be found, where for the space of six years together, within these twenty-nine years, a godly and learned minister hath executed the duty of a faithful teacher and approved his ministry in any mean sort. And what, then, should you tell me of abbey lubbers, who take no pains, though they be able? If I utter an untruth, let me be reproved and suffer as a slanderer; if a truth, why shall I not be allowed? I know very well that to speak anything at all in these days against clergymen is to speak in Bethel with poor Amos to prophesy in the king's court, and so to be busy in matters of State. Miserable days! Into what times are we fallen, that thieves and murderers of souls, the very patterns and patrons of all covetousness, proud and more than Pope-like tyrants, the very defeaters of God's truth, unlearned dolts, blind guides, unseasoned and unsavoury salt,

---

* An Exhortation unto the People and Governors of Her Majesty's Country of Wales, p.31, 1588.

drunkards, adulterers, foxes and wolves, mire and puddle; to be brief, the very swinesty of all uncleanness, and the very ignominy and reproach of the sacred ministry, cannot be spoken against, but this will be straightways made a matter against the State. And therefore all the misery, all the ignorance, all the profaneness in life and conversation, hath been, for the most part, by means of our bishops and our other blind guides; yet may not a man affirm so much with any safety, lest he be said to be a mutinous and factious fellow, and one that troubleth the State.'"

"That's a hard and rude style; there's nothing gentlemanly or refined about it, I think," said Swash.

"Yes, and they were hard and rude times in which Penry lived," replied Llewellyn Pugh. "They were not times for bandying compliments and doing the gentleman; a nation was being ruined in its highest, its eternal interests by the neglect of those who were professedly its teachers and guides. At such times God raises men of exceptional natures, men who are not well up in etiquette, who speak plain truths and not glib sentiments, men who, like the young Roman of old, will throw themselves into the yawning chasm that threatens to engulf a people, and let it close upon them and accept them as a willing sacrifice in the cause of their country. When such men use great plainness of speech we must not complain much since they purchase it at a high price— their life-blood. When a man like Penry is prepared to write his utterances with the very blood that bounds through his young heart, you must not be surprised if he speaks in words that burn.

"I heard Mr. Williams,* of Mountainash, once say—'When the Lord Jesus said to His apostles, 'Go ye into all the world,' there were not enough prisons in all the world to prevent them. 'Necessity is laid upon me,' said Paul, 'to preach the Gospel, yea, woe is unto me if I preach not the Gospel.' 'Woe to the Gospel,' as Cynddelw† once said, 'if some men preach it,' but woe to Paul, and woe to every man inspired with a message, if he preach not the truth. Such men cannot help themselves, they hear the word 'Go' come from eternity, so that it is easier to suffer martyrdom than to live in its sound without obeying it. The authority of the true preacher is that he cannot help himself, but is bound at all risks to speak for God. Paul's sermon at Lystra came back upon his

---

* Rev. W. Williams, Baptist Minister.

† The *nom de plume* of the late Rev. R. Ellis, Baptist Minister, Carnarvon.

head in a shower of stones from hearts of adamant. They had no better coins than stones to give by way of acknowledgment for the miracle and sermon of the great Apostle of the Gentiles. Though he was left as dead, yet on the following day, without staying to have his wounds healed, he and Barnabas went to Derbe determined to attack Satan's kingdom as long as there was breath in their nostrils. The command of the Great Master had come to Paul like a thunderbolt from the skies, so that it made him deaf henceforth to every other sound. Those heroic men were not sent out by any earthly senate, but went at the bidding of their King, when all the senates and kings of the earth were arrayed against them. Wounds and scars were the credentials of Paul and of the early preachers—'I bear in my body the marks of the Lord Jesus'—and mighty conviction attended the preaching of those days. Paul carried his clerk with him in the scars he bore, and he paid dearly for him, but he did good service, for his voice sent forth a clear 'Amen' at the close of every sermon and prayer. Paul was thus marked by the stones at Lystra in order that he might be distinguished as a noted preacher. Stoning was a very strange reward for preaching and healing, but it did not prevent Paul from completing his preaching tour. That shower did not quench the fiery zeal of the Apostle. The nearer he approached the threshold of eternity the more of the great Saviour came to view in his ministry. Thus he did not count his own life dear so that he may place the banner of Christ upon every towering height. Stephen lost his life beneath the shower of stones and thus could proceed no further. He had to go home, instead, to receive his crown. His mantle fell upon Paul to carry on the work at the cost of passing through many a shower himself as a reward for holding the clothes of those who put Stephen to death. Thus the message must be told though messengers fall one after another. And messengers must be prepared for this. Only death silenced Stephen, and only death could silence Paul. Men of such type do not wait until they are supplied with patent safety coverings before they will dare pass through showers of stones in the service of their Master.'

"All that is very true," continued Llewellyn, in a voice tremulous with emotion, "John Penry was one of that class. Listen to some of his last words to his countrymen, words which live, because he who uttered them can never die in their grateful memory and loving hearts. He says:—'The inhabitants of the city of Thasus being besieged by the Athenians made a law that whosoever would motion a peace to be concluded with the enemy should die the death. Their city began to be distressed, and the people to perish with the sword and famine. Hegetorides, a citizen, pitying the estate of his country, took a halter about his neck, came to the judgment-place and spake:—"My masters, deal with me as you will, but in any case make peace with the Athenians, that my country may be saved by my death." My case is like this man's. I know not my danger in these things. I see you, my dear and native country, perish—it pitieth me. I come with a rope about my neck to save you. Howsoever it goeth with me, I labour that you may have the Gospel preached among you. Though it cost my life I think it well bestowed!'

"Ah, a man who speaks like that," proceeded Llewellyn, "cannot be fashioned by the orthodox shape of the day. There is no running such a character into any other mould than that in which it was first cast. Such are the most uncompromising men of all. They speak out what's in them, though the heavens boom forth thunder, and earth and hell quiver with rage. Such a man was our martyred Penry. No, Mr. Swash, reformers are not distinguished for their politeness—Luther and Knox to wit. They are men raised by God to arrest the current of degenerate times, and to challenge sins which have become conventional and respectable; and therefore to tear in tatters sickly civilities and polite deferences which conceal beneath them a hell of sin and vice. They are no respecters of persons, but speak to king and peasant, priest and sinner, in the same dialect. Those men whom God has raised to speak for Him in times of degeneracy have always been scathing speakers, especially in addressing hypocrites. They scorch them with the burning words of their mouth. Listen again to Penry as he proclaims his sacred message to the unholy clergy of his day:—'I know you for the most part to be silly men—poor souls that make a means to live in the world. What should I say unto you who may say of yourselves as did the foolish prophets (Zech. xiii. 5). Though we wear a surplice and black garments to deceive, yet we are but plain husbandmen. Surely the people may ask counsel of their thresholds or desire their staff to teach them knowledge, as to come unto you for any instruction. You are no ministers as I have proved, and again will prove.'

"Addressing his countrymen in the same pamphlet he says:—'Let no man do me the injury that I deny any member of Christ to be in Wales. I protest I have no such meaning, and would die upon the persuasion that the Lord hath His chosen in my dear country, and I trust the number of them will be daily increased.' Then warning them against mistaking the hirelings for the true shepherds, he says:—'The outward calling of these dumb ministers by all the presbyteries in the world, is but a seal pressed upon water, which will receive no impression. Labour, then, to have true pastors over you, and rest not until you have brought this to pass... Difficulties in this case must not be alleged; for if you seek the Lord with a sure purpose to find Him, He hath made a promise to be found of you. Away, then, with these speeches, "How can we be provided with preaching?—our livings are unappropriated—possessed by non-residents!"—Is there no way to remove these dumb ministers, but by supplication to her Majesty, and to plant better in their stead? Indeed you will seek none—be it, you cannot remove them. Can you bestow no more to be instructed in the way of life than that which law hath already alienated from your possessions? You never made account of your tithes as your own. For shame! Bestow something *that is yours* to have salvation made known unto you. Contemn not the grace of God offered to you in these days of your peace.'"

"I have very little patience with that kind of thing," said Swash. "A raw young fellow from among the hills undertaking to rebuke bishops, dignitaries, and priests of the Church, many of whom were learned men; and then undertaking to give his countrymen a bit of gratuitous censure and advice. It's quite ridiculous."

"You speak about the raw young fellow coming from the hills of Wales to dictate to learned men what should be done," replied Llewellyn Pugh. "I would remind you that he had a University education, and that very early he was acknowledged to be 'a famous preacher' in the University—but that is nothing. I would remind you, too, that God does not confine His sphere of training men for a great work to the quadrangles of university colleges. He often trains in His own way amid the wild solitudes of the world, and not in the recognized schools of the prophets. Elijah of old, one of the grandest spirits of ancient times, and the father of the prophets, came forth from amid the wild and deep ravines of Gilead, and John the Baptist, greater than whom there has been no one born of woman, save He whose advent He foretold, emerged suddenly out of the solitudes of the desert. We are told that 'he was in the deserts until the time of his appearing unto Israel,' and when he appeared he was called 'a *voice,* 'because men knew little or nothing of the *man.* His identity had been all but lost, yet it was enough that they heard him; there was irresistible might in that voice—God had taught him to speak. What mattered it in what other school he was taught?

"Why, it was in the obscure home and the poor carpenter's workshop in despised Nazareth that the Lord Jesus Himself was prepared for His great task, and when at length He spoke to men they asked in wonder—and I have no doubt that you would have joined with them, Mr. Swash, judging from your objection to-night—'How knoweth this man letters, having never learned?' 'He is a young peasant from Nazareth, of all places in the land, and has never been in a college in his life,' said a young disciple who sat at some Rabbi's feet, and who had never heard his master say anything to compare with *this man's* utterances. 'Wonderful,' said Joseph of Arimathaea to Nicodemus, 'considering He has never been in our University in Jerusalem, and that none of the professors know Him.' 'Yes, wonderful indeed,' replied Nicodemus, 'I went to see Him last night, and He said to me strange things that I never knew before, "Except a man be born of water and of the Spirit he cannot enter into the kingdom of God." I never heard a Rabbi in my life say that. I showed some astonishment when I heard that and asked, "How can these things be?" He, with a look of sad surprise upon His youthful countenance, a look which made me ashamed of myself and all our schools, said, 'Art thou a master of Israel and knowest not these things?' Then in wondrous fashion He continued to speak things I had never heard before, and brought God so near to me that I lost all conceit for our schools, and sat at His feet a willing disciple—God speaks in that young man, and if I mistake not He is the Messias, "of whom Moses in the law, and the prophets did write."'"

"Yes, Mr. Swash, when God sent His own Son to the world as its Saviour, He ordained that He should be born in a manger and brought up in a humble cot in Nazareth. Ah, the world owes most to lowly cradles and obscure huts. Those mighty men who have led the world in leading strings—the true kings and rulers of our race—have in not a few instances been born in humble dwellings with thatched roofs and mud-built walls. From the lowliest circumstances there have arisen in times of danger and degeneracy prophets of the Invisible, holy and heroic men inspired with great thoughts and laden with solemn messages from God to man. Outward circumstances have never yet constituted the greatness or the smallness of a life. Man may rise above them or fall below them. In the history of the great past excellence has been confined to no locality or people, and there is no reason why it should be now. The testimony of bygone days, as one of your own writers puts it, is that 'the millstreams that turn the clappers of the world arise in solitary places.'

"Then with regard to his youth," continued Llewellyn Pugh, "remember that most of those who have done anything worth doing have done that when young. The inspiration of every life comes in youth, and all depends upon whether we catch it then or not. That is the period of enthusiasm, and there is but little done without that. The steady consolidating work of life is done later on, but the dash that storms positions which appear impregnable, and bounds from crag to crag until at length it plants the flag of victory on the very summit of the dizzy height, is got in youth, and all the enthusiasm we have in later life is but the remains of that, matured no doubt by passing years, but also weakened and modified. Look at the Reformers. Yes, look at the Lord Jesus Himself. He passed away from earth when He was but thirty-three years old, the same age as John Penry when he was martyred. Thus when God Himself chose the period of this mortal life in which to do a great work He chose youth.

"Penry, in advocating *lay agency and voluntary contributions,* struck the key-note of the Welsh Reformation, the advent of which he died to hasten. He had now crossed the Rubicon and cut the bridge behind him. The prelates treated this scheme of evangelization as a damnable heresy and a mortal sin. Henceforth there was no rest for him in her Majesty's dominions, for the chief priests and scribes were bent upon his death. His house at Northampton was ransacked, and an order was issued for his immediate apprehension, and of anyone who might be associated with him. He fled to Scotland, taking with him his wife and two infants. The Scotch people, however, extended to him cordial hospitality. When the Archbishop found that he had crossed the Tweed he persuaded the Queen to write to King James desiring him to send Penry back or to banish him from his kingdom. Meanwhile the Privy Council issued a warrant for his apprehension. King James, too, issued a decree of banishment against him, which he ordered the Scotch ministers to proclaim, but those intrepid men unanimously declined to do so. Thus while Penry was in Scotland he received kind hospitality and ready shelter. This Penry never forgot; even in his last letter to his children, which is copied in your Bible, Shadrach, he made touching and grateful allusion to it. Having remained there for over two years his enthusiastic desire to hasten the spread of Gospel truth in his native country led him back to London, hoping to obtain the Queen's permission to exercise his ministry among his countrymen.

"When he arrived in London he joined the Separatists, but declined to take any office among them, giving as his reason—'It hath been my purpose always to employ my small talent in my poor country of Wales, where I know that the poor people perish for want of knowledge.' On the 22nd of March, after a stay of six months in London, he was imprisoned, and was then subjected to a trial which Sir Thomas Phillips affirms 'disgraces the name of English justice.' He had violated no statute, and could not be legally condemned, yet at five o'clock in the afternoon of the 29th of May, 1593, Penry, the hope of his country, was hurriedly martyred chiefly at the instigation of the Archbishop and his priestly associates. Thus died in the thirty-fourth year of his life one of the noblest sons of Wales, who offered up his life in the cause of his country and of his God. It has been said that the blood of the martyrs is the seed of the Church. What wonder that such blood is productive of so much! You Englishmen ask why Nonconformity is so powerful in Wales. Let the immorality of the Welsh clergy in that and the two succeeding centuries, and the scaffold of our beloved John Penry, give you answer. I remember well hearing Mr. Williams, of Wern, once speaking of the Jews, God's chosen people, and saying that God did not forsake them until they themselves said, 'Away with him, away with him, crucify him,' adding the solemn words, '*God never leaves a people, a church, or a family until He is sinned out of it.*' That applied to the Established Church in Wales for almost three centuries; *God was sinned out of it,* hence He removed the candlestick and placed it elsewhere, never henceforth to be its exclusive possession.

"Penry, a few days before his death, wrote two letters—one to Lord Burleigh, the Lord Treasurer, and the other to his wife and children."

"Ah, yes, they are the letters which my father got copied into this Bible," said Shadrach, as his face beamed with delight, "and they read like the epistles of Paul."

Llewellyn opened the old Bible, and proceeded to read the letter written to Lord Burleigh:—

✳   ✳   ✳   ✳   ✳   ✳   ✳   ✳   ✳   ✳

"I am a poor young man, born and bred in the mountains of Wales. I am the first, since the last springing of the Gospel in this latter age, to have the blessed seed thereof sown in those barren mountains. I have often rejoiced before my God, as He knoweth, that I had the favour to be born and live under her Majesty for promoting this work.

In the earnest desire I had to see the Gospel planted in my native country, and the contrary corruptions removed, I might well, as I confess in my published writings with Hegetorides, the Thracian, forget mine own danger, but my loyalty to my Prince did I never forget. And being now to end my days before I am to come to one half my years in the likely course of nature, I leave the success of these my labours unto such of my countrymen as the Lord is to raise up after me for the accomplishing of that work, which, in the calling of my country unto the knowledge of Christ's blessed Gospel, I began.

"I never took myself for a rebuker, much less for a reformer of States and Kingdoms. Far was that from me, yet in the discharge of my conscience, all the world was to bear with me, if I preferred the testimony I was bound to yield unto the truth of Jesus Christ before the favour of any creature. The standing of the State, Kingdom, and Prince was always most dear to me, as He knoweth by whom States are preserved and princes do bear rule. The beginning of her Majesty's reign I never saw, and beseech the Lord that no creature may see the end of her prosperity. That brief confession of my faith and allegiance unto the Lord and her Majesty, written since my imprisonment and delivered to the worshipful Mr. Justice Young, I take, as I shall answer before Jesus Christ and the elect angels, to contain nothing but God's eternal verity in it, and therefore if my blood were an ocean sea, and every drop thereof were a life unto me, I would give them all, by the help of the Lord, for the maintenance of the same by confession.

"Yet if any error can be shewed therein that will I not maintain. Otherwise far be it that either the saving of an earthly life, the regard which in nature I ought to have to the desolate outward state of a poor friendless widow and four poor fatherless infants, whereof the eldest is not above four years old, which I am to leave behind me, or any other outward thing should enforce me by the denial of God's truth, contrary unto my conscience, to lose mine own soul, the Lord, I trust, will never give me over unto this sin. Great things in this life I never sought for, not so much as in thought. A mean and base outward state, according to my mean condition, I was content with. Sufficiency I have had with great outward troubles, but most contented was I with my lot. And content I am and shall be, with my undeserved and untimely death, beseeching the Lord that it may not be laid unto the charge of any creature in this land. For I do, from my heart, forgive all those that seek my life, as I desire to be forgiven in the day of strict account, praying for them as for my own soul. That although upon earth we cannot accord, we may yet meet in heaven, unto our eternal comfort and unity, where all controversies shall be at an end.

"And if my death can procure any quietness unto the church of God and unto the state of my Prince, and her kingdom, wherein I was born, glad I am that I had a life to bestow in this service. I know not to what better use it could be employed if it were reserved; and therefore in this cause I desire not to spare the same. Thus have I lived toward the Lord and my Prince, and thus mean I to die by His grace. Many such subjects I wish unto my Prince, though no such reward unto any of them. My only request, being also as earnest as possible, I can utter the same unto all those, both honourable and worshipful, unto whose hands this, my last testimony, may come, is, that her Majesty may be acquainted herewith, before my death, if it may be, or at least after my departure. Subscribed with the heart and the hand which never devised or wrote anything to the discredit or defamation of my Sovereign, Queen Elizabeth (I take it on my death, as I hope to have a life after this), by me,

JOHN PENRY."

"Now comes a still more touching letter to his dear wife and children; I have never been able to read it without shedding tears."

"Nor I," exclaimed Shadrach, as he brushed a tear with his rough hand from his manly countenance.

"The most touching words of all," said Llewellyn, "are those addressed by him to his four little infant daughters:—"

*   *   *   *   *   *   *   *   *   *

"Show kindness unto the kindred whereof you are come, both of your father's side and mother's also, but especially, if ever you be able, show all forwardness in doing good unto my people and kindred in the flesh.

"The Welsh nation now for many hundred years past have been under the Lord's rod, but I trust the time is come wherein He will show mercy unto them by causing the true light of the Gospel to shine among them; and, my good daughters, pray earnestly to the Lord when you come to know what prayer is, for this; and be always ready to show yourselves helpful unto the least child of that poor country that shall stand in need of your loving support... and be an especial comfort, in my stead, unto the grey hairs of my poor mother, whom the Lord used as the only means of my stay for me in the beginning of my studies, whereby I have come unto the knowledge of that most precious faith in Christ Jesus, in the defence whereof I stand at this present, in the great joy of my soul, though in much outward discomfort. Pray much and often for the prosperous reign and preservation, body and soul, of her right excellent Majesty, my dread Sovereign, Queen Elizabeth, under whose reign I have come unto this blessed knowledge and hope wherein I stand. The Lord show mercy unto her for it both in this life and also in that great day. Shew yourselves helpful and kind to all strangers, and unto the people of Scotland, where I, your mother, and a couple of you lived as strangers, and yet were welcome, and found great kindness for the name of our God. Be tender-hearted towards the widow and the fatherless; both because the law of God and nature requireth this at your hands, and also because, for aught I know, I am likely to leave you fatherless, and your mother a widow. Whatever becometh of you in outward regard, keep yourselves in this poor church where I leave you, or in some other holy society of saints... Although you should be brought up in never so hard a service, yet, my dear children, learn to read, that you may be conversant day and night in the word of the Lord. If your mother be able to keep you together, I doubt not but you shall learn both to write and read by her means. I have left you four Bibles, each of you one; being the sole and only patrimony or dowry that I have for you. I beseech you and charge you not only to keep them, but to read in them day and night; and before you read, and also in and after reading, be earnest in prayer and meditation, that you may understand and perform the good way of your God... From close prison, with many tears, yet in much joy of the Holy Ghost, this Tenth of Fourth Month, April, 1593, your poor father here upon earth, most careful to be joined with you for evermore in the kingdom of Jesus Christ.

JOHN PENRY,
A poor witness in this life unto the right
of Jesus Christ against the abomination
of the Roman Babel."

"What parting words were those to beloved children who did not know their meaning at the time, but who later on would understand all, and cherish as dearest the memory of that father, who, in laying down his life in the hour of its greatest promise, for the sake of the truth and his suffering countrymen, uttered his last and tenderest words to his young wife—his companion in adversity—and his infant children, who were so soon to be left widow and orphans in the land of his martyrdom. What a legacy to his orphan children were this letter and the four Bibles which he left behind for them. He had nought else to leave save the memory of a heroic life. But who that is wise would not have such a legacy with which to begin life? There is nothing so precious that a father can bequeath, or children inherit, as that. The allusion to his mother, too, is very touching, worthy of such a son and equally worthy of such a mother.

"Here, Shadrach," added Llewellyn Pugh, as he handed to him the Bible, "there is your Bible, and there the last utterances of John Penry, which will echo and re-echo among the hills of Wales for generations yet to come, and will rise up in judgment at last—though he prayed that his murderers might be forgiven—against the prelates of his day, who plotted against his life, as well as the Queen, who, at their instigation, consented to his death. He never meddled with politics, and had no quarrel with the State. A more loyal man could not be found within her Majesty's dominions than John Penry, the father of Welsh Nonconformity, and more loyal subjects than Welsh Nonconformists cannot be found to-day."

"But there isn't much known about Penry in England, is there?" asked Swash. "I never heard about him."

"No," replied Llewellyn, with a nod, "as a rule Englishmen haven't heard about him. Had he been an Englishman and had he been stealthily murdered at the instigation of a Popish Archbishop and his associates, and by the consent of a Popish Queen, due notice would have been taken of all by English historians, and proper emphasis would have been placed upon the criminality of the act, while all England would have rung with righteous protests as the ages passed; but as he was a Welshman, and though a Protestant was, by the consent of a Protestant Queen, hurried to death when no law of the realm condemned him, merely to satisfy the revenge of Protestant prelates, Englishmen find it convenient to ignore the whole proceeding, though his death was bewailed by a nation whose religious rights and liberties he lived and died to secure. Even when mention is made of his martyrdom, there is generally, by way of diverting the attention of the reader from the main point, a significant hint, or an explicit statement to the effect that he was the author of the 'Martin Marprelate Tracts,' a charge as unfounded as it is mean. Those tracts were written in a satirical and scoffing tone, a style never adopted by Penry; besides, in his Exhortation, published in the same year as the first Marprelate tract, he bitterly deprecated those 'busybodies who, increasing themselves still more unto ungodliness, think nothing so well spoken or written as that which is *satirical and bitingly done* against lord bishops.' The whole subject was far too heart-rending for a man like Penry to indulge in satire in treating it. All he wrote he did from an agony of spirit for his suffering countrymen and a righteous indignation toward those whom he called the spoilers and murderers of their souls, which did not admit of the play of satire, much less of scoffing tones. The man's heart bled as he wrote, and every sentence was projected by the accumulated energy of a soul that had gathered all its forces together for the desperate struggle to the death with sin and vice in high and sacred places. Those tracts, too, were written anonymously, while Penry appended his own name to all his writings—came out like a hero into the open field of battle, and never condescended to fight in ambush. That was beneath him—*beneath him.*

"Well, the time is gone, and we must think of home, but my story of those troublous times is but half told, and now that the subject has been brought up I should like to finish it on some other occasion, if agreeable to you."

"Hit the iron while it's hot, Mr. Pugh," said Shadrach, as he struck the glowing bar upon the anvil, and made the vivid sparks fly in all directions, "tomorrow night will do well, and all must make an effort to come."

It was unanimously agreed that on the following evening, at seven o'clock, they would meet again at the smithy, and all urged Llewellyn Pugh to come, as they had never been more delighted in their lives than that night.

Great was the surprise expressed by the little company after Llewellyn Pugh had left the smithy about his wonderful learning. Shadrach thought that there were very few in the country equal to him. John Vaughan, whose forte was Scriptural exposition and not history, said he never heard half as much about the Welsh Bible and John Penry before. Hugh Roberts said that when Llewellyn was a young man he was a wonder. Samson, as he hopped upon his crutch, hinted that he was like a walking dictionary, while Swash, in a patronizing tone, which greatly annoyed Samson, suggested that "dictionary" was scarcely the right word, but that Llewellyn certainly was well educated, and that he himself had an uncle very much like him—a remark which made David Lewis and Jenkin exchange looks and smile incredulously. Caleb Rhys said nothing.

The little group soon separated, each for his home, and the smithy once more was a deserted place.

CHAPTER IX

The Rise of Welsh Nonconformity

UST as the old clock in Shadrach Morgan's house struck five on the following evening he and Jenkin got up from the table, where with Mary Morgan, the affectionate wife and mother, they had taken their frugal meal in the united light of a home-made candle and of a blazing log of wood, which the good house-wife had placed upon the fire in anticipation of her husband's and son's return to tea. When they emerged from the warm light of that room into the outer world the day had all but closed—for it was early in December—and the night was descending upon the weary world as gently as a benediction. The stars had already commenced their nightly watch as they peeped down serenely from the infinite heights on the little smithy and its surroundings, and the hush of evening seemed to envelope the trees, the fields, and hills around in peaceful slumber, while the gentle breeze, half-awake and half-asleep, softly hummed a lullaby.

"What a beautiful night, father," said Jenkin. "How grandly the stars come out; just look, all the sky seems to be lit up. Do you remember what Mr. Kilsby Jones said about the stars, that they were the lamps on the highway to the King's palace?"

"Yes, my boy," said Shadrach, "and I thought it was very beautiful. So I spoke to John Vaughan about it, and he said that man everywhere points upwards when he points to heaven. 'How strange,' said I. He looked surprised, looked as only he can look on such occasions. His eyes quite sparkled as he replied, 'Not strange at all, Shadrach; all the light that touches the earth and blesses our life comes from that direction, and man naturally feels that *heaven must be somewhere in the path of light.'* Mr. Kilsby Jones gave the same idea, I think."

"Here's John coming, father," said Jenkin.

"So he is," said Shadrach, exultingly. "There's no one I like to see so much in the smithy, except, perhaps, old Hugh Roberts," he added in an undertone. "He's got a wonderful head on, and what a memory! He'll be sure to tell us something fresh now!" Then, turning to his cousin, he said "Good evening, John. I was just now telling Jenkin what you told me the other day about men everywhere looking *up* for heaven. I suppose we can look up for heaven *in the night* as well as the day—What do you say, John?—especially such a night as this. There's always light up there if we could but see it, and really those stars look as if they were keeping watch over us and saying—'The God who made us is taking care of you down there.'"

"So they do, Shadrach," said John. "I remember reading a letter written by Mr. David Rhys Stephen*—ah, he was an extraordinary man! I shall never forget many things I heard him say at 'Horeb.'"

"Who *can?*" exclaimed Shadrach.

"No," replied John. "Well, this was one of the letters he wrote to the *Merlin* under the name of 'The Welsh Pedestrian,' but everybody who understood English and had heard Mr. Rhys Stephen speak knew who it was. They said all the letters were written in his own beautiful way, so I got my eldest boy, who is a good scholar, to translate them for me. The ninth letter began, I think, something like this:—'It is very still—awfully still, just now, at four o'clock in the morning of the 23rd December, 18—. I have just turned out of a warm bed, in a house in a country place, and have several miles to walk to meet a train to carry me to Swansea. It is quiet, and it is not *very* dark, and should be good moonlight; but the clouds are crowding about and above me... I know the road and fear not; but it is very quiet. A man is now and here left alone to himself. Stay—do you see that star? There it is, in

---

* The late Rev. D. Rhys Stephen, who was minister of the Baptist Church, Mount Pleasant, Swansea, afterwards of the Church, at Commercial Street, Newport. He died April 24th, 1852.

its own unchanging mildness and purity—God's own sentinel, looking at me; yes, now, at *me!* How many hundreds of thousands of years did it take for thy light to travel immensity of space, ere we could see the gentle lustre of that steady and benignant look of thine? Tell me, how many worlds thy beams pass before they reach this remote portion of the universe, which God's hand hath created, and His right hand sustains? Wilt thou also let me, lovely star, know what is beyond thy dwelling-place, how many more systems are there still nearer than thou art to the *centre of light ineffable?* Still, thou lookest on and sayest nothing, but lookest—lookest still; but, though thou sayest nothing, nevertheless thou speakest clearly, distinctly, and emphatically—thou teachest me to borrow the words of a true bard,—God-inspired as he was, to address Him, who alike made thee and me, a worm of the earth, "Lord, what is man, that thou art mindful of him, and the son of man, that thou visitest him."'"

"What a memory you have, John; however could you remember that?" said Shadrach in astonishment.

"I've read it so often, Shadrach," said John. "When I think of Mr. Rhys Stephen and some of his sermons, and what he used to say at 'Horeb' in his wonderful language, I turn up those letters and a few other things of his, and read them through and through. I can't help remembering them. And I like him all the more because he taught so much from Nature. Mr. Williams, of Wern, used to say that one of the secrets of preaching was to know how 'to play skilfully on the great harp of Nature.' Mr. Stephen used to do that. Like the good Lord Himself he made everything in Nature preach the Gospel from a blade of grass to the sun.

"Yes, Shadrach, what you say is quite true, that you can look up for heaven *in the night* as well as the day. It's true in our *spiritual* life, Shadrach. It's the night that always brings out the stars. We should never see them if God didn't sometimes take away the day. There are times, like to-night, when God lights up almost every star of hope and promise, in order to make up for taking away the day from us, and every one of them says 'John,' or 'Shadrach,' 'God is taking care of you in the darkness, and He has told us to tell you so. What must man—yes, even man!—be in His sight, that he lights up a million stars to cheer his nights, as well as such a glorious sun to brighten up his day—the feeble child of earth the favourite of the skies!' Ah, yes, Shadrach, we can *took up* for heaven *even in the night,* I like that saying of yours. And even in the night we don't require *all* the stars to come out and tell us that our good Father is taking care of us. Sometimes one is enough, as on that dark morning Mr. Stephen spoke of; and sometimes when every star is hid behind dark clouds we don't fear, because we have seen them out so often we know they are there, though we can't see them. Besides, at such times, the good Lord Himself comes and whispers to us, *'The darkness and the light are both alike to me,'* and we reply—'Good Lord, if they are alike to Thee; they shall be alike to us.'"

"Well, I must make haste if I'm to be here by seven to hear Llewellyn Pugh, and that I must do if I can anyhow," added John. "Come, Shadrach, I want a pair of toe-tips that size," he continued, as he handed to him a bit of brown paper, "I saw some here the other day."

John was soon supplied, and hurried back to finish the boots in time for the meeting.

It was scarcely seven o'clock when Llewellyn Pugh arrived in company with John Vaughan, David Lewis, and Theodore Augustus Swash, who had met him at the smithy corner. A minute later came old Hugh Roberts and Caleb Rhys, and soon after Samson Lloyd brought up the rear.

No sooner had all arrived than David Lewis broke upon the desultory conversation by proposing that they proceed to business by asking "Mr. Pugh" to tell them a little more about old times, a proposal which was enthusiastically adopted by the company.

Llewellyn Pugh at once proceeded. "Well, last night I told you something about the charges which John Penry brought against the Welsh clergy. They seemed to be very severe, but they were as true as the Gospel. The assertions he made were never contradicted, and never could be, yet he lost his life for his faithful utterances. Indeed all that Penry stated was abundantly confirmed by numerous events, and the testimony of other holy men.

"In 1623—*thirty years* later than the martyrdom of John Penry— Dr. Lewis Bailey, Bishop of Bangor, took a tour through a part of his diocese to make inquiry into the state of the churches. His journal makes sad revelations, for instance:—In Anglesea, at Penmon, no sermon had been preached for five or six years, at Llangwyllog there was no preaching at all, at Llanddeusant and Llanfair-Ynghornwy Sir John Edwards, the curate, had omitted to read the services and the homilies, neglected baptisms and burials, and had not preached since the preceding Whitsun twelvemonths; he spent most of his time in public-houses and quarrelled with his neighbours and others. In Carnarvonshire, at Llanllechid, it was complained that Dr. Williams sent his horses to the graveyard, that he didn't see that it was cleaned after them, and that for the preceding two years he had not preached more than once. At Dolwyddelan, there was no preaching at all; at Dwygyfylchi it was complained that Sir Edward Jones, the vicar, mowed hay in the churchyard and converted it into a stack-yard, that he kept his saddle and bee-hives in the church, and that he neglected to hold communion the preceding Easter. At Aberdaron it was complained that Sir Griffith Parry had, through non-attendance, kept the corpse of a child named Hugh Thomas unburied from Saturday to Sunday, and that when he came on the Sunday he was drunk.

"Rees Prichard, the well-known Vicar of Llandovery, states in burning words, between ten and twenty years later, in the first two poems in the 'Welshman's Candle,' that not one in a hundred of his countrymen could read the Bible; that no copy was to be found even in the houses of the rich; that the clergy were sleeping, leaving the people to sin unwarned and unrebuked; that the upper classes, as a rule, were totally destitute of religion; and that the common people were ignorant, and did not love knowledge. He said, too, that it was difficult to decide whether the clergyman, the farmer, the labourer, the artisan, the bailiff, the judge, or the nobleman was the most daring in impiety.

"In a pamphlet* written in the year 1646 we read:—'A wretched sermon, now and then, and that by an ignorant or scandalous minister, or both, alas! what can it do, it being commonly, too, such stuff you know not whether it savours stronger of the *ale* or the *pocket.* In many places not a sermon is scarce to be had once a year. Half-an-hour's shower in a great drought will little avail the chapped earth. I must tell you, abating gentry and a few others that by the benefit of education may be otherwise, generally, I dare boldly say we can be but Papists or worse in Wales.'

"In addition to the charge of indolence and immorality which Penry brought against the clergy of Wales was that of being ignorant of the language of the people to whom they were supposed to minister. This charge is abundantly justified by the history of the Welsh Church from his day until now.

---

* "Contemplation on these Times, or the Parliament explained to Wales," by John Lewis, Esq., of Glasgrug, Cardiganshire. 1646, 27 p.

"The Established Church in Wales would be in a very different position to-day from that which it occupies, had the English Government and the Ecclesiastical authorities been half as anxious that the Welsh people should know the truths of the Gospel as that they should know English. The policy of the Government and, to an incredible degree, of the Church, has been to suppress the Welsh language. There are, I know, urgent reasons why the people of Wales should learn the English language. I only complain of the way in which the authorities have sought to secure this desired end, especially in relation to the religious life of the Welsh nation. There was, first of all, the neglect in obtaining for them a translation of the Scripture in their own tongue; and even when it was enacted by Parliament that the translation should be made, great prominence was given to the importance of having 'two Common Prayer Books in every Welsh church or chapel, one Welsh and one English, in order that *they may sooner attain to the knowledge of the English language.* *

"Dr. Morgan, in his Latin dedication† of his Welsh Bible to Queen Elizabeth gave words of solemn warning. I will try to translate them, although my Latin is stiff, for I have done but little to it for over thirty years. He says:—'If some persons desire that our countrymen should be compelled to learn the English language for the sake of closer union, rather than that the Scriptures should be translated into our language, I would have such, while they are zealous for union, to be more cautious

---

* v. Eliz., cap. 26. See also note p. 142, the last clause.

† "Si qui consensus rotinendi gratia, nostrates ut anglicum sermonem edifcant adigendos esse potius, quam scripturas in nostrum sermonem vertendas esse volunt; dum unitati student, ne veritati, obsint cautiores esse velim: et dum concordiam promovent, ne religionem amoveant, magis esse solicitos opto. Quamvis enim ejusdem insuæ incolas, ejusdem sermonis et loquelæ esse magnopere optandum sit; æque tamen perpendendum est, istud ut perficiatur, tantum temporis et negotii peti, ut interea Dei populum, miserrima illius verbi fame, interire velle aut pati, nimis sit fævum atque crudele. Deinde non dubium est, quin religionis quam sermonis ad unitatem plus valeat similitudo et consensus. Unitatem præterea pietati utilitatem religioni, et externam quandam inter homines concordiam eximiæ illi paci, quam Dei verbum humanis animis imprimit præferre, non satis pium est. Postremo, quam non sapiunt, si verbi divini in materna lingua habendi prohibitionem, aliena ut edificatur, quicquam movere opinantur? Religio enim nisi vulgari lingua edoceatur, ignota latitabit."

lest they hurt the truth, and while they promote unity I wish they would take care lest they drive away religion. For although it is greatly to be desired that the inhabitants of the same island should be of the same speech and language, yet it must be equally considered that it requires so much time and trouble to accomplish it, that to suffer the people of God meanwhile to famish with the most miserable hunger of the Word would be tyrannical and cruel beyond measure. Then there is no doubt that the likeness and agreement of religion tends more to union than that of language. Besides, to prefer union to piety, utility to religion, and a kind of outward concord among men to that special peace which the Word of God impresses upon human hearts is hardly pious. Finally, how unwise are they who suppose that the prohibition of the Word of God in our mother tongue, in order that another may be learnt, would avail anything. *For unless religion will be learnt in the vulgar tongue it will lie hidden and unknown.'*

"The warning words of Dr. Morgan were allowed to pass as an idle tale. Even when, through the zeal and indomitable courage of that holy man, the Bible was at length supplied to the people in a language which they could understand, the distribution of it was culpably neglected. Even as late as 1768 Dr. Thomas Llewellyn* says:—'It will appear from the following account that it is frequently impossible to procure Bibles for Protestants in Wales, and that this has been the case more or less ever since the Reformation, in which time the years of scarcity have been many more than the years of plenty.'

"But this is not the worst part of the story, I only refer to it as pointing, however slightly, yet very significantly, to a policy which has so frequently been adopted ever since the days of Penry—the appointment to Welsh livings of clergymen who were not conversant with the language of the people. The English Government has never gone so far as to deny the Welsh nation by any Act of Parliament the use of their own language in their religious services. After painful delay it even provided that the whole of Divine service should be used and said by the curates and ministers in the Welsh tongue through-out all Wales,† wherever that language was commonly used. It is the violation

---

* "Historical Account of the British or Welsh Versions and Editions of the Bible."—The opening words of the "Advertisement."

† "An Act to translate the Bible and Common Prayer into the Welsh Tongue. The Bishops of Hereford, St David's, Asaph, Bangor and Landaff

of this Act by bishops and patrons that I complain of, in sending clergymen who were ignorant of the language of the people. The appointment of foreign prelates to English sees during the times preceding the Reformation is well known to have occasioned much bitterness in the minds of the English clergy, and helped to estrange them from that religious system which could be guilty of such abuses. What applied to England in those days has applied to Wales in far more recent times, the only difference being that in the former case

---

shall take such order for the souls healths of the flocks committed to their charge that the whole Bible containing the New Testament and Old with the Book of Common Prayer and Administration of the Sacraments as is now used within the realm in English to be truly and exactly translated into the British or Welsh Tongue. And that the same so translated be by them viewed, perused and allowed be imprinted to such a number at the least that one of either sort may be had for every Cathedral Collegiate and Parish Church and Chapel of ease in such places and counties of every of the said Dioceses where that Tongue is commonly spoken or used before the first of March 1566. And that from that day forth the whole divine Service shall be used and said by the Curates and Ministers throughout all the said Dioceses where the Welsh Tongue is commonly used in the British or Welsh Tongue in such manner and form as is now used in the English Tongue and differing nothing in any order or form from the English Book for the which book so imprinted the Parishioners of every of the said parishes shall pay one half or moiety and the Parson and Vicar of every of the said Parishes where both he or else but one of them where there is but one shall pay the other half or moiety. The prices of which books shall be appointed and rated by the said Bishops and their Successors or three of them at the least. The which thing if the said Bishops or their Successors neglect to do then every one of them shall forfeit to the Queen's Majesty Forty Pounds, to be levied on their goods and chattels and one book containing the Bible and one other book of Common Prayer shall be bought and had in every church throughout Wales in which the Bible and Book of Common Prayer in Welsh is to be had by force of this Act (if there be none already before the first day of March 1566) and the said books to remain in such convenient places within the said Churches that such as understand them may resort at all convenient times to read and peruse the same and also such as do not understand the said Language may by conferring both tongues together the sooner attain to the knowledge of the English tongue, any thing in this Act to the contrary not withstanding."—v. Eliz. c. *28. See note, pp. 114, 115.*

the wrong was wrought by Papists, while in the latter case it is inflicted by Protestants. The evil is one, and its reward must be similar in both cases. You Englishmen, Mr. Swash, are surprised that the Established Church has no place in the affections of the great mass of the Welsh people. How could it be otherwise? What wonder that a Church whose whole machinery was worked so frequently for the purpose of conferring preferments upon English favourites, without regard to their ignorance of the Welsh language or their defects in morals, and as often for the sake of thrusting the English language under the cloak of religion upon a people proud of their own tongue, should soon have been looked upon in Wales—as well as in Ireland, where the same thing prevailed—as a mere instrument of the State! What wonder, too, that Welshmen should conclude that the chief aim was not the good of the people among whom the Church was planted, but the comfortable settlement in rich livings of those who in many instances would not be tolerated in England, and the strengthening of English rule by the forced adoption of what in such circumstances was sure to be regarded as the badge of an ignoble submission! Had I time I think I could prove that the policy of the English Government in matters of Church and State, and the grievances arising from it, have been identical in the case of Ireland and Wales. It is the Protestant Christianity of the Welsh people, as lived and taught by their religious teachers during the last two centuries and a half that has preserved them from ignorance, lawlessness, and irreligion, and made of them one of the most Scripturally-enlightened, loyal and religious nations on the face of the earth."

Here Samson became ecstatic, and jumping off the stool upon which he had been seated, so suddenly that it toppled over, he held up his finger before Swash and shouted vehemently, "That's it, that's it."

"But all these things have long since passed away," exclaimed Swash a little impatiently. "What you have been saying seems to me like digging up old grievances, which I think had better be untouched."

"I am glad and grateful to acknowledge," replied Llewellyn, "that the *immorality of the clergy* in Wales is no longer a stumbling-block or an offence to the cause of Christ here, but that the immorality and indolence of the clergy *were* the most powerful hindrances in the way of the spread and acceptance of the Gospel in Wales for over two hundred years after the Reformation in England—yea, even to this present century—no one can dispute; and as for the appointment to

Welsh livings of Englishmen ignorant of the Welsh language, why as late as 1849 Sir Thomas Phillips* wrote—'The inferiority of native Welshmen and their unfitness for stations of influence and authority are topics of an inviting description to English writers, and seem to have passed into axioms among English rulers. *For several generations no native of Wales has been appointed to a Welsh bishopric, and but rarely to any office of power or authority in the Church.'*

"What an anomaly," added Llewellyn, "that while the law of England ordains that all who are appointed to livings in those parts of the country where the Welsh prevails should have a competent knowledge of that language, the Sovereign, the conservator of all law, should appoint bishops who are ignorant of the language as the sole judges of their qualifications in that respect! Again, what an anomaly that the law which requires that Christian services should be held in Welsh has also appointed bishops, who, whenever they administered the rite of Confirmation, did it in a language which the candidates could not understand, and could not give the address except through one of their subordinates who had to translate it, because the Bishops forsooth would not condescend even to learn the language of the people! Is it surprising that the Welsh nation, in witnessing such incongruities, concluded that the whole thing as a religious institution for the welfare of the nation was a delusion and a snare! Is it not a significant fact that to this hour the Established Church in Wales is called 'The Church of England'† by the Welsh nation, who thus repudiate all relationship with it, save as an English institution planted in their midst?"

But then," said Swash, "it has been a moot point for centuries how long the Welsh language will continue as a living speech, and how long it will be used in places of religious worship. There is no doubt that ever since the conquest of Wales it has been dying out."

"Yes," replied Llewellyn Pugh, "six hundred years have passed away since Edward the First received in Carnarvon Castle the submission of the Welsh people, and three centuries and a half since the country was incorporated with and made part of the English realm. The English Church has been established in the midst of the people for the same period, and yet it is a striking fact that while the British language has

---

* "Wales—The Language, Social Condition, Moral Character, and Religious Opinions of the People," by Sir Thomas Phillips, 1849, p.59.

† "Eglwys Loegr."

vanished from Cornwall and Brittany, and only exists very partially in different dialects in Ireland, the Isle of Man, and the Highlands of Scotland, the inhabitants of Wales have clung so tenaciously to their language, that during the last fifty years they have formed a new literature in their own tongue. This, when we consider its youth, bears no mean comparison for insight, beauty, and force with the religious literature—for the literature of Wales is essentially religious—of any modern nation. The Welsh language, I have no doubt, will die out sooner or later like every other language, save the English, in the immortality of which some of the English people seem to believe a great deal more than in the immortality of their souls. It is, however, dying *slowly,* and Englishmen, acting on the principle that the Welsh was dying out, by sending English clergymen to minister to a people whose language they did not understand, or not to minister at all, as so many of the clergy did not even reside in their parishes, have sealed the Church's doom in our country. When the Gospel is taken to a people it should be presented to them in their own tongue, whatever its defects may be. No missionary society to-day is unwise enough to send the Gospel to a people in a language which they cannot understand, and by men who do not try or care to learn the people's own language. It may be a miserable *patois,* it matters little; the Scriptures are translated into that tongue, and educated men devote valuable time to master it, on the principle which Dr. Morgan so clearly and wisely stated three hundred years ago in his dedication to the first translation of the Bible into Welsh, that *unless a religion is learnt in the vulgar tongue it will he hidden and unknown.** Besides, the Welsh language is specially adapted for religious purposes. It has the advantage of being easily understood by those who use it, as I heard Mr. David Rhys Stephen once say—

[Here John Vaughan nodded significantly to Shadrach, evidently impressed with the strange coincidence of Llewellyn Pugh and himself having referred to Mr. Rhys Stephen that evening.]

"He said that the roots of our language are well understood by the common people, and so when we have to invent a term for a new science, a brief general use of it will not only cause it to be understood as to the sense intended to be conveyed, but the least learned of the people will understand it etymologically. The inconvenience consequent

---

* See page 141.

on the motley character of the English language, as it regards the
education and instruction of the English language, is beyond belief to
those who have carefully considered the matter. Thus, let us suppose
that a good man insists that he will have an evening school for adults
in some part of Herefordshire, say about Garway or Grosmont. A man,
a farmer's labourer, learns to read by slow and careful spelling as he
proceeds; by-and-by he says, 'Maister, I canna mind the meaning of
this here un,' pointing to a hard word. 'Oh, my good fellow, let me
see; *geography*—it comes from two Greek words, *geo* and *graphe.*' 'Aye,
zur, I heard un tell o' Greek, when I wur a buoy.' 'Well, Thomas, I'll
explain it to you.' 'Thankee, zur.' '*Geo* means the *earth.*' 'I mind it,
zur.' *Graphe* means the *description* of anything.' 'I zee it, zur.' 'Very
good, now bear in mind my good man; geography means an account
or description of the surface of the earth.' 'Aye, zur, and thankee too
a hundred times. I must say you takes a mighty lot of drouble wi' we.'
Thomas goes home with Jem, and on the way Jem says, 'Maister and
ye was main close in converzation tonight.' 'Aye, I reckon we was; he
wur mighty larned.' 'What did he tell ye.' 'Why, ye zee, I axed un what
a long word—a'most as long as my arm—meiant; and he zed as how it
meiant summat about concerning the earth.' 'Well, but what wur the
word itself?' 'Darn me, I canna for the life of me remember; but he
spoke of 'zurface of the earth.' 'D'ye know what zurface means?' 'I
dunna; I never heard it afore, in all my born days.'—In almost every
parish in England such a result must follow under the circumstances."

 "It's very easy," said Swash, "to conjure up a cock-and-bull story
like that to point a moral. I acknowledge that the Welsh imagination
is vivid enough to manufacture illustrations, but let us have them
from life."

 "I am glad that you give the Welsh credit for anything," replied
Llewellyn. "The instance imagined by Mr. Stephen is what might be
found in a thousand places in England. Instances of the same kind
occur every day. But we will leave the imaginative Welshman for his
more matter-of-fact and prosaic brother, the Englishman, for there is
another story given *from real life.* The following anecdote is found in
the Life of Berridge, a clergyman of apostolic simplicity, as well as of
apostolic zeal and fervency. The Rev. Mr. Venn, of Huddersfield, a
kindred spirit with Mr. Berridge, visited his friend at Cheriton, near
Cambridge; and notice was given to the villagers that there would be
evening service in the parish church. Before they went from the

parsonage the good incumbent said, 'We have but few small farmers and labouring men, who attend the church; they are all ignorant of Latinised English; talk in plain Saxon, and they will understand you.' 'Very well,' was the reply, 'I shall endeavour to do so; indeed, I like plain language.' The service being over, the visitor returned with his host to his residence, and said, 'I hope, friend Berridge, that I was simple and plain-spoken enough to-night even to please you.' 'Well, you certainly did your work successfully; there was one word, though, and you used it so often that the sermon could not be well understood, unless it was understood. 'I am sorry for that; what was it?' 'Omniscience.' 'Oh, nonsense, everybody understood that word.' 'My dear sir, of the persons at church, this evening, not twenty understood it.' 'I know not how to believe that.' 'I will, to satisfy you, call in my bailiff, an intelligent man, so far as a man can be so without learning, but the mere ability to read in his own tongue.' The bailiff was summoned—was asked, whether he understood the meaning of the word 'Omniscient,' which he used that evening in his sermon; he thought he did, and said, 'It is something inside of a pig.' Ludicrous though this anecdote be, it is pregnant with instruction on not unimportant points of vast public interest, to which just now we cannot advert in detail, but only in so far as it illustrates our position that it is a great advantage to have in common use a language that is self-included, and that cannot fail to be understood in any of its combinations and compounds, even to the full extent of modern discoveries, by the mass of the people. To revert to the word 'Omniscience,' is there a Welsh beggar-woman ninety years of age who could by any considerable possibility, misunderstand it? *Hollwybodaeth* * there it is patently and infallibly comprehended by all men of our nation. And so on, *ad infinitum.*

"The same applies," continued Llewellyn, "to 'Omnipresent,† and 'Omnipotent'.‡ Happily, however, you have in common use a word synonymous with the latter which every peasant can understand— 'Almighty.'

"But the Welsh language is not only *simple,* but also essentially

---

* "*Holl*" means "all," and "'*wybodaeth*" "knowledge," hence the word "*Holl-wybodaeth*" means "all-knowledge."

† "*Hollbresnnol,*" or "all-present."

‡ "*Hollalluog,*" or "Almighty."

poetic. You spoke just now about the Welsh people being imaginative. That is true; it is a peculiarity of our nation; we are gifted with a vivid imagination, which for generations has been quickened and developed amid the wild scenery of our native mountains and hills. The Welsh nature is exceptionally sensitive to mysteries, and has a keen appreciation of the superhuman. When the light of the Gospel was excluded this expressed itself in superstitions, wild or pathetic, but when the Gospel came that nature so sensitive to every touch of the mysterious was captivated and enraptured by the wondrous story of the Incarnation and of the Cross. But this story must be told in our own tongue, since our language is the exact counterpart of our nature. It revels in the superhuman and throbs with the fanciful and the mysterious. The Welsh language is intolerant of tameness, and applied to the Welsh people the saying of Sydney Smith is specially forcible, that 'the sin against the Holy Ghost in a sermon is tameness.'

"What wonder that the Welsh people, possessing as they did a language so congenial to their own nature, and so eminently adapted for religious purposes, should have clung to their mother tongue with a tenacity of purpose, which defied all efforts to deprive them of it in the most sacred relationships of life! What wonder, too, that they ignored a Church, which, in addition to its many other glaring defects added insult to injury by conferring the greatest honours and highest preferments upon strangers who were ignorant of the language of the people, thus employing its most sacred offices for the introduction of a strange language which, whatever may be its excellencies—and they are many—appeared to them, for religious purposes at least, tame and insipid compared with their own!

"The policy of suppressing the Welsh language was never so vigorously pursued in the Church as it was after the Revolution. The eighteenth century, that in which Welsh Nonconformity made such rapid strides through the great Calvinistic Methodist Revival, originated by Daniel Rowlands, of Llangeitho, and others of kindred spirit, was the worst of all in this respect.

"The other day," continued Llewellyn, "in reading a book written by a Fellow of Queen's College, Oxford, as late as 1768, I came across some very striking words, which I took the trouble to copy." Here Llewellyn once more brought out the old familiar note-book, and as usual translated into Welsh as he went on. "In speaking of the gentlemen of Wales, he says*:—'Destitute of friends and interest among the great, they cannot bring up their sons to any departments of the Law, the State, the Army or Navy, with any probable view of their succeeding. Placed in this disadvantageous situation to what profession can the gentlemen of that country educate their younger children? The eldest son is generally brought up to be a gentleman, to inherit his father's estate, and lead an idle life. The youngest are sent to college with a view to some ecclesiastical preferment, or lead a life of servile dependence on their eldest brother.' Further on he says:— 'We find the gay, the licentious, the man of this world acquire preferment by venial and simoniacal means, by borough interest, or if he can pander for the pleasures of a great man, if he can, with a spaniel-like adulation, that is a disgrace not only to Christianity, but to humanity itself, fawn and cringe to his patron, praise what he praises, and dislike what he dislikes. This is the broad road to preferment! Thus, when the inhabitants of Wales find that a door is shut upon them to exclude them from all preferment in the Church, they will not think it worth the expense and trouble of giving their sons a University education for a poor curacy of *twenty pounds per annum,* which in great condescension the rectors may permit them to enjoy.' That is written," continued Llewellyn Pugh, "by a Churchman and Fellow of his College, and as such carries considerable weight."

Samson Lloyd, who ever since his disappointment at not becoming parish clerk bore the Church a mortal grudge, nodded vigorously.

"What a view of the sacred ministry!" said Jenkin. "The youngest 'sent to college with a view to some ecclesiastical preferment, *or lead a life of servile dependence on their eldest brother.'* What an awful alternative! To become a legate of the skies, *or a hanger on!* a minister of grace, *or a humble settler on the bounty of a big brother, who is lazy, but rich!* Shocking! That's worse than *your* alternative, Samson, when you tried for the berth of parish clerk the other day—a *clerk* in the church giving the responses in the presence of the parson and the 'Squire, *or only a tailor* armed with needle and thimble, sleeve-board and goose, making your calling and election sure in sitting cross-legged on a table and sewing corduroys."

---

* "Considerations on the Illegality and Impropriety of preferring Clergymen who are unacquainted with the Welsh language to Benefices in Wales." By J. Jones, A.M., Fellow of Queen's College, Oxon, 1768, pp.45, 46.

Here Samson, who had greatly enjoyed Jenkin's introductory remarks, suddenly collapsed, and shouldering his crutch sat sulkily on the three-legged stool near.

"Shocking," added Jenkin, "to set aside for the Lord's work men who hadn't enough brain, or heart, or stamina to engage in any other calling. If that was the style in which men were chosen for the ministry, and if that was the class of men they got, it couldn't have mattered very much whether they understood English or Welsh or neither, they would do about the same good. And for *twenty pounds* a year!—poor pay after a University education, but about as much as they were worth, I expect. It's no wonder that the Church is where it is to-day; such men are bound to swamp any church."

"At it again, Jenkin," said Hugh Roberts gently. "Don't jump too readily at conclusions, my boy, that's the failing of impulsive young men. You conclude far too readily that the younger brother in each case had nothing in him. I admit that the system of setting aside for the work of the ministry those younger sons of gentlemen who couldn't find any other honourable employment was a dangerous and even a sinful one, and that very many of those who at that time, when all the best livings were in the hands of Englishmen, would seek a Welsh curacy at twenty pounds a year would be of the weaker sort. Yet in this matter, as in many others, there is danger of making sweeping statements, my boy."

"Quite right, Hugh," said Llewellyn, "Jenkin seems to have an unconquerable prejudice against two classes of men—hyper-Calvinists and lawyers—and I am inclined to think that with his Nonconformist leanings, he is too sceptical about clergymen. I confess I cannot refer to much that hyper-Calvinists have ever done, but in that they are consistent, as they don't believe very much in 'works.' I would remind Jenkin, however, that the first two printed translations of certain portions of the Scriptures into Welsh—if not, indeed, the first *books* printed in our language—were by two lawyers,* Sir John Price and Mr. William Salesbury, and that the first and second translations of

---

* See pp.110, 111. It is affirmed by some that in 1531 a Welsh school primer appeared, and in 1535 a second edition of it, entitled *"Salesbury's Primer,"* and thus that Sir John Price's so-called "Bible," referred to in pp. 104, 105, was not the first *book* printed in Welsh. Llewellyn Pugh leaned toward the other view.

the Bible ever given to Wales were given by two holy men, clergymen of the Church of England.* I would remind him, too, that even in the dark days which followed the martyrdom of John Penry there were, here and there, devout men in that Church who lifted up their voices against the iniquities of their age, and whose lives were constant protests against every evil. Lastly, I would have him remember that the great work which during the last two centuries has been growing in power in our country was commenced in the Established Church, although that community was not wise enough to encourage or even tolerate its promotion; and was originated, and to a great extent sustained, by zealous clergymen of that Church, although in the very furtherance of it they forfeited the favour of their Bishops and the ease of an ignoble conformity."

"The words of John Penry, written to Lord Burleigh within a week of his martyrdom, were not only the utterance of a strong faith in God, but were also as prophetic as anything ever foretold:—'I leave the success of my labours unto such of my countrymen as the Lord is to raise after me, for the accomplishing of that work which in the calling of my country unto the knowledge of Christ's blessed Gospel I began.' His bereaved country hadn't to wait long for at least a partial fulfilment of his prediction, for at that very time there was a lad of fourteen at Llandovery, Carmarthenshire, who in later years as Rees Prichard,† the vicar of the parish in which he was born and bred, was destined, by his preaching and by his spiritual songs, to shed a light into the surrounding darkness which will never die out."

"Those poems were his sermons turned into verse; so I heard my father say," said Hugh Roberts.

"Yes," replied Llewellyn. "There were no Bibles in those days in Wales, except in the churches, hence he put as much Scripture as he could into his sermons, and finding that the Welsh people were

---

* See pp.117-119.

† Rev. Rees Prichard, Vicar of Llandovery, Carmarthenshire, the eldest son of a gentleman of position, was born at Llandovery in 1579. He entered Jesus College, Oxford, in 1597, and was ordained at Witham, Essex, in 1602. In the same year he was promoted to the vicarage of Llandingad, the parish in which Llandovery is situated. As the chaplain of the Earl of Essex he held the rectory of Llanedi, as well as the vicarage of Llandingad. In 1614 he became Prebendary of the Collegiate Church of Brecon, and twelve years later Chancellor of St. David's. He died in 1644.

charmed by poetry, he converted his sermons into spiritual songs, some of which were published during his lifetime, and the others two years after his death under the name so well known, 'The Morning Star, or The Welshmen's Candle' ('Y Seren Fore, neu Ganwyll y Cymry'). These, comprehending almost every point of doctrine and practice, have been a rich heritage to the Welsh people. Next to the Bible, nothing has been read so much or has proved so great a blessing as these sacred songs. In every cot throughout the land they are known, and often on the field as well as by the fireside, in the smithy as in the sanctuary, those grand, inspiring words are repeated, and never without producing a powerful and hallowing influence."

"That's quite true," exclaimed Shadrach. "Why, there isn't a man here who doesn't know 'The Welshman's Candle,' and I'll venture Hugh could repeat it all word for word."

"Yes, I think I could," said Hugh Roberts; "they were among the first things I learnt, and they will be among the last things that I shall remember."

"No monument marks the grave of that holy man," continued Llewellyn Pugh "As in the case of Moses, even the exact spot in which he rests is unknown. Perhaps that is well. It is enough that his name is treasured in loving hearts, and his memory embalmed in the story of his country's progress from the darkness of superstition to the full light of Gospel truth and privilege.

"He alone of the clergymen of his day who sought to evangelize their country was allowed to remain in the Church till the close of life, and he probably was tolerated through the influence of the Earl of Essex, to whom be was private chaplain. The other holy men were driven out of the Church. The injunction of Archbishop Laud to the clergy to read the 'Book of Sports' was disobeyed by them, and thus they became exposed to severe persecution. At the instigation of the Archbishop, the Bishops of St. David's and Llandaff gave them no rest. William Wroth,* Rector of Llanfaches, near Chepstow, William

---

* William Wroth, Rector of Llanfaches, near Chepstow, was born at Abergavenny, Mon., in 1570. Entered Jesus College, Oxford, in 1586. The time and place of his ordination are unknown. Was presented to the living of Llanfaches about the year 1600. Very soon he became known throughout the adjoining Counties as a most earnest and powerful preacher, and multitudes flocked to hear him, so that in the summer he was obliged to

Erbury,* Vicar of St. Mary's, Cardiff, and Walter Cradock,† curate of the same church, were ejected. Walter Cradock, who was the most talented, and was destined to be the most useful of the three, was ejected in 1633, and William Wroth and William Erbury five years later. The ejection of these men resulted in the formation of Independent churches at Llanfaches and elsewhere. With these ejections the history of Nonconformity in Wales begins. The story of the heroic efforts of these devout men, and of others‡ closely associated with them, to evangelize Wales, notwithstanding cruel persecutions and severe hardships, is one of the brightest chapters in the history of our country. But I must not dwell upon this tempting theme. Their dauntless courage and patient endurance were productive of much good. Younger men followed their noble example, foremost among whom was Vavasor

---

preach in the churchyard, as his church was far too small to contain the people who assembled. During the primacy of Archbishop Abbot he continued to work unmolested, but after the elevation of Archbishop Laud he had no rest. Ejected in 1638, he formed an Independent Church at Llanfaches in 1639. This man was the father of Nonconformity in Wales, and not only laboured hard himself, but also trained young men, who became the distinguished evangelists of the succeeding age. He died in 1642, and was buried at his own request under the threshold of the parish church in which he had laboured so many years.

* William Erbury was born in the parish of Roath, Cardiff, in 1604. He was educated at Brasenose College, Oxford, was ordained at Newport, was afterwards Vicar of St. Mary's, Cardiff, and was ejected in 1638. Died April, 1654.

† Walter Cradock, described by the Bishop of Llandaff in 1633, the year he was ejected, as a "bold, ignorant young fellow," was born about 1610, and educated at Oxford. He was curate of St. Mary's, Cardiff, when ejected. In some way, not at present known, he was a little later accepted as curate at the parish church, Wrexham, and was greatly blessed during the one brief year in which he was permitted to serve there. After many journeys, during which he preached the Gospel with great results to his benighted countrymen, we find him in 1639 assisting the Rev. W. Wroth in organizing the Nonconformist church at Llanfaches. He was appointed his assistant, and at his death, in 1642, became his successor. He was a man of very exceptional gifts, and much fervour, and did more than any other, save, perhaps, Vavasor Powell, for the evangelization of his country.

‡ Marmaduke Matthews, Ambrose Mostyn, Henry Walter, Richard Symonds, Robert Powell, and others.

Powell,* who was imprisoned in no fewer than thirteen prisons, spending the last eleven years of his life in one or other of them, and at length, as the result of repeated and long confinements in most offensive and unhealthy cells, was released by death from all his sufferings.

"The Long Parliament, which assembled in 1640, proceeded to release the Puritans who had been imprisoned at the instigation of Archbishop. Laud, and to give freedom of utterance to those ministers who had been silenced during the preceding reign. The veteran William Wroth lived just long enough to see the Nonconformist ministers of Wales encouraged by Parliament in their noble efforts to evangelize the country, for, probably early in 1641, a year before his death, they

---

* Vavasor Powell was born at Cnwcglas, Radnorshire, in 1617. He was educated at Jesus College, Oxford. After leaving the University he kept a school for a while at Clun, Shropshire, during which time he assisted his uncle, Erasmus Powell, by reading the prayers. As yet he was unconverted. Having been rebuked one Lord's-day by a Puritan who saw him in his clerical dress looking approvingly on a number of people playing different games, his mind became seriously impressed. This impression was deepened when soon after he heard a holy man, probably Mr William Wroth, and still more when he read Sibbes' "Bruised Reed". He was at length converted under the ministry of Mr. Walter Cradock. From the year 1640 his history is one of unwearied toil and frequent imprisonments. In 1656 he was baptized by immersion and joined the Baptist denomination, an event which greatly promoted their cause in Wales. Referring to that period of his life from his return from England at the close of the Civil Wars in 1646, to the Restoration in 1660, Dr. Rees writes:—"On his return to Wales he became a most indefatigable and active instrument in propagating the Gospel among his fellow-countrymen. He very often preached two and three times the same day, and was seldom two days in the week, throughout the year, without preaching. There was scarcely a church, chapel, or town-hall in the Principality in which he had not preached. He also often preached at fairs, markets, in fields, and on the mountains, and wherever he could find a number of people to preach to. It is impossible to form an adequate idea of the extent of his labours in Wales from the year 1646 to 1660." His history after the Restoration of Charles II. is one of a long series of imprisonments and sufferings, alternating with renewed efforts to evangelize his country. The cruel imprisonments he received impaired his health, and brought his life to a premature close in the Fleet Prison, Oct.27, 1670. He was buried in Bunhill Fields.

were authorized to preach in Wales, and in the September of the same year it was further '*Ordered* that it shall be lawful for the parishioners of any parish in the kingdom of England and dominion of Wales, to set up a lecture, and to maintain an orthodox minister, at their own charge, and to preach every Lord's-day, where there is no preaching, and to preach one day in every week, where there is no weekly lecture.

"The Civil Wars, which began in 1642, brought the greatest suffering upon the Welsh Nonconformists. Dr. Rees, in referring to this period, says:*— 'As almost all the clergy, the gentry, and the people generally throughout Wales were violent Royalists, the Nonconformists, who were comparatively few in number, and scattered over extensive districts of the counties of Monmouth, Glamorgan, Brecon, Radnor, and Denbigh, had nothing but death, in its most cruel form, to expect at the breaking out of the war, if they remained in the country. The ministers, and as many of the members of their churches as could do so, fled for refuge to England... Our information in regard to the condition and sufferings of those Welsh Nonconformists who were unable to escape to England at the breaking out of the war is very scanty. That they were great sufferers is beyond doubt. Vavasor Powell tells us that their goods and cattle were seized upon by their adversaries, and that their wives and children were necessitated to live in distress and danger till the war was over. We are also informed that Prince Rupert, in his expedition through Wales, "drove away the people's cattle, rifled their houses, and spoiled their standing corn; that aged and unarmed people were stripped—some murdered in cold blood, and others half hanged and burnt, and yet suffered to live." Inasmuch as the mass of the Welsh people of all classes were Royalists, who then, but the poor Nonconformists, could have been subjected to that cruel treatment? Yet, notwithstanding their great dangers, privations, and sufferings, these good people not only adhered immoveably to their principles, but also traversed the country to make known the way of salvation to their fellow-countrymen. When the ministers returned to the Principality after the war, they found that religion had made remarkable progress during their absence, through the humble instrumentality of these sufferers.'

"After Oliver Cromwell had overcome the Royalists in the year 1646, Parliament, having ejected a large number of ministers, most of whom

---

* "History of Protestant Nonconformity in Wales," pp. 75, 76.

were notorious for their immorality, appointed preachers under the Act for the Propagation of the Gospel in Wales, and in every way encouraged devout men to engage in itinerant preaching throughout Wales. Two Nonconformist churches* sent out seventeen of their most gifted members to engage in preaching the Gospel to their countrymen. This is the first instance recorded of systematic itinerant preaching in Wales, but not the last, for it is to this instrumentality that our country owes those great revivals, which occupy so glorious a place in the history of its religious life. These lay preachers were led by seven young Puritan clergymen, and others of ability and repute, and such was the success that accompanied their united labours that in 1662—only sixteen years later—when the Act of Uniformity was passed *one hundred and six* Welsh clergymen were ejected from their livings for refusing to submit to its conditions. These heroic men, under the severest persecution, visited all parts of the country, and with Apostolic zeal preached the Gospel to their countrymen in the thousand secluded nooks which are to be found in the glens and valleys of our native land. Multitudes were converted through their faithful labours, and Christian communities were formed everywhere, so that when the Toleration Act came into force, hundreds of chapels were built, and a large number of dwelling-houses recorded for preaching.

"Unfortunately, however, lay preaching, which had been so blessed in times of persecution, fell into comparative disuse during the time of peace which followed. The ministers who came after those holy men, who had so toiled and endured in troublous times, did not adequately realize the value of this powerful agency, and in many instances even discountenanced it. In times of rest those who succeeded the grand confessors of 1662 became cold and formal. The result was that the spiritual life of the churches began to decline, and that the people partly relapsed into a state of indifference. This continued until the time of the Great Revival, which began in 1735, and lay preaching has ever since occupied a very important and prominent place in the religious activities of the Welsh people.

"It must not be disguised, however, that the revival of lay preaching by Daniel Rowlands, of Llangeitho, Howell Harris, of Trefecca, Peter Williams, of Carmarthen, William Williams, of Pant-y-celyn, and others who promoted that great Revival, was as distasteful to some of the

---

* Llanfaches, and Mynydd-islwyn, near Cardiff.

Nonconformist ministers as to the Church clergy, though many others warmly approved of it, and threw themselves heartily into the work.

"But I have finished. I cannot tell anyone here much that he doesn't already know about Daniel Rowlands, of Llangeitho, and those grand men who were his fellow-workers. That Revival, like others to which I have already referred, began in the Established Church, but it could not be carried on there. Her bishops and dignitaries became impatient of such an innovation, and her forms and rules were too contracted and rigid for the free exercise of that mightier energy and fuller life which now began to develop so rapidly within her pale. Hence, once more, she rejected her noblest sons, and deprived herself of the foremost position in a movement that will never be forgotten in that country which it has so much blessed."

"If what you have been saying is correct," said Swash—"and I have no reason for questioning it—you Welshmen know nothing about the real Church of England; you have had only a caricature of it in Wales, and a very miserable one, too."

"I very readily admit that," said Llewellyn. "The history of the Established Church in England—though by no means free from serious blots—bears no comparison with that of the Established Church in Wales for disgraceful abuses. Had the history of the two been similar probably the result would have been much the same. I have gone more fully than I otherwise should have done into the story of the abuses within the English Church in Wales, in order to show that the Welsh people were *forced* to separate themselves from all relationship to it, in the interests of morality and religion. They could not have belonged to it and be devout. Hence they held themselves aloof from it, and to this day they call themselves by no other name than *'Separatists.* *

We, as Welshmen, have to do with the Established Church *in Wales,* and it is from our standpoint that I have spoken to-night. I have also referred to those abuses within the pale of that Church which gave rise to and did so much to further Welsh Nonconformity during the last three centuries, and not to the *Church as it is now in Wales.* Those evils to which I have referred—the immorality of the clergy, their non-residence in their parishes, and their culpable neglect of the duties of their sacred office—have, during this century, disappeared, I think, almost entirely, while the appointments of Welshmen in recent years

---

* "Ymneillduwyr."

as bishops in Wales are additional and very gratifying proofs that those in high places have at length realized that the policy so long adopted of placing Englishmen in all positions of honour and influence in the Welsh Church was as fatal to the interests of that Church as it was unjust and insulting to us as a nation."

"You are quite right," exclaimed Hugh Roberts, when you say "that the Church in Wales has greatly improved of late years. If the clergymen of this parish many years ago had been like our present Vicar, the old parish church would look far better on Sunday than it does now."

"Why," said Shadrach, "the present Vicar preaches exactly like our ministers. I heard him the other day in a funeral. He gave us a sweet little sermon, it did me good to hear it, and he hadn't a bit of paper before him, but spoke right out of his heart; besides, there isn't a kinder man in all the parish than the Vicar."

"The present 'Squire, too, is very different from the old one," said Hugh. "*He* doesn't tell his man to bring the hounds in time for the close of the service as the old gentleman used to do, but takes his young family to church and returns home quietly with them. Ah, things have mended very much in the Church the last fifty years. But then, you see, it's almost too late now. All the people go to their chapels, and a clergyman may be as good as he can be, they never think of going to hear him except when there is a funeral in church. They have their own places of worship to go to, where they first found peace for their souls."

"The fact is, from all I can see," said Swash, "the Nonconformist chapels have emptied the churches."

"That is scarcely correct," exclaimed Llewellyn. "The clergy emptied the churches of old, and the Nonconformist chapels have been filled by those who attended the fairs, the public-houses, and such places. The Welsh people left the Church before ever Nonconformity sprang into existence. Nonconformity in Wales was a *necessity* of the times. So far from having militated against any *good* which the Church may have desired to accomplish, you will find—strange as it may seem—that as a rule where the Nonconformists are strongest the Established Church is more awake to its responsibilities, and, as the result, their services are better attended, than in those districts where as yet Nonconformist causes are few and feeble.* All points to this, that up to the present age

---

* "In the district of Newcastle Emlyn, where the mass of the people attend Dissenting Chapels, we find that ten per cent. of the population

at least little would have been done in Wales by way of evangelizing the people, apart from the Nonconformist denominations, who, at the cost of much toil and self-denial, have built thousands of sanctuaries on hill and dale throughout the land, and sent forth a host of preachers to proclaim the love of God to their fellow-men."

"We must hear a little some other night," said Shadrach, as he rested his arm upon the handle of the smithy bellows, "about Daniel Rowlands, of Llangeitho, and the great Revival of his day."

"Hugh Roberts and Caleb Rhys could tell you more than I can about that," replied Llewellyn, "but I will gladly join with them and tell all I know on some future occasion."

It was now late, and the company began to show signs of moving, but not before they expressed their thanks to Llewellyn Pugh for all he had told them. At other times, John Vaughan, Hugh Roberts, Caleb Rhys, and Shadrach had much to say, but on this and the previous night they had been almost silent, because they felt that it was better to let Llewellyn say what he had to tell them in his own way. Besides they knew that there was no one who knew so much about the old times as he did. Swash had been placed in a very awkward and disadvantageous position, for he was not only in the miserable minority of one as a Churchman, but as an Englishman he knew very little about the subject under consideration. No one regretted this more than Llewellyn. He only wished that Englishmen *did* condescend to study the ecclesiastical history of Wales for the last three hundred years; they would then marvel less about the prevalence of Nonconformity in that land, and would no longer mistake it and its thousand ramifications for a political organization, whose chief aim was to sow discord and encourage strife. The Welsh nation, he affirmed, could boast of a history which, for fidelity to the throne and willing recognition of all authority and law, cannot be surpassed by the history of any people.

---

were present at the services of the parish churches on the morning of the Census Sunday, March 30th, 1851, while on the same morning, in the district of Rhayader, Radnorshire, where the Dissenting congregations are few and small, the attendance at the parish churches was less than six per cent. of the population."—*Dr. Rees's Miscellaneous Papers, p. 54.*

CHAPTER X

John Vaughan and his Bible Class

Or an "Association of Sunday Schools," was advertized to he held on Christmas Day at Peniel Independent Chapel, a little way out of the village. A minister of note had been announced to catechize the united Sunday Schools of the district on "The Parable of the Prodigal Son." Great were the preparations in the different schools in anticipation of the event, and not least at "Horeb." In addition to the preparation in each class, there was a final review held on the Sunday preceding the "Association," when the pastor of the church questioned the whole school on the lesson.

John Vaughan's large Bible Class was better attended than usual, and nothing pleased him more than to prepare his class for an examination similar to that which they, in common with so many others, would have to undergo on Christmas Day. John had unbounded faith in the well-known minister who had been chosen to catechize them, and he warned them that they must know the subject thoroughly if they wanted to satisfy *him.*

His Class, numbering about forty, consisted of men, varying in age from twenty to seventy. In it were Shadrach Morgan, his son Jenkin, David William, of Ty-mawr, and almost every man who attended the services at the chapel, with the exception of those who were engaged in teaching in the Sunday School. There was no Bible Class like this in the whole neighbourhood. The fact was that John was exceptionally gifted as an expositor. When a young man, although poor, he had been encouraged by his pastor and by the church at "Horeb" to engage in preaching, a step toward being sent to college and entering the ministry. The sudden death of his father, by which the cares of a long family were thrown upon John as the eldest son, put an end to this project, but to this day the villagers look upon him as one of God's own gifted men, whose calling it is to explain His Word.

A large number of Commentaries were consulted in anticipation of the Class, prominent among which were Dr. Lewis's Commentary, and Robert Ellis's, as well as Welsh Translations of Albert Barnes's and of Matthew Henry's Commentaries. Old David William, of Ty-mawr, believed only in one Commentary, and that was Dr. Jenkins's, of Hengoed, which he carried with him to Class—a ponderous quarto volume. Jenkin Morgan called that Commentary, which was hyper-Calvinistic in tendency, *"The burden of the Word of the Lord,"* and by way of explanation used to repeat in high glee a story to the effect that Dr. Jenkins, when he brought out his Commentary, sent a large number of 'parts' to Llanwenarth, to Mr. Isaac Hiley, the brother of the Rev. Francis Hiley. Llanwenarth in those days was the stronghold of high doctrine, and Dr. Jenkins concluded naturally enough that there would be a great demand in that district for his Commentary. The sale among those farmers, however, was far from encouraging, and notwithstanding repeated efforts on the part of Mr. Isaac Hiley to sell the books, the market was very dull, and the poor man, though he sought often, and almost with tears, could scarcely find a purchaser. Meanwhile, Dr. Jenkins was impatient for the returns; he sent hint after hint in apostolic fashion to Mr. Hiley, but did not receive a reply, as the good man was loath to confess to Dr. Jenkins that the sale was hanging fire; besides, he hoped that the decrees would smile more favourably by-and-by. Dr. Jenkins, receiving no reply, and not having the least doubt that *his* Commentary had been bought up at once, became somewhat suspicious that Mr. Hiley, prompted by motives of strict economy, was reaping a little temporary advantage by turning over in the interests of farming the proceeds of the books he had sold. Hence he wrote to him, no longer in a theological and apostolic fashion, but in a very practical matter-of-fact tone, asking Mr. Hiley to send the money or to return the books forthwith. Mr. Hiley, on receiving the letter, at once called his manservant, and asked him to bring the mule to the door of the house—there were no railways in those days—and having put into a sack the 'parts' of Dr. Jenkins' Commentary he, with the help of his servant, placed them across the mule's back, and then, having written in a clear round hand on a piece of paper the words, 'THE BURDEN OF THE WORD OF THE LORD,' he stuck it on the sack, and dispatched the man, the mule, and the 'burden' to Hengoed, where Dr. Jenkins lived.

The afternoon's work always began with devotional exercises, in which the whole school joined. When these were over, John announced the lesson to his Class. This was read through by the members verse by verse. Then John began again by reading a few words with his well-known emphasis and clearness, and, throwing up his spectacles on his forehead, would proceed to question the Class. Few things pleased him more than to arouse a discussion, for he said that when they discussed the lesson they were interested in it; besides, forty or fifty people could never *think* for themselves about a lesson without having some differences. Thus it took many Sundays for John and his Class to go through the lesson thoroughly. He would not be hurried in those matters. He could never have adapted himself to the Sunday School Union Lessons. He would say about them, "Ah, too much at a time, people can never digest so much at once. There's no wonder that so many suffer from spiritual dyspepsia and sluggish livers if they swallow the Word in such lumps as that." When the Class had spent a few Sundays in going over the subject thoroughly, John would give a concluding lesson, which consisted of a running comment on the whole passage. This was always highly valued by the Class. Never were there so many present as on such occasions when John brought out his own individuality into special relief. His comment generally occupied a whole afternoon, especially at such times as this. That was the case on the last Sunday preceding the final review by the Pastor. There were scarcely any questions asked when John gave his running comment. He was allowed to rove at his own sweet will and pleasure, for never was he so interesting as when that was done.

John, who had his own way of looking at things, protested against the name given to the parable under their consideration. He said the Lord Jesus never called it "The Parable of the Prodigal Son," that He would have probably called it "The Parable of the Two Sons," because He began it by saying, "A certain man had *two* sons," and He never lost sight of the two from the beginning of it to the very close. The boy who ran away from home was not the only sinner in the parable. There was another at home who wasn't much better, if at all—indeed, John believed he was the worse of the two. But the world as a rule only recognizes one kind of sinners—the *prodigals.* Those who were too cunning to be prodigal, and whose whole life was a life of policy, passed, he said, for good moral men. This was the general theory with which John started.

"You see," said John, as he commenced his exposition, "how very near the Lord Jesus comes to us in His parables. This great Teacher is always near us. He has just been speaking about a house-wife, then about a shepherd, and now about a father. He doesn't bring His illustrations from the skies, and such as only angels can understand, but those which men, women, and even children can remember. There are some good people who, when they want to explain some simple truth, are always up in the clouds, or higher still, with what they call 'the sweeping comets, and the eternal stars, and the planets revolving in their orbits,' till some of us poor souls get so puzzled and so giddy with it all that we begin to think our heads are revolving in orbits, too. Those teachers never come near the earth, or if by hap they do, they rush off to Greece and Rome to the old philosophers and the gods, that, for all we learn from it, they might as well be still riding a comet. The good Lord is very different from that. He comes with us to the fields and mountains and our very homes and talks to the house-wife, the shepherd, and the father.

"Now," continues John, "let us try to go as simply as possible over the story, if we don't understand that we can't learn the moral. The Lord Jesus begins by saying 'A certain man had two sons.' There wasn't a father there who didn't prick up his ears when he heard that. If you want to interest fathers tell them something about another father and his boys. They may not know anything about him, but the fact that he is a father, and that he has some boys, is enough to secure their attention. Ah! how all the fathers would listen who heard our blessed Lord tell this story.

"'*Two* sons'—not a very big family; but a small one sometimes costs a deal of trouble, as this did. There's nothing said about the mother. There's no doubt that she was dead, or depend upon it the father wouldn't have been the first to meet the returning prodigal, and to fall on his neck and kiss him. The mother would have seen the boy long before the father, and had a mile's start of him. No, there couldn't have been any mother in that home. Those boys, no doubt, had missed her influence, good soul, so that one became a prodigal, and the other a selfish boy. But, remember, that's no *point* in the parable. We mustn't try to spiritualize everything in it. I only say this by way of trying to understand the story, and think of it as if it happened to our next-door neighbour. There's such a thing as people when they don't understand the real meaning of a passage rushing at spiritualizing it, and so ignorance passes very often for devotion. We must try not to fall into that mistake.

"Well, there were *two* sons. 'How are they going to turn out, I wonder?' asks some father. 'I have two sons, and they are as different as chalk from cheese.' These were different, too, but there wasn't very much to choose between them to my mind. Now, let's see. The *younger* of them said, *'Father.'* "Ah,' says the father, 'I'll warrant that boy wants something; I know by the way he calls me.' He was quite right. The boy came and said, 'Father, give me the portion of goods that falleth to me.' You see, he thought he could do better with his portion of goods than his father could. He's not the only boy who has thought that. There's a time in the lives of us all when we think no end of ourselves; that's when we are about sixteen or seventeen, when we look out every morning to see if the whiskers are coming, and when at last we find there is a little down on the upper lip and about half-a-dozen hairs on the chin, that's the time we are on good terms with ourselves! There's nothing we can't do then, and there's no responsibility we won't undertake. What's wanting in wisdom is made up in conceit. 'The old man,' says the young stripling of seventeen, meaning his father, 'is *too slow;* he belongs to the time before the flood;' and then the boy grins and thinks he has cracked a good joke. Then he continues, 'Just imagine a young man of *my* abilities boxed up here all my life! What *a scope* outside.' Yes, fine scope! There's plenty of room outside. Well, give the boy a chance! Let him find out for himself. The father 'divided unto them his living.' 'Them'—*both.* It was only fair that the one who didn't ask should have his share.

"'And not many days after.' Not *many days*—there wasn't much delay after he had his goods. Bless you, no. The young man was in too great a hurry to have his *'scope'* and make his fortune.

"'The younger son gathered all together, and went into a *far* country.' Of course he must go to a *far* country to make his fortune. There wasn't enough *scope* for his energies nearer home. He arrived at last, and all the village was in a consternation. 'I say, Jack,' said one idler to another, 'There's a young Jew come to the village—quite a gentleman!' 'Good natured?' asked Jack. 'He just is,' said Will, 'he spends like a good one; he treated us all round last night. He's a jolly good fellow.'

"For a time everything went on well, the young man spending, and his boon companions patting him on the back and calling him the best fellow out. How delighted every idler in the place was to see him. But by-and-by the money ran short, until at last there was nothing left; and, still worse, bad times came on, and he couldn't get any respectable work, so that he was forced to go to the fields to feed swine. Where were his companions now? Why, they helped him, of course. Not a bit of it. Jack said to Will, 'That young swell who cut such a show, and that you thought so much of has come to nothing. I thought that would be the end of it.' 'Ah, yes,' said Will, 'A fool and his money are soon parted.' 'Have you heard the last news?' said another. 'That young Jew who sported his money so much the other day has run down the scale pretty fast, and what do you think he's doing?' 'Don't know,' said his friend, ''twould puzzle a lawyer to tell; some stupid thing, I expect.' 'Why, he's out in Farmer So-and-So's fields feeding swine— fine work for a would-be gentleman, especially a *Jew.* Ha, ha!' 'Why the other day,' said another, 'I was passing, and there was my gentleman eating carob-pods with the swine—select company! What do *you* think. Ha, ha!' And so the laugh goes the round of mockers.

"And when he came to himself," read John, slowly. "I remember reading this when I was a boy, and saying to myself, 'He hadn't to go very far to come to himself,' but I have been learning ever since that most of us live very far from ourselves, and that, like the Prodigal, we have to go a very long way sometimes, and have a great many trials and disappointments—of ups and downs in life—before we know very much about ourselves. Here was this young man. Bless you he was a perfect stranger to himself, and if he could have met himself on the way, he wouldn't have known who he was. We are all too ready to mistake ourselves for somebody else, who is very much better and wiser than we are.

"Well, I must go on with the story. 'He said how many hired servants of my father's have bread enough and to spare.' Ah, that boy never knew the value of home till now. He had to miss its comforts in order to know its worth; and for the same reason he never knew how to value his father till now.

"'I will arise and go'—to my *companions?* Oh ,no, 'to my *father.'* Companions were good enough when everything went on well and he had plenty of money, but they have turned their backs now. He had seen one of them look over the fence at him and laugh as he was feeding swine, and that laugh pierced his heart. That man was the man who patted him most vigorously on his back only a fortnight before when he was fooling away his last penny. Ah, he thought, there's no heart in such companionship; but there was *one* who would pity him, though he had been treated ill, for not only had the prodigal left his home, but he had never sent a message from the distant land to tell his father what had become of his prodigal boy, yet *he* would not despise or fail to pity. 'I will arise and go to *my father.'* I should like to have heard him say *'my father'* just then. The boy's heart melts when he thinks of his father, and his soul goes out in the words— *'my father.'* Well, of course, he must put on a bold face, hold up his head, and make the best of a bad job, and say, 'Father, I've come back, but remember I could get on very well where I have been. There was a splendid *"scope"* there, but I thought I would come home for *your* sake, father.' Oh, no, he will not talk like that, he's got all the conceit dashed out of him at last, and he's disgusted with shams and lies, so he decides to make a clean breast of it, and say, 'I have sinned against heaven and in thy sight, and am no more worthy to be called thy son; make me as one of thy hired servants.' Poor fellow, he must have been pretty hungry before he could be brought to say that. It's wonderful how much starch a thorough bout of hunger takes out of a man, and how limp it makes him."

"There's a saying, isn't there," said Jenkin, "that an empty sack won't stand long."

"Yes, there is a saying like that, my boy," replied John, "and it illustrates this very truth that human nature—with all its pride and conceit—is very weak on an empty stomach. Well, I've often thought of the prodigal as he returned home step by step, how he would say, 'I had a mighty opinion of myself when I passed this way before, and I thought—'I shall never have occasion to travel *this* road back again. I've had quite enough of the old country and the tame life at home. I believe in seeing a bit of the world.'—Ah, I've seen quite enough of the world now it's cold, bleak, and selfish enough in the country in which I've been. There's no place like home—no, *there's no place like home.'* And then he would begin to think about the old home, and about the reception he would have, wondering whether his father would take him back as he was—rags and all. And so I can imagine him often looking into a pool of water, or the smooth part of a stream or river, to see what sort of a figure he would cut when his father saw him; poor boy, he would start back half frightened, but even then he would say, 'Well, my ragged clothes are a poor recommendation enough, but then my father—my *father* didn't love me in the first place because of my fine clothes, and he isn't going to reject me now because of these poor rags.' And so he would go on his way with a new heart.

"'When he was a great way off his father saw him.' *A great way* off—who will say love is short-sighted after that? A father's love sees a long way when the prodigal is on his way home. How did he know him so far off? Why, by his clothes, of course. Bless you, no, he was all rags and tatters. The father had never seen his boy in such a plight as that before. Oh, no, nobody would have known him by his clothes. Well, that father was on the flat roof of his house walking up and down, thinking no doubt about his poor boy who had gone away, and who hadn't as much as sent a letter home to say how he was. Ah whenever that father was alone he was sure to think about his lad, and would often look out beneath the clear Eastern sky in the direction the boy had gone, to see if he was coming back. He had looked hundreds of times in vain, but there's nothing so persistent as a father's love, except a mother's. So on this afternoon, when the day was just fading, the father was once again on that roof thinking about his boy, and walking up and down—up and down. He looked eagerly along the road by which his lad had gone, and all at once, just at the spot on the dusty road where he had seen the last of his boy, he saw someone come. His face brightened in a moment. But was this to be another disappoint-ment, or was this his very lad? The father looked and looked. At last he said to himself, 'He walks like my boy, though not quite so erect; besides he appears, as he comes nearer, to be ragged and poor, but I think I can account for all that.' Then the father was silent, and strained his eyes as he looked anxiously. Then he said, 'Ah, if his mother were living she would have known him long ago.' At last he said, 'He is my very boy, I'm sure of it,' and down he rushed to the road, ran—he never ran in his life like that—and met the prodigal on the way, fell on his neck and kissed him.

"And the son said 'Father, I have sinned against heaven, and in thy sight, &c.' This was the old confession which he had uttered first in the far distant land among the swine, and which he had often repeated on the way, but mark, he didn't say all now. Those words, 'Make me as one of thy hired servants' were forgotten—no, not *forgotten,* the father had kissed him and made it impossible for him to repeat those words ever after. His father wouldn't have kissed him if he only meant to make a servant of him. Bless you, no, and the boy knew that very well.

"Mark you, the Father said nothing to *him,* he felt too much to say anything; he could only caress the boy whom he had given up a hundred times as lost; but turning to the servants he said, 'Bring forth the best robe and put it on him, and put a ring on his hand and shoes on his feet.' The poor boy had come back in a poor plight. He hadn't brought with him anything worth keeping; not a bit of clothing, or even a pair of shoes—and when a man hasn't a pair of shoes on," added John, authoritatively, as one who knew something about that, "he's a poor object to look at."

"Well, did the servants do as they were bidden? Of course they did, and were delighted to do it, too. And that was not all, for they killed the fatted calf, prepared a glorious feast, and began to be merry. They had caught the joy of their Master, and there was nothing they wouldn't do to give the prodigal a welcome home. All joined in the gladness, but one, and that *one* was the elder brother. Some wish the parable had closed before any mention was made of this brother. Depend upon it the Lord Jesus knew where to finish His parables, and there's a reason why the elder brother should be included in this parable. If it had ended here it would have been only an encouragement to publicans and sinners, but, finishing as it does, it is also a rebuke to Pharisees and self-righteous men. It shows that sinners are not only those who are known by everybody as such, but also those who pass for respectable people, who have good names, who are never brought to rags and hunger by their sins, who don't sin so much as that against themselves, but who are yet far from being what they ought to be in charity and goodwill. The Lord Jesus, in this parable, denounces sin which passes under the name of piety, and to my mind that's as bad as the other. Sin, as I take it, is to be out of sympathy with the mind and spirit of our heavenly Father; and if that's right the elder brother was a sinner as well as the younger one. The only difference is that each sinned in his own way, the one as a sinner, the other as a Pharisee.

"Now I think we must remember this before we understand this parable; as old Mr. Ishmael Jones once said, when preaching at the Methodist Chapel—'The Holy Spirit has taken care to present the key to every parable; but it doesn't always put it in the same place. The wife is sometimes heard to say to the husband when both go out of the house together, 'If you are back before me the key will be above the door,' or sometimes, 'The key will be under the door.' The Holy Spirit has sometimes hung the key of a parable 'above the door,' at other times 'under the door.' In Luke vii. 4-50, it is *'beneath* the door' that the key is hidden. The good Lord gives the parable first, and then says:—'Simon, I have somewhat to say unto thee,' and thus he catches him unawares. Now the key of this parable is *'above* the door.'

"The chapter begins with the words, 'Then drew nigh unto him all the publicans and sinners for to hear him.' The world's notorious sinners were charmed by the blessed Lord, but the story doesn't end there. 'And'—*'and,'* notice. *'And* the Pharisees and scribes murmured, saying, This man receiveth sinners and eateth with them.' Don't you see the parable of the prodigal son in these two verses? Sinners were no sooner received by Jesus than pious people began to grumble about it. There are some good folks who are well up in murmuring. If there were a crown in heaven for grumbling they'd bid fair to win it. Those Pharisees belonged to that class, and they never grumbled so much as when poor prodigals were received by the great Saviour.

"Now there are two classes of sinners in the world, and *only two*—notorious sinners and respectable ones; the prodigal belonged to the former class, the elder brother to the latter. Now respectable sinners always disclaim all relationship to the notorious ones, as the Pharisees did on this occasion. Our Lord gives this parable to show that they were closely connected, and that there wasn't very much to choose between them.

"He pictures, first of all, the wilful sinner who commits himself to a ruinous course, cuts himself away from all submission to his heavenly Father, and openly severs himself from Him and from all the sacred influences of the Father's house. It is a sad story—a man foolishly bringing about his own ruin, wasting valuable time and priceless gifts in riotous living; a man who for the time being seems to be given up to the devil. Everybody gives him up but the good Father Himself. *He* still hopes, and longs for his return.

"For a time the story saddens as it goes on, and the prospect becomes darker and darker; the man comes down almost to the level of the beast. 'He would fain have filled his belly with *the husks that the swine did eat.'* He couldn't fall lower and be a *man.* But at that moment, when all hope seemed gone, the story brightens. 'He came to himself'—to *himself* mark, at that moment he rose to a higher level than that of a companion of swine, and that was the turning-point of his life. It was then that he said, 'I will arise.' *'Arise'*—grand word! After that his path was an upward one; he had reached the lowest point, every step he would now take would be to purity and joy. 'I will arise and say *Father.'* Ah, that's the secret. All hope lies here in his being able to say 'Father.' He has gone far, but he hasn't forgotten that word. He said 'Father' before he left home. 'Father, give me, &c.,' but in what different tones does he say it now! How much more meaning and love he finds now in the word! Ah, we are a long time in life before we learn how to pronounce the word 'father.' Sometimes it's over his grave, at other times over the grave of some conceit. Depend upon it, the *fatherhood* of God is man's only hope in all his wanderings.

"The prodigal no sooner came to himself than he began the way to his father. It was because he had forgotten himself that he ever left his father in the first place. Now he came back to his old home. I once heard Mr. Roberts,* Wrexham, preach from these three parables. He spoke of the father keeping the home together, and the door open for his foolish lad, during all the time he wandered, and how the prodigal as he drew near, looked out eagerly to see if the old home was just the same as when he left it. He then added 'Thank God! He has not broken up the old home, and made a new heaven for other beings, and left us for ever out, but the old home is kept, so that " *Welcome Home* " may be given to thee, poor sinner. Return, oh prodigals to-night.'

"I said, in going over the story, that there was one part of the confession which the boy didn't repeat when his father had kissed him. But there was another part that he was bound to give all the more because his father had fallen on his neck and kissed him. He never felt so much as now what a wicked boy he had been. Thus he said, *'I have sinned against heaven and in thy sight.'* Ah, it's so with us—nothing brings our sins as prodigals so much to light as the patient and tender love of our heavenly Father. The forgiving kiss makes us more than ever ashamed of ourselves, and forces us to say, 'I have sinned.'

"The father said nothing to the boy in reply; words would only weaken the meaning of that kiss and that embrace, and so he was silent in his love. There are times when love can't speak, but that is

---

* Rev. D. Roberts, Congregational Minister, Wrexham.

when it's deepest. Had the father of the prodigal boy felt less he would have spoken more. He had already spoken in a kiss and a loving embrace. Words would only weaken the meaning of that speech. It's exactly so with our heavenly Father. There have been times when He has spoken in words, there are other times when He doesn't utter a word, but gives the kiss of peace, and there is heaven in that kiss. It seems to me that when our heavenly Father is at His best, and is bent upon producing a masterpiece of love, He is generally silent. He spoke out a great deal of His love through the prophets and through His Son, but when He wanted to shew His love at its best, He lifted up the cross and *said* nothing—He spoke no longer in words, but in *blood.* He could afford to be silent then; it's just so, when He kisses the prodigal son and clasps him in His Almighty arms, He need say nothing, *He can afford to be silent; the poor prodigal knows what He means.*

"'But the father said to the servants, "Bring forth the best robe and put it on him; and put a ring on his hand and shoes on his feet."' *'The best robe!'* The kind father didn't think that any old suit would do for the boy instead of the rags in which he came home. Oh, no. Bring forth *the best robe.* When the prodigal was welcomed home, he was welcome to the very best that his father could provide for him. Again—*Ring on his hand!* Ah, He wouldn't have said this had he thought of making him as one of his 'hired servants.' The ring was a sign of sonship, which the lad could show to anyone who would be unkind enough to remind him that he was only a poor prodigal. Caleb Rhys told me once about a gentleman who owns an estate in Glamorganshire. I think he called him Mr.——, and told me he was a magistrate. On this estate an old man lived for many years, who used to go to the chapel along the gentleman's private walk, because he saved a considerable distance by going that way. Some unkind neighbour told the magistrate about it, who on one day when the poor old man was going to the house of God, met him on his private walk, and said, 'What right have you on this path?' 'No right at all, Sir,' he answered, 'but I thought you wouldn't mind an old man who has lived on your estate so many years going this way to the house of God, especially as it's so very far the other way.' 'Give me your stick,' said he, sternly. The trembling old saint gave him his stick, not knowing what to expect next. Then, to his surprise, the gentleman, with a kind smile upon his face, and in the gentlest tones said to him, as he gave him in return his own walking-stick, mounted with gold and bearing his own crest, 'Here my good man; when anyone asks you again what right you have this way shew them this, and tell them that Mr.———— gave it to you.' That was exactly what the father did to this poor prodigal boy. He told his servants to put the ring on his finger, so that he could shew it to anyone who might tell him he had no right there, and say that it was his own *father's* gift. *'And shoes on his feet!'* Here again he was not treated as a 'hired servant,' but as a son. Servants wore no shoes in the East, but this boy was a *son,* though he had wandered, and must be treated as a *son.* Ah, he never went again along the old paths once he had the new shoes on!"

"Oh, no, he never wandered again," said David William, of Ty-mawr, who had all along been comparing John Vaughan's remarks with Dr. Jenkins's exposition, and had occasionally sighed as he thought he detected a taint of Arminian heresy in John's teaching. For the first time during the lesson he felt sure that John was right, for he now taught the *'final perseverance of the saints.'* David William would overlook a great deal for that.

John Vaughan, pulling down his spectacles from his forehead, continued to read from his well-thumbed little Bible—"'My son was dead and is alive again, was lost, and is found.' 'My *son'*—he had wandered far, but he was his *son* still. How sacred are those ties which bind the father to his child. God said long ages ago, 'When Israel was a child then I loved him... I taught Ephraim also to go (or *to walk),* taking them by their arms; but they knew not that I healed them. I drew them with the cords of a man (or with *leading-strings),* with *bands of love.'* Then He asked, 'How shall I give thee up, Ephraim?' Ah, *'How?'* indeed! The *leading-strings* by which He had in days gone by drawn Ephraim towards Himself still united that wayward boy to the great Father's heart. He had taught him *to walk,* too. Then He was bound to love him now. What! giving up loving him after having taught him to *walk!"*

"No, *Never!"* exclaimed Shadrach Morgan.

"No," replied John, *"Never.* Ephraim in one sense was 'dead' and 'lost,' but he wasn't 'dead' or 'lost' to his father's love. He perhaps almost gave up *hoping* about him, but He never almost gave up *loving* him. It's just so with our heavenly Father and ourselves. It's the same God that spoke in the days of Hosea as He who spoke in this parable and speaks to us to-day. The gracious Father would have no one—not even the prodigal who has wandered farthest—doubt His love. All that the good Lord expects of us is to trust in His forgiving grace. I heard Mr. Henry Rees* preach from the words, 'Beginning at Jerusalem.' He imagined Peter saying in surprise, *'Jerusalem!*—Good Master, the chief priests and scribes, and those who crucified Thee are there!' 'Yes,' replied the Master, 'Go and tell *them* that God so loved the world that he gave his only begotten Son that whosoever believeth in him should not perish, but have ever lasting life.' 'But,' said Peter, 'Pilate is there. He gave Thee over to be crucified when he knew that Thou wast innocent.' 'Yes,' answered the gracious Lord, in the tenderest tones, 'Go to *Pilate;* tell *him* there is enough virtue in My blood to wash away his sin, and tell him further that if he refuses to believe this that he will pierce My heart with a thousand wounds worse than any I received upon the cross.'"

"That's just like the blessed Lord," said Shadrach.

"Yes," replied John. "It is just like Him and like no one else. Llewellyn Pugh told me the other day that the greatest god of the old Greeks and Romans was noted for *thundering.* That's a great deal to do, no doubt, but it would be a poor thing if our God couldn't do anything better than thunder. I'm sure I couldn't love such a god. There's nothing in a clap of thunder or flash of lightning to melt my heart and to win its love—*Nothing!* No doubt it's god-like to thunder, and this old Book says that our God 'thundereth marvellously with his voice,' but that isn't His favourite way of speaking. He loves to speak in a still small voice, the voice of love and mercy. Let the old Romans boast in a god who could *thunder,* we will glory in the God who can *sigh,* and *pity,* and *love.*

"I thank God for a Gospel that has in it this parable. Such parables are only found in the Gospel of Jesus Christ. As I heard Mr. Ishmael Jones once say at the Methodist Chapel, 'Our religion is a religion for *men,* not for angels. They have a religion, but God has made no provision for failures in theirs. Forgiveness forms no part of it. But God has made a merciful provision for *failures* in man's religion. It's a Gospel for prodigals—for broken-down men. Though we lose the path and wander far away there is forgiveness still, and another chance given if we but repent; but for angels there's no second chance, at least, so far as we know. Thank God that we are men, and that we have a Gospel for prodigals.

* The late Rev. Henry Rees, Calvinistic Methodist Minister, Liverpool.

"I heard him say at another time," added Shadrach, "that when God forgives He does it Himself, and does not ask any angel to do that. 'God alone,' he said, 'is great enough to forgive sins.' Angels have ministered to man in God's service, but whoever heard an angel say, 'Thy sins are forgiven thee?' There are no angels in glory with shoulders strong enough to bear the burden of forgiveness to man, and even if there were, and God gave them permission, who knows but that they would carry it to their fallen brethren, instead of to men, for 'nearer elbow than wrist'* even to the angels, my good people. But He didn't entrust *this* to angels, and when He came Himself, 'Verily He took not on him the nature of angels; but he took on him the seed of Abraham.' Forgiveness is so priceless and great a gift that God reserves for Himself—*Himself*—the privilege of bestowing it."

"'They began to be merry. Now his elder son was in the field, and as he came and drew nigh to the house he heard music and dancing.' All this, remember, was over the boy's return. Some might think that the anxious father and the poor prodigal couldn't enter into such joy at once; but that's a great mistake. The moment they saw each other they lost their sorrow, and even the remembrance of it only added to their joy. It's exactly so with the heavenly Father and the returning prodigals to-day. How sweet the music that is born of sorrow! It's all the sweeter for the recollection of the hunger—and the grief. There is a song in heaven which angels cannot sing, which only those from the land of tribulation are able to learn. The voices that can give the sweetness of the minor in heaven must be got from earth. An angel can never touch the minor key in the anthem of the blest, because he has not touched sorrow. This is a secret in harmony which they have never found out. The eldest brother in the parable didn't understand this.

"'And he was angry'—'*angry,*' mark—because his poor prodigal brother had returned home, and his father and the servants were glad, and had killed the fatted calf, because he had been received safe and sound. *Angry*—the one who was so fond of telling how good he was and what he had done! 'Lo, these many years do I serve thee, neither transgressed I at any time thy commandment.' What a wonderful young man he was! Quite perfect; and yet he gets into a vile temper. From all I have seen, people who think themselves perfect are rather given to that. They as a rule—so far as my experience goes—have

* "Nes penelin na garddwrn."

dreadful tempers; if you offend half a dozen of them you may as well disturb a colony of hornets, but remember they *don't sin. I don't like perfectionists,"* added John, emphatically, "I like people who can be agreeable, kind, and forgiving, and I never saw a perfectionist of that sort, yet I'm looking out for him."

"Yes, there's room for improvement in this direction," said David Lewis, who was the superintendent of the school, and who in his round of visits to the classes had come to John, and had been listening for the last few minutes. "There are some pious people who have very bad tempers, and are always ready to get into a rage at anything, but then they are miserable specimens of Christians. Joseph Thomas,* of Carno, was quite right when, about five years ago, he represented the Methodist denomination as a deputation to the Welsh Congregational Union at Portmadoc, and said—It's a great pity we can't agree better. They are small insignificant beings who quarrel oftenest. Abraham and Lot were friends to the last, but their servants and shepherds were always quarrelling; and they represent the people who quarrel in all ages. There's a magnificent breed of cattle in the vale of Clwyd— the most beautiful vale in Wales. They have scarcely any horns, but an abundance of meat; yet if you ascend the hills on every side, there on the heights you find a breed which grows scarcely anything but horns, and from morning tonight all you hear is the constant din of clashing weapons. There are many Christians who live on *the heights,* but on very cold and barren ones. Everything they eat grows into horns, the strength of which they are constantly testing."

"That's all very true," said John, as he looked again at his Bible, "and it would be well if we all remembered that. Now mark you, the prodigal boy returned at last, and was restored after all his wanderings, but what of the other—the self-righteous son, who was so ready to tell what a good son he was, and how faithfully he had served his father—what of him? I ask. The parable closes, while as yet he is outside. It is for him to decide whether he will go in. He cannot make the company less by excluding his brother; he can only do so by excluding himself. I don't say that such men will be lost, far from it. Didn't the father say, 'Thou art ever with me?' The father who forgives the wayward boy also bears with that son, who, though he has never demanded his portion and spent it prodigally, yet, even beneath his

---

* Rev. J. Thomas, Calvinistic Methodist Minister.

father's sheltering roof, cherishes anything but his father's disposition, and becomes a sullen, narrow-minded man. That the great God bears with such is as great a proof of His patience as that He receives back the prodigal, every bit, and that's the point of the parable.

"The younger son is one of those who without much thought bring about their own hurt, who sin, perhaps, more against themselves than against anyone else, except the good Lord. Those soon reap the fruit of their folly, for nothing brings a crop so quickly as the wild oats sown early in life. The other brother is one of those who are too cunning—calculate too carefully—and love themselves too dearly to leave their comfortable home, but who, even within the walls of God's own house, and while they pass muster as the good sons of His family, cherish a spirit which divides them—almost, if not quite—as far from the loving Father whose name they bear as the prodigal boy ever was. The love of the Father must triumph over these two classes of sinners, or neither of them will be up to much. Oh, depend upon it, the bigotry and hypocrisy of so-called good people are more trying to the gracious Father than even the wanderings of His prodigal ones."

"Listen how the elder brother speaks to his father:—'But as soon as this thy son was come which hath devoured thy living with harlots, thou hast killed for him the fatted calf.' What venom in those words! *'Thy* son,' not *'my* brother,' *'thy* living,' not *'his* portion of goods,' 'with *harlots,'* not 'with *riotous living.'* Everything is distorted. What he says is a hideous caricature of truth, and that is the worst form of a lie, and yet he passes for the good son in the family."

"There's a great deal of daubing other people's characters, which passes for piety," said Jenkin. "You remember hearing Mr. John Stephens,* one of 'the three brothers,' speaking at 'Peniel' on the duties of the church toward its pastor. He gave a capital story. He said:—'Do you know the old saying about Aberdaron, in Carnarvonshire, a district noted for its dirt? The people of Aberdaron generally carried long walking sticks, and were noted for being inquisitive. People who passed through to Pwllheli on the way to market were often accosted by the inhabitants of Aberdaron. The stranger was greeted at the outset with, "How are you to-day?" At the same time he was pushed with the dirty end of the stick. Again, "Where are you going to-day?" Another push with the dirty end of

---

* The late Rev. J. Stephens, Congregational Minister, Brychgoed.

the stick. Then, "What are you going for?" Another push. Meeting with another a little further on the same process was repeated. The third he met added his share to the number of spots already on the garment, until at last when he reached Pwllheli everybody knew he had passed through the neighbourhood of Aberdaron that morning, for he bore upon him the dirt of that district. Dear brethren, you are having to-day a young minister who has a clean coat without a spot upon it. He comes to you with a bright character, let him be among you "without fear," that you will ever mark him with the dirty end of your walking sticks in quizzing rudely into his affairs.'—I've no patience," continued Jenkin, "with people who with such an air of piety throw dirt on other people's characters."

"No," said John, "you and I haven't, but our heavenly Father has patience even with them. Listen:—"And he said unto him, Son thou art ever with me, and all that I have is thine.' Here the love of the father appears to me greatest of all. We blame the prodigal, and are tempted to despise his elder brother, but he neither blames the one nor despises the other; and the greatest wonder of all to me is that he doesn't do the latter, that he can give such a tender reply to such bitter and unkind words from the lips of his eldest son. Even when he rebukes, the sting of the reproof is dipped in honey. 'It was meet that we should make merry and be glad; for this thy brother'—notice, *he* had said '*thy son,*' now the father says '*thy brother,*' thus reminding him that the prodigal boy he so despised was still *his brother.*

"The parable is now finished. The Pharisees and Scribes had murmured, saying, 'This man receiveth sinners and eateth with them.' This is Our Lord's answer to them, an answer to which the other two parables only prepare the way. Our blessed Lord would have them remember that the love that forgives poor wayward ones who are called 'the lost' is the only love which *could* bear with the pride, coldness, and bigotry of self-righteous men, who are too cautious to wander into the wilds of sin, and are too wide-awake to sell their birthright for a mess of pottage, or, like the prodigal, to waste their substance in riotous living."

Just then the superintendent announced the time for closing the school. John took down his spectacles, folded them, and put them into a leathern case of his own making; David William, of Ty-mawr, shut Dr. Jenkins's big Commentary and placed it carefully in the green baize bag in which it was generally carried; while all the Class, laying aside their Bibles, prepared for the concluding prayer and hymn.

CHAPTER XI

The Great Revival

N two or three occasions some of the old friends had visited the smithy, but nothing of special interest had occurred till a few evenings before Christmas, when the whole company met, with the exception of John Vaughan and Swash. John was very busy just at that time. There were so many who ordered new shoes and boots for that, wonderful to relate, he had not been in the smithy for over a week. Swash, too, had to make arrangements for a sale, which was to take place the first week in the new year. Besides, there was no special arrangement to meet at the smithy that night, and Swash was not one of the most regular attendants there.

Although there was no general understanding that anything of importance would then take place, yet there was a good muster early in the evening, and when Llewellyn Pugh looked in a little later Shadrach accepted this as a good opportunity for ventilating the subject to which the old schoolmaster had recently referred.

"The other night, Mr. Pugh," said Shadrach, "you began to tell us about Mr. Rowlands, of Llangeitho, and the Great Revival of his time. I for one should like to hear a little more about that."

"Caleb knows far more than I do about Daniel Rowlands, of

Llangeitho," said Llewellyn, "as he was born in the neighbourhood, and knows all the local traditions about him."

"I have very little to tell that I haven't told before," said Caleb. "I spent the first thirty years of my life at Llangeitho, and of course can remember well what my father, grandfather, and others used to say about the old times, and especially about Daniel Rowlands. Wherever I went they used to tell me something about him—'There,' they said, 'Daniel Rowlands preached on such an occasion when so many were converted—in this field he used to study his sermons—and in that field the Communion Service was held during the summer months, when as many as three thousand met to take part in it—and along that road he walked last of all before he passed away.' Almost every spot within many miles of Llangeitho is connected with some event or other in his life. I used to feel that I was treading upon holy ground, and very often would look up from the village at the wooded slopes around; or when I climbed one of the hills would gaze upon the hamlet sheltered in the hollow beneath, and would watch the lovely Aeron winding its course through the valley, and murmuring on its way to the sea as it skirted the meadow in front of Mr. Rowlands' house, and then I would wonder whether all appeared to him as they did to me. At other times I have looked at the grey old church in which, for twenty-six years after his conversion, he used to preach the Gospel so mightily, and near which his ashes now rest, though he himself during his life was excluded from its ministry. I have stood by his grave at the north end of the churchyard, round which there is an iron railing, and at the head a simple stone bearing the name of that holy man, and I have felt as if I would give all the world could I but hear him speak. But all is silent now; that powerful voice is still, and the surrounding hills will never again ring with the echoes of his mighty appeals. But there, I forget myself when I talk about dear old Llangeitho. I feel towards it very much as the Jew did towards Jerusalem."

"Go on Caleb, I like to hear you talk about it," said Shadrach, "it does my soul good."

"Yes, go on, Caleb," said his old friend, Hugh Roberts.

"Well, Mr. Rowlands was born at a farm-house called Pant-y-beudy, between Nantcwnlle and Llangeitho. I have often seen the old house, with its thatched roof and its mud-built walls covered with ivy, but I have been told that only a small part of it stands now. They have built a new house on the old spot. I don't think I was ever told when he was born or where he was educated; you, Mr. Pugh, could tell that, no doubt."

"Daniel Rowlands," said Llewellyn," was born in 1713. His father and grandfather were clergymen. When as yet a youth he was intended for the Church, but his father was too poor to send him to Oxford or Cambridge; he was therefore sent to the Grammar School at Hereford, and when about twenty-one years of age was appointed curate of Nantcwnlle and Llangeitho, at a salary of *Ten Pounds* a year.

"Big pay," interjected Jenkin, as he threw the hammer on his shoulder ready to strike alternately with his father the glowing iron on the anvil.

"Yes," replied Llewellyn, "and he never got a higher preferment than that in the Church."

"When he entered the ministry he didn't deserve that," said Caleb, "for he wasn't morally qualified for his sacred calling. As yet Mr. Rowlands looked upon the ministry as a mere profession. Like the majority of Welsh clergymen in his day he hurried through the service—prayers, lessons, and sermon—and at the close of all would say a hearty 'Amen,' the only hearty thing he did in the service, and then would resort with the men of his congregation to the village ale-house close by, in order to prime themselves for a good game at football. He soon took the lead in the field, and the little parson of Llangeitho became a favourite throughout the whole neighbourhood. Finding, however, that the popularity of Mr. Pugh,* his Nonconformist neighbour, who drew large crowds, was far greater than his, football notwithstanding, and becoming heartily dissatisfied with the part he had taken in desecrating the Lord's Day, he gave up the sports and devoted himself to preaching. He tried to find out the secret of Mr. Pugh's popularity, and hearing the people say 'Mr. Pugh thundered terribly to-day,' he resolved upon choosing for his texts the most solemn and terrible passages within the covers of God's Book. He had a voice like thunder, and an eye that flashed lightning. Soon he created a powerful sensation, and those who heard him began to say, 'Mr. Rowlands thunders too, now.' Just about this time the Rev. Griffith

---

* The Rev. Philip Pugh was born near Llangeitho in 1679, and was educated for the ministry at the Academy at Abergavenny. In 1709 he was appointed co-pastor with Mr. David Edwards and Mr. Jenkin Jones over the churches at Cilgwyn, Cae'ronen, Llwyn-y-piod, and others. He continued to labour in this sphere with increasing power and usefulness for over half a century. He died in 1760 in the eighty-first year of his age.

Jones, of Llanddowror, in this county, a mighty man in the Scriptures, came to Llanddewi-Brevy, a little village in which, over thirteen hundred years ago, a synod of British bishops was held. You could tell us something about that, Mr. Pugh."

"Not much," replied Llewellyn, "except that it was held in the year 519, in order to suppress the heresy of Pelagius, and that St. David on that occasion, to use the words of an old chronicler, 'confuted and silenced the infernal monster by his learning, eloquence and miracles.'"

"Well," continued Caleb, "when Mr. Griffith Jones, in 1737—more than twelve hundred years later—visited that spot the church could hold almost three thousand people. The name of Griffith Jones was enough to fill the church to overflowing with an attentive congregation. Preaching was a novelty in Wales, especially such preaching as his. The people came from the surrounding country, many as far as ten miles, to hear this wonderful preacher. Among those present was the young parson from Llangeitho, then nearly twenty-four years of age, who, on account of the crowded state of the church, had to stand opposite the pulpit. Mr. Jones was much struck by the haughtiness of the young parson, and in the midst of his discourse was moved to offer a silent prayer on his behalf. He paused, clasped his hands and closed his eyes, his heart meanwhile pouring out in silence its request to God. The prayer was heard, and from that hour Daniel Rowlands, of Llangeitho, was a changed man. The effect produced by the powerful sermon which was then preached was to humble him in the dust. In a moment of despondency vowed to himself he would never preach again.

"The warm and unbounded approval of the sermon by all those who accompanied Mr. Rowlands on the way home from the service helped to humble him still more. At length one man who rode by his side broke upon the chorus of praise and said, as he placed his hand on Mr. Rowlands' shoulder, 'Well, you may say what you like; I have reason for ever thanking God for the little parson of Llangeitho. I have often felt much more serious under his fiery and powerful ministry than I have felt to-day.' This may have appeared very insignificant at the time, but taking place just then it had a great influence upon the mind of the young man. By that friendly touch his hope revived and he said within himself, 'Who knows, perhaps God will make some use of *me*—poor creature!' After this Mr. Rowlands preached with increasing power in his own church, which was crowded by those who came from all parts of the country for many miles round. As yet he never preached outside his own parish The story is often told in the neighbourhood of the first circumstance which led Mr. Rowlands to preach from home. A young woman from Llangeitho had married a farmer who lived in the upper part of this country. During one of her visits to her former home she was greatly impressed under the ministry of Mr. Rowlands, who was then known in the neighbourhood as the 'cracked parson, and whom she had been moved by curiosity to hear. She returned home the following day but next Sunday morning she came again on horseback to Llangeitho, much to the surprise of her sister whom she had visited. When asked why she had come so unexpectedly and whether all was well at home she replied 'All is well at home, but something that your 'cracked parson' said last Sunday has brought me; I *must* hear him again, for I have spent a most miserable week.' She heard him that day and found rest for her soul. In a short time she went again to Llangeitho, and during the Sunday spoke to Mr. Rowlands, beseeching him to visit her neighbourhood as it was in the most deplorable condition. He told her that if her clergyman would invite him to preach in his pulpit he would gladly do so. This was readily done by the parson of the little chapel-of-ease at Ystrad-ffyn, for that was the name of the parish where the farmer's wife lived.

"Great was the expectation during the week before the Sunday in which Mr. Rowlands was to occupy the pulpit at the 'old chapel of Ystrad-ffyn.' Already the fame of 'the cracked parson of Llangeitho' had been spread far and wide, and now that he was to come to their neighbourhood the people assembled in large numbers from all directions. Long before the time for service the chapel was crowded. Mr. Rowlands had to travel on horseback that morning over twenty miles of rugged road, over hill and dale. Owing to the roughness of the journey he was late for service. The large crowd became restless, and began to show signs of impatience. Men were sent along the way by which he was to come, and were stationed at different points from which they could see each other. The advanced guard was to signal to the next, and so on, in order that the large congregation in and around the chapel might hear as soon as possible that the wonderful preacher was near. At length he appeared at a spot I know very well, and which I passed scores of times when I was a young man. It is where the road is highest, and on the very summit of one of the two hills which hide Ystrad-ffin from the world's gaze, and only allow the heavens to peep down into the deep glen. In an instant the news was signalled along the line, and in less than a minute it was known in the chapel that the preacher was coming.

"Mr. Rowlands soon arrived. The crowd without and within the chapel immediately made way for him. It was a motley throng that had gathered together on that occasion. Many of those present had never heard a sermon in their lives. Some of the oldest and most daring sinners of the neighbourhood came to hear the 'cracked parson.' There they were, young and old, rich and poor, mixed together in strange confusion. Never before had there been such a congregation at Ystrad-ffyn. Every possible space near the chapel was filled with the vehicles of farmers and others who had come from a distance.

"Among others present was one gentleman who was accustomed to hunt on Sundays. After he and his companions had started that particular Sunday morning, he heard that the young 'cracked parson of Llangeitho' was to preach there on that day. Returning from the hunt, he went to church with his dogs and his companions. He was there early, and, in order to confuse the preacher, stood up on a form right in front of the pulpit, and began to make grimaces at him. Mr. Rowlands took no notice, but proceeded at once to read the lessons and prayers. The people had never heard such reading before. They had often used the phrase 'he can read like a parson,' but until now they little knew what that meant. They had never known a parson who could read like that. When he read the Scriptures it seemed as if God was speaking to them, and when he read the prayers they felt as if they were speaking to God—they couldn't help it. But the sporting gentleman who stood on the form opposite the pulpit, and a few of his companions, were still unmoved, and continued to jeer at the preacher. He began his sermon as if he hadn't noticed them, yet he was aroused by their conduct to speak more powerfully than ever. He seemed to speak like a being from another world. Some of his words sounded like a crash of thunder, and lightning flashed in every sentence. The congregation was soon brought to tears, and an occasional cry breaking like a jarring discord upon the harmonious voice of the preacher told that conviction was at work. The feeling spread, and all present hung helplessly upon the preacher's words. Meanwhile the sportsman who had come to disturb the service ceased to mock he became pale with fear, then his tears began to flow, and trembling like an aspen leaf he got down from his exalted position and sat out of sight, glad to hide his head for very shame. At the close of the service he went to Mr.

Rowlands, confessed all with many tears and sighs, and besought him to forgive him. He also invited him to his home, and to stay under his roof that night. Mr. Rowlands consented, and this was the beginning of a life-long friendship between the preacher and the would-be disturber. For many years after this there were none who attended the monthly Communion Service at Llangeitho more regularly than this gentleman, although he lived twenty miles away. Ah, that was a day which will never be forgotten at Ystrad-ffyn. The story is handed down by parents to their children as generations come and go, and there is scarcely a young man or woman in the place to-day who doesn't know about the 'cracked parson of Llangeitho' and the sporting gentleman farmer who went to mock him, but who was caught in his own net."

"I should like to see that old chapel-of-ease," said Hugh Roberts tremulously, "as it was the first place in which the great apostle of Wales in the last century preached the Gospel beyond his own parish, and so revived itinerant preaching at a time when it seemed to be fast dying out of our land."

"Yes," said Caleb, "the little place is sacred because of its associations, but when one draws near to the old chapel in that lonely glen the silence seems to be unbearable. One wants to hear that voice which less than a century and a half ago echoed and re-echoed within those ancient walls, but everything is terribly still now. Yet there is one comfort, that the voice which was once heard there, and in a thousand places besides, hasn't died out of the land; the words which Daniel Rowlands spoke sank deep into the hearts and memories of men, who in their turn told the glad tidings to others, so that to-day there is scarcely a nook or corner of our dear country where the Gospel isn't preached by some faithful messenger."

"The sporting parsons of his day were greatly displeased. 'A clergyman,' exclaimed they, 'preach beyond his own parish! Who ever heard of such a thing? Worse than all, here was a clergyman encouraging men who had never been episcopally ordained to conduct religious services! Shocking! A clergyman might get drunk occasionally, it was an infirmity of noble minds, or he might join in the game of football on Sunday afternoon, law and custom justified that, but neither law nor custom justified a man preaching the Gospel outside his own church! The Bishop, too, protested. Mr. Rowlands pleaded the ignorance and depravity of the Welsh people as a sufficient reason. The Bishop reminded him that that was no business of his, but of those clergy who were appointed over them. 'Then, my lord,' replied Mr. Rowlands, 'the clergy themselves are so bad. They have no grace; they never preach; they get drunk.' 'Leave that to me,' replied the Bishop. He was deprived of his living because he would not give up preaching the Gospel to the thousands of his fellow-countrymen who were perishing around. Two clergymen appointed by the Bishop entered the church at Llangeitho one Sunday morning. The church was filled. When Mr. Rowlands was on his way from the desk to the pulpit they delivered the Bishop's letter to him. He read it, and having told the congregation that he was forbidden to preach or officiate in that church any more he immediately dismissed them with a blessing. My grandfather often used to tell me the story. His father was in the church at the time, and he said that no one but those who were there could imagine the effect that was produced upon the crowded congregation. Well, said they, 'the Bishop can stop him preaching in the church, but he can't prevent us building him a chapel.' The chapel was built, and my grandfather was taken as a little child in his mother's mantle to the opening services. The building was too small to contain the people who came from all parts of the country. When Mr. Rowlands was thrust out of that church the glory departed from it. God removed the candle-stick to the chapel close by.

"Daniel Rowlands had no wish to leave the Church. He loved it to the last, but like the great and holy men you spoke about the other night, Mr. Pugh, he was driven out of it. As long as he lived, and for many years after his death, whenever the service was conducted by an *ordained clergyman* the Litany was read in the chapel, so that there was no difference between the service observed there and that held in the parish church close by. Indeed, the services which were conducted by 'exhorters,' and at which, therefore, the Litany was not read, were considered incomplete. It was not until many years after Mr. Rowlands' death that the Church Service was discontinued in the chapel which is so sacredly associated with him and his glorious work."

"There was a similar complaint against Mr. Jones, Llangan," said Hugh. "Representations were made to the Bishop (Dr. Barrington) that he went out of his parish to preach, that he preached in unconsecrated places, and without a book. The Bishop summoned Mr. Jones to his presence, and said, 'I am told, Mr. Jones, that you preach in unconsecrated places.' 'No, never, my lord,' replied Mr. Jones, 'I believe that when the Son of God set His foot on the earth he consecrated every inch of it, so that the whole earth is holy ground.'"

"Have you heard the story." said Caleb Rhys, "of Mr. Jones and the aged woman who came to him at the close of an Association meeting at the little village of Niwbwrch, Anglesea. He had preached very powerfully, and the poor old saint was delighted. She went to him and asked him when he would come again. Mr. Jones smiled and said, 'When you come to Llangan to fetch me.' He thought no more of it. But she did not forget his promise, and concluding that the man of God could not withdraw from it she determined to go and fetch him. Before she went she announced to the whole neighbourhood that Mr. Jones was coming. Llangan was *one hundred and fifty* miles distant, and she had only a pair of clogs on her feet, and very little, if any, money in her pocket with which to proceed on her journey. She walked, however, all the way, and one day, as Mr Jones was looking through his study window, to his great surprise he saw the poor old woman with walking stick in one hand and wallet in the other coming toward the house. Imagine his surprise! Her faith overcame him and it was amply rewarded, for she thus succeeded in inducing not only him, but also Mr Rowlands, of Llangeitho, and Mr. Lloyd, of Henllan—three of the greatest evangelists of their day—to visit her little village, and the whole of Anglesea reaped the fruits of poor Anna's faith."

"Wonderful," said David Lewis. "Speaking of Mr. Rowlands, Mr. Philip Pugh, who was then drawing near the close of life, was very helpful to him just after his conversion, wasn't he?"

"Yes," replied Caleb, "for some time after his conversion, Daniel Rowlands preached from such themes as the Curse of the Law, Death, The Judgment, Hell, and kindred subjects. The people who heard were terrified beyond endurance. His neighbour, Mr. Pugh, the aged Nonconformist minister, warned him kindly against mistaking these terrors and threatenings for the Gospel. He said, 'My dear Sir, preach the Gospel to the people, and apply the balm of Gilead, the blood of Christ, to their spiritual wounds, and show the necessity of faith in a crucified Saviour.' 'I am afraid,' confessed Rowlands, 'that I have not that faith myself in its full vigour and scope.' 'Preach on it,' said Mr. Pugh, 'till you realize it by so doing; it will be sure to come.' The young man received thankfully the hint given by his venerable and experienced friend, and with what results all Wales can testify."

"Ah, that was one of the secrets of his success," said Llewellyn, "that he was willing to learn from older and wiser men. It is interesting to notice that many years later Mr. Rowlands was permitted to extend to Mr. Pugh's successor the same friendly aid and counsel as he himself had received when a young man from Mr. Pugh, for he was not only the means of producing deep impressions upon the mind of Mr. Thomas Grey when a student at Abergavenny, but also when he settled at Llangeitho, as the successor of Mr. Pugh counselled and befriended him in every possible way. But I am taking up time. Tell us something, Caleb, about the Communion Sunday at Llangeitho; that to my mind is the most interesting part of all."

"Ah, yes," replied Caleb, earnestly, "that was always a wonderful day. Thousands came to partake of the Lord's supper. It was the great day of the Feast for the whole country within a distance of thirty miles or even more. Many reached Llangeitho in time for the 'preparatory meeting' at noon on the preceding Saturday, at which Mr. Rowlands preached. The afternoon meeting, which was conducted by lay preachers, was also largely attended, and on Saturday evening hospitality was freely extended to the strangers who had arrived. The following day, however, was the day on which the people came in throngs from all points of the compass. It is said that Mr. Rowlands was up earlier than usual on that Sunday morning. He spent most of the time before the morning service in front of his house in the meadow, which the clear waters of the graceful Aeron touch as they flow gently by. There, within sound of the meandering stream, the great man of God pondered over his message until he heard among the hills the echoes of the Psalms of Praise, as sung by large companies of joyful pilgrims on their way to the Feast. The hour was at length come. The apostle of his country would listen to the sound growing louder and louder as the numerous bands drew near, until at last the glen was flooded with the gladsome music. He would then exclaim, in an ecstasy of delight, 'Here they come; here they come! bringing heaven with them!' The service was generally held on such occasions in a field close by, as the sanctuary was far too small to hold the multitude who congregated together. The introductory part of the service was conducted by some minister or lay preacher from a distance; when that was over Daniel Rowlands would announce his text and preach like an apostle to the thousands present. Then came the most imposing service of all. Upon the grassy field the thousands sat to partake of the bread and wine. The sun in the heavens seldom looked down upon a sight so beautiful as that which it witnessed once a month at Llangeitho every spring and summer about a century ago—seldom since the day it saw the Lord Jesus feeding the needy multitude upon the grassy slopes of ancient Palestine. He who fed the hungry throngs eighteen hundred years ago on the wild eastern shore of the Sea of Galilee also fed the thousands who, in a secluded glen amid the hills of our native country, met together to partake of His own appointed Feast."

Yes," said Hugh Roberts, "and long before Mr. Rowlands died people went to Llangeitho to some of the Communion Services, even from Carnarvonshire in the north and from Glamorganshire in the south, aye, from almost every county in Wales. There were many who travelled for days and nights in order to reach Llangeitho on Sunday morning. My father and many of the old people have told me how the company grew in number as they drew near Llangeitho. Like the streams that rush down the hill-sides after rain, and unite on their way to the sea, these little streams of worshippers met and blended on their way to Llangeitho, until at last they became a multitude of people. And I have heard them often speak about the Mr. Edmund Pryse's psalms, and the hymns of Mr. Williams, of Pantycelyn—those Welsh 'Songs of Degrees,' which they, like the Jews of old, used to sing on their way to the House of the Lord. They loved to tell, too, about their halting places, especially the last on 'The Little Mountain'* near Llangeitho, and by 'The Communicants' Well,'† where on the morning of the Lord's Day, they ate their frugal meal, consisting generally of barley bread and cheese, and quenched their thirst with the water from the well."

"It is said that the Revival began on one Sunday morning," added Caleb Rhys, "just as Mr. Rowlands in reading the Church service repeated those solemn words, 'By thine agony and bloody sweat.' He uttered them with such over powering feeling and thrilling tenderness that the people could hardly bear them. They seemed to he in Gethsemane with their Lord, far in amid the darkest shades of that awful garden. A cry of agony went up from the whole congregation, and it seemed as if *there and then* they were filling up that which was behind of the affliction of Christ. Mr. Rowlands had to pause and it was some time before he could go on with the service. Ah, the old people used to say that that was a wonderful occasion and that ever after when Mr Rowlands read those words strange mysterious feeling came over them."

---

* "Y Mynydd Bach."
† "Ffynnon y Cymmunwyr."

"I have heard them say," said Hugh Roberts, "that he was very often so filled with the spirit of his subject that he had to pause for a moment fairly overcome and wondering how he might tell his thoughts and feelings as they rushed upon him. The awful period in his sermon was *that* silence, similar to that which is felt in the brief pause between the flash of lightning and the crash of thunder; all knew that something terrible was coming."

"Howell Harris too was an extraordinary preacher, wasn't he, Hugh?" asked David Lewis.

"Yes", replied Hugh, "I've heard my father speak much about him. He heard him many a time, and he used to say he hadn't such deep thoughts as either Griffith Jones or Daniel Rowlands, but that he had greater power to sway a multitude than both. It was he who founded our denomination. But no one here knows so much about him as you, Mr. Pugh."

"Mr. Howell Harris, the founder of Calvinistic Methodism* in Wales," said Llewellyn, "like so many others who did a great work in our country during the last century, was brought up within the pale of the Established Church. He entered St. Mary's Hall, Oxford, with a view of being educated for the ministry. While there he had the promise of a benefice, but, to use his own words, in reviewing that time, he says, 'Although I was encompassed with fair prospects, yet when I saw the irregularities and wickedness which surrounded me, I became soon weary of the place, and cried to God to deliver me from thence; and thus after keeping that term I was again brought to my dear friends in Wales.' Returning to Wales, he engaged in evangelistic labours, a work which he had begun even before he entered Oxford, but which he now undertook with greater energy than ever. He went about, to use his own words, 'from house to house,' until he had visited nearly the whole of the parish in which he was born, together with some of the neighbouring ones. The people crowded to hear him, so that the houses in which he addressed them were far too small for the congregations. He was then invited to all parts of the country, and spoke to crowded congregations, four, five, and even six times a day.

---

* By *Methodism* is meant *Calvinistic* Methodism. No Welsh *Wesleyan* Church was formed in Wales till the beginning of the present century, notwithstanding that John and Charles Wesley frequently visited the Principality during this revival.

This led to better attendances at the parish churches and to family worship being held in many homes. Yet the clergy became embittered and preached against him, while the magistrates threatened to fine him, and all who received him into their houses. The mob, encouraged by these chief priests and rulers, waylaid him in many places. His own account of this period of his life is very interesting." Here Llewellyn took out his familiar pocket-book and began to read:—

"'During all this I was carried, as on wings of an eagle, triumphantly over all. I took no particular *texts,* but discoursed *freely,* as the Lord gave utterance. The gift I had received was as yet to *convince* the conscience of sin. There appeared now a general reformation in several counties. Public diversions were laid aside, religion became a common subject of conversation, and places of worship were everywhere crowded. The Welsh Charity Schools, by the exertions of the Rev. Griffith Jones, of Llanddowror, began to spread; people in general expressed a willingness to receive instruction; and societies were formed in many places.

"'About this time I heard by a friend that came from London of a young clergyman, namely Mr. Whitefield, that preached four times a day, and was much blessed. My heart, on hearing this, was united to him in such a manner as I never felt the like with anyone before; but I had not the least prospect of seeing him, being informed that he had gone beyond the sea; it was his first voyage to America. However, in the beginning of January, 1738, I was agreeably surprised by a letter from him. He, having providentially heard of me, wrote in order to encourage me to go on. I was at this time greatly distressed as to my itinerary way of preaching. Yet I went on with the work most actively. Thus I went on, having sweet fellowship with God daily in private prayer, and at the Sacrament, which I constantly attended. Yet still I was, not being satisfied as to my method of proceeding, shaken by Satan, and by a sense of the greatness of the work; but still I was constrained to go on, by the importunity of the generality of the people, and by the visible good tendency of my labours, and the united call and approbation of many whom I esteemed as gracious ministers, and by the *continual power* I felt with me in the work. Thus my spirit was much enlivened, especially when in the Lord's work: and I feared neither men nor devils. Such power and courage I had not by nature; therefore it appeared to me to be undoubtedly supernatural, and from God.

"'As to the subject of my discourse, it was all given me in an extraordinary manner, without the least premeditation! It was not the fruit of my memory, for naturally my memory was bad: therefore it was the effect of the immediate strong impulse, which I felt in my soul; indeed, I was not able to rest, consequently necessity was laid upon me to go and awaken souls. Thus I went on, though with fear and trembling, lest others of bad intentions should take occasion to go about after my example. I therefore prayed that I might know the will of God more perfectly, and whether His glory and the salvation of my fellow sinners were the only objects in my view. I had power, after examining the matter thus, to rely in all things on the strength of the grace that is in Christ Jesus for power to carry me through the great work; and if His honour should call me to suffer—to be imprisoned and tortured—I should find Him a faithful friend in every trial, in death, and to all eternity. Thus, though I had many comfortable assurances that my commission was from above, yet I was not thoroughly satisfied in my own mind until summoned before a person of distinction to give an account of my going about as I did, when these words forcibly came into my mind,—"Behold I have set before thee an open door, and no man can shut it." And by the effect produced on my soul I am persuaded that the passage was applied to me by the Holy Ghost.'

"In August, 1739, he writes—'*After this I was more satisfied than ever that my mission was from God, especially as I had so often applied for Holy Orders, and was rejected, for no other reason than my preaching as a layman.* I saw, both from Scripture and the practice of the Church, that the preaching of laymen was proper in times of necessity. I saw in the Acts of the Apostles the account of Apollos and others who were scattered by the death of Stephen, having no other mission than being moved by the Holy Ghost, and love to the immortal souls of their fellow creatures. I thought that a *greater* time of necessity could hardly be than the present, when the whole country lay in a lukewarm and lifeless condition. In many churches there was no sermon for months together; in some places nothing but a learned English discourse to an illiterate Welsh congregation! And where an intelligible sermon was preached it was generally so legal, so much in the spirit of the old covenant that should any give heed to it they could never be led thereby to Christ, the only way to God. Seeing these things, and feeling the love of God in my heart, I could not refrain from going about to propagate the Gospel of my dear Redeemer.'"

"Here is another instance," continued Llewellyn, as he closed his book, "of the Established Church in Wales depriving herself of the services of her noblest sons. Mr. Howell Harris was one of the most successful preachers that ever addressed a multitude, and was to the last a Churchman in most of his sympathies, although by the force of circumstances, which none deplored more than himself, he left its pale and became the founder of Calvinistic Methodism in Wales. For some years he never took *a text* for his discourses, thus avoiding every pretence of being an ordained minister; he merely spoke as *man* to *men* about sacred things. This early habit of speaking informally accounts to a great extent for the fact that to the close of life his sermons were not so orderly or carefully prepared as those of the other great preachers of his day, but, as Hugh Roberts said just now, none of them spoke with so much effect. He was raised by God for a special work, and he was specially qualified for it."

"That was a very interesting event," said Hugh Roberts, "when Howell Harris and Daniel Rowlands met each other for the first time. I remember, Mr. Pugh, that on one occasion you read to me Mr. Harris's own account of it. You have it in your pocket-book somewhere."

"Yes," replied Llewellyn, as he put his hand into his deep coat-pocket for the book that had been his companion since his student days, and to which he had committed most things about the religious history of Wales that were worth preserving. "They were both converted about the same time, and both had gained much popularity in the districts in which they lived for more than a year before they were known to each other. This is Mr. Harris's account of the first time they ever met:—'Mr. Daniel Rowlands was awakened about the same time as myself in another part of Wales, namely, in Cardiganshire, where, by reason of there being but little correspondence between that county and Breconshire, he went on gradually growing in gifts and power without knowing anything of me, or myself knowing anything of him, until by Providence, in the year 1737, I came to hear him in Devynock Church, in the upper part of our county, where, upon hearing the sermon, and seeing the gifts given him, and the amazing power and the authority with which he spoke, and the effects it had upon the people, I was made indeed thankful, and my heart burned with love to God and to him. Here began my acquaintance with him, and to all eternity it shall not end.'

"On one occasion," said Caleb, "Mr. Harris was expected to preach at a place not far from 'The Garth,' the residence of Mr. Marmaduke

Gwynne. Mr. Gwynne had heard a great deal about him as an enemy of the Church and a disturber of the country, and concluded that his purpose in coming to that district was to incite ignorant people to tumult. He therefore took the Riot Act in his pocket, intending to read it and then to disperse the people. He said, however, to his wife before he started, 'I shall hear the man for myself before I give him into custody.' He did that. Mr. Harris preached with great power. Mr. Gwynne was much impressed, compared him to the Apostles of old, and said that he had never heard anyone speak before like that. He went to him at the close of the service, shook hands with him, and invited him to 'The Garth' to supper. From that hour Mr. Gwynne was one of Mr. Harris's firmest friends and stoutest supporters against all the calumny and cruel persecution of his foes. One of his daughters, years after that, was married to Mr. Charles Wesley, and a noble wife she proved to be."

"Did you ever hear of him when at Swansea preaching on a spot called Cryg-glas?" asked Hugh Roberts. "A drunken man came who had been sent by some reprobates to shoot Mr. Harris. This he tried to do, but he missed fire. Mr. Harris in a moment commanded the man in an authoritative tone to 'point the gun in the other direction, adding that the charge would then go off immediately. He did so, with the result which Mr. Harris had foretold. No one was more surprised than the man himself. The event was in one sense trivial, but it shewed, like many others in his life and in the lives of the other great preachers of his day, how ready he was to adapt himself to any circumstance that might arise, and to turn it to the best possible use.—Ah, Daniel Rowlands and Howell Harris were wonderful men."

"Yes," said Llewellyn Pugh, "and in addition to these great men there was another—William Williams, of Pant-y-celyn—who not only preached but sang the songs of Zion in his native tongue, songs that will never be forgotten. He was born near Llandovery, and the mantle of 'the old Vicar of Llandovery' seems to have fallen upon him. There is scarcely a land where his hymns are not sung. There is that hymn,

'Guide me, O Thou great Jehovah!'

It has been translated into English and even into other tongues. So has that hymn,

'Jesus lead as with Thy power
Safe into the promised land.'

And that hymn,

> 'O'er the gloomy hills of darkness.'

What a missionary spirit breathes in that. Yet missionary societies were unknown when that was written by the servant of God at Pant-y-celyn in the very heart of Wales. He was educated for the medical profession, but his conversion, under the preaching of Howell Harris in Talgarth churchyard, gave a new turn to his life. Being a member of the Established Church he sought ordination and deacon's orders, which he received, but was refused priest's orders, an event which severed him from the Church. He then joined the Methodist body and was very useful. It is said that he travelled during the forty-three years of his ministry over ninety-five thousand miles, and that at a time when there were no railways in the country. Those many miles were chiefly travelled on horse-back along the narrow lanes and the rugged and steep roads of our country."

"Have you ever heard," asked Caleb Rhys, "of Mr. William's visit to Llangefni, in Anglesea? It was before any Methodist cause had been established in the place. On that occasion Mrs. Williams was with him. After the service they both went into a well-known inn* for the night. His persecutors fixed upon a plan for annoying him. They engaged a fiddler who went before them into the inn, and opening the parlour door stood before Mr. and Mrs. Williams. When Mr. Williams saw him, and his companions behind him jeering, he said, 'Come in, my man.' The fiddler with mock politeness asked them if they would like to have a tune. Mr Williams replied, 'By all means, we should like to hear you play.' 'What tune?' asked the fiddler. 'Any tune you like, my man,' said Mr Williams, 'and we'll sing.' 'Nancy Jig?' asked the fiddler with a smile, while those behind him were greatly enjoying the joke. 'Very well,' said Mr Williams. While the man was tuning his fiddle, Mr Williams said authoritatively to his wife, 'Now, Mary, sing

> 'Gwaed y groes sy'n codi fynu,
> 'R eiddil yn gongcwerwr mawr.'"
> [Blood of Christ it lifts the feeble,
> Makes him more than conqueror.]

---

* "Pen-y-bont" or "Bridgend."

They both had excellent voices and they sang that glorious hymn with such thrilling effect that the fiddler soon gave up fiddling, and he and his companions were glad to beat a hasty and ignominious retreat."

"I should like to have heard Mr. Williams, of Pant-y-celyn, sing that, and have seen the fiddler and his companions sneak away," said Shadrach. "I can well believe that the old fiddler couldn't get 'Nancy Jig' to fit in with that hymn and tune, especially when sung by that holy man and his good wife. The devil's songs are poor and tame things by our grand old hymns. A Christian need only sing about the blood of Christ in right earnest to send the old Tempter flying. We owe more than we think to the dear old hymns our mothers taught us when we were children."

"Yes," said Llewellyn Pugh, "You are quite right, Shadrach. And as a nation we owe as much to the psalms of Edmund Pryse, the spiritual songs of Rees Prichard, the 'old Vicar of Llandovery,' and the sweet, charming hymns of William Williams, of Pant-y-celyn, as we do to all the sermons ever preached in Wales, greatly as they were blessed. During the Great Revival, which began with Daniel Rowlands and Howell Harris, hymns occupied a more important part than ever in the religious life of the people, and in the grand services that were held they were no longer given out of books to be sung, but were learnt by heart, and given out from memory. In the intense heat of religious feeling in those days the last few lines of the hymn were repeated over and over again, just as in the case of the enraptured multitude whom John heard sing in heaven—'And again they said, Amen.' Some of the most glorious awakenings were the result, under God, of this hearty singing. Whole congregations were moved to tears by the hymns sung to our well-known plaintive or joyous tunes. People could easily remember the truths of the Gospel as given in these simple songs; even when they could not take away very much of the sermon they were sure to carry the hymn and tune with them to the fields and to their workshops all over the land.

"Those were glorious days! In them Calvinistic Methodism in Wales was born. It was the offspring of the simple and earnest Christianity of those times. Other denominations who had already done a great work in the country were greatly blessed by that revival; they were aroused out of the formality into which many of the churches and ministers had fallen. They caught the spirit of those great men, and became a mightier power for good in the land. The Established Church was the only religious community which gained nothing from that memorable movement. She seems to have been doomed to blindness in deliberately and repeatedly casting from her bosom loyal children who sought her loving shelter, but who, whether nursed by her or not, were destined to be giants and the rulers of their race. They were rejected by the Church, and thus the Church was rejected by the people."

"That's it, that's it," shouted Samson, who not only rejoiced in anything that might be said disparagingly of the Established Church, but who also, since he had re-united himself with the Independent Church of 'Peniel'—after his varied wanderings—felt a brotherly interest in Llewellyn as a member of the same church. Hence the vehemence with which he endorsed Llewellyn's remarks on this occasion.

Jenkin was amused at Samson, but said nothing.

All the others felt that no exclamation or words of theirs could add force to the indictment which Llewellyn Pugh had brought against the Established Church in Wales; and it being already late, they felt instinctively that the subject had better be left where he had left it. Thus they separated, each for his home, impressed with the solemnity of a great fact, to which the English people and the authorities of the Church in Wales are only just beginning to awake.

CHAPTER XII

𝔐𝔞𝔯𝔶 𝔍𝔬𝔫𝔢𝔰 𝔞𝔫𝔡 𝔥𝔢𝔯 𝔅𝔦𝔟𝔩𝔢

"BEIBL i bawb o bobl y byd'* ('A Bible to all the people of earth') is a grand saying," said old Hugh Roberts to the company who had met at the smithy on New Year's Eve. "I was very much struck by it on Christmas Day when so many schools met at Peniel, and when, by-the-by, John's Class came out right well. There were many hundreds of children there, and what was the most pleasing part of all was that every child who could read had a Bible of his own. I couldn't help thinking of the story of little Mary Jones who walked more than twenty five miles to Bala in the year in which I was born in order to buy a Bible, and then only got it through the kindness of the good Thomas Charles, who, although every copy was sold, could not refuse her, but gave her one he had promised to keep for a friend. I remember well hearing my mother tell me about it when I was quite a little boy, and how I wished I could see the noble-hearted girl who walked that journey on such an errand—a wish that was never gratified, though I was almost sixty-eight years old when she died. I've never been fifty miles from home in all my life, and I don't suppose

---

* This is one of the many striking alliterative sayings of the Welsh language.

Mary Jones ever was, so that there was but little chance of my ever seeing" her on this earth. You, Caleb saw her many times."

"Yes" said Caleb "During my travels I've exchanged many a piece of flannel and had many a chat with Mary Jones. She was a weaver like myself, and I felt all the more interest in her for that."

"I've heard you tell a few things about her," said Shadrach "and I make bold to say that nothing would interest us here to-night more than to hear you tell the story of Mary Jones's journey to Bala as she told it to you herself."

"Hear, hear," exclaimed Hugh Roberts, John Vaughan, Llewellyn Pugh, David Lewis, and Jenkin, simultaneously. Samson Lloyd and Swash were absent.

"Now then, Caleb," added Shadrach.

"Nothing will please me more than to tell the story, which may be partly new to you," replied Caleb, "although a very interesting little account of her life has lately appeared.* She was the daughter of a poor weaver living in a humble dwelling called Ty'nyddol, in a small village† at the foot of Cader Idris. She was born in 1784, and early in life began to learn her father's trade. When very young she was taken regularly to religious services by her mother, who, as well as her husband, was a devoted member of a little Calvinistic Methodist Church. Just at that time Mr. Charles, of Bala, instituted one of his Circulating Schools‡ in the village of Abergynolwyn, about two miles

---

* "Mary Jones, Y Gymraes fechan heb yr un Beibl," gan Robert Oliver Rees, Dolgellau.

† Llanfihangel-y-Pennant.

‡ The Welsh Circulating Schools were first formed by the Rev. Griffith Jones, of Llanddowror, already referred to in pp.182, 191. The plan on which Mr. Jones proceeded is thus explained in "Johnnes's Causes of Dissent in Wales:"—"He first engaged a body of schoolmasters, and then distributed them in different directions over the Country. The duty of these men was to teach the people to read the Scriptures in the Welsh language, to catechise them, to instruct them in psalmody, and to promote their religious advancement by every means in their power. They were sent, in the first instance, to the nearest town or village where their assistance had been requested; and then, having taught all who were desirous of instruction, they were to pass on to the next district where a similar feeling had been manifested. In the course of time they were to revisit the localities whence they had at first started, and resume the work of education anew on the

distant from Mary's home. A young man named John Ellis was appointed schoolmaster. He, like all those employed by Mr. Charles to teach the young, was a very devout and earnest man, and soon began a Sunday school in connection with the day-school. Mary was one of his first scholars, and was soon distinguished by her readiness to learn and repeat large portions of the Word of God. As yet, although there had been many editions of the Welsh Bible published, it was an exception to see a copy in a poor man's house in Wales. There was no Bible in Ty'nyddol. There was, however, a farm-house about two miles away where there was a Bible, which Mary had permission to read as often as she wished. Frequently she might be seen during summer and winter for six years wending her way to that house to read the Bible, and to commit portions of it to memory for the school on Sunday. Meanwhile she carefully set aside all her pence, determined, if possible, to buy a Bible which she could call her own. After years of saving she succeeded in making up the sum necessary to buy a copy of the Welsh Bible. It was with a proud heart that on one day she went to a Methodist preacher* in the neighbourhood to inquire of him where she might get one. He replied that Bala was the nearest place in which a copy might be got, and that probably she could not obtain one even there, as it was then more than a year since Mr. Charles had received the parcel of Welsh Bibles from London, and there was no likelihood of his having another parcel soon. Not in the least daunted she started shortly for Bala. It was a bright morning in the spring of the year 1800, when Mary began her journey of over *twenty-five miles* in her sixteenth year. She walked all the way foot-bare, and carried in a wallet lent for the occasion her boots which she had taken in order to put on her feet just before entering Bala. I've often heard Mary tell the story of that journey. She told me that it was one of the most beautiful

---

youth who had sprung up during their absence; and thus making a continual circuit of the whole country, to present to every generation as it arose the means of knowledge and the incentives to virtuous principle." These schools, once so prosperous, gradually declined after the death of Mr. Jones, and when his friend, Madam Bevan, died in 1779 they ceased to exist. The schools established later by Dr. Williams, of Oswestry, were converted into Circulating Schools by Dr. George Lewis, Llanuwchlyn. About the year 1788 Mr. Charles established schools on the same principle. These have proved to be an inestimable boon to Wales.

* Mr. William Hugh, Llechwedd.

mornings she ever knew. She was up early and saw the day dawn; she said it opened like a rosebud and seemed to fill the air with sweetness. Everything was bursting into bloom. The wild flowers blossomed in the hedge-rows by the wayside, and the pale green blade of corn peeped out of the soil; the birds sang sweetly, and the voices of merry herdsmen and milkmaids rang among the hills; the lambs gambolled on every hill-side, and the speckled trout played merrily in every stream. All Nature that morning seemed to be in the same mood as Mary's heart, and to say to her, 'Be of good cheer, Mary. Go on thy journey. Thou wilt be rewarded yet. Everything is full of promise to-day. It is spring with us, and it is springtime with thee, too. Who shall despise the day of small things?' Mary returned the smile of sympathy, and marched on step by step, sometimes well-nigh lost in the very heart of the wild mountains, at other times climbing the steep slopes, now passing through shadowy glades, now walking on sunny heights, but everywhere she heard the same cheering voices urging her on her way. Ah, I know the district well, and have carried many a heavy bundle that way, but I've never passed along that road without thinking of Mary Jones, and I've always felt stronger to carry my burden for that recollection.

"Well, she arrived at Bala late in the evening. She inquired for Mr. David Edwards, an old Methodist preacher, who was held in high esteem in the district, and to whom Mary's friend—the Methodist preacher at Llechwedd—had directed her. It was too late to see Mr. Charles that night, therefore the good man gave her shelter under his roof; but before dawn on the following morning Mary and her old friend were on their way to Mr. Charles's house. Mr. Charles was always up very early, as David Edwards well knew; and since Mary had to return home that day no time was lost. 'We shall be sure to see a light in his study,' said old Mr. Edwards to Mary. 'Mr. Charles is a wonderful man; he is in his study for hours before most people are awake. He'll let you have a Bible, too, if he can, for he's the kindest man I've ever known, especially to young people; the only fear I have is that he has sold every copy, but we'll try, my child, we'll try.'

"They soon reached the house. There *was* a light in the study, as old Mr. Edwards had said. He knocked at the door, and I've often heard Mary Jones tell her feelings just then, how her heart beat in anticipation of seeing the wonderful Mr. Charles about whom her parents and her schoolmaster at home had told her so much. She was glad he was *kind* as well as great. Most great men, she thought, were not so, at least she was always afraid to speak to them, but Mr. Charles was *kind;* perhaps he would shake hands with her, and he would be sure to sell her a Bible if he had, one—Mr. Edwards had told her so, and he knew him well. These thoughts were rushing through her mind, when lo! Mr. Charles himself opened the door, greeted his old friend and young companion with a smile, and invited them into his study. Mr. Edwards told him their business, and explained why they had called so early. Mr. Charles questioned Mary very kindly, and was greatly moved by her simple story. At length he said, 'I am heartily sorry that the little maid has come all the way from her home to obtain a Bible, and that I have no copy to give her. All the Bibles I received from London have been sold months since, excepting one or two ordered long ago, which I have promised to keep for friends. I do not know what I shall do to obtain Welsh Bibles again.'

"Those words, sadly uttered by the great man, were more than the little maid could bear. She could walk once or twice a week for six years, winter and Summer, a distance of two miles each way to read her Bible, could save her halfpence for that long period, and at the close of all walk to Bala and back, a distance of over fifty miles, to buy a Bible, and not give up or falter in her purpose, but now, when she was within reach of the Great Prize, to have it snatched by a dark Providence out of her grasp was more than she could endure. She wept bitterly. The plan of years seemed to be rudely shattered. The disappointment was all the more trying because of the long time in which she had cherished the fond hope, and given it time to take root in her soul. Those tears! nothing could withstand them. Mr. Charles was moved to greater sympathy than ever. He was overcome by the tears of the little maid just as One greater than he, in days of old, was vanquished by the faith of woman. 'My little maid,' said he, 'I see that I am bound to let you have a copy, though that will be at the sacrifice of my word to another friend. I must break my promise and give you the Bible. I cannot say No.'"

"Break his promise! Of course he did," said Jenkin. "If he hadn't I should have doubted his Christianity."

"That's rather strong, my boy," said Shadrach. "A promise is a sacred thing."

"Yes, father," replied Jenkin, "and men should be cautious what promises they make, but there are some promises which the sooner they are broken the better. If Herod, about whom John Vaughan was talking the other day in class, had broken his promise he would have been a better and wiser man than he was. If he had dared to say before the big folks who had come to spend his birthday with him, 'Gentlemen, I must break my word; I never bargained for this when I made the promise you heard me make. John the Baptist's head is worth a great deal more than my word; here goes my word, and you may think what you like of me, but I *must* save John's life'—if he had said that—he would have done a noble thing; but he was incapable of that; he was too great a coward. 'He was sorry, nevertheless, for the *oath's sake, and them which sat with him at meal he commanded it to be given her.'* So he gave John the Baptist's head for the sake of appearance, in order that the big folks may say, 'Herod is a rare man; he beheaded a prophet the other day rather than break his word.' Poor fool; how he has been despised ever since! Yes, and if even Mr. Charles had sent that little girl away for the sake of his word he would have been despised for his conceit. But he was too great a man, and too much like his Master to do that."

"You've come down on your feet at last, my boy, I think," said old Hugh Roberts, tenderly, "though I wasn't at all sure of it when you started. Go on with the story, Caleb; there are but few things which have ever moved me like that."

"Well," said Caleb, "Mr. Charles then handed the Bible to Mary and told her to read much of it, and to treasure its truths in her memory and in her heart. He was moved to tears, and, stepping aside, he said to his old friend, Mr. Edwards, 'Is not this enough to melt the hardest heart? A poor and intelligent young maid having to walk fifty miles for a Bible, and then with the probability of being disappointed. The Society for the Propagation of Christian Knowledge, which has been accustomed to print Welsh Bibles and Testaments since the beginning of the last century, has decided not to print another copy for the schools of Wales, but this little maid has so moved me that I cannot rest until some other means are found by which the great need of our country may be supplied.' Mary placed her Bible carefully in her wallet, and bade 'good-bye' to the great man whom she had overcome with her simple story and her tears. Mary loved to talk about her return journey; how often she took the book out of her wallet to read it, and then placed it back again with the feeling that she was far richer now than when she passed that way the day before. She no longer needed the songs of birds to cheer her; she had a Bible—all her own—in that wallet, and what joy could compare with that!

Her visit to Mr. Charles left a lasting The impression upon both. They never forgot each other. Whenever Mr. Charles visited Llanfihangel or the neighbourhood to catechize the schools or on a preaching tour, there was no face more welcome to him than Mary's, and there was no one so likely to be present as she was. Mary Jones was never so delighted as when she could talk about the great Thomas Charles, and he was never so moved as when he mentioned her name. Often after this did he refer to that touching incident and repeat her thrilling story, in order to convince his English friends of the great need and the intense craving of the Welsh nation for the Word of Life. In December, 1802, Mr. Charles preached in the Spitalfields, London. He availed himself of the opportunity thus offered of attending the Committee of the Religious Tract Society, and of laying before them the pressing claims of his country. He dwelt largely upon the fact that there were no Bibles for the people, although through the recent revivals there was a great craving for them throughout the land. Among the most striking proofs he gave of this was the story of Mary Jones's life, and of her visit two years before to Bala. The simple yet telling story of the Welsh maid as given by Mr. Charles awakened sympathy in every breast. All present were deeply affected, some to tears, and were on the point of granting Mr. Charles's request, *'that a Bible Society should be instituted for Wales,'* when one of their number* exclaimed with much feeling, 'Mr. Charles, if a Bible Society for Wales, why not for the whole country, and why not for the whole world?' 'Why not?' replied Mr. Charles. *This was the origin of the Bible Society.* The visit of the little maid to Bala touched a secret spring, which in due time set the vast machinery of the Bible Society in motion. All Nature seemed to say to Mary on her way to Bala, 'Who shall despise the day of small things?' Who indeed *could* after this? Who would have thought that little Mary Jones's journey on that bright spring morning, when she walked barefooted to Bala, would have supplied the important link which until then had been wanting in the chain of events before the great Bible Society could spring into being?"

"What became of Mary Jones in after life?" asked David Lewis.

"In due time," replied Caleb, "she was married to Thomas Lewis,

---

* The Rev. Joseph Hughes.

a weaver, who lived at Bryncrug, a neighbouring village. In her new home she maintained her love for her Bible, read it much, and was acknowledged by all in the village to be quite an authority in Scriptural subjects. Mary was very fond of bees, and during the many years she lived at Bryncrug was very successful in the management of them. She became noted for the large number of bee-hives she kept, and the superior quality of her honey and bees-wax. She was on the best terms with the little creatures of her charge. I've often seen her go to the garden to them. She no sooner approached the hives than the bees came out in battalions to give her hearty welcome. They would play around her head, and alight in scores upon her face and arms, and they were never known to sting her. Sometimes she would close her hand upon them and press them gently, and they would run in and out between her fingers, as if her hand were a bee-hive. When once I asked how it was, she smiled and said, 'They seem to know that a part of their earnings is spent in making known their great Creator's name in the world.' And it really *did* seem like it. Ever after that I used to call them 'Mary Jones's Missionary Bees.'"

"I understand that she felt a special interest in the Bible Society till the end of life," said Hugh Roberts.

"Yes, Hugh," replied Caleb. "In 1854 there was a collection made in the Methodist chapel towards the *China Million Testament Fund*. One half-sovereign was found in the plate. The congregation consisted of poor people; and it was feared that some one had made a mistake, but on inquiry it was found that Mary, 'the poor widow,' had given it. It was a part of the proceeds of the honey. Poor as she was she always divided the money she got from the sale of the bees-wax between the Bible and the Foreign Missionary Societies, and nothing gave her more joy than to be able to give a large sum as the result of a successful season with the bees.

"Mary lived to an old age, and was eighty years old when she died on the twenty-eighth of December, 1864. The Bible she bought at Bala was by her bedside on a little table when she passed away. That book, which had been the companion of her youth and old age, was her comforter in death. She no longer required to read it; she knew all its promises and consolations by heart. The statutes of the Lord were her song in the dark valley. She no longer needed the old Bible. It had rendered all the service it could to her, but still she cherished it as the most sacred treasure she possessed on earth, and with her dying breath bequeathed it as the mark of her high esteem to Mr. Robert Griffiths, the Methodist minister at Bryncrug; he bequeathed it to Mr. R. Oliver Rees, Dolgellau, who placed it in the library of the Calvinistic Methodist College at Bala. Very recently it has been handed over to the British and Foreign Bible Society, with the formation of which that Bible has so sacred a connection. The Book consists of the Old and New Testaments, the Apocrypha, John Canne's Marginal Notes, the Common Prayer, Edmund Pryse's metrical version of the Psalms, and various Church tables. It also contains, written in Mary's own handwriting on the blank page at the close of the Apocrypha these words:—

Mary Jones was
Born 16th December 1784

I Bought this in the 16 year
of my age I am daughter
of Jacob Jones and Mary Jones
His wife the Lord may
give me grace Amen

Mary Jones His the True
Onour of this Bible
Bought In the year
1800 Aged 16

Not long since I passed on my journey through Bryncrug, but it seemed then like another village. Old Mary Jones's house had no longer any interest for me, *she* was not there. I went to the graveyard where her body rests, and stood by her grave. It is surrounded by a handsome iron railing, and at its head is a large stone, upon which an open Bible is engraved, and arching it like a 'Bow of the Covenant' are the words, 'GWYWA Y GWELLTYN, SYRTH Y BLODEUYN, OND GAIR EIN DUW NI A SAIF BYTH.'— 'The grass withereth, the flower fadeth but the Word of our God shall stand for ever.' Then come these words, written in Welsh and English:—

MARY

GWEDDW THOMAS LEWIS,
GWEHYDD, BRYNCRUG,
BU FARW RHAG. 28, 1864,
YN 82 OED.
CYFODWYD Y FEDDFAEN HON
TRWY DANYSGRIFIADAU
Y METHODISTIAID CALFINAIDD
YN Y DOSBARTH A CHYFEILLION
ERAILL, YN DYSTIOLAETH
O BARCH I'W CHOFFADWRIAETH
FEL Y GYMRAES FECHAN

MARY JONES,

A GERDDODD O ABERGYNOLWYN
I'R BALA, YN Y FLWYDDYN 1800,
PAN YN 16 OED, I GEISIO BEIBL
CAN Y PARCH THOS.CHARLES
B.A. YR HYN A FU YN ACHLYSUR
I SEFYDLIAD Y FEIBL
CYMDEITHAS
FRYTANAIDD A THRAMOR.

MARY

WIDOW OF THOMAS LEWIS,
WEAVER, BRYNCRUG,
WHO DIED DEC.28, 1864,
AGED 82.
THIS TOMBSTONE WAS ERECTED
BY CONTRIBUTIONS
OF THE CALVINISTIC
METHODISTS IN THE
DISTRICT AND OTHER
FRIENDS, IN RESPECT TO HER
MEMORY AS THE WELSH GIRL

MARY JONES,

WHO WALKED FROM ABERGYNOL
-WYN TO BALA IN THE YEAR 1800
WHEN 16 YEARS OF AGE,
TO PROCURE A BIBLE OF THE
REV. THOS. CHARLES, B.A., A
CIRCUMSTANCE WHICH LED
TO THE ESTABLISHMENT OF THE
BRITISH AND FOREIGN
BIBLE SOCIETY.

"There she rests, but her name is not forgotten, for it is written not only on the stone that is placed over her grave, but also upon the hearts of thousands who love to tell their children of little Mary Jones's journey to Bala over eighty years ago, and of her interesting and devout life at the villages of Abergynolwyn and Bryncrug for fifty-five years after that; and that simple story never loses its charm. Children crowd eagerly to hear it, though it be for the hundredth time, for it ranks with the story of the little Israelitish maid in the house of Naaman the Syrian in ancient days, and is in no respect inferior to it for tenderness and beauty, while it gains interest from the fact that the event to which it refers occurred in much later days, and in this old country, which is so dear and sacred to all its children. I don't think I have any more to say. I've told you all I can remember."

"Thank you, Caleb," said Hugh Roberts. "That's the kind of story to tell our children; one that will do them good all through life if they will only remember it; not like the stories which were told us when children about giants ghosts, goblins, and all kinds of horrible things which used to make us mistake every tree we passed at dusk for a bogie, and run away for our lives from our very shadows in broad daylight.—Well, I must go, there is a storm gathering, and we shall have a heavy fall of snow I think before the morning. I must wish you all a 'Happy New Year' if you live to see it. As for me I have almost seen the last of new years, and I don't care how soon it's all over. My old friends are almost all gone, and my turn can't be far distant now."

"Now, Hugh," said Shadrach, "we've heard enough of that; haven't I told you that we want you here, and that God isn't going to take you away just yet for our sakes? There's no knowing what would become of us if you were to go, Hugh."

"That's all very well," said Hugh, "but almost all my old companions—and among them your father, Shadrach—are gone, and though I enjoy coming to the smithy and having a chat with you and others, my boy, yet I sometimes long to see those old friends who have gone before; there are so many treasures laid up in heaven that my heart goes up after them. I often think that I'm not ripe yet for glory, or the good Lord would not keep me here so long after my companions if I had been fit for His home. We must be *'made meet* for the inheritance of the saints in light' before we can enter upon it. That's what the gracious Father is doing with me, I trust, making me 'meet'— ripe—for Heaven. It's a long process, but then, He has had such a sour, crabbed nature to work upon in me that there's no wonder He's longer in ripening me than most others. The great Husbandman will not gather me in with the ripe fruit until I, too, am ripe, and it seems to me sometimes as if that will never come, it's so long to wait."

"That's the common impression of old Christians," said Llewellyn Pugh. "I heard Mr. Kilsby Jones once repeat what the Rev. John Evans, of Llwynffortun said in a sermon delivered in a village, which he said was situated in one of the most romantic glens in Breconshire. Mr. Jones described him as a man of princely presence; his figure tall and commanding, his features regular and well-defined, his eyes large and lustrous, and his voice unusually rich in the melodies of the minor key. His temperament was intensely melancholy, and his face and voice were in perfect harmony with his habitual pensiveness. Mr. Jones said that on this occasion he was labouring under an unusual depression of spirits, which tinged his allusions with more than sombre hues. Just at that time every Christian denomination had lost one of its mighty men. 'I understand,' said the preacher, 'that the Established Church has lost one of its ablest preachers and most devoted pastors—*he has gone home.*

Our Baptist brethren have been called to mourn the loss of one of their distinguished men—*he has gone home.* And I have just learned that the Independents have lost, in the person of the late Mr. Breese, of Carmarthen, a man of eagle glance, glowing enthusiasm, and surpassing eloquence—*he has also gone home.* And it pains me to inform you that our people have lost in Cardiganshire a young man of great promise, 'mighty in the Scriptures,' earnest, devout, and popular; 'His sun is set while it is yet day.' He died in the prime of manhood—*he has gone home.* All these beloved brethren and fellow-labourers died comparatively young, and had entered the spiritual battle-field long after I had put on my armour, but they have already changed the war-song for the hymns of triumph. Beloved souls! I am a long while growing meet for heaven. I sometimes think I am like 'winter apples'—a long time getting ripe. From the surrounding trees all the fruit has long been gathered, while I still remain *un*ripe and *un*gathered; but I do devoutly hope that though the days are shortening, and there is less strength in the heat of the sun, there is the less need for that heat, and that I, even I, shall be gathered in ere the sere and yellow leaf has fallen, and the earth has been wrapped in her winding sheet.'"

"Ah, there's more truth in that than some are apt to think," said Hugh, "but there, I have no doubt I shall be ripened at last, and *that's enough.*"

"Yes, *quite enough,* Hugh," said Shadrach, "and remember that the apples that take longest to ripen are often not a bad sort after all."

"You remind me, Hugh, of old William Rees, Landore, a well-known character among the Methodists in that district," said Caleb. "On one occasion Mr. R. Roberts, Llangeitho, was preaching at Landore on the resurrection of the dead. During the sermon Mr. Roberts said that we could now only see through the medium of the body, which, like a window, darkened as well as revealed; he added that soon the window would be broken, and that then the spirit would see clearly—no longer through a glass darkly, but face to face. Suddenly old William Rees, who was now fairly carried away by the *hwyl,* shouted, 'O, my dear boy, break it *now.*'It seemed for the time as if the shout of old William Rees had broken it, and as if the land of light had been fully revealed."

"Dear old soul," said Shadrach, "he wanted to be in heaven too soon, very much like Peter on the Mount, but there, the good Lord isn't hard on those who make that mistake. Tell us more about him, Caleb, I've heard you mention his name before."

"Mr. Henry Rees, of Liverpool, was once preaching at Morriston," replied Caleb. "Old William Rees had walked from Landore to hear him. The text was 'Our friend Lazarus sleepeth; but I go that I may awake him out of sleep.' Before Mr. Rees had closed his sermon, old William Rees had broken out into the *hwyl* and responded vigorously, until at last his voice drowned the preacher's voice, and the congregation for some time were captivated by old William Rees's *hwyl*—not least 'the man of God' in the pulpit, who looked at him with intense delight. At the close of the service Mr. Rees said, 'That's more than I have seen for the last twenty years.' In the chapel-house he had a long chat with the old pilgrim. At last William Rees got up, and wishing the preacher good-bye, he said, 'Farewell, Sir, I shall never see you again,' 'Oh, yes, William Rees,' said the Rev. T. Levi, 'you shall see each other again in heaven.' 'I don't know about that,' replied William, because *he will be so much higher than I there.'* On another occasion he was rebuked by William Hopkin, one of the elders, for shouting so loud as to unnerve a young local preacher, so that he couldn't proceed with his sermon. 'My dear friend,' said William Rees, 'I couldn't help it; everybody gets distracted when heaven appears in sight.'

"On another occasion," continued Caleb, "Dr. J. H. Jones Was preaching, and in his sermon said that Jesus Christ and the Christian lived next door to each other, that there was only an earthen wall between them, and if that were taken down they would be in the same room. This was more than William Rees could bear. He shouted—and his whole soul seemed to go out in that shout—'Down with it *now,* then.' I was at that service myself, and I shall never forget it. The whole congregation were in tears, and William Rees was in raptures singing old Simeon's song, 'Now lettest thou thy servant depart in peace, for mine eyes have seen thy salvation.' You often remind me of old William Rees, Hugh, you get quite impatient of earth when you think about heaven."

A smile passed over the old man's face; he and his friend Caleb bade the company 'Good-night' and 'A Happy New Year,' and arm-in-arm left the smithy.

Just as they were leaving the snow began to fall thickly, the strong breeze, already blowing, speedily freshened into a gale, and everything seemed to promise a dark, cold, and boisterous night. The old year was growing angry as it drew near its close and seemed to threaten, in the extremity of helpless peevishness, to die in a rage.

The company separated earlier than usual for their homes that night, and Shadrach and his son were left to finish the work they had on hand, and thus add another year's toil to the many that had been completed in the old smithy. It was half-past nine before Shadrach and Jenkin put aside their aprons, closed the door of the workshop and went into the house to partake of their evening meal.

CHAPTER XIII

𝕳ugh 𝕽oberts in "𝕿he 𝕮loud"

ILD and 'weird was the night in which the old year died and the new year was born. The whole creation seemed to groan and travail together in pain in the double conflict of birth and death. When at last the old year expired it was with a desolate sigh that rent the air as if the soul of things was passing away with it; and when the new year was born in the dead of night it was received into the cold snowy swaddling clothes which the wild hurricane and blinding storm had snatched from the storehouses of the clouds, and hurled recklessly on the desolate earth.

It was a night of desolation everywhere, but at Pentre-mawr it was doubly so. In that old homestead there was a night within a night. Scarcely had Hugh Roberts returned home from the smithy early in the evening than his daughter, his sole stay for many years in the home, who throughout life had suffered from a serious affection of the heart, and who had been complaining of a slight indisposition during the day, sank suddenly into her chair, became unconscious, and showed unmistakable signs that the feeble heart had at length collapsed in the exercise of its functions, and that soon it would be at rest for ever.

A messenger was at once sent on horse-back for the doctor, who lived two miles away, but when he arrived he shook his head and said there was no hope, that the life was fast ebbing, and that the heart was far too weak ever to recover its action. The storm grew more and more furious without, but to Hugh it was only the deep undertone of the more awful storm that raged within. He remembered the time when, years ago, his wife had passed away in that room, and when his daughter, then a little girl, softened her pillow, and moistened her lips in the dying hour. That service he insisted upon performing himself now, as there was no hand so tender, or heart so loving as his. He forgot all about the dying year as he stooped pensively over his dying daughter, but to those who stood round it was a question which would expire first. Moment after moment passed away, and each threatened to be the last. At length as the clock struck the death-knell of the old year the dying form upon the bed gave one deep sigh and all was over. It was an awful moment. There was a silence in the room like the pause of death. It lasted for a few seconds, but to those who were present it seemed like an age. Meanwhile, Hugh's countenance changed the anxious, cloudy look melted away into a serene, placid expression as he lifted up his eyes to heaven, and in clear tones exclaimed, "Shall I receive good at the hand of God, and shall I not receive evil?" "I was dumb, I opened not my mouth, because thou didst it." While he spoke a soft, mellow light passed over his countenance as if God had smiled upon it, and thus illumined the face of his aged servant with the light of His own countenance. There it shone in the chamber of death like the face of an angel.

Early on the following morning the sad news spread rapidly through the neighbourhood. Shadrach was one of the first to hear it. Immediately he went to John Vaughan, and both hurried to Pentremawr to see "dear old Hugh."

When they arrived Hugh was seated in his arm-chair beneath the large open chimney in the kitchen, looking steadfastly into the fire that blazed upon the hearth.

"Taken into 'the cloud' again, my dear old friend," said Shadrach, as the tears flowed down.

"Yes, my boy," replied Hugh tenderly, "but the good Lord is with me *in the cloud.* I was just now thinking about the words, 'I will appear in the cloud upon the mercy-seat.' I never saw so much beauty in those words as I do now. It's well worth going right into the cloud to see *Him and His mercy seat.* This is the second time I have been in it, and both times I have found *Him* there."

"Quite true, Hugh," said John Vaughan, "and as I heard Mr. Roberts, Wrexham, once say, 'Every cloud that rises in this world leads toward that mercy-seat.'"

"Yes," replied Hugh, "even the cloud that rises from the dark valley of the shadow of death leads to the mercy-seat and rests over it as a symbol of God's presence. Every cloud I have ever seen has had God in it. He comes to us every day 'with clouds,' and it is that fact that makes them bearable to us. That's my comfort now. I heard that sermon to which you referred, John, and I remember, too, that the preacher spoke about the clouds which gathered once above the head of the great Saviour, clouds which had no mercy-seat connected with them. God did not appear in that terrible cloud above Calvary; the Saviour of man cried beneath its chilling shadow, 'My God, my God, why hast thou forsaken me;' yet it was there, that a mercy-seat was associated once for ever with the darkest clouds of our mortal life."

Just as Hugh was uttering these words his old friend Caleb came in, shook hands with him, and looking affectionately into his face said, "No chastisement for the present seemeth joyous, but grievous, nevertheless afterward it yieldeth the fruit of righteousness unto them that are exercised thereby.' That's a precious truth for you now, Hugh."

"Yes," replied Hugh, "and it is in times of chastisement that we find such truths precious to us; they are like the stars which come out *in the night* and cheer us *in the darkness.*"

"I heard Mr. Herber Evans, Carnarvon," said Caleb, "a short time ago refer to those words of the Apostle in his own chapel, on the occasion of his occupying his pulpit after a very long and trying illness. He said, 'Let us always remember that as there are justice and goodness in God's character so He has created us not to make us happy merely, but also to develop in us nobility of being. That is a key which has of late opened a very difficult lock in my earthly life. I am not here for the sake of happiness—but for the sake of developing a *good character.* More than that, it is by forming in us a noble nature that God gives us heavenly bliss on earth. Now the formation of such a character costs us all very much. It is through much tribulation that we must not only go to heaven but also possess a heavenly character here. It is a costly thing to form in us such a nature as you and I should possess, but it is worth all the expenditure. It is worth going through every discipline, brother, in order to become a good man—so that the good Lord may rejoice in thy fellowship for ever. And it is evident that such a character cannot be formed except in the midst of difficulties, temptations, and sufferings. While we see suffering and pain on all hands we see characters ennobled by them everywhere.'

"'Come with me to a house in the town where the father is bad-tempered, and harsh in speech, and the mother a talkative woman, fond of criticising and finding fault with her neighbours. One day the fond child of those parents was taken very ill; she was confined to her room for months. There was *one* chamber in that house those months in which no loud, harsh word was heard from the father—that room softened his voice and exalted his character. In that chamber too the mother did not dare to run down her neighbours—the glance of the sick child made her leave all slander outside. Look at that father in the beginning of spring hastening through the chilly air over the fields to look for the first primroses and violets for the child who is a prisoner in the upstairs room. He knows well the field in which they grow first, and great is his fear lest someone else has been there before him; when at length he finds them he thinks of nought save the pride with which the little sick one will receive the posy; and long before he reaches the house the flowers are wet not only with dew but with the tears of that father. Listen to the tenderness of his whole nature in the words, 'Here, my dear, are the first flowers of the spring for you.' See the eyes of the sick child and of her father glisten alike with tears. After months of sickness that child has changed the character of the whole household, and ennobled the natures of her father and mother. Suffering and affliction are thus the means of changing and exalting characters about us throughout the world and during all ages.'

"Mr. Evans then went on to warn us against the mistake of looking for the fruit of our afflictions and griefs while we are in them; at such times the mind is often too agitated, as the Apostle said, 'No chastisement for the *present* seemeth joyous but grievous, nevertheless *afterward—afterward* the fruit is promised. The gardener goes out to prune the fruit trees in the autumn. His child goes after him, and says with some surprise, 'Although you have trimmed those trees, father, there's no fruit there.' No, but *afterward* cometh the fruit;—and perhaps *we* shall never see all the fruit that has been ripened by the burning sun of trial until we reach the country above. It is *thus* that those who arrive there from this old earth will be recognized—'These are they which came from the land of great tribulation.' I should not like to go there without bearing the mark of the old family. I should not like an angel to point to the redeemed, and *not* to me, and say, 'These are they which came out of great tribulation.'"

"Ah, that's it, '*Tribulation*' is the old family crest," said John Vaughan, and we mustn't lose that among the big families in heaven. We never need be ashamed of it among the angels. Why the Lord Jesus himself has worked it into His *coat-of-arms,* as the Man of Sorrows and the King of once sorrowing but now redeemed men, for *the cross* and *the crown of thorns* are the arms of our exalted Prince and Saviour. I love to read those words, 'They sung as it were a new song before the throne... and no man could learn that song but the hundred and forty and four thousand which were redeemed from the earth.' This is one of John's visions; he sees heaven from *our* point of view not from an angel's. To him, next to the great Saviour Himself, there's nothing so interesting in heaven as man. Well, I am glad that there is given us in this sacred Book, not an angel's, but an inspired *man's* view of heaven, for that interests us above everything else. Now the first thing about these words that cheers me very much is that *earth will never be ignored in heaven.* Learned men say that, as a material world, if it dropped out of existence it wouldn't be missed in the vast universe—that it is only like a leaf in the forest; but as a world in which Jesus has died and man has been redeemed its story will be the most thrilling of all in the land of light. Ah, yes, and the sweetest song that will be sung in heaven will be from the old country, and will be sung only by its old inhabitants. 'No man could learn that song but the hundred and forty and four thousand which were *redeemed from the earth.'* I like to repeat those words 'redeemed from the earth.' *From the earth*—Ah, heaven, thy harmonies would be poor indeed if earth withheld its song.

"'*Redeemed,'* too. Mark, it is redemption that will inspire the sweetest song in heaven. It will be 'the song of Moses and the Lamb.' This is the only song of earth that will outlive it. How many of its songs die in their infancy and no one sheds a tear over their grave, but the song of Moses and the Lamb—the song of the *old* and *partial* redemption at the Red Sea, and of the *new* and *complete* one on Calvary will ring out in heaven for ever. Now these words seem to show that earth is the only scene of redemption, and therefore is the only world that can produce this song. Ah, it's our *copyright*—our *copyright*— and angels, and principalities, and powers will never be allowed to infringe upon it. There's no angel in heaven that can throw so much love and tenderness into the name *Jesus* as we can. He is their *Lord,* but He is our *Saviour.* They excel in *strength,* but not in *tenderness. Redeemed man* excels in that. They have never been at the foot of the cross and there learnt how to love.

"I went the other day to hear a noted English preacher in Carmarthen, and I enjoyed the sermon very much as far as I could understand it. The hymns too were very good, but they sang one which had these lines—

> "We long to love as angels do,
> And wish like them to sing."

Now I can't understand what that writer could have been thinking about when she wrote that; the good Lord expects of us greater love than He does from the angels. "To whom little is forgiven loveth little," are His own words; but he to whom much is forgiven loves much, and we belong to the last class. ' *We long to love as angels do!'* Ah, it would be a poor thing if we didn't far outstrip them in love by-and-by. It would be a poor result for our blessed Lord, after all His suffering and shame if we didn't love Him more than the angels do. *"And wish like them to sing!"* Hugh, we shan't be satisfied with that, shall we? There'll be strings in our harp which the fingers of angels will never be able to touch, and notes in our song that they will never be able to reach—*never.*

"Redeemed from *sorrow,* too, Hugh," added John, warmly, as he looked at his bereaved old friend. "How sweet that music which is born of sorrow will be in the land of light. We know something about the sweetness of 'songs in the night' now. There would be less music and brightness in our life even now if there were less affliction and fewer dark problems. Even the clouds of sorrow look beautiful when touched up by Christian joy. There's a beauty in the blending of light and darkness, of sunshine and cloud. I heard Captain Jones say that we have far grander sunsets in this damp old country than they have in the east, where there is nothing above but cloudless skies for many weeks together. Now if you notice there's no grand description of a sunset in the Bible. If there were it wouldn't be true to fact. The eastern sky is far too clear for a gorgeous sunset. It requires the clouds of our damp climate to make the setting of the King of Day glorious. *Without a pillar of cloud by day he wouldn't have a pillar of fire at even.* It's exactly so with us; the dark clouds which have grieved us so much during our short day will appear glorious at the close, they will

be touched and made beautiful with heaven's own light, and angels
will look on in wonder.

"And then as to the *song* we shall sing—why, Hugh, you'll be able
to sing all the sweeter for this terrible trial. The brook that runs at
the bottom of your garden and murmurs—no, not murmurs, but
sings—on its way to the sea draws its music from the pebbles and
sharp stones that resist its course and cut its waters. Without those
hindrances the brook would have no music. So it is with us. Hindrances
and trials are those which give sweetness to our song even here, how
much more yonder. David said, 'I will open my dark sayings upon the
harp.' That's exactly what the world can't do. It can't set its *'dark
sayings'* to music. It has no harp for its problems, no song for its
sorrows. But *we have,* Hugh."

"Yes, bless the Lord," said Hugh, as his countenance shone with
an unearthly joy, "Yes, like the blessed Master Himself we can 'sing a
hymn' even just before entering our dark Gethsemanes."

"You are right, Hugh," responded John, "and we shall thank God
for our Gethsemanes by-and-by; an angel never entered Gethsemane
or stood by an open grave, and therefore knows nothing about the
song which is sung by those only who know the meaning of such
experiences."

"I shan't easily forget," said Caleb, "hearing Mr. Thomas Jones,*
then of Swansea, speak by the graveside of Mr. Davies, Llandilo. He
said, 'The English people have a hymn—I trust it is not to be found in
Welsh—

> "I would I were an angel,
>   And with the angels stand."

We do not want to be angels; they are excellent beings in their way,
but we want to be perfect *human* beings. We should never know our
friend were he an angel, but he is not an angel. The angels have never
buried a brother—there are no graves in the angels' land—I should
not like to be an angel, and I say this by the *graveside of a friend.'"*

"That's very beautiful and very true," replied Hugh. An angel has
never stood by the graveside of a dear friend and wept bitter tears as
the earth closed coldly over that which was mortal of him or her, and

---

* The late Rev. Thomas Jones, the well-known Congregational minister,
firstly of Morriston, then of London, afterwards of Swansea.

therefore an angel can't set those words to music, 'O death where is thy sting? O grave where is thy victory? The sting of death is sin: and the strength of sin is the law: but thanks be to God which giveth us the victory through our Lord Jesus Christ.' An angel can't do that, but *we* can, Caleb, and I can even *now.* Ah, it's quite true. An angel has never buried a friend or shed a tear by a graveside. No, an angel never has, but our blessed Lord has, and *I would rather be like Him than like an angel."*

"'He took not on him the nature of angels,' Hugh, 'but the seed of Abraham,'" exclaimed John Vaughan. "That was a very striking illustration which Mr. Thomas,* of Liverpool, used the other day at 'Peniel' chapel. He said that on the centenary of the birth of the great Robert Stephenson at Newcastle-on-Tyne a short time since, there was a very large demonstration. The town was paraded by a vast procession, who carried banners in honour of the old distinguished engineer. In the procession there was a band of peasants, who carried a little banner of very ordinary appearance, but bearing the words, *'He was one of us.'* They were inhabitants of the small village in which Robert Stephenson had been born, and had come to do him honour. They had a right to a prominent position in that day's proceedings, because he to whom so many thousands did honour was one of them. Even so, whatever praise the thrones, dominions, principalities, powers, and all the grades in glory can ascribe to Christ, and however glorious the banners they will display in that grand celebration when time shall be no more, we from earth can wave our banner with the words written upon it, *'He was one of us.'* None but redeemed men shall wave *that."*

"As Mr. Jones,† of Talsarn, once said," added Caleb, "Heaven must come to earth in order to have its mansions filled. Thus it constantly robs the earth of its best things. If one flower blooms more beautifully than another, heaven is sure to take it away."

"Yes," replied Hugh, "and who shall complain if from our little gardens, where the easterlies blow and the blight consumes, the Great Husbandman transplants our choicest flowers into His own paradise, where they will bloom with a celestial beauty? Who shall complain if He takes from our poor earthly homes the most loving presence of all, with which to enrich His home above, and thus deprives us of the

---

* The Rev. J. Thomas, Congregational minister, Liverpool.

† The late Rev. John Jones, Talsarn, a distinguished Calvinistic Methodist minister.

sweetest voice in order to add to the harmonies of the blest. I cannot complain even now, and *will not.* He has taken from me my best. It is enough if the good Lord hath need of her, and could I but realize it, it is a high honour which He confers upon me in choosing my home from which He sees fit so soon to draw the reserve for heaven."

"Ah, it's wonderful," said Caleb, "what the gracious Lord will yet be able to make of us. We are poor creatures here, but He has a glorious purpose, which He will yet fulfil in us. As Mr. Jones said in the same sermon:—'The golden vessels which adorn the tables of dukes and lords on festive occasions are made from the metal obtained in an exceptionally poor country—Peru, and from the *dust* of that country. The Great King will have upon his table in His banqueting hall, beyond the veil, golden vessels to honour. Even the angels of God cannot surpass them in brightness, yet their material is obtained from a poor world—the earth, and from the *dust* of that earth. His attention is fixed upon the old diggings still, desiring to obtain more of the same kind to adorn His table.' Then the preacher shouted as with the voice of an angel, 'O God, take us too—*us too.*' Here a loud 'Amen' that rent the air went up from the vast congregation.

"I shall never forget that sermon," continued Caleb, "especially that part of it in which he said:—'It is probable that in the world to come we shall derive happiness from the recollection of many things which occurred here. I shall never forget this old earth. I have seen things here which will be worth remembering for ever. It will be impossible to be silent about this dear old home. It was here that we saw Jesus Christ first of all;—here we were wedded to Him; this old earth is the parish church where we were united in sacred matrimony, the union which gave us a right to the great inheritance. I do not know in what condition this globe will be after the judgment day, but it will be worth remembering *then,* and in heaven for ever.'—I felt, as I listened, as if I were in heaven already.—But tell us now, Hugh, how your dear daughter passed away."

"Passed away!" exclaimed Hugh, as a sweet smile lit up his countenance, and heaven's own light was reflected in his tears. "'Passed away!'—She passed away in a sleep which we call *unconsciousness,* Caleb, but before she fell asleep she sang as I never heard her sing before—feebly, yet so sweetly. It was the 'Song of the Redeemed,' which John has been speaking about. It came like celestial music from the dark valley. I shall never forget it. It reminded me of

what I heard Mr. Phillips, of Newcastle-Emlyn, say about a little girl
he knew who was ill of consumption. During her sickness she found
much comfort in singing hymns which she had learnt when she was
well. At last the disease got such hold of her as to deprive her of her
voice, yet she wanted to sing, and was very grieved and cast down
that she had no longer a voice with which to praise her Saviour. One
day her mother heard faint whistling, as she thought, outside. She
went to see who it was, anxious to prevent any annoyance to her child,
but there was no one there; again she heard a similar sound. At length
she entered her little daughter's room, and asked her tenderly, 'Did
you hear someone whistling just now, my dear?' 'Yes, mother,' said
the child faintly, 'It was I that whistled.' ' *You,* 'asked the mother, 'and
why did you *whistle?*' 'You know,' she whispered, 'that I have failed
to sing for many days now, and I *did* want so badly to sing that hymn,

> 'Mae'r gwaed a redodd ar y groes,
>   O oes i oes i'w gofio.'
> [The blood that flowed upon the cross,
>   From age to age remembered.]

so I whistled it; I felt sure Jesus would know what 'words I meant
and I am happy now.' 'So you whistled it,' said the mother, in surprise.
'Yes, I did,' said her little daughter. 'YES,' added Mr. Phillips, 'She *did*
whistle it, till the old valley of the shadow of death became as bright
and as cheerful as the valley of Teivy on a bright morning in May.' Ah,
I thought of that when my dear one was passing through the valley,
and when drawing near the dark river, sang faintly yet so sweetly,

> 'Yn y dyfroedd mawr a'r tonau
> Nid oes neb a ddeil fy mhen,
> Ond fy anwyl briod, Iesu,
> 'Rhwn fu farw ar y pren.'
> [In the deep and billowy waters
> There is none can hold my head,
> But my dear Redeemer, Jesus,
> Who once suffered in my stead.]

    "Religion has the best of it at such times, Hugh," said John, "as
Mr. Williams,* of Newcastle-Emlyn, once said in a sermon at 'Peniel'

---

* The late Rev. J. Williams, Congregational minister, Newcastle-Emlyn.

chapel. 'Place an aged Christian and an aged infidel side by side. Who shall the infidel be? John Hobbes; I've no doubt that if there were an association of infidels here they would be willing to have him as their representative. Who shall 'we have for a Christian? David Edmunds, of Llansadwrn mountain. John Hobbes, with his great mind, goes deep down beneath the different layers of rocks, and all the formations that go to make the earth's crust. He knows something of geology. *Geology,* indeed! What does David Edmunds know about geology? His investigations extend only to the depth of his spade in the garden, to see how many potatoes he can find. John Hobbes with his great mind ascends to the region of the stars, understands something about the movements of the worlds on high, and the numberless systems that revolve at the bidding of our Father. *Astronomy* indeed! What does David Edmunds know about astronomy? Nothing but—'Mary, see if the moon is up to light us through that dark glen to the prayer-meeting to-night.' David Edmunds went once to London to the Exhibition, and lost his way in *Paddington Station* among the lamps and the grand folks, nobody understanding his language, and he not understanding theirs; while John Hobbes, in his day, knew the twelve best hotels in London, and the best rooms in those hotels. But by the time they both draw near to death's dark river, ask John Hobbes what he thinks about it, he replies, *'I am about taking a leap in the dark.'* All is dark with him now. But ask David Edmunds 'What is that old river?' 'O, it is the old river Jordan.' 'Who is that One walking on the surface of the water?' 'The Great Saviour, come to break the force of the dark current.' 'Who are those on the other side?' 'The old saints from the neighbourhood of Llansadwrn welcoming me home to know a little of the history of the good cause in the old country.'"

"That's very true," exclaimed Hugh. "Atheism may do very well for fine weather, but not for the night of sorrow and the valley of shadows, while faith brightens as the darkness gathers; and though it is hard to part, the joyous welcome on the other side makes up for all the bitterness of the separation here."

Thus the friends who had gone to Pentre-mawr to comfort the veteran in his sudden bereavement found that a greater Comforter than they could be had been there before them. They at length bade him good morning, and commending him to the care and keeping of that God whom he had trusted and served for so many years, they left the house together.

"It is more than fifteen years since last I came to see my old friend in bereavement," said Caleb Rhys. "It was when he lost his wife—one of the best women that ever trod the earth—and it's very interesting to notice how much he has ripened in experience since then. He found it hard then to reconcile Divine love with the terrible mystery of his bereavement, but you see that he's no longer troubled with any doubt or misgiving. He is now at perfect peace, because his mind is stayed on God."

"I remember his wife's funeral well," said John, "and especially Mr. Ishmael Jones's sermon in the chapel."

"Ah, that was a wonderful sermon," said Shadrach, "I've forgotten most of it, but you remember every word of it, I'll venture. Repeat some of it, John."

"Well," replied John, "he began in his peculiar way by saying:—'The text is the experience of a godly man, and the cream of religion is to be found in that. This is Paul's experience—Paul *in gaol.* He wasn't ashamed to be there for the sake of Jesus Christ, my friends. When a man has been in gaol people are likely to remind him of it ever after, but, mark you, Paul stole a march on his greatest foe, Satan, so that he mightn't have a chance to laugh at him,—"Ha, ha! Paul is in gaol." He himself says, "Paul a *prisoner* of Jesus Christ." His friends didn't know what would befall him, whether he would be offered up or released, but he was as prepared for the one as the other. In the text he is in a strait betwixt two. Paul's dilemma was not like David's. David was in a strait between two judgments, but Paul between two blessings. "What I shall choose I wot not," says he. He holds the scales in his hand. Mark, friends, what is in the scales; the best thing that earth can give on the one hand,—a life of usefulness for Christ, and the best that heaven can give on the other hand—the bliss of being with Christ for ever. For a moment the scales seemed to balance, but in our text they turn in favour of departing and being with Christ, *which is far better.*

"That's not the *usual* experience of even Christians, John," said Caleb Rhys. "I recollect hearing when quite a boy, Mr. John Jones, of Holywell,* preaching from *Job* vii. 16—'I would not live alway.' He said, 'What a striking resolution; here is a man who would not live for

---

* Rev. John Jones, a distinguished Calvinistic Methodist minister. He died August 2nd, 1830.

ever on the earth. If two books were taken through our towns and villages, the one a big book bearing the words *"To live for ever,"* and the other a small one, and upon it the words *"Not to live for ever;"* I know well in which people would put their names. The young and middle-aged would be foremost in putting their names in the big book—" *To live for ever.* "But yonder is an old and infirm woman, who has coughed herself almost to death all through the years; it's possible that we shall have her name in the little book. We ask, "Where shall we put your name; here is one book, which says *'To live for ever;'* and another that says *'Not to live forever;'* which will you say?" "Well, I don't know," she replies, "but here, put me down with my neighbours— *To live for ever.* "And to tell you the truth, dear friends, if the books were brought this moment to the pulpit, it's very likely that it is in the big book that I, too, would put my name with the rest. Yes, we all want to live for ever. But not so Paul—"I have a desire to depart and to be with Christ, which is far better." Paul had been in heaven once, and there was never any satisfying him here after that till he was allowed to go again to heaven. A boy from Wales has gone to London, remained there for years, and has got into the spirit of the business and style of London; he comes home to visit his friends in Wales, but he cannot be happy again among the old mountains of his native country. "I must go back to London," he says. "My dear boy," replies his mother, "you must stay a little longer; there are seven years since you were at home last." He stays a few days more, but at last the yearning for London becomes too strong for him to stay away any longer, much as he loves his friends in the dear old country. "I *must* go back, now, mother," he says—and goes. It was exactly so with Paul, my friends; having been once in heaven he had a desire to depart and to live there ever after, which, he said, was much better.'"

"That's very good," said John, "Ishmael Jones, too, spoke very effectively from those words of his text—"'I have a desire to depart' (Welsh Version—to be *loosed* or *untided).* He said—'Death is the *loosening* of all earthly relationships. Death has many names. There is a reference here to taking down tents. This was a very familiar figure to the Apostle, friends. He knew a great deal about tents, and how easy it was to take them down. A tent was seen last night very neatly fixed, but this morning it wasn't to be seen anywhere. It only left behind a small red spot on the soil. Death sometimes unties very suddenly, at other times gradually. Have you ever watched the doctor trying to tie the loose knots, and death silently but persistently going on untying? Death untied two knots for everyone he tied, poor man. Some of you complain sometimes that your sight fails you. My friends, haven't you thought that it is death who has cast his heavy shadow over your eyes? We hear another say, "I am losing my hair fast, and am almost bald." Hast thou not thought, friend, that it is death who has placed his cold hand upon thy head? Not a hair will grow again after the touch of that hand. Death takes the body apart piece by piece. Man, in coming into the world, brings a stock of life with him. Mark you, that stock doesn't increase here like a farmer's or a shopkeeper's stock. It becomes less every year, and every day; and in proportion as the stock of life decreases earthly treasures become less valuable. Someone here may have hundreds of pounds more in the bank to-day than twenty years ago, yet they are of less value to thee, my friend, because thou hast twenty years less of life in which to enjoy them. And death will soon put an end to every enjoyment of that nature here—it loosens us from all earthly treasures. No one takes anything with him out of the world save his *character*—"Their works do follow them."'

"He paused for a moment and then went on saying—'*Death loosens or unties every earthly bond.* When the mother weeps bitterly as she buries her babe don't be unkind to her and say she weeps too much; that babe will never be her's again. Even Mary is not the mother of the Saviour in heaven. It was only here that she was His mother. She is not a nearer relative to Him there than any other saint.'"

"Yes, I remember that now very well," said Shadrach earnestly, "and still better what followed, when he said:—'*Death unties the bond between soul and body.* This is a wonderful union, and as far as we know unlike anything in God's universe, my people. It is a very near and dear one—the house and the tenant. Those are very striking words in the Book of Job, "His flesh upon him shall have pain, and his soul within him shall mourn." The old partners cannot separate without signs of intense grief—the soul failing to leave the old house lived in so long, and the house on its part keeping its hold of such a faithful and dear tenant. Yet, notwithstanding the hard struggle to maintain the union, death at length gains the day—"Thou prevailest for ever against him: thou changest his countenance and sendest him away."'"

"That was very good. But the best part of all the sermon, I think," said John, "was that in which he said:—'*The Christian when loosed by death from all these things goes to be with Christ in heaven.* It is a glorious thing to be with Christ. It is not something common-place, my friends. I remember reading about a godly mother—the wife of a doctor—who called her children to her bedside when she was dying in order that they might see their mother going to heaven! Wasn't it a grand sight! It was worth more than all the world to those children to see their mother go to heaven! They felt that the greatest thing of all was to go there. There is nothing common about heaven—heaven with all our debt fully paid and our sins forgiven without a slur being cast upon the everlasting Throne! Heaven prepared for the saints, my people. God took Abel to heaven after the fall by the new and living way as a specimen of the work of Divine grace upon poor fallen humanity. The Holy Ghost insisted upon giving him a name—*righteous* Abel; he was so righteous through grace that the God of all grace was not ashamed to acknowledge him before the thrones, dominions, principalities, and powers in glory.

"'I dare tell you, my friends, that to go to Christ in heaven is *"much better"* than the highest enjoyment of religion on earth. I would not speak anything disparagingly of thy religion, Christian, but thou hast not had the best yet. Drops as compared with the vast ocean are all that thou hast yet had. Thou hast had glorious things on earth, thou hast had the forgiveness of all thy sins—justification—peace of conscience—and a foretaste of the everlasting inheritance. But much as thou hast had, by far the best is yet in store. Five minutes of the enjoyment of heaven will be more than all—*all*—thou hast had here. Heaven, too, improves constantly. When redeemed man first went in the door was but slightly opened. I've thought that Abel must have felt somewhat shy at first in heaven without one companion from earth; that the angels wondered at him, gathered round him and shook their fiery pinions above his head, asking in wonder, "Who is this? Whence has he come? We never saw one here like this one before." But as they were thus questioning in astonishment, me thought I heard a voice from the great white throne, answering, "He is the *master thought* of the great *King—the first fruit of redeemed humanity.*"'"

"Ah, that was glorious," exclaimed Shadrach, enthusiastically, "I remember it now."

"Yes, it *was* glorious, Shadrach," replied John. "The preacher continued:—'A large multitude of saints went to heaven under the Old Dispensation—"Many sons to glory"—but they went *on trust;* the debt had not yet been paid, and the fountain was not yet opened. But on Calvary the books were settled; the fountain was opened; and when Jesus ascended the gates were opened wide. I hear the heavenly hosts exclaim—"Lift up your heads O ye gates and be ye lift up ye everlasting doors, and the King of Glory shall come in!" Heaven still continues to improve. Eternal life has not commenced yet, and will not until all the saints, as a whole, reach home. There are chambers there that will not be opened until the Judgment Day has passed. There are viands upon the table that Abraham has not tasted yet, my friends. Mark those words, "And the *dead* in Christ shall rise first"—that is, before those who are alive shall be changed. One saint shall not complain to the other, "What a pity that thou wast not awakened sooner; many of the wonders of the second Advent have passed; we saw the Son of Man come upon the white cloud before thou didst awake." No, no, my people, every child of His shall awake in time to see it all. "They without us cannot be made perfect." The doors of the grave will not be kept closed a moment too long.'"

"When Mr. Jones at the close of his sermon," said Caleb, "repeated those words 'That they without us should not be made perfect'; and said that heaven will be incomplete until every saint will enter it, that when the Lord Jesus shall come we shall all see Him, and that not even the humblest Christian will be kept a moment too long in his grave so as to miss the sight, I couldn't help thinking about the old patriarch, Enoch Jones, of Bala. Mr. Henry Rees, of Liverpool, called upon him on his way to one of the monthly meetings. Old Mr. Jones was very ill. Mr. Rees asked for a message to convey to the Conference. 'Tell them,' said he, 'that I know full well they will not miss Enoch Jones, they can preach as happily without him and transact business quite as well without him, but tell them, too, that *they cannot be made perfect without Enoch Jones.*'"

The smithy corner was now reached, and the three friends parted each for his home.

During that day and all through the following night the snow continued to fall thickly, so that on the morrow the earth presented a beautiful sight; but to Hugh all appeared desolate and cold.

❋   ❋   ❋   ❋   ❋   ❋   ❋   ❋   ❋   ❋

A few days later the funeral took place. Notwithstanding the inclemency of the weather a large number of friends met at Pentre-mawr to pay their last tribute to the memory of the departed, and to express their sympathy with the aged and bereaved father. Before the procession was formed the minister of the Baptist Church at "Horeb" read a portion of Scripture and offered prayer in the house. Mr Phillips, of Newcastle-Emlyn, who, in accordance with the itinerant system so largely adopted among the Methodists in Wales, was to preach on the following Sunday in the Methodist Chapel, had come a day earlier at Hugh's request to be present and to preach at the funeral. At the close of the brief service in the house the procession was formed, the most intimate friends of the deceased taking their position in front of the bier, Hugh and a few relatives following immediately after, while the remaining friends formed the rear of the *cortége*.

The black mourning contrasted strongly with the snow which covered everything around. The road along which they passed was a lonely one at all times, but was the very picture of desolation now. On every side death seemed to have vanquished life, and to triumph over its grave with grim and cruel joy. The silence* with which the procession advanced—a silence which was only occasionally relieved by subdued voices of those engaged in brief conversation—made the heavy fall of footsteps in the deep snow sound painfully like the dull tramp of death. All the surroundings seemed to conspire to make the funeral of a young person who had been cut down in the strength of life exceedingly sad and touching.

Among the first who followed the mourners were John Vaughan and Shadrach Morgan, who walked arm-in-arm all the way from the house to the chapel.

For some time the two cousins walked silently side by side. At length Shadrach said:—"The funeral of the son of the widow of Nain must have been a wonderful one, John. I shall never forget the sermon I heard Mr. Jones,† of 'Zion' Chapel, Merthyr, preach on that subject, when he described the procession wending its way to the burying-place, and the widowed mother following the bier, and especially when speaking of the great One who met that funeral and bade the procession stand still. He asked in his powerful way, 'Who ever heard

---

* In Glamorganshire appropriate hymns are generally sung at intervals from the house to the graveyard. In Carmarthenshire and some of the other agricultural counties there is a strong objection to singing in funerals.

† The late Rev. John Jones, Baptist minister, "Zion" Chapel Merthyr Tydvil.

before of anyone stopping a funeral on its way? When a funeral moves along everyone stands aside and uncovers his head, the gentleman in his carriage bids his coachman turn the horses toward the hedge to remain there until the solemn procession has passed. There is nothing that is allowed to stay its course until the grave is reached. But behold the funeral from the little village of Nain is *stopped!*—It was impossible that the King of Terrors, while he displayed a single trophy in his triumphal march, should be allowed to pass "The Resurrection and the Life." The prophet of Nazareth—the Son of God—bade the young man "arise." The young man heard that voice, rubbed the sleep of death from his weary eye-lids, arose, and sat upon his bier. The conqueror was vanquished in his own triumphal march, and the young man returned home from *his own funeral* with his mother leaning upon his arm.'"

"I heard Mr. Roberts, of Wrexham," said John Vaughan, "preach once on 'The son of the widow of Nain.' He imagined the mother and her son by themselves, when all the excitement was over and the neighbours had returned to their homes. 'Mother,' said the son, 'tell me how it all happened.' 'Well, my boy,' answered the mother, 'at such an hour you became unconscious. I called the next-door neighbour in, not knowing what to do, and she hurried and fetched the physician. When he came he shook his head and said all hope was gone. Just as the day dawned you passed away, and I was left alone to break my heart almost with weeping. In the afternoon of the same day the neighbours came to the funeral. Your companions kindly bore you on the bier, and I walked behind them in the sad procession. I thought of the time when I followed your father's body to the burying-place when we walked along the same way, when you were a little boy by my side, and all my hopes clustered round your head; but now I was *alone*—a childless widow—in my sorrow, following the mortal remains of my only boy to the sepulchre. When we had passed through the gate and were going down the hill to the burying-place, Jesus of Nazereth chanced to meet us on His journey—nay, it was no *chance,* for I believe He knew all about it. His face beamed with unearthly tenderness. He looked on the bier and then at me, and then again on the bier, and with his hand motioned your companions to stop. They obeyed, and He, placing his hand upon the bier, said in a voice that I never shall forget, there was so much tenderness and yet so much authority in it—"Young man, I say unto thee, arise."'—*'I heard that, mother,'* replied the son. I shall never forget, Shadrach, the impression which those last words left upon all who listened."

The solemn procession had now arrived at the chapel, which was soon filled to overflowing. A portion of the eleventh chapter of the Gospel according to John was read and prayer offered by the minister of "Peniel" chapel, after which Mr. Phillips took for his text the words, "Keep back thy servant also from presumptuous sins." The preacher began by stating some of the hindrances to sin, which God mercifully places in the way of men, and said—

"There are first of all *natural* hindrances to sin, for notwithstanding man's fall, there is still a kind of *delicacy* in his nature, which often feels the shock of sin and a keen pain which comes in the train of sinning. Then there is *the voice of conscience* that makes it impossible for man to transgress God's Law and be at ease.

"Again there are certain *outward* hindrances to sin. *Sleep* is a merciful hindrance. Few imagine what value there is in six or seven hours sleep. How much impatience, soreness, and bitterness is taken from us in this way. Again the *Sabbath* the one day of rest in seven— is a gracious barrier. Who could tell what a blessing the Sabbath is to man? All Wales has been anxious that this barrier against sin should not have a single defect in it, and desires at least that one serious gap should be filled up by the passing of that salutary measure—'The Sunday Closing Bill.'*

"Again, there are *social barriers* against sin mercifully erected by God. The *Christian home* with all its hallowing associations, *the Sunday school,* and the *presence of good men* are among those social hindrances to sin which God places in the way of young people especially. They cannot rush on in their sinful career without being checked by these barriers at every turn."

Then coming to *Providential barriers,* he said, "God by His *Providence* checks much of the world's wickedness. He prevents the ungodly for many years from rushing wildly on his downward course. In some cases the ungodly man is thus effectually checked, and his course turned for ever. In other cases, alas, the barrier only *delays* the sinner's onward sweep, for, like a river whose progress is barred, he gathers strength by the delay, until at last he rushes madly over every barrier or carries all before him, and descends in wild cataracts over the brink of ruin.

---

* This was spoken before the passing of the Act.

"But my text speaks about God keeping back His *servant* 'from presumptuous sins.' Ah, it is the gracious Lord that preserves the *greatest saint* from sinning. In a very special manner does He keep His child from a sinful course. He checks him very much as He does the river. If many a river were to flow in a straight course from its source to the sea it would rush on at a terrific speed. It has been said, for instance—with what truth I am not able to tell—that if the river Thames were to flow in a straight line from its source among the Cotswold Hills to the sea it would rush through London at the rate of from forty to fifty miles per hour. Such a river would be dangerous, unnavigable, and a curse to our country; but the great Ruler says to the river Thames, 'I will put a few curves in thy course. Thou shalt visit the foot of yonder slope, and then thou shalt cross the valley and touch the dark rock on this side. I will curve thee on thy journey, so that thou shalt pass through London, the great Metropolis of a great country, in a quiet and majestic way.' God does very much the same with His child. If he were allowed to go straight on according to his own impulse he would rush on sometimes at a dangerous speed, but his heavenly Father says, 'I will put a few curves in thy course; thou shalt pay a visit to the graveyard on this side of life's valley and leave thy wife or child—little John or Jane—there, and then cross the valley and come into contact with the black, frowning rock of temptation or trial on the other side. I will make thy course a winding one all along, so that thou shalt appear calm, dignified and stately when thou shalt enter the heavenly Jerusalem, the Metropolis of the great King.'

"It would be the extreme of folly to complain of these windings. They are those which will make the review very charming from the hills of immortality. There would be but little beauty in a river that had no windings. No one feels much interest in looking at a straight canal extending far into the distance. It has no curves in it. The eye soon tires in looking at a straight line. Curves are ever the conditions of beauty. Thus we never grow tired of looking at a meandering stream or river. So shall it be at last, it will be the windings in life's stream that will appear the most beautiful of all from the everlasting hills. In reviewing our life from that vantage ground how beautiful will that bend in the course of life's river be when we touched the graveyard, or that curve when we passed beneath the dark and chilling shadow of the frowning rock of affliction and trial. Those windings will be the most charming parts of all our course.

'O fryniau Caersalem ceir gweled
Holl droion yr yrfa i gyd.'"
[From Salem's high hills we shall witness
The windings of life's river through.]

The service having been closed, the congregation left the chapel for the graveside. The coffin was lowered, and Mr. Phillips broke upon the silence which followed by repeating the words, "Our life is hid with Christ in God." He added, "There is a sound of *safety* about these words. That is one reason why our thoughts and aspirations as Christians should go forth and find a resting-place where our life is hid—yonder with Christ in God.

"There is also a sound of *mystery* about these words, and that is another reason why they should draw to themselves our solemn thoughts at this hour. While the source of the river Nile was a mystery it was an object of intense interest to the civilized world. The very mystery increased the interest felt; so the mystery that attaches itself to God helps to draw us to Him. It is the glory of God to conceal as well as to reveal a thing. All the harps in heaven would be silenced if there were no heights and depths of mystery to be found in Him. So, too, this life that is *hid* becomes all the more absorbing in its interest, because we cannot fully comprehend it now. It gives scope to faith, and inspiration to hope.

Remember, too, that this is hidden in order that it may be *revealed* more fully by-and-by. Every life is hidden at first—the seed falls into the ground and disappears from sight, but it appears again in the blade, the stalk, and the full ear of corn. The glory of that life would not come to sight apart from that concealment... Christ Himself is hidden at present. The last sight that *the world* had of Him was on the cross and beneath the crown of thorns. The life of the saints is hid *with Him.* But when He 'who is our life shall appear then shall ye also appear with him in glory!' Even inspired men did not speak much about heaven under the Old Dispensation—there was no Christ revealed in it, and thus it was scarcely worth speaking about. But since Christ has entered the third heaven, and the fact has been made known, heaven has had an unutterable charm for His followers. It is *He* that makes heaven a place of intense interest to us. May we learn, my friends, to be content here with a *hidden* life for a little while—hidden by grief, afflictions, &c.—it will yet appear as surely as that He will."

A brief prayer, in which the mourners were commended to God, brought the service to a close, and the large gathering separated.

Caleb, John, and Shadrach having expressed their sympathy with their old friend Hugh, and shaken his hand warmly, walked quietly together through the village engaged all the while in close converse.

"We've had a very solemn service to-day," said Shadrach. "It's sad to see young life cut short like this. There are too few like that maid in the world already, without having them taken away from us so soon—but there, God does all things well."

"Yes, He *does,* Shadrach," replied John, "and remember her life is not cut short—she lives more gloriously than ever before. You've forgotten your faith in your sorrow, Shadrach."

"That's true, John," exclaimed Caleb. "I told you the other night something that Mr. Jones, of Swansea, uttered by the graveside of his old friend, Mr. Davies, of Llandilo. He also said on the same occasion, 'Our friend lives. Life was delightful to him in this world; it is still more delightful to him, now. I do not believe one word of Watts's hymn,

"Oh, what a wretched land is this."

It is a libel on this delightful and grand world. It is not a wretched world. It was in it that I learnt to walk, to feel, to see, to act... I remember the early days of my childhood when I used to play on the old hearth at home. This world was a beautiful world to me at that time—fifty-four years ago. God placed a cup in my hand then, filled with the luscious wine of life, and I took a draught of it in the days of my childhood, and another draught in the days of my youth, and another when I became a man; and now that the face is somewhat furrowed and the hair is becoming grey I love life more than ever—life, sweet life. Mr. Davies is not dead. The cup is in his hand filled with the sparkling wine of life, and he drinks of it now in the land of light.'"

"God has always been giving hints of this to man," said John. "Of course it is the resurrection of our blessed Lord that has taught us the glorious truth that there is life beyond death, but I believe that God long before that took Enoch and Elijah to Himself without seeing death, in order to teach men to look for *life* yonder. You remember, Shadrach, the sermon which Mr. Thomas, of Narberth, preached a few years ago at 'Horeb,' from the words, 'He was not, for God took him,' when he said:—'Our text implies that Enoch's life was progressive, "he walked with God." Every step he took was a step to higher truths, richer experiences, and a more perfect character. No one *stands* with God. If you desire to be with Him you must walk with Him, for He ever moves on in glorious manifestations of His wisdom, love, and purity. Enoch walked with Him on this earth for three hundred years. It was a long walk, but no walk, however long, with God, is tiresome, for He leads on to scenes ever new, to pastures ever green, to waters ever still, and to skies ever bright.

"'His departure was only a continuation of his holy and consecrated life—"God took him"—took him further on and higher up. This was not a sudden transition, or an unexpected change of his course. Oh, no, only a continuation of his long walk with God, the dawn brightening into day, the stars melting into sunshine, the old walk of time lengthened into eternity. He had gone far with God often before now, he had walked with Him to the very threshold of heaven, but this time *he lost his balance and stepped in*—'God took him." He had walked so well and so far that he had but a *step* at last. His holy and devoted life had made a coward of death, so that he was afraid, but allowed him to pass through the gate without paying the usual toll exacted of mortal men.'"

"I heard Mr. Williams,* Ruthin, preach once from that subject," added Caleb. "He said, 'Enoch often walked with God. They walked so long together one day that God said to him, "Thou hast come so far to-day there's no need for thee to return any more. Thou shalt come all the way with me to my home."—"He was not, *for God took him."*'"

"Yes, that's very good," said John. "I should like to have heard Mr. Williams preach from that subject.—Well, Mr. Thomas went on to say in his sermon at 'Horeb':—'Enoch had received some intimations that he should not die like others. I imagine God calling him one morning in the early dawn to come for the usual walk. He went up to a neighbouring mountain—his customary retreat—reached its very summit, and there in solitude and in the ecstasy of devotion prayed. "Father, take me now." I seem to hear the Father reply, "Come on, my child, give me thy hand."

"'With this he found a sweet change coming over him, heaviness giving way to buoyancy, and mortality to life. He felt all soul, and yet as if still in the body. He ascended... until at last there opened to him the indescribable scenes of the better land, whose sky was bright,

---

* The late Rev. Robert Williams, Baptist minister, Ruthin, North Wales.

whose climate was genial, and whose air was redolent with the sweetest perfume, and bracing with the currents of life. He found himself entering a gorgeous city—the metropolis of the land—and the King's temple, wherein worshipped thousands of thousands and millions of millions, and in the midst of the throne saw One of peculiar beauty, more beautiful than the morning, the chiefest among ten thousand, and altogether lovely. He did not ask where he was. He knew that he was in Heaven—the home of God—and *his* new home. All to him was a source of wonder, and heaven was not a greater wonder to Enoch than Enoch was to heaven. The angelic hosts had never seen such a thing before, the oldest inhabitant had never witnessed such a spectacle; they had seen many before coming from earth, but he was the first to stand among the princes of Heaven in the *full costume* of his native land. Paul's account is:—"By faith Enoch was translated that he should not see death." Enoch was the first complete translation of man heaven ever had.

"'His loss *was felt,* he was missed. "He was not," or according to Paul, "he was not found." His departure caused a great consternation, and a diligent search was made, a sad wail of grief went forth from the family, and even the wicked neighbours, who had in the days gone by sneered at him, now joined in the sorrow, for they held Enoch in high esteem, and cherished a kind of affection for him. But all was in vain—"He was not, for God took him."'"

"Ah, that reminds me of what I heard Mr. Thomas, of Cardiff, say," said Shadrach, "when preaching from the subject:—'There appears to have been a considerable stir and commotion about him on earth. The words "he was not" (seen), and "was not found" suggest to us the idea that there was some searching for him as there was for Elijah when he had been taken in his fiery chariot. His family was full of trouble and anxiety as to what had become of him. It was getting very late at night. I can imagine his wife becoming very uneasy about him and asking, "Methuselah, when and where did you see your father last to-day?" and her son, replying, "I saw him in the afternoon, mother, just about the time of the evening sacrifice. I thought at first that he was speaking to some one, but I could not see anyone with him." Later still she asks some of the neighbours, "Have you seen Enoch tonight anywhere? I can't imagine what makes him so late. We have been married now more than three hundred years, and I never knew him to be out so late before. He has always come in time for evening prayers. Something very strange must have happened to him, otherwise he would have returned home long before now."' The preacher then paused and said—'Ah, she little knew the secret—"He *was not, for God took him.*"'"

"Well, go on, John."

"I only remember the words with which he concluded," replied John:—"'God *took* him, not drove, or tore him away, but took him gently, as ripe fruit is taken from the tree, or a pretty flower from the stalk, or as a mother takes her babe into her arms, or a father his little boy across the stream.'"

"The death of Mr. Powell, of Cardiff, was a death of that kind—one of the most beautiful I can well imagine," added Caleb. "One Saturday he went to the little village of Bonvilstone to preach there on the following day. On the Sunday morning, he preached a very interesting sermon in his own quaint style. He returned with his host to dinner, a distance of about a quarter of a mile from the chapel. Shortly after dinner he expressed to the friends at whose house he stayed his intention of going to the Sunday school. They tried to dissuade him, assuring him that the school was in such a lamentable state that only a very few attended it. He replied that that was an additional reason why he should go. When he arrived there were only five children present. He opened the school with prayer, then he and the children sang a hymn as best they could. After that he gave them a very interesting little lesson, closed the school, and left with them. As they walked together along the greensward by the wayside, Mr. Powell began to address his little companions, and said, 'You are very good children in coming to the Sunday school, and I must reward you for your conduct this afternoon;' then taking some pence from his pocket he added, 'I have here *seven pence.* Here is a penny each for you, and I have *two* pence for myself. You are all very rich, and I am still richer, you see, and more than all I have a Father in heaven who will give me all I want.' These were the last words he uttered. He fell gently on the grass, the children called for help. When friends came to the spot Lewis Powell 'was not, for God took him'—he had gone to *his* reward; his Father there and then gave him *all he wanted.* What a glorious translation and an infinite surprise that must have been to Mr. Powell—one moment on the lonely road near the little village of Bonvilstone, the next in heaven."

"Yes, Caleb," exclaimed Shadrach, "and yet heaven wasn't

altogether new to him; he had got a few glimpses of it before from this old earth."

"Very true," replied Caleb. "When Mr. Phillips repeated that hymn,

'O fryniau Caersalem ceir gweled,'

I was reminded very forcibly of what I heard Mr. Morgan Howell* once say in a sermon in a monthly meeting. He was in a glorious *hwyl* when he repeated that verse, and seeing two well-known poets in the gallery he addressed them and said—'I want one of you to compose another verse, which shall be a counterpart of that. That verse speaks of seeing the wanderings in the wilderness from the eternal hills; we want another verse which shall tell of seeing the everlasting hills while yet in the wilderness.'"

"Ah, the great thing," said John, as the friends parted, "is to be always, as David Rowland, of Bala, once said, like the swallow about to take wing for foreign lands—*everything ready.*"

---

*The late Rev. Morgan Howell, a distinguished Methodist minister.

CHAPTER XIV

Some of Caleb's Reminiscences

OME weeks passed by after the funeral of Hugh Roberts' daughter during which nothing of interest occurred. Death had cast its chill shadow not only on Pentre-mawr farm but also over the little company who usually met at the smithy. Hugh was absent, and so was his friend Caleb, who had gone on a journey to "the hills" to close accounts with those who had for so many years bought flannel of him. Caleb was getting old, and as he had by a life of much industry saved just enough to maintain his wife and himself in their latest years, there was no need for him to toil any longer. Besides, he felt that the eventide of life was the time in which to forget its bustle and tumult, and in which to pause and consider before the head was laid in sleep upon the lap of death; as he himself put it, "Now that I am old I don't want to have anything more to do with flannel, nor do I want to pass away in a rush, but calmly and reverently into the presence of my God."

The circle of friends was for the time broken, and with the exception of a few conversations between Shadrach and his cousin John nothing transpired at the smithy worth recording, and even those we must now pass over.

The first evening after Caleb's return was the one in which the prayer-meeting was usually held in the Methodist chapel. There Hugh and Caleb met each other, and at the close walked arm-in-arm toward Pentre-mawr. The road passed by the smithy, and as a matter of course they called there. Shadrach and Jenkin were busy at work, but the moment Hugh and Caleb appeared at the door Shadrach dropped the tongs and greeted them right heartily.

A few minutes later John Vaughan entered the smithy. He had finished his work for the day, and had come to have a chat with Shadrach. To his surprise Caleb had returned, and, as he said, "of course Hugh was with him."

"Tell us something, Caleb, about your visit to Glamorganshire," said Shadrach. "How is the good cause getting on there."

"Exceedingly well," replied Caleb, "especially the cause of temperance. I spent a Sunday at Swansea, and every other person almost wore the blue ribbon. As I hadn't heard Dr. Rees for many years I went to hear him instead of going to one of our own chapels. He preached an excellent sermon, and there was one thing he said which struck me very much. He was speaking of the drunkard and the reprobate, and said that he was one of the saddest sights in God's creation. Then he said, 'When I see a worm wallowing in the mire the sight does not affect me, because the worm is in its congenial element, but when I see a beautiful bird with clipped wings struggling helplessly in a muddy puddle my heart is moved to pity, for I know that it is not made for that but to soar aloft into the pure air and clear sunshine. So when man's aspirations are clogged with earthliness, and he wallows in the mire of sin, it is a sight which may well make angels weep and fill the heart of God with pity. Man is not made for that, but to soar heavenward and hold fellowship with his God.'

"But the most interesting meeting of all that I attended was one held in a coal-pit. There was an open place there set apart and roughly furnished for that purpose. On every Monday morning a short service is held there, over which one of their own number presides. On this special occasion the meeting held was in connection with the Gospel Temperance Movement, and was a very enthusiastic one. After reading and prayer there were two short addresses given. The first was based upon Deut. xxii. 8, 'When thou buildest a new house then thou shalt make a battlement for thy roof, that thou bring not blood upon thine house, if any man fall from thence.' The speaker, who was rather advanced in years, gave a very forcible address, shewing that if neglect on the part of a man to build battlements on the flat roof of his house brought upon his own head the blood of anyone who might fall over, a similar neglect on our part to protect by example as well as by precept the souls of our dear ones will bring their blood upon our heads if they are lost. The second was a very homely and powerful address. There was one thing in it which interested me very much. The friend who spoke repeated with great force Christmas Evans's dream, one that I heard the old dreamer repeat himself when I was quite a lad on a journey with my father. The story as told in the coal-pit brought back to me that crowded meeting in which Christmas Evans told that dream for the first time, and when looking up to the gallery at the close his one eye flashed as I have never seen any other eye flash in my life.

"Ah, that was the eye, Caleb," said John Vaughan, "of which Robert Hall once said that it was bright enough to light an army through a desert."

"Yes," replied Caleb, "his eye was a wonderful one.—Well, he was announced to speak at that meeting; people came from far and near to hear him. Mr. W——, of A——, a well-known minister, said at first that he should not be present for he anticipated a personal reference to himself, yet such was the fascination that he could not stay away. He came to the meeting late and crept into the gallery, where the preacher's eye, which had been long searching for him, at length discovered him. Christmas Evans at once proceeded to say, 'I had a strange dream last night. I dreamt that I was in Pandemonium, the council chamber of Hades. How I *got there* I *know* not, but *there* I was. I had not been there long before I heard a thundering rap at the gates. 'Beelzebub! Beelzebub! you must come to earth directly.' 'Why, what's the matter now?' 'Oh! they are sending out missionaries to the heathen.' 'Are they? Bad news that. I'll be there presently.' Beelzebub rose, and hastened to the place of embarkation, where he saw the missionaries and their wives, and a few boxes of Bibles and tracts, but, on turning round, he saw rows of casks piled up, and labelled gin, rum, brandy, &c. 'That will do,' said *he,* 'there's no fear yet. The casks will do more harm than the boxes can do good.' So saying, he stretched his wings and returned to his own place. After a time came another loud call. 'Beelzebub!' 'Yes.' 'They are forming Bible societies now.' 'Are they? Then I must go.' He went, and found two ladies going from house to house distributing the Word of God. 'This will never do,' said he, 'but I will watch the result.' The ladies visited an aged woman who received a Bible with much reverence and many thanks. Beelzebub loitered about, and when the ladies were gone, saw the old woman come to her door, and look around to assure herself that she was unobserved. She then put on her bonnet, and with a small parcel under her apron, hastened to a public-house near, where she exchanged her Bible for a bottle of gin. 'That will do,' said Beelzebub with a grin, 'no fear yet,' and back he flew to his own place. Again a loud rap came, and a more urgent call. 'Beelzebub! you must come now, or all is lost; they are forming teetotal societies.' 'Teetotal! what is that?' 'To drink no intoxicating liquors.' 'Indeed! that is bad news. I must see to that.' He did; but soon went back again to satisfy the anxious enquiries of his legions, who were all on the *qui vive* about the matter. 'Don't be alarmed,' said he; it's an awkward affair, I know, but it won't spread much yet, for *all the parsons* are with us, and Mr. W——, of A—— (here the preacher's eye glanced like lightning at him) is at the head of them." 'But I won't be at the head of them any longer,' cried Mr. W——; and immediately walking down out of the gallery, he entered the table pew and signed the pledge."

"It's slightly different now from then," said Shadrach. "Christmas Evans couldn't have dreamt such a dream as that now."

"No, the times are changed, Shadrach," replied Caleb. "Total abstinence is considered respectable now, but I honour those who stood the brunt of the fight forty or fifty years ago, men like Christmas Evans and David Rowland, of Bala. David Rowland joined the 'Teetotal Society soon after its formation. I heard him say at a public meeting once that, at the beginning of that movement, some who had been notorious drunkards, but who were then teetotallers, came to him asking him to sign the pledge. He answered, 'I won't give my name to such as you are, but,' he said, as he told us the story 'when I saw from the Old Book that it was my duty to abstain I should have been willing to write, if necessary, in letters of pitch on my hat, "DAVID ROWLAND, TEETOTALLER FOR EVER."' At another time he said in his quaint way, 'Years ago a drunken man could fall from his horse without being much injured. Before "teetotalism" came a drunkard was like a young calf, fall as much as he might he was but little hurt comparatively; but now, since "teetotalism" has come, he breaks his leg or his neck by the least fall. There are judgments befalling the drunkards now as they never did before. God passed drunkenness over in the times of ignorance, but now that the light is come he punishes fearfully.' The last time I ever heard him speak was on total abstinence. It was near the close of his life. I shall never forget one thing he said. Referring to the great progress which the cause of temperance had made he added in his own peculiar style, '"Teetotalism" has made such a rent in the devil's kingdom, that there are not sufficient tailors in hell to sew it up again.'

"I remember on another occasion hearing him speak about Job and referring to the words with which the Book begins said that if some people had written it they would have dwelt largely at the outset upon Job's wealth, position, and influence, then they would have given an account of the children, one a lawyer, another a parson, &c., and then the little religion would be allowed to sneak in at the tail, 'but here,' he added, 'we read, "There was a man in the land of Uz whose name was Job." Well, what about him? "And that man *was perfect and upright, and one that feared God and eschewed evil.' Religion in the forefront, you see."'"

"It was then I suppose," interjected Jenkin, "that he referred to Job's words, 'Though he slay me, yet will I trust in him,' and said, 'Ah, if the old tempter had only known that Job would have said this he would have put a boil as big as a turnip on the tip of his tongue.'"

"No Jenkin," replied Caleb, "that was on another occasion when he preached from the words you have just repeated, and that was how he began his sermon. He riveted our attention in a moment."

"Mr. John, of Cilgerran, gave a capital speech on temperance in your chapel years ago," said John. "He told us that he was once on the coach from Newcastle-Emlyn to Cardigan. There were three dogs tied together near him, and being rather interested in them he asked the driver where they were going. He answered, 'I can't tell you, Sir; they have eaten their addresses.' 'I couldn't help thinking,' added Mr. John, 'about some men who go to the public-house, and who do very much as the dogs did—not *eat*—but *drink* their addresses, they do not know themselves which way to take, and nobody else knows where to send them, thus it's never certain that they'll ever reach their destination.'"

"There's a very good story told about him," said Jenkin. "They say that he was very ugly, and that on a certain occasion he was in North Wales on one of his preaching tours. It was getting dark, and Mr. Thomas John was astride his little pony passing along a lonely road. It was very cold, and he wore a long, thick overcoat and was heavily muffled. Nothing but his long nose and staring eyes appeared in the twilight, and they looked dreadful. Mr. John also stooped very much, and leaned forward over the pony's head, as he rode. A gentleman chanced to be passing in his carriage, the horses threatened to shy, and the gentleman himself looked at him with astonishment. He had never seen such a sight before; he became terrified, but at last understanding that what appeared so hideous was after all a man riding by, he recovered his speech and said, '*Why,* man, you are enough to frighten the devil!' '*That's my mission, Sir,*' replied Mr. John."

"That story, as well as a great many more, *is* told about him, Jenkin," replied Caleb, "and though you have drawn upon your imagination rather freely in your description, yet I believe that the story is substantially true, and the answer he is said to have given the gentleman who accosted him is just such an answer as he would give. Ah, he was a wonderful man; a grand soul in a frail body, one of the aristocracy of heaven occupying a very dilapidated earthly holding. I have seen him before now hold a congregation spell-bound. He was a wonderful man at illustrations, which he drew from all quarters.

I heard him once preach a very powerful sermon from the words, 'If they do these things in a green tree what shall be done in the dry.' He described in a thrilling way the sufferings of the great Saviour—repeated the story of the betrayal and crucifixion in such a way as to make us all feel that we were eye-witnesses of the awful tragedy. Then he contrasted His sufferings with the far more fearful ones which are in store for the wicked. He spoke of one Francis Spira, who became a prey to his own passions. The lamp of hope was extinguished in him, he could not take his food, sometimes he would search for his sword to slay himself with it, and would then shout, 'Oh, that I were stronger than God.' A cold sweat would then cover him, and he would fall down as dead, then arousing himself would shout in his fury, 'Oh, that I were stronger than God, for I know He will not have mercy on me.' This, the preacher said, was an earthly story which might explain more fully than we think what hell may be. And then he told us about some great emperor very long ago. I don't remember his name nor much about him, except that he turned from Christianity to heathenism, and became very cruel toward the church of God. He shed much innocent blood; but one day he was overtaken and wounded. Looking at his wound, when he saw that all hope was gone he grew furious in his despair—and I'll never forget the look of the preacher as he described him. This wicked emperor, overcome by his own evil passion, held his hands to receive his own blood, and then cast it up in handfuls toward heaven and blasphemed

God. The preacher said, 'You need not go further for an exposition of the words which God grant we may never more fully understand:—"There shall be weeping and gnashing of teeth."'

"Speaking a little further on to Christians, he gave words of terrible warning, and said:—'If you would go on straight to perdition, cling to ordinances, and live all the while in your sins, and you will be as certain to reach it as that Beelzebub himself is there. That is the devil's turnpike road to lead professors to destruction. I have never understood that the Gospel of Jesus Christ grants special opportunities for sinning. I remember reading about sacred groves that were set aside for the special protection of criminals, but which at length were so infested with evil doers that it was dangerous for virtuous people to live near. If I thought that our religion was based upon a similar principle I should like to see every chapel throughout our land in flames at this very moment, and I would shout Hallelujah over the conflagration.' Ah, that was an overpowering sermon from beginning to end," added Caleb, "I shall never forget it."

"And I shall never forget one thing he said at your chapel, Caleb," said John. "Speaking about the Cross, he said that it was the master-thought of God, that there is nothing great when placed by it, and that its brightness will cast all the other glories of heaven into the shade; then each redeemed spirit will exclaim—'God forbid that I should glory save in the *Cross* of our Lord Jesus Christ.'—Just now when you were telling us about the solemn warnings which you heard Mr. John give his hearers, I was reminded of a sermon I heard Mr. Thomas Rees Davies* preach at 'Horeb.' Before announcing his text—'How shall we escape if we neglect so great salvation,' he said:—'I have in my text a question which you cannot answer (he then gave a nod, which, as you know, was familiar to all his hearers) yet I will ask it; no mortal can answer it—(another nod)—still I will ask it; an angel cannot answer it—(another nod)—yet I will ask it; yea with reverence I will say God Himself cannot answer it—yet—yet I will ask it, for it is God's own question,—"How shall we escape if we neglect. so great salvation?" There it is. It is a question here in this Book, and it will remain a question for ever.'"

"Mr. Hughes,† formerly of Machynlleth, was once preaching on the

---

* The late Rev. T. R. Davies, a quaint and popular Baptist minister.

† Rev. Thomas Hughes, Calvinistic Methodist minister, now of Tremadoc, Carnarvonshire.

responsibilities of hearers of the Gospel," added Caleb, "and gave this very forcible illustration:—'I was once on the top of Snowdon, and noticed different fossils of shell-fish there. I said to myself, "This high summit has been beneath the sea at some time or other, and it tells the story now though thousands of years have passed away since then." So, I thought, those who have lived in Wales during these times of Gospel privileges will bear evidences of it to all eternity. It will be easy *then* to see that Wales has been beneath the flood of Gospel truth, and those who go to the next world without accepting its blessings will be their own condemnation, the Bible, the Sabbath school, the prayer meetings, other services, and all the gracious privileges received, will no longer be living things, but will have been converted into fossils—*dead records* of a once living but now wasted past.'—The effect of that sermon was overpowering.

"But the most powerful sermon I ever heard was when I was quite a youth. It was preached by Mr. John Jones, of Talsarn, the Calvinistic Methodist minister, who was one of the most distinguished preachers which the Welsh pulpit has produced. He was emotional, and thoughtful, was endowed with a fine imaginative touch, had a good presence, and withal possessed a powerful as well as a musical voice. One of the most effective discourses he ever delivered was the sermon I heard him preach on 'The claims of Jesus to be supreme in the affections of men.' In the middle of his discourse he expressed his fear that many in the congregation were servants of Satan. Then in the most touching manner possible he urged all his hearers to examine themselves, whose servants they were, adding that if they served sin they ought to have some reason for so doing. 'And if,' said he, 'you are servants of Satan you ought to stand for him now publicly. If he has any claim to the allegiance of your souls it is only right that you should acknowledge him.' Then, in his own powerful way, he repeated a prayer to the Evil One—'O, Prince of Pleasure thou hast promised us great things, days of joy and merriment, we will serve thee faithfully to the end, and take our chance with thee at last.' Then looking straight into the faces of his hearers he said—'Let all who are followers of Satan say Amen.' But a stillness like the silence of the grave prevailed. Then he turned to the other side, and addressing the Saviour of men, said—'O, Jesus of Nazareth, Thou hast suffered the death of the cross for us, and bidden us bear our little crosses for Thee; we will follow Thee faithfully in this world through good and evil report. If we have to go through the flood we will follow thee. Do Thou guide us by Thy counsel, and afterwards receive us to glory.' Then he added—'Let all who are anxious to follow Jesus say Amen.' The effect was irresistible, and a chorus of Amens rose like the voice of many waters and mighty thunderings from the whole congregation. It required a great preacher to attempt such a method in his endeavour to win souls, but all who heard that wonderful sermon felt that the speaker was intensely in earnest, and many were converted that night.

"You, John, spoke just now of Mr. Thomas Rees Davies—generally called the 'Black Cap.'* I knew him very well. He was a remarkable man, was tall, and of very commanding presence. He was one of the most popular preachers of his day—though he used to repeat the same sermons often. One of his favourite discourses was from the text, 'And upon this rock I will build my church.' '"Who is this rock?" he asked. "Peter," says the Pope. "Jesus Christ,"' says Thomas Rees Davies. 'I am willing that Peter should be a "stone" and a "lively stone," though he had a serious flaw in him, but I am not willing that he should be "this rock." Who shall decide the matter between us? Shall Paul? Yes, I am willing. Is the Pope willing? Yes; valuable paintings of Paul are hung up in the Vatican, which shows that he is respected there. Then shall he decide? Yes. "Paul, what hast thou to say about the foundation upon which the church is to be built?" "Other foundation can no man lay than that is laid," says Paul. "Then there is one laid, Paul?" "Yes, oh, yes!" "But there can be no other?" "No." "Then who. is that foundation, Paul?" "Jesus Christ." You all hear,' exclaimed the preacher in a triumphant tone, his voice meanwhile reaching its full compass and rich modulation, 'You all hear, *the Pope has lost, and Thomas Rees Davies has won the day!'*"

"I remember him, too, preach on one occasion in North Wales on the free invitations of the Gospel of Jesus Christ to all. He said that near Menai Bridge he had seen a hospital, and inscribed upon it were the words, 'For-invalids from the counties of Anglesea and Carnarvon.' There was no room there for the invalids of the other counties of North Wales. Every human institution is necessarily limited, but the hospital of Jesus is free to all— '*Whosoever.* 'He then read the words of Jesus in *Matt,.* xi. 28, 'Come unto me'—a *few*—(a nod)—no—*many*—(another nod*)—no, no* ALL—I have it now, 'Come unto me ALL ye that labour and are heavy laden, and I will give you rest.'"

---

* Mr. Davies generally wore a black velvet cap in preaching.

"Those grand old preachers," said John, "were very clear in proclaiming the love of God and His gracious invitation to sinners, and the Lord never failed to bless them."

"Very true, John," said Caleb. "They spoke of the rich provisions of Divine grace, not merely as being just enough to satisfy our wants, but as far exceeding our utmost need. I well remember hearing Mr. Hughes,* Pont-Robert, preach at Rhyd-y-berau on the Atonement. He was carried away in the *hwyl,* and exclaimed very powerfully and effectively, 'It is enough for God—*enough for God.'* Two godly sisters forgot themselves and shouted, 'Then it's enough for us—*enough for us!'* The old preacher got impatient for the moment and replied, 'Silence, silence, sisters, it isn't much to say that it is enough for *you,'* and then he shouted with his mighty voice, 'IT IS ENOUGH FOR GOD— *and that's more than enough for all, for* ALL *besides.'"*

"Ah, those men preached from the heart," exclaimed Shadrach, "and therefore *to* the heart. They composed their sermons not in studies, but in the fields, the workshops, and often during their weary journeys. Edward Coslett,† the blacksmith of Castletown, and one of your best preachers, Caleb, was one of that sort. He used to strike off his sermons like sparks from the anvil. 'Edward,' said the famous Mr. Jones, of Langan, to him once after a very stirring meeting, 'Where did you get that sermon?' 'In a study where you have never been, Sir.' 'Where is that study, Edward.' 'Between the fire and the anvil, Sir.' The result of this was that when Coslett wanted an illustration he didn't go far for it over hill and dale, but took the nearest at hand. It was sometimes very plain and homely, I know, but always striking, and people didn't go to sleep in hearing it. 'Don't serve the devil, boys,' said he on one occasion in a sermon to young people. 'I served him for many years, and I never received from him as much as a nail to put in a tip.'"

"Coslett was a genuine character," said Caleb. "Have you heard of him at the Quarter Sessions applying for a license to preach? It was necessary for him to have the protection of the law, as he had received

---

* Calvinistic Methodist minister.

† Mr. Coslett was one of the most popular Calvinistic Methodist preachers in the early part of this century. He was a working blacksmith to the close of life; was a man of great physical strength, and often walked between thirty and forty miles on the Saturday, and as many miles on the Monday to and from the place where he preached on Sunday.

many threats. When one of the magistrates saw his countryfied look he said with surprise, 'You preach the Gospel! God help you!' 'Amen,' said Coslett, 'His help and your good wish, Sir, will do.' He had the license without delay.

"I remember hearing of him once on a visit to Pembrokeshire. In one place he was asked to conduct a service throughout in English. The old, unassuming blacksmith did not much relish the request. At length, however, he consented in part. 'I am willing,' he said, 'to preach in English, but I will not *pray* in English. I'll speak in English to you, but I never in my life said a word in that language to my heavenly Father.'"

"That's very good," said Shadrach. "He was a quaint old man.—I suppose, Caleb, that during your travels through Glamorganshire you often heard Mr. David Stephens, one of 'The Three Brothers,'* who were brought up at Capel Isaac. I liked to hear him. He had always a good story to illustrate his point; one never forgot what he said."

"I knew him well, Shadrach," replied Caleb. "I heard him soon after his settlement at Glantaff. Mr. Oliver,† of Pontypridd received from his friends a large presentation of books. A meeting was held on the night of presentation. Mr Stephens was one of the speakers. He said:— 'There was an old man who lived in the neighbourhood of Capel Isaac who used to haul coal. He and his wife had lived very comfortably together for many years. But one day as he was hauling coal he saw Lady Dynevor driving by in her carriage. He was greatly impressed by her exceptional beauty. When he returned home his wife was delighted to see him but he appeared very disconsolate and could not speak a word. "Jack, dear," said she, "why don't you say a word to your wife?" "Wife, indeed! It's Lord Dynevor that has a wife," said Jack, at the same time lifting up his walking-stick. I shall do the same thing,' said Mr. Stephen, 'with my library when I go home. I shall lift up my stick before my own books and say, "Library, indeed! It's Mr. Oliver, of Pontypridd, that has a library!"'"

"On another occasion he was speaking of those who will never give up their plans, and upon whom all persuasion and warning are lost, but who at length, when all else has failed, have their plans upset, and their selfish persistency frustrated by Providence. By way of

---

* The late Revs D. Stephens of Glantaff, J. Stephens, of Brych-goed and N. Stephens of Liverpool, all Congregational ministers.

† Rev. H. Oliver, B.A., Congregational minister, now of Newport, Mon.

illustration he described a scene he had witnessed at Llandilo fair when he was a boy. Some old woman from Carmarthen, bolder than the others, placed her table further out in the road than the rest. They complained, and requested her not to go beyond the proper bound, as it placed them at a disadvantage. The policemen warned her, but she still persisted. At length the mail coach came—the wheel struck against the table, upset it, and smashed everything that was on it. Because she would not listen to anyone she had to suffer for it; she came in the way of the mail coach of the Government. 'So,' he said, 'the people who consult only their own interests and try to occupy more than the place allotted to them by Providence sooner or later get into difficulties. The mail coach of the Divine Government topples their little tables over, and they have to bear humiliation as the reward of their folly.'

"I heard him also preach from the text, 'Give me neither poverty nor riches.' He said:—'If you offer this prayer be sure that you offer it all. Don't take a part of it and forget the other. Be honest. Don't be like the hearers of Mr. Jonathan Jones, of Rhyd-y-bont. When the old man quoted the words, "Give me neither poverty," all the farmers responded vigorously; "Amen, Amen," but when he went on to repeat the words "nor riches," their voices subsided into a moan—"H'm! H'm!" They lost the *hwyl* and collapsed all at once.'"

"Ah, they have had some quaint preachers in Glamorganshire, Caleb," said John, "such men, for instance, as Mr. Evan Harris, of Merthyr, and Mr. Powell, of Cardiff."

"That's true," replied Caleb. "Have you ever heard the story of Mr. Harris and Mr. Powell travelling together one Saturday on their way to the places where they were to preach on the following day? Just as they were parting Mr. Powell said to Mr. Harris, 'Good-bye, my friend; I hope we shall have the Master's face to-morrow.' 'I hope so,' replied Mr. Harris, 'but if not we must do our best to speak well of Him *behind His back.*'"

"Those preachers visited different parts of the country years ago, far more than they do now," exclaimed Shadrach. "They used to send their 'publications' to preach here on week-nights on their journey, but now we seldom hear them except at Anniversary or some big meetings. There's one comfort, we shall hear some of our very best preachers at the Association this year. It will soon be here—only six weeks before it comes. Ah, it's twenty-five years since our last Association was held here, but I shall never forget it, not if I live to be as old as Methuselah."

"I hope we shan't be able to forget this one," added John; "I'm expecting a good time of it, Shadrach."

"If we *expect* it, John, in right earnest we shall have it," said Shadrach, as he laid aside the tongs for the night and leaned for a moment against the anvil.

In a few seconds the conversation was brought to a close, and the smithy was left to darkness and to silence until the dawn of another day.

CHAPTER XV

The Association

"ONLY six weeks before it comes," said Shadrach when speaking of the Association at the last meeting in the smithy. Since then the friends had been very busy. The days were rapidly lengthening, and the evenings were so short that the smithy was all but deserted by the company who had met there so often during the winter nights.

On a few occasions a friend or two had exchanged words with Shadrach in passing; but with that exception the smithy was for the time being forsaken.

Of course, Shadrach and his cousin John had many conversations on the way to and from the services at "Horeb", especially during the week preceding the Association, when special prayer-meetings were held to ask the Lord's blessing upon the services.

The meetings were conducted on the Sunday by ministers from a distance, and were continued on the following morning, but the Association proper began with a conference, which was held in the chapel in the afternoon, and a public service at night.

On "the second day of the Feast" the meetings were held on "the field", with the exception of the first, which was held in the chapel at seven o'clock before the dew had evaporated from the grass. On that morning the sun shone in a clear, cloudless sky, and poured down his gladdening beams into the hollow among the hills where the little village lay. It was a very beautiful day in spring; life quivered in every leaf, and glistened in every dewdrop; each blade of grass nodded to its fellow, and every flower waved its censer of rich perfume as its morning sacrifice. Everything seemed to burst into an intense and powerful life. The pale green corn started from the soil, the violets and primroses adorned the hedge-rows, the birds sang their songs, and the air was pregnant with the sweetest scents and the most harmonious sounds of gladsome spring.

The village had for some weeks shown signs of preparation for the Association. One or two of the houses had been newly thatched, and every cottage had been whitewashed, so that the whole village on that spring morning appeared as "white as snow in Salmon". There had also been extensive preparations in every household for receiving guests during the meetings. The humblest host had provided a joint of fresh meat for the occasion; there was an additional supply of provisions in the larder, the bake-stone and oven had, on the preceding days, been called into special requisition, the oaken dresser, table and chairs had received an extra bees-waxing, while the fire-place and hearthstone bore an ornamentation in chalk, specially designed by the busy house-wife.

During Monday a large number of persons had arrived in time for the meetings, but the bulk, saving the ministers and delegates, were from the immediate neighbourhood. It was on the following morning that those from a distance came, arriving in time for the ten o'clock service in the field. Many had started from their homes before dawn in order to be in time for that. They came from all directions; every road, by-lane, and path pouring in its quota of worshippers.

Jenkin and Samson Lloyd were standing at the smithy corner as the stream of people on foot, on horseback and in conveyances of every conceivable shape and description, from a carriage and pair to a donkey cart, came in. "That's a shaky concern; it reminds me of the story of stammering Jim's cart," said Jenkin, as he looked upon an ancient conveyance, whose several parts threatened to dissolve partnership, and which was drawn by a rickety and antiquated horse. I've heard my father say that in the time of 'Rebecca and her children'* there was an order given' that all conveyances should bear the names of their owners, so that when any mischief was done by young farmers they could be identified more easily. Jim omitted to put his name upon his cart, and was summoned before the magistrates for his omission. He was asked by the presiding magistrate why he had neglected to put the name on his conveyance. Jim stuttered, 'Who-o-o-se name shall I put on it?' 'Why yours, of course,' replied the magistrate. 'B-b-b-but it isn't my cart, your worship,' said Jim. 'Who's the owner, then?' asked the magistrate impatiently. 'Ah, th-th-that's the difficulty, Sir,' said Jim. 'The old sh-sh-shafts belong to David Thomas. The wh-wh-wheels belong to Hugh Jones, the old axle b-b-belongs to William Bowen—the t-t-t-tub belongs t-t-to Joshua Morgan—the t-t-tail-board b-b-belongs to Rees Davies, and only the old nag belongs to me. Who-o-o-se name shall I put on, Sir?'"

"Ah, I expect there will be a few sermons at this Association like Jim's cart," said Samson—who, as we have seen, since he had failed to become a local preacher had never lost any opportunity of reflecting upon the ministry generally—"The shafts will belong to Matthew Henry, the wheels to Dr. Lewis, the axle to Dr. Jenkins, the tub to Robert Ellis, the tail-board to Albert Barnes, and only the old nag will belong to the preacher."

Jenkin, who on his part was equally anxious to avail himself of every opportunity of having a joke at Samson's expense; winked at David Lewis, and said, "Ah, Samson, it's a great pity no church has been fortunate enough to find out your talents. They ought to have put you to preach; you were never cut out for a tailor. Your sermons

---

* The "Rebecca Riots" took place about the year 1843, and continued for some time. They resulted from local grievances especially to small farmers in the counties of Cardigan, Carmarthen, and Pembroke by way of exorbitant exaction of turnpike tolls.

would be all your own, I'll venture; *you'd* never borrow another man's cloth, would you?"

David Lewis, who was evidently afraid that the little tailor would, in the blindness of his conceit, take this as a compliment, interjected, "I'm afraid, Samson, you're like the man who was a member of Mr. Joseph Harris's* church at Swansea, and who was always dissatisfied with the ministers who supplied the pulpit in his pastor's absence. On one occasion, when Mr. Harris intimated at the church meeting his intention of being away from home on a certain Sunday, this man, who had no small estimate of himself and of his qualifications for judging the comparative merits of every preacher he heard, got up and said that the ministers who supplied Mr. Harris's pulpit on those occasions were such poor preachers that he felt bound to express his regret that their pastor left his pulpit so often. Mr. Harris whispered to one of the deacons, then got up and said that he sympathized with much that brother So-and-So had said. It must be very trying for a man of his exceptional gifts to listen to poor sermons, they all knew how well qualified their friend was to preach himself if he could only he induced to do so. He therefore proposed that their brother be asked to occupy the pulpit on the particular Sunday in question. The deacon to whom Mr. Harris had whispered got up and seconded the proposal. The complaining brother was very pleased with the compliment, and promised to do his best. The Sunday came, he ascended the pulpit and went through the devotional part of the service very fairly. Then he read his text—'Unto you that fear my name shall the Sun of righteousness arise with healing in his wings.' He read it in a strong voice, then pause—looked confused—cleared his throat—then repeated the words—'Unto you—*you*, my friends—*you*. That fear my name— that *fear*, my friends—h'm. My name—*My* name—h'm—my *name*— dear friends—precious truth—h'm—shall the Sun of righteousness— *Sun*—h'm—Sun of *righteousness,* dear friends—h'm—precious truth, dear friends—h'm. *Arise*—h'm—arise—h'm.—Well, my dear friends, I hope it has risen on you, for it has set on me right enough;' and down he came from the pulpit considerably humbler than when he went up. Never after that did he complain of the ministers who occasionally occupied Mr. Harris's pulpit."

---

* The late Rev. Joseph Harris (Gomer), a distinguished Baptist minister and writer, and the originator of Welsh Periodical Literature.

This was more than Samson could bear. Taking to his crutch he went off in a rage, much to the amusement of David Lewis and Jenkin, who also soon separated for their homes.

Long before ten o'clock every available space was occupied by conveyances, while the road which ran through the village was filled with people who were bent on arriving early in "the field".

The platform, which had all the appearance of a grandstand, was firmly constructed and made to accommodate about fifty ministers and the same number of singers. In front was a neat desk covered with scarlet cloth, and having upon it a Bible and hymn book for the preacher, while above all was a tarpauling covering, securely fastened at the four corners. This stand was erected at the lowest point of a hollow which formed a kind of amphitheatre on the slope of one of the surrounding hills. Above, and on the right and left of this hollow the hills rose majestically toward the sky. Within hearing a torrent rushed down over huge boulders and steep descents from the heights above, and then, finding a smoother course, it murmured on its way down to the valley beneath, where, clear as crystal and sparkling with perennial youth, it became the favourite haunt of the merry trout, and the frequent resort of the cunning angler.

Circumstances conspired to make this Association exceptionally interesting. There had been a Methodist monthly meeting in the district a few days before, at which a very large number of ministers—some from a great distance—were present. A large Eisteddfod, too, had been held about the same time in a town a few miles away in another direction. Thousands of people had been attracted to it. Among the adjudicators of compositions in prose and poetry were two or three of the foremost ministers in Wales. In addition to these there was one minister of note in the neighbourhood seeking a little rest from overwork. Thus some of the leading representatives of each of the three large denominations in Wales were present at the Association. Such is the cordiality which exists between all denominations in the Principality that on those occasions a minister of distinction who chances to be present is always requested to take part in the proceedings irrespective of the particular church to which he belongs. Thus, though this was a Baptist Association, there were among the fifteen or so that preached three congregationalists and two Calvinistic Methodist ministers. This admixture, which was made practicable by the circumstances already referred to, added greatly to the interest and the effect of these Association meetings.

The service began with the singing of the grand old hymn,

> "R wyf yn dechreu teimlo eisoes
> Beraroglau'r gwledydd draw."

There, in Nature's glorious temple, beneath the dome of sky, with the rocky buttresses of the hills on both sides and the mossy earth beneath their feet, over five thousand people lifted up their voices in praise to God. The plaintive tune, with its oft-repeated refrain, sung to the accompaniment of the bounding mountain torrent close by, ascended like incense in eddying circles to the skies. The birds flew from tree to tree and crag to crag in strange surprise, and poured forth an occasional note as if anxious to join in the song, while the heavens above seemed to kindle into a smile of love, and shed their own benediction in sweetest sunshine upon the assembled throng. After the singing of the hymn a chapter was read and a prayer offered, at the close of which another hymn was sung.

The first preacher was the Rev. F. Herber Evans. He stepped forward toward the desk like one ready for his work. There he stood before the vast throng a man in the prime of life, tall, robust, and of fine muscular development. His broad, open, genial face beamed with kindliness, and was in itself a message of "peace on earth, and goodwill toward men." His voice seemed to embrace the whole gamut, and to be capable of almost every variety of expression, now subsiding into a pensive whisper of grief, now swelling into an ecstatic burst of triumph—the climax and anti-climax vying with each other in their exquisite beauty and thrilling effect. His subject was "The Mind of Christ"* (II. Phil. iv. 5), and his treatment of the theme was such as to gain the unbroken attention of the whole audience, and at times to arouse within them the most powerful emotions.

The next preacher was the Rev. F. J. Kilsby Jones, a man every inch, and blessed with twice the number of cubic inches of humanity possessed by ordinary men. His hair bore traces of having been bleached by the heat of life's day, but there was scarcely a sign of his having borne its "burden," for he still stood as stalwart and erect as an ancient Briton, from which race he proudly claims descent. His massive, powerful countenance revealed in a *humanized* form the same

---

* See Appendix, p. 308.

rugged reality and volcanic strength as the everlasting hills and hoary mountains among which he was born and bred. When he spoke his words and thoughts flowed out in torrents, shocking men with the suddenness with which they leaped from point to point, and then charming them with the grandeur of their erratic course. His text was "Away with him, away with him", (John xix. 15), and never did he take a theme more favourable for the manifestation of those characteristics or style which are peculiarly his. The sermon produced a powerful effect, especially the closing part, which consisted of an irresistible appeal to those who despised the Christ.

After the singing of another hymn, Dr. Owen Thomas* stepped forward to the desk to take his text. He presented a striking contrast to the two preachers who had preceded him, being a short man below the average height. His white hair, however, and his expressive classic features were very imposing, and his voice, while by no means powerful, was exceptionally clear and effective, especially when the preacher was fully animated with his theme. His text was, "Why will ye die?" His exposition—always a strong point in Dr. Thomas's sermons—was masterly. At length as the preacher gained in fervour the clear exposition gave way to powerful and ringing appeals, culminating in each case in the question, "Why will ye die?" which was echoed and re-echoed by the surrounding hills. No one who heard that discourse could be surprised at hearing that elsewhere when the Doctor preached the same sermon a man who accidentally passed through a neighbouring wood within hearing of the preacher's voice was so impressed by the powerful repetition of the appeal "Why will ye die?" that he became a changed man from that hour.

At the close of the sermon a short prayer was offered by the preacher; the announcements were made; and after the singing of a final hymn the vast concourse separated.

The afternoon and evening services fully maintained the interest and enthusiasm so characteristic of the morning service, some of the most eminent ministers in the Principality being the preachers, among whom were Dr. William Rees† (Hiraethog), who preached a very

---

* Rev. Owen Thomas, D.D., of Liverpool, Calvinistic Methodist minister, and well-known Welsh author.

† Rev. William Rees, D.D., formerly of Liverpool, now of Chester, Congregational minister, and one of the foremost Welsh poets of the day.

striking and characteristic sermon on Psalm ciii. 20; Dr. Roberts,* of Pontypridd, who gave a masterly discourse on The Miracles, and the Revs. E. Thomas,† of Newport, and Dr. Hugh Jones, President of Llangollen College, who preached powerful sermons from John i. 10-12,‡ and II. Cor. iv. 7,§ respectively. Those speakers, and others whose names are not mentioned here awakened within that vast concourse during the day the best thoughts and holiest aspirations. A detailed record cannot be given here of all the services held and the sermons preached on that day; such may be found in hundreds of memories which thrill with the recollection of them. For many years to come the story of that Association will take no unimportant part among the inspiring reminiscences of glorious services which have been held amid the grand solitudes of the Welsh mountains.

One of the features of such gatherings is that they help to keep alive the memories of similar meetings held in earlier days. This was the case on this occasion.

Hugh Roberts, on the way home from the afternoon service, in company with Shadrach Morgan and John Vaughan, seemed to find unspeakable delight in relating his recollections of other Associations, which during his long life had been held in that field. He said, "Ah, I've heard some grand men in my day preach on that very spot. I recollect when quite a youth hearing Mr. Titus Lewis,¶ of Carmarthen, at an Association, and I remember the sermon now as if I had heard it only yesterday. The subject was 'The betrayal of Our Lord' by Judas. In one part he was speaking of Judas taking the money back to the priests. He said:—'He had been accustomed to steal for many years, but not money like this. He had neither bag nor pocket in which he could keep the price of innocent blood. Ah, behold a lover of money— a *miser*—failing to keep money! He must rid himself of it, and that in haste. Because no one would take it he cast it upon the floor. But where did he go? He went and hanged himself. It was not necessary

---

* Rev. Edward Roberts, D.D., Baptist minister, and a large contributor to Welsh Literature.

† Rev. Evan Thomas, Baptist minister.

‡ See Appendix, p. 351.

§ See Appendix, p. 298.

¶ The late Rev. Titus Lewis, a noted Baptist minister, Carmarthen. He died in 1811.

that anyone should capture him, bind him, and bring him forth to judgment. He did all this himself. He hanged himself, and thus went to his *own place.* Judas, until now, wasn't in his own place. I see him among the disciples, and walking with Jesus from place to place, but he wasn't in his own place... Judas is in his own place now—in his own place in the pages of history, in his own place in the judgment of all succeeding ages. He is known for ever as the betrayer. Remember this, my friends, every one of us shall have his *own* place at last. We shall not rest until we come to that. The end of all will be every man in his own place. We all in our life make our future *our own.'"*

"That was a wonderful sermon," continued Hugh, "and I recollect another which I heard Mr. Williams, of Wern, preach in the same field some years after in an Independent Association. Strangely enough I forget most of what he said, but I well remember one thing. He was speaking about the miser and said:—'The king's officers are out in search of this old offender, but in consequence of the numerous aliases which he assumes they find it difficult to take him. They are told he lives in No. 14, *Greedy Street,* but when they enquire if such a character lives there, they are answered in the negative. "But *who* then does live here?" ask the officers. "Oh, *Mr. Pay-his way."* "Well, *where,* then, does Mr. Miser live?" "Mr. Miser? Mr. Miser? Why I have heard speak of him—he lives in this street. Try No.10." They call at No. 10, and ask if Mr. Miser is in? The answer is—"No such person resides here." "*Who,* then occupies this house?" "Why, *Mr. Provide-for-his family."* "You know that a man called Miser *does* live somewhere in this street?" ask the officers. "Oh, yes, try No. 7." No. 7 *is* tried, but with the same result, for the occupier's name is *Provide-against-a-rainy-day. Nobody owns the name of Miser.'"*

"Yes, Hugh," exclaimed John; "some grand men have preached in that field, and some glorious services have been held there. I shan't easily forget one sermon I heard Mr. John Jones,* of 'Zion' Chapel, Merthyr, preach at the last Association, which our denomination held here more than twenty-five years ago. He spoke wonderfully on the Deluge. He pictured Noah going on building the ark for one hundred and twenty years, and how when he chanced to pass through the village some would mock him, and others, looking significantly and pointing to their heads, would say, 'Poor man, he's weak there.' Another would

---

* The late Rev. John Jones, Baptist minister.

exclaim, 'Who ever heard of a ship being built upon the top of a mountain?' Mr. Jones then paused, and said—'There was no wonder that people mocked, and yet it was a wonder when we remember that Noah only did what God had commanded him. Noah persisted in building. In the clear eastern sky the people could hear in the valley the echo of the hammer—knock—knock—knock. They laughed; and yet every knock said that the Deluge was coming and hastened the event. One hundred and twenty years thus passed; Noah had finished the ark, and he and his family, as well as the creatures which were to be saved had safely entered. The people laughed more than ever, gathered round the ark, asked him how his family was, and said, "Thou dost only want water now, Noah, to float it. Ha! ha! Ha! ha!" The heavens were as bright as ever; not a cloud as big as a man's hand was to be seen anywhere. "It's a fine day, Noah," said they; "no prospect of a flood yet." Noah gave no reply. He let God Himself give the answer, and that answer came from the frowning sky and the heaving earth—"The same day all the fountains of the great deep were broken up, and the windows of heaven were opened"—and mocking men were silenced in the terrible flood.'

"That was the only time that I heard Mr. John Roberts,* of 'Tabernacle', Merthyr. He was an exceptionally big, broad man, with a very strong and rugged countenance. He had serious shortcomings, but was one of the most eloquent and powerful preachers that ever ascended the Welsh pulpit. His appeals were awful. He often revelled in the fearful and the terrible, in the vicinity of Sinai and the judgment to come. The thunder would roar, the lightning flash, the storm howl, the thunderbolts fly, so that flesh and blood could scarcely stand the effect. At that Association he preached from the words, 'Verily, this was the Son of God.' Taking up the sneer that Jesus was an impostor he said, 'Thou veil of the Temple, thou hast seen many an eminent priest and prophet die, and hast remained whole until this hour, but why rend when that *impostor* dies! Thou ancient earth, thou hast witnessed the death of thy greatest sons, yet thy huge foundations have stood as firm as ever, but why shake and tremble like an aspen leaf when that impostor dies! Ye dead of Jerusalem, many of the mighty, yea, some of the mightiest the world ever saw, have passed away and joined you since you have slept there, but why move and rise when

---

* The late Rev. John Roberts, Baptist minister.

that impostor breathes his last! Ye adamantine rocks of Judea, you have seen patriarchs and prophets, priests and psalmists draw in their feet to die, and have stood unmoved, but why rend when that impostor dies on yonder tree! Thou great sun, the king of day, thou hast seen the mightiest in song, in learning, and in power—poets, philosophers, and kings—thou hast seen Homer, Socrates, and Alexander the Great draw their last breath beneath the cold hands of the King of Terrors, and thou didst not put on mourning, but why dress in black, why draw the veil of mourning over that bright face of thine when that impostor dies between two malefactors on yonder cross?'"

"Ah, we've had glorious preachers," said Shadrach, "and there are as good to-day as ever, I think."

"Then you don't agree with the great Ebenezer Richard," said Hugh. "He once said that the Lord in the last century had kindled about half a dozen torches that lit up all the Principality, but he was afraid that they had given way to candles twenty-four in the pound."

"Well, of course, *they* were wonderful men," replied Shadrach, "and I'm not surprised that anyone should doubt that God would send the like of them again. They were bright lights, and they could be seen more easily then, because the darkness was greater, but there are bright lights in Wales still, and, judging from to-day, God isn't going to allow them to come down to small candles yet."

The village being now reached, the friends parted.

CHAPTER XVI

The Ministerial Chat

Gladly do ministers avail themselves of the opportunities afforded by such meetings for social intercourse. On this occasion a goodly number met in David Lewis's parlour for a chat and a homely cup of tea. The conversation first turned upon the services of the day, then upon the preachers of other days, especially the three great princes of the Welsh pulpit in the early part of this century—Christmas Evans, John Elias, and Mr Williams, of Wern.

"I was delighted to see old Mr. Robert Jones, of Llanllyfni, on the 'stage' to-day," said one of the older ministers. "He preached a very powerful sermon in that field twenty-five years ago on the text, 'The Lord hath anointed me to preach good tidings unto the meek,' and taking those words as prophetic of Christ, he said, 'The Lord of heaven had only one Son, and He anointed Him to be a preacher. Young men in the ministry think very highly of your calling.'—The effect was thrilling."

"He is a sturdy old Puritan," said another with a smile. "He can hit hard, but the honesty of his intention, the purity of his life, and his kindness of disposition secure to him the goodwill of all lovers of truth. Lecturing on one occasion on the Church of England in Wales, he created great amusement by stating that he had no idea what a canon was. 'But,' said he, 'there's a good opportunity of knowing to-night,' and addressing a clergyman present asked, 'Will you kindly tell us what a canon is?' The clergyman shook his head. 'O,' said Mr. Jones, 'M—— does not know.' He addressed the same question to another clergyman present. He did not reply. 'Then,' said Mr. Jones, 'there are three of us here who cannot say what a canon is; the probability is, my dear friends, that no one can tell. But,' said he further, 'I know something of it, too; there are four of these gentlemen at Bangor, each of them receives £350 for three months' service, and were he to retire to bed for the other nine months no one would miss him.'"

"He is a gem in the rough and has worn well," said another old minister. "When he was a young man he was friendly with the great Christmas Evans. The first time I remember him was preaching a sermon before that grand old dreamer and one-eyed seraph. Ah, that's nearly fifty years ago. Robert Jones was then a promising young man, and Christmas Evans was in the height of his popularity, drawing thousands after him wherever he went. Christmas preached wonderfully at that morning service, his subject being 'Satan walking in dry places.'* The same evening he preached a striking sermon from the words, 'Behold I stand at the door and knock.'† Those who had often heard him said that he never preached more powerfully than on that occasion. The thousands present were fairly carried away by the rich imagination and fervid eloquence of the greatest preacher that God has ever given to Wales."

"I've read most of the 'Lives' of Christmas Evans,‡ but I forget where he began preaching just now," said one of the young ministers.

---

* See Appendix, p. 342.   † See Appendix, p. 345.

‡ The leading "Lives" of Christmas Evans are those written by the Rev.

"In connection with the Baptist church at Aberduar," replied the speaker; "the minister who baptized him was a remarkable man, and came from a well-known family which has produced a succession of exceptional men. I refer, of course, to Mr. Timothy Thomas. He was a wealthy man, and lived on one of the best farms in the vale of Teivy. He would often go on horse-back on Sunday mornings a distance of forty miles to preach, and return to his home the same evening. He was exceptionally tall and powerful, and was distinguished for his energy, wit, and tact. The anecdotes told about him are very numerous. On one Sunday he was preaching in the neighbourhood of Llandilo. The morning service was a baptismal one, and, of course, was conducted in the open air. It was a very beautiful summer day, and many hundreds of people had assembled. At the close of the service Mr. Thomas was told that owing to the crowd the clergyman had been unable to pass on his way to the church, and that he had been present during most of the service. He immediately said—'I understand that the esteemed clergyman of the parish has been present with us during our service, we will return the compliment and go to church with him.' The church and even the graveyard were crowded. The clergyman made no mention of the annoyance, but only expressed his high appreciation of Mr. Thomas's catholicity.

"This was the illustrious man who, in the first place, discovered and turned into the right channel the exceptional gifts of his still more illustrious disciple. Had Mr. Timothy Thomas done nothing more he would have accomplished something well worth living for in befriending and imparting an inspiration to the greatest giant of the Welsh pulpit, while as yet his grand soul had not developed its resources or revealed its strength.—Ah, we shall never have the like of Christmas Evans again."

"No, it's not very likely that we shall," added another minister. "He was a man specially raised by God for a great work, and so were Mr. Williams, of Wern, and John Elias. We have never had a trio like them; God doesn't send such men in every age; He is not so lavish as all that in sending great souls. Speaking of Mr. Williams, of Wern, I once heard

---

R. Ellis (Cynddelw), in Welsh, and by the Revs. D. R. Stephens, D. M. Evans, and Paxton Hood, in English. These, especially the two last-mentioned, include about all that can be told about that great man, whose name occupies the foremost place among those of the leading preachers of Wales.

Mr. Kilsby Jones, who is well qualified to judge, say that among other high qualities for which that great man was distinguished as a preacher, was the quickness with which he detected the analogies existing between *human* and *spiritual* operations. If there was one thing more than another in which he excelled as a preacher it was in the *novelty* and *pertinence* of his illustrations. Never, perhaps, since the days of the Great Teacher did any preacher lay the objects of Nature and the pursuits of men under greater contributions for the exposition and enforcement of religious truth. To simplify a subject was his great aim, and hence the rejection of mere *flowers,* and the employment of only *expository* images. His mind was of too masculine a cast, and too solemnly *pledged* to usefulness in all pulpit engagements, to admit of his dallying with the mere ornaments of oratory. When he said that one of the secrets of preaching from the *human* standpoint was to play skilfully on the great harp of Nature, he gave expression to one of his leading characteristics as a preacher; for instance, when speaking once from the text, 'Despise not the day of small things,' he said, 'The Wye and the Severn when they start from their wild moorland mountain home for the Bristol Channel are thankful for the aid of the *tears of rushes.'* Often, too, he obtained his figures from the different industries of daily life; for example, when he preached that sermon on Christian character at Bala, then noted for stocking-making, he said, 'How does a man form his character? Just as you Bala women knit stockings—a *stitch at a time.'* His sermon on the text, 'Beginning at Jerusalem' is another illustration of this kind. Sometimes he would condense a sermon into a phrase, for instance, when speaking from the words, 'Vanity of vanities, all is vanity,' he began by saying—'This is *Solomon's farewell sermon to the world.'* On another occasion he said, 'Eternal mid-day is the hour of heaven—its sun never declines; eternal midnight is the hour of hell—its clock will never strike *one!'"*

"John Elias, too, was a very powerful preacher. I remember him very well," said a Methodist minister present. "He had a strong, tall body, and a noble and commanding appearance. His face and eyes beamed with an unearthly earnestness and solemnity, and he had a strong voice, which was fully at his command. Thousands at a distance

---

* The Rev. T. John, of Cilgerran, once spoke of it as having no dial to tell the passing moments, but as consisting only of a pendulum ticking solemnly, *"Ever—for ever; ever—for ever."*

could hear his words distinctly. He gained attention at once, then rivetted it, and roused it into enthusiasm by degrees. He worked one theme after another into a series of climaxes, each one enhancing the interest of the hearer up to the last climax, which generally and fully captivated every heart in his audience. Every attitude, every look and every cadence, were natural as life. People felt the electric effect of his earnest heart to such a degree that they forgot his oratorical power. There was a kind of mesmerism in his oratory which put his audience *en rapport* with him. It seemed as if some invisible, subtle spirit, which no one could define or explain, went forth with his words, that made them to possess a peculiar charm and power, which they had not when uttered by ordinary preachers. I heard him preach once at Bala Association from the words:—'Shall the prey be taken from the mighty?' &c. He looked with scrutinizing gaze right into the heart of the vast congregation, and asked if there was anyone present who could answer the question. The vast throng stood breathless. Then he turned to his brethren in the ministry who sat around him, and asked if one of them could give an emphatic reply to the audience—their *life* depended upon the answer. There followed a profound silence. Then reaching out his hand and pointing with his finger toward the heavens, he said, 'Oh, heaven, what hast thou to say to us—hast thou hope? No one here on earth can answer the question. Gabriel, thou mighty archangel and messenger of the Most High, thou who seest Him face to face and dwellest in the ineffable brightness of His presence. Canst thou give a reply to the anxious throng?' The silence during these pauses was almost unbearable. At length the preacher exclaimed: 'There is only one more that we can ask; we will pass by Gabriel, and go to Gabriel's God, and say, "O Lord, who art our only hope, wilt Thou in mercy answer Thine own question? Shall the prey be taken from the mighty, or the lawful captive delivered?"' The preacher paused, looking into the heavens; then, as if catching the Divine answer from the skies exclaimed with the full compass of his voice—a voice like that of an archangel— *'Even the captives of the mighty shall be taken away, and the prey of the terrible shall be delivered: for I will contend with him that contendeth with thee, and I will save thy children.'* The vast multitude who had all but fainted in the fearful suspense that he created, now broke forth into torrents of praise, so that Elias was silenced. He sat down to let the people rejoice over their escape, like the Israelites of old on the banks of the Red Sea.

"On another occasion he went to Rhuddlan to preach in the open air on Sunday during which a fair was held there to sell and buy articles used in the time of harvest. Scythes, sickles, &c., were sold there on that day. Crowds of ungodly people were present. Mr. Elias ascended some steps near a public-house as a messenger of God to denounce the desecration of His day. His prayer arrested at the commencement the attention of all present. He acknowledged with trembling voice and with floods of tears how the people in the fair were bringing God's wrath upon their heads by violating His holy day. The contagion of serious apprehension of danger spread through the throngs in the fair. They hid their sickles and scythes as if the Judge of the world had come to call them to account for their rebellion against Him. Mirth and music were hushed under the power of the dread which ruled all hearts. At the conclusion of his discourse the people quietly but quickly wended their way toward home, glad that a storm of fire and brimstone had not consumed them. One person, in going home, imagined that one of his arms holding a sickle had been paralyzed. He could not venture to put it on the other arm lest that one should be paralyzed, too. He therefore threw it away. That effort on the part of John Elias put an end to that harvest fair on Sunday from that day to this, nearly eighty years ago."

"That must have been a wonderful meeting at Anglesea," interjected a young man who had been listening eagerly to the others. "I heard Mr. Parry, of Conway, once speak about it. It was a meeting of the Bible Society. The Marquis of Anglesea was invited to preside. He immediately consented, promising a liberal subscription. His Lordship had recently received numerous titles and honours in recognition of his brilliant services at the ever-memorable battle of Waterloo. His statue had just been erected on the summit of Craig y Ddinas on the banks of the Menai, in Anglesea. The meeting was crowded, and all classes of society were represented. The noble Marquis arrived punctually, and delivered a short and pithy speech. At length John Elias was called. He began by reviewing the history of Wales before the Bible was given until then. He then proceeded to speak of the moral condition of the country at that time as being in a state of war between light and darkness, Christ and Belial. He said that the two armies were approaching each other with great speed, that the intervening space was becoming daily narrower, that the climax was at hand, and that the victory must finally be on the side of truth. The happiness of the world depended upon the issue of this stupendous conflict. The plan of the battle and the final issue had been illustrated of late on the field of Waterloo. The vast audience were electrified by this sudden turn. All the great people forgot their prejudices against the Nonconformist minister as he went on to describe the recent conflict in Waterloo, and showed how the fate of nations, the peace of the world, the progress of commerce, the success of trade, the growth of knowledge and the advancement of the Gospel turned on that important hour. There the hand of Providence had been plainly seen. Their officers had been gifted with the wisdom and power necessary for the stupendous task—'The Lord is a man of war, the Lord is His name.' Then describing the gallant officer going forth into the front at that moment when the scale was about to turn for ever, he repeated the description of the war-horse in the Book of Job, and applied it to the steed upon which the noble Marquis rushed into the thick of the fight, and amid the smoke and din of battle led his men to victory. Gathering strength the speaker rose from height to height of oratory, and exclaimed, 'Methinks I hear the shout of victory before it was won. Yes, but victory at the cost of losing the life of one of the choicest sons of the nation. No, not the life, only one limb. Now death comes forward and hurls a ball which severs the arm of the gallant soldier, but what of that? Providence steps in at once, and exclaims, "Thus far shalt thou go and no further. Touch not his life. Do not go a step nearer his life than his arm. I need his services yet as an officer in a far nobler conflict than this. I shall require him to occupy the chair in the Bible Society meeting at Anglesea. I want him to lead an army that shall carry the Word of Life to every country, and tongue, and people, and nation over the face of the whole earth."' Then the preacher in a mighty but pathetic voice shouted, 'What see we now? *The enemy is bound, but the Word of God is not bound.*' The whole audience had by this time lost all control. The Welsh hearers were thrilled by the oratory, and the English overcome by the mystery of the influence and the pathos of that voice. The noble chairman made a sign to a friend near who understood Welsh, and asked for the secret of that extraordinary sensation, to which he replied, 'It was an allusion to yourself, my Lord, and the accident at Waterloo, where by the interposition of Providence you were spared to preside over this meeting.' The noble Marquis, who had stood the terrors of war without quivering, wept like a child. There was not enough force in all the cannons of Waterloo to make him betray the softer feelings of his nature, but this touching allusion vanquished him."

"Have you ever heard the story about an old Methodist minister baptizing an infant?" asked a mischievous Baptist minister, who had been taking a kindly interest in the preparations for tea which had been going on. "He took the babe in his arms very affectionately, and addressed in a paternal fashion a few words of advice to the young parents—'See that you train up the child in the way that he should go, that you surround him with the best influences, and that you give him a good example. If you do so who knows but that he may become a Christmas Evans or John Elias! What is the name of the child?' '*Jane,* Sir,' replied the mother."

This anecdote put an end to the conversation, while the hearty laugh it elicited prepared the way for the social cup of tea, which was now ready.

We have had only a glimpse of the services and social meetings in connection with this Association, but that must suffice for the present.

CHAPTER XVII

The Harvest Field

LADSOME spring, so full of song and vigorous energy, had ushered in the summer with its mellower music and maturer life. The young birds that a few months ago twittered in their infancy had now learnt the song of life, and carolled it forth in all the fullness of its melody, and the green blades that then peeped above the ground modestly asking for a place in the world of life and beauty had now developed into the ripe grass, or the tall stalk bearing upon its head its crown of golden grain.

At this season the quiet and peaceful villagers obeyed the friendly summons of the neighbouring farmers to the harvest-field. Shadrach's smithy was unceremoniously closed, and John Vaughan and his apprentices quitted the workshop for the more inspiring activities of the harvest season. The village was deserted save by the aged, who had done with harvesting, and had laid down the scythe and the sickle for ever. They had remained at home to see that the children did not carry away the houses while the bread-winners were in the fields.

On this particular day Shadrach Morgan, John Vaughan, their wives, Jenkin, and other villagers started early in order to reach a field three miles distant, where the corn of a friend of theirs was ripe for the sickle. They had promised him a few days in harvest, and he had sent to them the preceding week urging upon them to give him that day without fail. They arrived early in the field ere the freshening breeze and the morning sun had lifted the white mist which during the night had enveloped the sleepy hill close by, and which still fluttered in tatters on its flanks and crest, and before the glittering dewdrops, sown broadcast in the harvest-field when the stars were out, had been wooed and snatched away by the million sunbeams that came in bright battalions from the source of day. It was a spot which had a peculiar charm for a typical Welshman. At the foot of the sloping field in which they toiled, and sheltered by the projecting shoulder of the opposite hill, is an ancient sanctuary, which was built in that lonely dale in the times of severe persecution, but which since then had undergone several enlargements. It is so secluded a spot, so much out of the world, that it is just the place where man would find it easy either in times of deep sorrow or exultant joy to worship God. The old chapel is situated on a narrow slip of ground between the two hills, the one, upon the slopes of which they harvested, being little more than a hillock, the other being of considerable height and steep withal. Around the chapel is a graveyard adorned by a stately yew-tree, which overshadows many a resting-place, and skirting the graveyard is a tiny brook, which has just emerged from the bosom of the earth, and which has already learnt to babble musically through the narrow and winding glen on its way to the stately Towy. There are no human sounds heard there save the occasional voice of the herdsman or shepherd, the annual din of harvesters in the fields close by, the music which at service-time floats upon the breeze from the little chapel under the hill, and the numerous voices of the worshippers on the way to and from the lonely sanctuary. Those sounds are only occasionally heard. At other times that brook sings its song to the varied accompaniment of the whistling breeze or the sighing wind, the bleating of a wandering sheep on the hillside or the lowing of the cattle that browse on the neighbouring slopes, the song of the lark as it pours forth its thrilling carol to returning or departing day, or the still sweeter and fuller music of the nightingale who sings her lullaby over her native glen, while for a few brief hours it lies asleep in the dark mantle of the night.

It was natural that the conversation that morning between Shadrach and John while they were waiting for the dew to evaporate from the grass should derive its character from the associations of the harvest-field and of the little chapel at the foot.

"I heard Mr. R. Thomas, of Bala, preach once," said Shadrach, "from the words, 'As the earth bringeth forth her bud, and as the garden causeth the things that are sown in it to spring forth, so the Lord God will cause righteousness and praise to spring forth before all the nations.' He referred to the certainty of the growth in each case, and if man could not prevent the growth of the kingdom of Nature how could he expect to prevail in reference to the spiritual kingdom? He said that rather than oppose the Gospel, which is the work of God's mind, infidels should first try their hands on the work of God's fingers. He imagined a number of infidels assembling in the Vale of Towy in the month of May, and doing their utmost to prevent the growth of the grass; *the grass would grow* notwithstanding their efforts, the sun would shine manifesting God, and the clouds would drop rain, every drop saying in effect to unbelieving man, *'Do not deny my Father.'*"

"I recollect Hugh Roberts once repeating to me," said John, "what Mr. Evans, of Llwynffortun, said in this chapel many years ago. He was speaking about those who doubted whether Christians would ever attain unto perfection, and pointing to this very field in which the green corn was just appearing above the ground, he said:—'As well might you entertain doubts as to whether that field of wheat will ever become fit for the sickle. I know that it will have to encounter bleak winter, with its nipping frosts, its howling tempests, and deluging rains. I know that the unfriendly east wind will blow harshly over it, but despite all this I dare promise there will be a glorious crop. For did I not hear the earth, the sun, and the clouds enter into a solemn league and covenant that they would take charge of it until it was fit for the reaper? "I will nestle it in my bosom," said the earth; "and I," said the mist-cloud, "will spread a counterpane of white driven snow over it to keep it warm;" "and I," said the sun, when the balmy spring shall set in, will visit it with my fructifying beams;" "and we," said the clouds, "will water it with showers;" and thus, through the joint agencies of earth, sun, and shower, that field of wheat, which has now only just sprouted, shall become a waving, golden-eared crop, gladdening the heart of the hard-working husbandman. Equally sure is it, my precious souls, that the Christians will be made ripe for heaven; for heard I not "all things" on earth solemnly engage "to work together for their good?" and heard I not "the Keeper of Israel, who neither slumbereth nor sleepeth," swear by His unchangeableness, "I will never leave them, I will never forsake them?" and heard I not the Sun of Righteousness say, "I will visit them with my beams?" and heard I not the Holy Spirit promise, "I will be to them as the early and latter rain," and "as the dew?" and thus, through the united influences of earth and heaven, Christians shall be made "white unto harvest," and shall be gathered in amidst the triumphant shoutings of gladsome reapers.'"

Soon the harvesters entered heartily upon their work. As the day advanced the sun beat down with concentrated heat upon them, and scarcely a breeze passed into the narrow glen, yet they seldom paused save when they withdrew for refreshments. During these intervals John and Shadrach resumed the talk about the preachers they had heard in the chapel at the foot of the hill.

"Many a time, John, have we heard old Mr. David Evans preach there,"* said Shadrach. "Ah, he was one of the wittiest men that ever lived. He made people laugh and cry the same minute. That was an extraordinary sermon of his on Jonah, wasn't it?"

"Yes," said John, "and that on The Deluge,† when he talked about the different creatures going to the ark."

The two old friends continued cross-questioning each other:—"Do you remember Mr. Ambrose, of Portmadoc, preaching that wonderful sermon about The Women standing by the Cross,‡ or 'Mathetes' on The Dead Flies, or Dr. Ellis Evans on the Man of Macedonia?"

"Ah, John," said Shadrach, "there's a danger of becoming too familiar with sacred things. I shall never forget a story I heard Mr. Benjamin Thomas, the Methodist minister, give about a blacksmith's dog. He said that the dog used to spend most of his time in the smithy, and that he got used to the fire. Other dogs came, and the moment the sparks flew they ran away in terror, but the smith's dog would sleep in the midst of all undisturbed. He would scarcely leave the smithy, but used to stay in it all night. One night the smithy caught fire, and the dog lost his life in the conflagration. 'How many of you hearers,' asked the preacher, 'have got too familiar with the warnings of the Gospel? Many others have taken warning, but you sleep amid the sparks.'"

The sun was drawing near its setting. Its slanting rays brought into relief the deep furrows on the brow of the opposite hill which looked with lofty disdain upon the humble toilers below. A gentle breeze arose, which, shepherd-like, drove before it a flock of fleecy clouds.

---

* Rev. David Evans, of Ffynonhenry.
† See Appendix, p. 360.   ‡ See Appendix, p. 339.

Then there was a lull, and the clouds seemed to pause and congregate in the far west round the setting sun. There was a holy calm as the evening drew on and the shadows gathered. The weary harvesters left the field for their evening repast in the homely farm-house. John looked at the towering hill as in the peaceful hush he passed out of the field, and said to Shadrach, "'The mountains shall bring peace to the people.' How true that is! And again, 'The mountains shall depart, and the hills be removed; but my kindness shall not depart from thee, neither shall the covenant of my peace be removed, saith the Lord, that hath mercy on thee.' Ah, there's a great deal of Gospel, Shadrach, written on these old mountains and hills."

What the old friends further said on that and many subsequent evenings must now be left untold. If what has been repeated receive a kindly hearing that will be an encouragement to tell more at some future time.

APPENDATORY

The following selections are appended in order to illustrate more fully than could be done in the preceding pages some of the leading characteristics of the Welsh pulpit.

Characteristics of Welsh Preaching

By the Rev. J. R. KILSBY JONES,
Llanwrtyd Wells.

THE influence of the pulpit in Wales, in telling beneficially upon the masses of the people, originated unquestionably with the founders of Calvinistic Methodism; and properly dates from the time when they laboured, which was the middle of the last century. Most of these excellent and energetic men, "of whom the world was not worthy," were originally attached to the Church of England, at whose altar they ministered for a season, and would probably have continued to serve, had not its secularised spirit and morbid dread of innovation denied them range for their enterprising measures. The few dissenting ministers that were to be found at that time were in general formal and dry, and stood much in need of the fire and zeal of such men as Howell Harris, Daniel Rowland, and other kindred spirits. And they caught to a considerable extent the contagion of their holy and kindling enthusiasm. The bold impetuous style of Whitfield's associates was much more agreeable to the temperament of so excitable a people as the Welsh, than the cold lifeless precision which had hitherto marked the pulpit exercises of the early representatives of the present Baptist and Independent ministers of Wales.

The indifferent morals of the clergy at that period, and the utter

NOTE.—The above essay, which appeared twenty-one years ago in *The Homilist,* has been placed at my disposal with characteristic heartiness by its gifted writer. I accept it gratefully as by far the ablest contribution I have seen on the subject, and as strikingly corroborative of much that is contained in the preceding pages.—D. D.

absence, with lamentably few exceptions, of anything like the Gospel from the pulpits of the Establishment, together with the too prevalently cold and, in certain cases, Laodicean temperature of the ministerial exhibitions of even the Nonconformist pulpit, opened a fine field for the energies of these holy, devoted, and impassioned men. And nobly did they respond to the calls of the times. Boldly did they attack every species of iniquity; and by the blessing of heaven upon their efforts they succeeded, in an incredibly short space of time, in turning the Principality "upside down".

Various circumstances contributed to give them unexampled power and influence. Their holy life enabled them to speak with authority. Their eloquent and burning discourses were seconded by a life and conversation that spake still more eloquently and influentially. Their self-denial and disinterestedness told mightily in their favour, as the almost extravagant expenditure of their physical strength in journeyings and toils, undertaken solely to promote the interests of others, contrasted impressively with the indolence and self-pleasing of those who had given too many convincing proofs that the fleece was to them an object of far more vital importance than the flock. There were not wanting many other equally striking evidences of their noble contempt of ease and of their generous self-oblivion; whilst the very opposition which they encountered, and the spirit in which it was offered, served only to impart a bolder tone to their denunciations of evil, and a more uncompromising character to their representations of truth. They felt the elevation and confidence attendant on a consciousness of being "endued with power from on high", and they boldly advanced against the fortresses of the foe under the full influence of the persuasion that Providence had called them to accomplish a great work, and that accomplish it they must, or honourably perish in the effort. The sacred enthusiasm which they communicated to others returned to themselves, like the stream to the ocean, and they waxed bold at the sound of their own thunders. On a people like their countrymen, though sunk at the time in ignorance and depravity, their preaching could not fail of making an impression. Apart from a higher influence, there was a direct tendency in the very *novelty* of the thing to startle them into thought and awaken them to inquiry. And when once "the truth as it is in Jesus" had taken a saving hold of their minds, there was sure to spring up between the preacher and his audience the strongest attachment. It would have been his fault if it was not moulded to his will and made obedient to his touch. Rival teachers had not yet sprung up, neither had the influence of the pulpit to compete with that of the press. The masses of the people were not then able to read; and if they had been, there was no available provision in their own language to meet the wants they had been made to feel. The pulpit was the only fountain of religious knowledge accessible to them, for they were *hearers* and not readers. And when they were brought to thirst for the waters of life, it is not difficult to imagine what "heed they would take to the things which they heard", and how they would "open their mouths wide for the doctrine, as for the latter rain".

These were some of the causes, if not the principal ones, which under the leadings of providence served to elevate the Welsh dissenting pulpit into a position of authority and influence.

It will not perhaps be found altogether unworthy of inquiry how the successors of the founders of Calvinistic Methodism, and their contemporaries, the ministers of other denominations in Wales, have been enabled to exercise so much power over the people by means of the pulpit. There has been, and there still is, much more preaching in the Principality, according to its size and population, than in any other country in Christendom. In what other country could even a *popular* man attract a crowded congregation at 12 o'clock at noon, and during the busy season of hay or corn harvest? And yet the Welsh are not idle or reckless of their temporal affairs, as any one who has mingled with them can testify—far from it; they are hard-working and industrious: but they *will* make any contrivances to redeem the time, and to *time* their arrangements, so that they may but hear the eloquent and popular preacher. And this is not all;—they attend with almost mechanical constancy on the humbler ministrations of less gifted men.

In endeavouring to account for the ascendant influence of the pulpit in Wales, it will be necessary to correct certain errors which prevail on the subject in the religious world. It is an ungracious task to destroy pleasing illusions, but it becomes an imperative duty when appearances have been falsely or too favourably interpreted. Truth requires that an attempt should be made to assign a just proportion between the contributions of the different causes which have secured for the ministrations of the Welsh preacher so deep an interest and so multitudinous an attendance. It will be found, on even a slight examination of the present circumstances of the inhabitants of the

Principality, that their extreme attachment to preaching does not arise exclusively from the pre-eminence of their religious character. That they are religious there is no question; but to suppose them to be more so than other people professing a pure form of Christianity, is altogether a mistaken, though a charitable notion.

It is not impossible, but on the contrary, highly probable, that there is something in the very temperament of the Celtic family, of which the Welsh are a branch, which pre-disposes them in favour of religion; or if not of religion itself as such, yet in favour of the *poetry* of religion, and of the gorgeous poetical costume in which Scripture has arrayed a multitude of its announcements. The character of their country; may have helped to give a peculiar complexion and excitability to their minds. The crag, the cliff, and the lonely glen—the heath, the lake, and the mountain;—the mist rolling up the hill side, the mournful gust sweeping over its brow, and the thundering brawl of the cataract; would all tend to quicken their imagination into a keen and even feverish susceptibility of impression from the creations of poetry. The rich and varied imagery of the Bible could hardly fail to arrest the attention and appeal to the whole soul of the mercurial Celt.

It is characteristic of the Celtic mind to prefer poetry to science. It has been, with rare exceptions, constitutionally shy of the latter, while it has cultivated the former with passionate fervour and devotion. The Welsh have been, and still continue to be, a poetical rather than a scientific people. And as religion is more nearly allied to poetry than science, it is found, in one sense, to harmonize well with the predispositions of their temperament, though, in another, it encounters of course the same kind of opposition as from any other section of Adam's apostate family.

The interest they take in religion arises also no doubt, in some measure, from the extreme *paucity* of other objects of interest. Occupying a secluded and distant part of the country; slow to adopt all improvements; debarred the advantages of intercourse with their educated, advanced, and still advancing neighbours, the English, through ignorance of their language; moving mostly in the humbler walks of life, where, if ambition in any form existed, there is no scope for its aspirations, and little prospect of realizing its visions entirely dependent for information and culture on the miserably scanty, and, till lately, heathenish, resources of their own language; we need not be surprised that, since *all* men must have some object to interest them, they should all feel that religion with its present advantages and future prospects, is almost everything to them—high enjoyment, as well as perhaps a kind of pastime. About politics they know nothing, and, if possible, care still less. Most of them are engaged in a very small way of business. They know nothing of the racking anxieties of the merchant and the manufacturer. To the joys—such as they are—of sudden and extraordinary prosperity they are equal strangers. The state of the funds does not affect many of them. They have no capital invested in daring speculations. They are not likely to be stunned by the perusal of a letter announcing their bankruptcy and poverty. They have but little at stake in this world. Between them and this earth the ties, save those of kindred and friendship, are few and frail. For their toil and sweat they have little beyond food and raiment. Though industrious and thrifty, they are utterly destitute of an enterprising spirit. They "live, move, and have their being" in a little monotonous contracted world of their own, and the natural result is that all their notions partake of the same limitation. In their own language, copious, expressive, and beautiful as it is, there are no scientific works of any account, nor any indeed of much value that contain miscellaneous useful information. Only a few years* have elapsed since the first Welsh periodical was set on foot; now there are several religious magazines in circulation. If the people were ever so disposed to read, none but religious books could be put into their hands. And the consequence is that the Welsh people (I mean those who do not understand English, for it is to them I refer) are grossly ignorant of almost everything save Theology, of which they certainly know a great deal, and for which they have a great taste. They are intimately acquainted with the Scriptures—can discuss, with considerable ability and skill, even knotty points in divinity; and some few, here and there, venture so far as to dabble a little in metaphysics. Take them from these subjects, and they are remarkably innocent, and very little superior to babes.

It also deserves mention that places of public amusement in Wales are few, and the range of social entertainment very limited. The theatre and the racecourse find little favour in the eyes of the Welsh people. Games and holidays have become well-nigh obsolete. Little remains besides the village and town fairs and the festivities of a wedding. Add to this the favourable circumstance, that, to the best of my

---

* This essay was *written* about 25 years ago.—D. D.

knowledge, there is not in the Welsh language a single infidel publication, either original or translated.

These facts, which have been stated with all possible brevity, are important items in the account to be taken of the *real* causes which have served to present that appearance of extreme religiousness in the people, with which strangers have been struck on visiting the Principality. While they cannot but modify the conclusions which had been previously drawn from that appearance, they will set in a clearer light than anything else could have done, the *kind* of materials upon which the Welsh preacher has to work, as well as the many signal advantages which he has in addressing, on religious subjects, a people who have both inclination and time to hear him, and whose minds are not pre-occupied and poisoned by infidelity. And allowing for a measure of sadness which may well come over the mind of a serious observant man, as he is forced to suspect the motives of numbers who help to swell the congregated throngs that attend the more public religious services, still there is the counterbalancing consolation that they are there—within sound of the truth which has made thousands free, and where the "breath from the four winds of heaven" has been wont to "come and breathe upon the slain".

Such are the present characteristics and circumstances of the Welsh people, and such are the facilities which religious teachers enjoy for influencing their minds and forming their habits. But their intellectual and religious character are on the eve of being considerably modified, if not substantially altered. Already are there indications that their minds are in a transition state. The increasing influence of even the *Welsh* press encroaches on that of the pulpit, and gradually undermines the pre-eminence it once enjoyed as the enlightener of ignorance. Entirely new classes of influences are about being introduced into the Principality. Railroads are to traverse its hitherto comparatively retired vales and glens, while more English capital will soon be devoted to eliciting the wealth of its "everlasting hills". Many a lonely, barren, mountain will be made to teem with population, and the clang of machinery will speedily break on the silence of many a spot of delicious seclusion. The available mineral resources of the country, together with its charming scenery will, it is confidently expected, tempt the wealthy capitalist to make his home among the mountains. The subject of education is also engaging the attention of those who have the best interests of the rising generation at heart. Schools conducted on broad enlightened principles, and under the superintendence of educated pious masters, are about being established through the united efforts and pecuniary aid of the different denominations of Dissenters. In the meanwhile the English language will make rapid progress in the country, as its acquisition will soon come to be regarded as the only open path to wealth, influence and honour.

Its prevalence will sweep away much ignorance and prejudice, as well as numerous existing obstructions to affluent attainments and intellectual pre-eminence. For the Welshman, no longer impeded by the difficulties and disadvantages imposed by his isolated position, and no longer restricted to the stinted provisions of a language, whose literature consists of only romances and fragments of ancient poetry, will enter the field of science or of art on equal grounds with his hitherto more privileged and prosperous neighbour, the Anglo-Saxon.

Even the rapid and imperfect survey which has just been taken of the mental character and social position of the Welsh people, will have enabled the reader to anticipate, in some measure, the kind of preaching that is adapted to their capacity and agreeable to their taste. The extraordinary effects which are produced by a popular Welsh preacher must be attributed to the excitability of the people, very nearly as much as to his rousing oratory. Their feelings are like their own mountain torrents—subject to sudden floods and equally sudden ebbs. I have known instances in which a single sentence has run like wild-fire through a Welsh audience. The late Griffith Hughes, of Whitecross, near Cardiff, often ignited a whole congregation by simply giving out one stanza of a striking hymn. The very appearance of a favourite preacher in the pulpit moves them, and no sooner does he announce his text, than they give unequivocal signs of the presence of a latent heat which he may fan, if he choose, into a crackling flame. Their extreme inflammability renders it very difficult for an impassioned speaker to keep up their attention to the close of a sermon unless he have great self-possession, for if an explosion take place about the middle of the discourse, it brings on a reaction which frequently ends in utter listlessness and inattention. Daniel Rowland, of Langeitho, according to Christmas Evans's account of him, possessed the happy but almost unattainable gift of controlling, as well as of exciting the feelings of an audience. He permitted the tide to rise to a certain height but not to overtop it. The spirit he raised he could allay. He did not allow the feelings to overflow their banks, until he had enlightened the judgment and informed the understanding.

A style of preaching which eschews comparisons and figures, and makes no appeal to the feelings would not, for reasons already stated, be popular in Wales.

The people like reasoning and argument very well, but they are certainly more partial to the striking illustration and pertinent anecdote, and they fully calculate upon being *warmed* by some part of a sermon. A dry essay, or a cold elaborate dissertation, would be sure to act upon them very efficiently as opiates.

It is quite necessary to apprise the reader that in the remarks I am about to offer on the characteristics of Welsh preaching, I have in my eye only the master preachers of the Principality. Now I shall have in view a Baptist, now an Independent, and then a Calvinistic Methodist;— now deceased, and now living, preachers.

So well established is the character of the Welsh pulpit for *Evangelicalism* that it is not deemed necessary to dwell upon it in this paper. Suffice it to say, that its absence would soon entail upon the hapless preacher the dismal task of addressing himself to empty seats and echoing walls.

Self-possession is a striking characteristic of Welsh preaching. Welsh ministers enjoy very favourable opportunities for acquiring this enviable, invaluable power. With the exception of those settled in towns and populous localities (and they are often relieved by strangers—for itinerating is not yet out of fashion) they are not required to preach so often to the same people as their English brethren. A thin and scattered population compels them to be pluralists; and as their chapels lie sufficiently distant from each other to admit of their preaching the same sermon twice on the *same* day, increased confidence is necessarily gained, as a discourse will be delivered the second and third time with greater freedom and boldness than the first.

The acquisition of self-command is further facilitated by frequent engagements at public meetings, of which there is no lack in Wales; and also by the practice of taking preaching tours, when the ministers almost invariably preach the same sermons. They thus become so sure of their ground by going over it so repeatedly, and so accustomed to address large miscellaneous congregations in the open air and elsewhere, that they are not easily disconcerted. In fact it requires a very serious interruption to throw them out of joint.

Perhaps a secret consciousness of superiority to his audience, with the composing persuasion that he has no doubting sceptics to hear him, may have something to do with the look and tone of assurance for which the Welsh preacher is in general distinguished.

It appears that Whitfield was not in "full sail" till he had preached a sermon some thirty times: and I know a Welsh minister now living, whose invariable practice, when he has to preach on a public occasion, is to train himself for the engagement by delivering the sermon over and over again till he is perfect master of it. He preaches it first of all to his own people, and then to several congregations on his way to the place where he has to fulfil his engagements. Like the majority of his brethren in Wales, he travels on horseback, and holds a service wherever he halts for the night, of which due notice is sent to the pastor of the place. This practice, with the usual attributes of his discourses, is the true solution of his wondrous ease, volubility, and power.

The late John Elias made half-a-dozen sermons serve him from Holyhead to Cardiff.* They were elaborated both as to matter and style, and told amazingly upon the people. And no wonder,—for the preacher knew every inch of the path along which he had to travel. Nothing was forgotten, nothing misplaced, nothing mistimed, and nothing damaged, through the speaker's want of self-control. But he was excelled in point of self-possession by the late lamented Ebenezer Morris. This magnificent preacher, of whom, when living, the Calvinistic Methodists were so justly proud and passionately fond, and whose memory they love and venerate, had, among other high endowments for public speaking, a voice of almost matchless volume and melody over which, as well as himself and audience, he exercised perfect mastery. It was only when about reaching a climax, that he would let out the thunderings of his voice, and then the effect was indescribable. But it was only for a moment, for he would instantly check himself and descend, apparently without effort, to tones as calm and subdued as those of a quiet fireside conversation. The object of the periodic swelling note was only to help a sentiment to work its way into the heart. The constant bridling in and restraining of his power when the people were impatient for its clearing the barriers to dash off at full speed riveted their attention whilst it kept them in a state of breathless suspense, which was only partially relieved by another rolling and still grander burst with which he would abruptly close his discourse.

Adaptation is another characteristic of Welsh preaching. The

* The John-o-Groat's and Land's-End of Wales.

generality of the sermons preached bear evident marks of having been composed in view of the real exigencies and capacities of the people for whom they were intended. Speculative views and refined disquisitions are not allowed to pass in lieu of evangelical sentiments and Scriptural statements. Those aspects of truth with which plain people cannot be expected to have much sympathy, are seldom, if ever, presented before an audience. Points of established and prevalent belief are wisely left undisturbed. Matters unto which ordinary minds "cannot attain" are not brought down from their elevation. The illustrations employed are drawn from incidents, scenes, and occupations, with which the parties for whose instruction they were borrowed are supposed to be intimately acquainted.

The *style* is simple and homely;—for the preacher feels no pleasure and finds no interest in employing words which the people do not understand. The appearance and manner of the Welsh preacher are admirably adapted to secure for him a candid hearing. He stands before his audience more as a friend than an official. The people feel that he is *of* them, and with them, and that their interests are one and undivided. In general he is a plainly-dressed and plain-spoken man. To the *refined* he *may* appear unceremonious and blunt, if not even deficient in courtesy but he is never effeminate, finical, or affected. He may be rough but he is ever manly. His is not the strutting gait and mincing enunciation; and he is about the last man in the world to be concerned about the appearance of his drapery when his subject has warmed him into eloquence. He would as soon think of playing with a white handkerchief in the *pulpit* or of applying it in dandy-fashion to a puckered mouth after pronouncing a few icy sentences, in a strain *meant* to be very energetic, as the captain of a vessel would of trimming his whiskers or of adjusting his shirt-collar amidst the perils of shipwreck.

Another very prominent feature in Welsh preaching is the prevalence of the *illustrative style*. But here the preacher must battle, as best he can, with the difficulties arising from the limited range of objects from which his illustrations are to be drawn. The people that flock to hear him know nothing of the arts and sciences. Sealed to them are the languages containing the wealth of history. The pages of nature's book are opened before them, and she has issued some of her works in Wales in so large a type that "the reader may run and read them." Rocks and mountains are characters she has frequently employed. And it is nature with her varied appearances, together with the ordinary pursuits and avocations of life, that the preacher must lay under contribution, if he would expound "the things which are not seen by the things which are seen". While the outlines and features of the external world remain substantially the same, the uses to be made of them in illustration of truth, are as new and varied as the minds by which they are contemplated. It is the province of genius to apply old materials to new purposes. To what may seem, to the less reflective, "old and ready to perish," the creative mind can apply its plastic touch, so that out of it should arise, as if by magic, a well defined and beauteous structure. Of how many things is the rock an emblem! But it is not to be supposed that its symbolical power is yet exhausted. It is more reasonable to believe in the limitation of the suggestive power of the most observant mind, than to conclude that nature's expository resources have been all employed. And the Welsh preacher may possibly find more cause for lamentation in the absence of a fixed habit of observing things around him, and of tracing resemblances between natural and spiritual objects, than in the circumscribed territory to which he must confine his explanatory references.

It is unnecessary, after what has been said about the predispositions of the Welsh people, to state the reasons why their ministers have adapted the illustrative style of preaching. Let it not, however, be supposed that they cultivate the imagination to the neglect of their other faculties, or that they allow themselves to be carried away by its witchery into the regions of improbability and fiction. No such thing. With rare exceptions the imagination is employed as the handmaid of the reason and judgment, and restricted pretty closely to its own legitimate and proper province, which is to *illustrate.* What logic is *exclusively* to a cold unimpassioned mathematical mind, *that* is imagination *subordinately* to the Welsh preacher.

The unpoetical reasoner arrives at conclusions by means of a series of *therefores,* as stepping-stones; the man of imagination establishes his points by an apt illustration. Concatenated argumentation will frequently weary the attention, or escape the memory, of thousands to whose minds a pertinent comparison will cling through life. To a public speaker imagination is of incalculable service. It certainly has a great deal to do with the complexion and costume of the pulpit exhibitions of the Principality. It is a constant attendant upon the mental excursions and public exercises of the more popular Welsh preachers. No sooner is a principle evolved, a position chosen, or a startling statement made, than they draw on their imagination for the requisite imagery for exposition, confirmation, or embellishment. What is recondite is brought to the surface—what is ideal is arrested and not allowed to escape till invested with form; and what has been used by the commonalty of minds till worn out to a threadbare commonplace, is clothed afresh with novelty and beauty.

Great *aptness* is also displayed in interpreting and turning to practical account the facts and historical parts of Scripture. The narratives and facts of the Bible are treated as the exponents of principles and the expositors of human nature. The doctrinal part of the Sacred Volume is illustrated by means of its recorded incidents. Circumstances and events which had suggested no useful lessons to less reflective minds are so expounded that they become "profitable for doctrine, for reproof, for correction, for instruction in righteousness." The people are made to see *how* the "things which were written aforetime were written for their learning."

If there was one thing, more than another, in which the late Williams, of Wern, excelled as a preacher, it was in the *novelty* and *pertinence* of his illustrations. Never, perhaps, since the days of the Great Teacher, did any preacher lay the objects of nature and the pursuits of men under greater contributions for the exposition and enforcement of religious truth. All things seemed to whisper something to him which had never been disclosed before, and to point out for his occupation new and highly advantageous points of observation. Some men appear to examine the same objects always from the same spots, and hence the sameness of their reflections; but Williams seemed to look at everything from unfrequented points that commanded fresher and bolder views. Every object in nature, every human avocation, every incident in life, seemed to have fastened on it some new and striking truth. To simplify, rather than embellish, a subject was his great aim, and hence the rejection of mere flowers, and the employment of only *expository* images. His mind was of too masculine a cast, and too solemnly *pledged* to usefulness in all pulpit engagements, to admit of his dallying with the mere ornaments of oratory. *His* use of comparisons was sufficient to convince anyone that he attached no value whatever to them, except so far as they subserved the explanation or application of truth. Unlike certain showy but weak-minded preachers, who are so enamoured of tinsel and glare that they often employ even religious truths only as pegs on which to suspend a *fine* simile; he, on the contrary, with almost instinctive severity of taste, allotted to figures only a subordinate department in expounding the great verities of the Bible.

It would be worse than superfluous, formally to advocate a style of preaching adopted by him of whom it is said—"Never man spake like this man." Truth never yet suffered any damage by being elucidated by means of simple and even *homely* comparisons; and the sooner the illustrative style of preaching supersedes that affected, would-be, philosophical mode which too much obtains in certain quarters, the better for the interests of religion and the great purposes of the Christian ministry. "The common people" at any rate will always feel that William Dawson and men of his stamp come much nearer to the human breast with its tide of tumultuous passions, than the poor pitiable drivellers who more than insinuate that human nature has never yet been properly understood and treated, and who attempt to make up the deficiency by experimenting upon it with semi-political, semi-heathenish, unctionless, essays and dissertations.

Passion is another feature in Welsh preaching. This capital quality, so necessary to effective speaking, is quite natural to a genuine Celt. An unimpassioned Welshman is a singular phenomenon; and when *he* is cold, as well might a spark be elicited from an icicle. He will not stop short of the freezing point. The usually ignitable temperament of the Cambrian preacher is of signal service to him in addressing an audience. It gives an air of unmistakable earnestness and of reality to all he says. Words of import so momentous that an angel might well tremble as he uttered them, are not pronounced listlessly and allowed to drop like snow from his lips. It makes his "thoughts breathe and his words burn". It is this which produces, and renders appropriate, the bold burst—the abrupt apostrophe—the glowing description—the passionate declamation—the burning invective—the rousing appeal and the impetuous thundering charge. It was his tremendous passion, in conjunction with a peerless imagination, that gave Christmas Evans so much power over a congregation. To see his huge frame quivering with emotion, and to watch the lightning flash of his eye—that lustrous black eye of which Robert Hall said it would do to lead an army through a wilderness—and to listen to the wild tones of his shrill voice as he mastered the difficult *prosopopœia,* was to feel completely abandoned to the riotous enthusiasm of the moment. Abstractions, dry as the bones which Ezekiel saw of old in the valley, he could clothe with sinews, flesh, and skin, and breathing life into them, make them stand on their feet. Of scenes enacted centuries ago in the glens and on the hills of Judea, his fire and fancy enabled him to furnish so vivid a representation that all sense of the distance both of time and place was entirely lost; and though he was frequently guilty of the grossest anachronisms, yet so admirably sustained were the parts assigned to the different characters, and so lifelike and natural were the sentiments put into their mouths that the discrepancy, however glaring, did not damage the effect. So genuine was the fire that burned within him, and so completely did he throw the whole of his impassioned soul into his descriptions, that even the fastidious critic was "taken captive", and compelled to become his admirer.

The situation in which Welsh preachers often address their audience must be inspiring to men of their mercurial constitution.

The yearly associations in Wales are held in the open air. I have a very distinct recollection of being present some years ago at one of them, which was held that summer at Gwernogle—a romantic wooded glen situated to the North of Caermarthen. An unusually large number of ministers was present, and the congregation consisted of several thousands. A covered platform had been erected in a field not far from the chapel for the accommodation of the ministers, from which the different speakers addressed the assembled multitude. There was a gradual ascent in the field which made it an admirable rising gallery. Into it opened several winding glens; and the sides of the hills which crowded on us in every direction were clothed with luxuriant trees in full foliage. It was a beautiful day in June. The sun shone brightly— the winds were asleep, and nothing broke on the silence of the spot save the voice of the preacher as it echoed in the wood, and the subdued murmurs of the people as they expressed their approbation of what he advanced.

The singing also aided the general impression. It commenced on the platform, whence, as simultaneous starting was out of the question, it rolled wavelike over the congregation, on whose outskirts in the distance the strains had scarcely died away ere they were resumed by the parties who raised the tune, the custom being to repeat the same stanza several times over. The man that could have preached to such an assembly and on such a spot without being roused into passion and fire must have had a soul of ice and a heart of stone.

The practice of giving audible expression to their approval, which prevails among the Welsh people, and which, with the exception of being much less noisy, answers to that of "cheering" in England, is not without its effects in kindling the mind of a speaker.

The *delivery* of a Welsh sermon is usually marked by great *variety of intonation.* The ear is entertained while the mind is informed. The charms of sound secure a hearing for sense. The attention of an audience is sustained to the close of a discourse without weariness or flagging, as the speaker's tones are constantly varying with the varying aspects of his theme. Welsh ministers need not have any fears that mellifluous and varied sounds will be thrown away upon a people devoted like their countrymen to melody and song. And so sensible are they of the value of a well-trained voice to a public speaker, that they pay particular attention to its improvement. It may be all very well for parties not blessed with this fine instrument to sneer at the effects produced by a judicious use of it in preaching, and flippantly to dismiss the whole thing with a "*vox el præterea nihil:* "but they should bear in mind that Braham if he were to sing to an English audience even in Hebrew, would afford a splendid instance of the influence of "voice", though unaccompanied by anything else. Let the argumentative or metaphysical preacher, who professes generally to esteem but very lightly the usual auxiliaries of effective public speaking, please to remember that his discourses would be none the less welcome to an audience if they were pronounced in tones enlivened by variation and melody. And persons who have neither ear nor taste for music should accustom themselves to speak of its effects as things which they do not properly understand, and upon which therefore it becomes them not to pronounce any decided opinion.

I do not exactly know the date of the recitative style of speaking prevalent in Wales, but it was probably introduced by the founders of Calvinistic Methodism. The *judicious* use of it is confined to the more passionate or pathetic parts of a discourse. When *genuine* it is the speaker's spontaneous and almost involuntary mode of throwing off his views and feelings when greatly interested and warmed by his subject.

The Welsh preacher, in his expository approach to the selected topic of discourse, is in general cool and collected, and speaks in a quiet and somewhat low tone of voice. But even here there is sufficient variety of intonation. The frequent use of interrogatives, with the adoption of the conversational style, adds to the liveliness and cheerfulness of the Welsh accent, saves the tones of the speaker from the disagreeableness and soporiferousness of monotony. As he advances in his sermon and fairly gets into the *"hwyl"*, he nearly exhausts the variations of the gamut. Now there is the shrill startling alarm; and then the deep sepulchral tones of solemnity. Now we have the dash of defiance; the shout of triumph; the dance of joy; and then the tremulous accents of tenderness; the earnest tones of remonstrance and the muttering of the thundering denunciation. Now we have the plaintive melancholy of bereavement's soliloquy—the wail of sorrow and the cry of despair; and then the wild ecstatic notes of the Christian pilgrim, as with a tear in his eye he sings of the dawning of the morn that will set him in heaven's bowers of repose. Now we have the loud voice rending the sky and awakening the echo; and them the "still small voice" and the whisper of confidence. In short there is all the variety both of manner and tone that disinterested love or friendship would employ in private, in attempting to dissuade a person from pursuing a suicidal course, or to persuade him to look after things in harmony with the tremendous destiny of an immortal creature.

All these transitions are effected with perfect ease and without the slightest semblance of clap-trap or affectation. All is natural. The variations in the speaker's tones are sudden and unexpected, and occasioned solely by his own emotions at the moment of utterance. Ample range is provided for all the capabilities of a voice of the greatest compass and power by the nature of the Welsh language, of whose beauties the reader, if ever he came in contact with an educated patriotic Cambrian, must have heard *ad nauseam,* and to the exhaustion of his patience. It affords special facilities for speaking in the major key. Its pronunciation requires a disposal of the organs of speech very favourable to the emission of a *volume* of sound. The mouth is more open in general than is required for speaking English. The ascent to the topmost note of the gamut is rendered comparatively easy. The prevalence of consonants, of which a goodly number consists of gutturals, with the great abundance of words of more than one syllable, admits of that waviness of sound which, without a break in the swell, gracefully laves the summit of the scale. The reader may possibly recollect that in singing a very high tune he has experienced much more difficulty in one stanza than another. This was owing to the difference in the *words*—some of them allowing of a more opened mouth in the enunciation than others. Let anyone try to pronounce in an elevated tone such words as *speak, neat, believe, sing, wheel, note,* and a host of others which might be named, and he will

find the sounds become highly nasal and fine-spun. Let anyone witness
the effort which most English speakers are obliged to put forth in order
to make themselves heard in a large place, and compare *that* with the
ease with which a Welshman addresses a numerous assembly in the
open air, and he will be struck with the difference. The fact is that the
English language, owing to the silken fineness with which its vowels
require in general to be pronounced, cannot be spoken easily, fully, and
musically except in the minor key. *There* it is incomparable; but if a
speaker aim at the major key to which it is natural he should resort in
moments of passionate excitement, there is instantly more or less
appearance of straining and high pressure which detracts from the effect
that would have been otherwise produced. Mere noise and loudness of
tone are not of course advocated here; but there are seasons of such
intense irrepressible feeling with a speaker and his congregation (as on
the question of slavery with Mr. Knibb) that they would not only tolerate,
but even hail the use of the thunder's voice—if he could but borrow it
to give additional force to the sentiments announced.

The speaker who can bring *sentiment* and *music* to bear upon an
audience, is in possession of two splendid instruments for influencing
the human mind. Such is the privileged position of a gifted Welsh
minister with a fine voice.

In addition to the acknowledged expressiveness of the Welsh
language and its adequate copiousness for all the purposes of the
highest style of oratory, it has two other features to which a passing
reference must be made. Its extreme *flexibility* admits of great variety
in the style of composition. The verbs, adjectives, and prepositions
can be made to occupy very numerously different positions in the
construction of sentences.

Its mode of denoting the *genitive* case is even simpler than the
construct state of the Hebrew, as a string of words may be linked
together without a preposition, or change of termination. The definite
article "y", or "yr", placed before the final word is the only sign of
possession.

Here is an example—

"Ardderchawgrwydd braich Arglwydd y lluoedd."

(The excellency of the arm of the Lord of hosts).

Here is another—

"Cawr-lais udgorn y cur-wlaw."

(The giant-voice of the trumpet of the pattering rain).

These properties of the language are not without their uses to a public speaker. The one, by providing against sameness in the form of constructed sentences, produces the pleasing effects of novelty; while the other, by dispensing with a number of connecting links, throws the words into one continuous unbroken line, along which a speaker, when impassioned, may dash with the rapidity of lightning.

It remains to notice very briefly the *character* of a Welsh preacher's *application* of his subject, and I shall have done with this desultory and imperfect sketch. The social equality, in general, of ministers and people, is not without its influence in giving to the ministrations of the pulpit a tone of unmincing fidelity and unfaltering boldness. The major part of Welsh ministers are engaged in some kind of business, and consequently not strictly dependent for their support on the contributions of their flock. Let it not, however, be supposed that undue advantage is taken of this circumstance to address an audience in a rude and blustering style. The people are treated with all becoming deference and respect; but the preacher is not guilty of a cowardly or temporising adjustment of his discourses to the complexion of their prejudices and passions. They may be sometimes handled somewhat roughly, but then it is by the hand of generous and well meaning friendship. A drowning man must not complain of the hard grasping of his deliverer. Where there is peril, the person who gives the alarm does not think it necessary to use much ceremony. An apology for roughly shaking a drunken man found sleeping on the sand where the tide is wont to come, would be singularly and almost ludicrously inappropriate. If a neighbour's house were enveloped in flames and the family fast asleep, a man might well be pardoned for crying fire with all his might and main, and for making unauthorised efforts to save life and property.

The *appeals* of a Welsh preacher are in general of the most uncompromising character. They are not frittered away by apologetic disclaimers of "this, that, and the other". They come with the suddenness and disclosing glance of the lightning, and with the terribleness of thunder. Sometimes the preacher holds before his congregation a picture which he has been painting, and while they are wrapt in silent admiration of its fidelity and beauty, there comes to many a conscience the rapier thrust of; "Thou art the man." No one knows where to look for the application, for it is not confined to the close of a discourse. There is nothing to indicate the direction from which the preacher may come, or in what way he will make his attack;

and nothing in the nature of the subject chosen for discussion, or in the manner of illustrating it, that offers security against his onsets. The hearer can never make sure but that he may, by an unexpected and dextrous application of the point in hand, however apparently remote from practical purposes, plunge his "two-edged sword" into his very heart. There is no room for one class in a congregation to indulge in self-gratulation at the expense of another. The miser is smitten in the very act of applauding the preacher's eloquent denunciation of drunkenness. Many a hand ready to seize a stone to cast at the discovered offender is made to hang nerveless by the side. To the malicious joy of the reprobate at witnessing the unmasking of the hypocrite, succeed "shame and confusion of face", on account of his own delineated character. The enemy of religion is made to quail while rejoicing over the fall of "the saints".

It may not be altogether out of place in closing this unpretending paper, to express the persuasion that there is now open to the man who shall combine in himself the requisite qualifications, an untrodden path to usefulness and eminence as a preacher in England. While the "high places" of the field will be wisely left by every modest person in the undisputed possession of Robert Hall, and others of stately endowments;—and while the more retired posts of ministerial service are efficiently occupied by men of less mark and stature, there is a broad midway, not so thronged by distinguished preachers, but that the rightly qualified individual may find sufficient room for striking out a new course. The path, thus but dimly defined, will run in the main through unfrequented ground, while, in several points it will coincide with that so usefully trodden by the celebrated Whitfield. Whoever shall unite in himself *even* the characteristics of *Welsh* preaching, will not be found very meagrely equipped for the duties of the pulpit. The resources of *manner* and *intonation* have not as yet been worked to exhaustion; on the contrary there is an ample residue of latent forces awaiting evocation, and ready to do the bidding of any man who shall be but wise and bold enough to employ them as the auxiliaries of sacred oratory.

The Gospel Treasure

By the Rev. HUGH JONES, D.D.,
President of Llangollen College.

"But we have this treasure in earthen vessels, that the excellency of the power may be of God, and not of us."—II. *Cor.* iv. 7.

E learn from the preceding verses that the Apostle deeply felt the goodness of God in saving him from his unbelief, and in committing to him the ministry of the Gospel. "*Mercy*" is the term by which the Apostle characterises such conduct on the part of God towards him; his sense of his own unworthiness kindles his gratitude, and his gratitude stimulates his activity in the work of God. "Therefore, seeing we have this ministry, as we have obtained *mercy,* we faint not."

His conduct was perfectly disinterested and straightforward: "We have renounced the hidden things of dishonesty, not walking in craftiness, nor handling the word of God deceitfully, but by manifestation of the truth, commending ourselves to every man's conscience in the sight of God" (*v.* 2).

If his ministry was rejected by men the defect was not in the ministry, but in themselves; it only proved their blindness and their being the slaves of Satan: "But if our Gospel be hid, it is hid to them that are lost: in whom the god of this world hath blinded the minds of them which believe not, lest the light of the glorious Gospel of Christ, who is the image of God, should shine unto them" (*v.* 3, 4).

Those, on the other hand, who received the Gospel were enlightened and illumined by the Spirit of God, that they might see the glory of God as revealed in the Person and work of the Redeemer, and feel the saving power of His grace: "For God, who commanded the light to shine out of darkness, hath shined in our hearts, to give the light of the knowledge of the glory of God in the face of Jesus Christ" (*v.* 6). "But we have this treasure in earthen vessels." The light of life was at first deposited in "earthen vessels" belonging to the terrestrial world, and not in the golden vessels of the celestial city. Had it been placed in the shining vessels of the city of God, many of the spectators would have ascribed the brilliancy of the light to the shining quality of the vessels, and not to the supernatural brightness of the Divine light itself. But God ordained that the vessels should be made of clay, that the glory might be ascribed to the light, and not to the vessels in which it was deposited: "that the excellency of the power may be of God and not of us."

    I. THE TREASURE.
    II. THE TREASURY, AND THE REASON ASSIGNED FOR CHOOSING IT.
    III. THE VALUE AND EXCELLENCY OF THE TREASURE ITSELF.

We shall consider:
I. THE TREASURE.
    1. *The Gospel is the Treasure.* We are not to understand by it the soul of man, though that is an invaluable treasure, placed in an earthen vessel; but the Gospel of our Lord and Saviour Jesus Christ, as entrusted to the Apostles. This is evident from the context. The Apostle has been treating of the Gospel under different aspects, and describing it (1) *as excelling the law,* since it is the ministry of justification and of life (II. *Cor.* iii. 6-8); (2) as *the hope of the world,* and the *Gospel, or glad tidings of great joy,* since no other scheme holds out the hope of escape for the guilty (II. *Cor.* iii. 12., iv. 3); (3) and as *the revelation of the glory of God,* in the face of Jesus Christ (II. *Cor.* iv. 6): and then to show his sense of the value and importance of it to mankind, he calls it a "*treasure.*" In the context the words "*hope,*" "*ministry,*" "*gospel,*" "*light of the knowledge of the glory of God,*" and "*treasure*" are synonymous terms, setting forth the different aspects of the scheme of salvation.
    2. *Why the Gospel is called a Treasure.* (a) Because it is *a mine of Divine riches.* The word *thesauros* (*treasure*) is used in the New Testament in a two-fold sense—to denote a *repository* for valuable things, and for *the valuable things themselves.* The wise men from

the East opened their *treasures,* that is their *boxes, chests,* or *trunks,* in which their gifts were kept (*Matt.* ii. 11). The minister of the Gospel, duly instructed for the ministry of the kingdom of heaven, is compared to a householder who bringeth forth out of his *treasure* a variety of things according to the needs and circumstances of his family—so is the minister of the Gospel to bring out of *his treasure*—of his mind and memory, in which stores of religious knowledge and Biblical truth have been laid up—"things new and old" for the instruction and edification of his hearers (*Matt.* xiii. 52).

The word means also *valuable things in themselves.* Moses disregarded the *treasures* of Egypt, for the sake of Christ (*Heb.* xi. 26). The kingdom of heaven is like unto *treasure* hid in a field (*Matt.* xiii. 44). The saints lay up for themselves *treasures* in heaven (*Matt.* vi. 20). And all the *treasures* of Divine wisdom and knowledge are laid up in Christ (*Col.* ii. 3). They are valuable things which, for the most part, are treasured up and carefully guarded and protected by men; and God's valuable things—the riches of Divine grace, the treasures of Divine wealth—are treasured up in the Gospel, in which they are concealed from the wise and prudent, and preserved from being corrupted by men.

The word treasure is used in the text in both these senses. The Gospel is itself the *repository* in which Divine things are accumulated and laid up for future use—a *casket* of Divine jewels—a *storehouse* of spiritual blessings—a *magazine* of Divine wealth—and a *mine* of inexhaustible riches, that will yield support and enjoyment, position and protection to mankind for all time to come. The Gospel is thus in itself a treasure of the highest value, and of unspeakable importance. It is *God's cabinet,* in which God's gems are preserved; the *focus,* in which the rays of Divine light are concentrated; and *the fountain* of the water of life, from which the healing streams issue forth.

(b) The Gospel may be called a treasure *on account of what may be realised by means of it.* The value of things in this world is estimated in proportion to their usefulness; and according to this rule gold is most valuable. Gold may be converted into almost every other earthly blessing—food or raiment, or health, or knowledge, or influence, or position. If we estimate the value of the Gospel—the treasure of our text—according to this rule, we shall find its value to be infinite. It becomes the source of every blessing and enjoyment to the true believer.

II. The Treasury, and the Reason Assigned for Choosing It.—
"Earthen vessels, that the excellency of the power may be of God."

It is probable that Paul was suffering from bodily weakness while writing this epistle, and that there is a reference to his infirmity in the text and context. It is probable also that there is a reference in the expression, "treasure in earthen vessels," to some fact in the annals of history, or to some custom among the ancients. (*a*) The allusion may be to the custom of Eastern nations of putting their money and treasures in earthen vessels and burying them in the earth in times of revolution and war, in order to conceal them from the enemy and preserve them for future use. (*b*) Or to the conduct of Gideon's soldiers, carrying their lighted lamps hidden in earthen vessels when they went out against the Midianites, and when God so marvellously delivered Israel. (*c*) Or to the custom of victorious generals distributing gold and silver on their return from war. On such occasions it was usual to carry in the procession vessels of gold and silver filled with small coin, the conqueror dispensing the money to the spectators on his triumphal march. We have an instance of this in the account of the return of Paulus Æmilius to Rome, after his conquests in Macedonia, when Perseus, the defeated King of Macedonia, with his family, was dragged through the streets of Rome before the chariot of the Roman general, who with a lavish hand distributed pieces of gold and silver to the inhabitants (B.C. about 160).

If the allusion be to such a custom, the meaning seems to be this:—
"We, the apostles, carry the treasure of Christ in the procession of his victorious march through the world; but we bear it not in vessels of gold and silver, like those in which the treasure of earthly conquerors is borne but in vessels of clay; that the excellency of the power may be found to proceed from God and not from us.

It is impossible now to arrive at positive certainty with regard to the allusion; but there is no uncertainty with regard to the treasure spoken of. The treasure is the Gospel, and its design is to enrich mankind.

1. *The Earthen Vessels were the Apostles.* There are two important truths involved in the fact that God put this treasure in earthen vessels:—

(*a*). *The Divine Origin of the Gospel.* The treasure was *deposited* by God in these earthen vessels. It did not grow out of them, and it was no part of them. The Apostles were not the authors of the Gospel, they were only vessels to carry it to the nations of the earth. The faith of the Gospel was given once for all to the saints, and not invented by them. The Gospel is a scheme infinitely above the ability of man to contrive—a scheme which has struck angels with adoring wonder—a scheme entrusted to the Apostles by the inspiration of God, and based on the incarnation, obedience, and death of Christ.

(*b*). *The equal authority of all the Apostles*. All the twelve had the Divine treasure deposited in them, and no distinction of power belonged to any one of them. Each of them was honoured with a throne, from which he judged the twelve tribes of Israel. The vessels may have varied as to their size or dimensions—the natural abilities of the Apostles may have differed; but when they spoke on behalf of God and in the name of Christ they were all equal.

2. *The insignificancy of the means and the magnitude of the result prove the work to be from God.*

(*a*). *The insignificancy of the means*. "Earthen vessels." Here is a treasure more precious than the world—a jewel from God's crown—a gem from the Divine throne, deposited in frail earthen vessels, which are hurled about, and liable to be broken every moment; but are, nevertheless, encompassed with Divine strength, and preserved and defended by Divine power, for the sake of the treasure placed in them. The Apostles in themselves were but weak, frail earthen vessels, often persecuted and imprisoned, and frequently discharging their duty with fear and much trembling (I. *Cor.* ii. 3., *Gal.* iv.13), yet God saved them often from the very jaws of death, for the sake of the treasure deposited in them.

The expression "earthen vessels" may be used to denote *the lowly and humble social position of the Apostles,* as contrasted with that of the rich and mighty. The phrase is sometimes used to denote what is mean and contemptible in the sight of the world. "The precious sons of Zion, comparable to fine gold, how are they esteemed as earthen pitchers, the work of the hands of the potter" (*Lam.* iv. 2), and "Thou shalt break them with a rod of iron; thou shalt dash them in pieces like a potter's vessel" (*Ps.* ii. 9).

With the exception of Paul, all the Apostles were men of humble birth, destitute of great educational advantages, earning their livelihood by their labours and occupations; and when they went forth to preach they had no earthly authority to enforce their message or defend their persons, and were liable day by day to be cut off by their adversaries, yet God protected them and abundantly prospered their labours, to the confusion alike of the wise and of the mighty, "that the excellency of the power may be of God and not of us."

The expression may refer *to men as contrasted with angels*. They are "earthen vessels" and not the golden vessels of the celestial city; they are men "that dwell in houses of clay, whose foundation is in the dust, which are crushed before the moth" (*Job* iv. 19), and not "angels that excel in strength".

The fact that the Apostles were men indicates their infirmity. Had God chosen angels to be the heralds of the cross, they would have been free from the trials to which the Apostles were exposed. Neither exposure to inclement weather, persecutions, journeys, storms at sea, nor privations on land, would have interfered with the work of an angel; yet, it was not these sons of heaven, but the recipients of Divine grace on earth that God chose to proclaim it to the world, "that the excellency of the power may be of God, and not of us."

(*b*). *The insignificancy of the means securing the glory to God.* It is assumed here, as it is taken for granted throughout the Bible, *that the glory of God is the ultimate end in view in all the Divine dispensations towards the world.* The insignificancy of the means by which God works enhances the glory of his achievements. *When there is no proportion between the power of the means or instruments employed, and the greatness of the results achieved through them, the hand of God is unmistakably conspicuous.*

When we see mighty miracles in Egypt following the movements of the rod in the hand of Moses—when we see the walls of Jericho falling at the sound of rams' horns—when we see the hosts of Midian destroyed before Gideon and his little band, without their striking a blow—it is impossible for us not to see the arm of God made bare, for there was no other power at work to effect the deeds.

Thus, also, was the hand of God manifest with the Apostles. God made use of "earthen vessels" to humble the pride of heathendom, to destroy Jewish prejudice, and to dethrone the god of this world. Their ministry effected a moral revolution in Europe and Asia. A few fishermen, tax-gatherers and tent-makers, without arms, without money, without intrigues, contemptible and persecuted, triumphed over the whole world with the mere sound of their voice! Idols fell before them; the temples were deserted; the oracles were struck dumb; the ancient habits of nations were changed, and their morals reformed;

the wisdom of the world was made foolishness; the devil's charm was broken, and multitudes flocked to adore the crucified Nazarene. No wonder, then, that Paul "glorified in his infirmities, that the power of Christ might rest upon him" (II. *Cor.* xii. 9). The Apostles prospered because God was with them: "And the hand of the Lord was with them: and a great number believed and turned unto the Lord" (*Acts* ii. 21). He that kept the key of the heart followed them; He that circumciseth the ear spoke through them; and the Quickener of the dead exerted His power through their ministry.

3. *The present repository of this treasure.* It is important for us to remember that there is no class of men in our day who stand in the same relation to the Gospel and to the Church of God as the Apostles did. They stood in the same relation to the Church in the Apostolic age as the New Testament does to us now; the word of the Apostles was the rule of the Church in the Apostolic age, as the instruction of the New Testament is our law. When they died the treasure was not removed from one set of earthen vessels into another, but was transferred to the parchment of the New Testament. The Holy Spirit had instructed the Apostles before their death to transfer the treasure from themselves to the New Testament, and it is to the New Testament that we are now to look for it, and not to any so-called successors of the Apostles, or ministers of the Gospel in general.

It was to the twelve Apostles only that Christ gave thrones, from which they were to judge the twelve tribes of Israel; it was to them only that the gift of inspiration was promised; and no class of men can now affect the infallibility of their teaching without blasphemy. The Apostles are still enthroned in their office, acting as Apostles through the New Testament. John says in the Book of Revelation (xxi. 14), which was written after the death of most of the Apostles, that the names of the twelve Apostles of the Lamb were engraved on the twelve foundations of the city of God, a fact which indicated their authority in the Church to the end of time.

The treasure was not kept in "earthen vessels" longer than the end of the Apostolic age; it was then transferred from the vessels to God's Book, so as to be safe from injury and accessible to all mankind.

This written Word follows us to our homes, to refresh our memories and correct our mistakes. So that, in one sense, the treasure, instead of being confined to a dozen earthen vessels, becomes the inheritance of all God's children throughout the world.

It is true that the great impression produced by the oral testimony of the Apostles, and by their earnest personal appeals to the heart and conscience of their hearers, is lost in a large measure in the written Word; but the great Head of the Church has preserved and perpetuated the essentials of this influence by instituting the Christian ministry as a permanent ordinance in His Church. The glow of sympathy—the enthusiasm of zeal—the intensity of conviction—the earnestness of conscientiousness—and the ardour of love are still preserved through the living ministry of the Gospel to co-operate with the truth; and the greater the reality of these subordinate auxiliaries, the greater the impression produced by the message delivered. Man is still to preach to his fellow-men, and the sympathy and enthusiasm of a living herald is still of the greatest importance to further the work of grace in the world.

III. THE VALUE AND EXCELLENCY OF THE TREASURE ITSELF. Let us inquire in what this treasure consists:—

1. *It is a treasure of light for the instruction of the world.* The world was enveloped in darkness till God commanded this light to shine upon it. *The Gospel is the only source of true light to the world.* Without the Gospel the world would be like a firmament without a sun, or a temple without light in it. But through the Gospel the day-spring from on high has visited us; the Sun of Righteousness has risen, and chased away the shades of night. "For God, who commanded the light to shine out of darkness, hath shined in our hearts, to give the light of the knowledge of the glory of God in the face of Jesus Christ" (v. 6). Here God, the eternal source of all light, is represented as making the Apostles a number of luminaries, by treasuring in them the light of Divine wisdom and knowledge, and then placing them as minor lights in the dark moral, intellectual, and religious sky of this world, that they again might reflect this light on the world, that the way of salvation might he revealed to all mankind.

2. *The Gospel is a source of power for the salvation of the world.* As to the constituent elements of its power we may notice:—

(*a*). *That its revelations are according to truth.*

(*b*). *Its purity is another element of its power.*

(*c*). *The first publication of it was accompanied with signs and wonders.*

(*d*). *The saving power of the Holy Spirit worked gloriously through the preaching of it.*

(*e*). *But the great secret of its power as a testimony is the old story of Jesus and His cross.* "For the preaching of the cross... is the power of God" (I. *Cor.* i. 18). The philosophy of the heathen world was but a collection of theories and maxims, the product of man's ingenuity, but the Gospel is a summary of the marvellous facts of the Incarnation, Life, and Death of the God-man; it is the history of Jesus Christ living and dying for His enemies, "that whosoever believeth in Him should not perish but have everlasting life."

There is life in the story of the Cross, which no other history can produce. The account of the death of Socrates is very affecting. He was one of the purest characters and brightest lights of the heathen world; he was a teacher of virtue, and died a martyr for his principles. But who ever heard of a reformation in any town or country in consequence of reading an account of his death? Even at Athens, where the writings of Plato and Xenophon were in every house, and the name of Socrates a household word, four hundred years after the death of Socrates the people were the slaves of idols! Paul's "spirit was stirred in him when he saw the city wholly given to idolatry" (*Acts* xvii. 16).

All the efforts of Zoroaster in Persia, of Confucius in China, and of Socrates in Greece had turned out a complete failure. But the writings and preaching of a few despised Jews, giving an account of the career of the Lord Jesus Christ, regenerated the world. When Paul raised his voice at Athens to preach the true God and his Son Jesus Christ, Jehovah made bare His arm, and many believed. When he preached at Corinth multitudes believed and turned to the Lord. And so everywhere. When the story of the death of Jesus Christ was proclaimed thousands were won to love Him as their only Saviour. And while the account of the death of Socrates had left no impression whatever on the world four hundred years afterwards, the record of the death of Jesus before the end of three hundred years had won the Roman Empire, from the shores of Britain to the banks of the Euphrates, and from the north of Germany to the deserts of Africa, to pay homage to the religion of the cross. Verily, "Christ was the power of God and the wisdom of God," to save the nations (I. *Cor.* i. 24).

3. *The Gospel is an inexhaustible source of consolation to God's people.* It is the ministration of *justification—of life—of hope.*

4. *This treasure is of abiding worth.—It* "*remaineth.*" "The word of the Lord *endureth for ever.*" "For if that which is done away *was* glorious, much more *that which remaineth* (*tò ménon*) is glorious" (I. *Peter* i. 25; II. *Cor.* iii. 11). This treasure is spiritual, heavenly, and Divine, so that

time cannot affect it. Though the inhabitants of the world fade away and disappear, the everlasting Gospel will remain the same through all generations. The discoveries of the ages cannot falsify this testimony, the needs of the world cannot exhaust this treasure; no inventions or progress in arts and sciences can ever render this economy needless; it is the one thing needful for a lost world. While there is thirst in man's bosom for immortality, while there is guilt to be removed and a soul to be saved, the Gospel must be accepted as the only and infallible remedy for our fallen race till time shall be no more.

The Mind of Christ

By the Rev. E. HERBER EVANS, of Carnarvon.

"Look not every man on his own things, but every man also on the things of others. Let this mind be in you which was also in Christ Jesus."—*Phil.* ii. 4-5.

VERY good teacher is, to a certain extent, a man before his age. Human teachers, however, anticipate the world only by a few years, the age soon grows up to them. But what is remarkable in the teachings of Christ is that he has anticipated the world, not by a few years, but by centuries, and that the world does not outgrow Him, on the contrary, that after eighteen centuries of patient waiting it has not yet grown up to Him. Take any great question, and see the many centuries He has had to wait before the foremost minds of the foremost nations have been ready to adopt His teaching. I know not how much longer we must wait before any great power in Europe becomes convinced of the wisdom of "beating their swords into ploughshares, and their spears into pruning hooks", to turn all arms into useful implements, so that if a king or emperor becomes distracted he will not be able, for want of arms, to rush to war. How far are we now from all this, from *"not learning war any more!"* Looking at these sham campaigns in England and at the learning of war in every country in Europe, we cannot but see how slowly the world grows up to Christ. Whenever humanity, however, reaches the noble platform of universal peace it will feel, as it has always felt when shaking itself loose from every old prejudice and tyranny, how foolish, how blind it was not to have adopted His teaching sooner. How great must He have been who has been obliged thus to wait for thousands of years for the world to come up to His own level upon every great question! What a glorious country to live in this England would be were we but to unite to live out the principles of Christ, and is it not this slowness to accept His teaching that keeps us back, that clogs our highest progress. It is said that one of our eminent statesmen has been permitted to live long enough to see his country adopting all his great thoughts. He was laughed at and ridiculed when he first enunciated them, but his countrymen have seen that it was advantageous to turn one after another of his proposals into law, and they have done so occasionally without acknowledging the originator. Jesus Christ was the truest, the highest reformer this world ever saw. He enriched it with more original thought than all other teachers combined. He was ridiculed and persecuted when He first taught His wonderful truths, "Love your enemies, bless them that curse you, do good to them that hate you." "What foolishness! such lessons never can be practised." Yet the farsighted of one country after another, of one age after another have adopted His thoughts one by one, and found the country growing better, and the age growing higher; and many a time have his thoughts been taken acknowledged— but heed not that. Every time this has been done the world has risen from a lower to a higher platform. It has taken another progressive step onwards and upwards.

The text just read to you calls our attention to one of these reforming thoughts of His. "Let this mind be in you." Entertain the mind of Christ in yourselves—*This mind.* It was the grand thought of His life, it was the thought of His death, and it is the great thought of His Gospel—*This mind.* "Look not every man on his own things, but every man also on the things of others"—not that He expects us to neglect our own families, our own affairs, but rather not to confine ourselves to them. "Do not be selfish, self-seeking. Be generous, broad-hearted. Be not like the slimy pool by the roadside, full of unhealthiness, because always receiving in and never giving out. Be like the clear crystal well, always giving as well as always receiving." It was a new thing to see a teacher who had been brought up as a Jew in the midst of Jewish prejudices, anxious to turn the whole world into one great Fatherland—one great Brotherhood. The Jews of that age were exceptionally selfish and bigoted. They never could conceive of a Saviour anxious to bless a Gentile. "Wilt thou at this time restore again the kingdom to Israel?" was their loudest prayer at the close of

His ministry. Their sympathies were confined to Israel and Israelites. John was the son of a Jew, so was Peter, and so was James, but Christ was the *Son of Man,* who could look upon the Samaritan—upon man everywhere—as a brother. Dean Stanley has well said that Christ introduced one word that was new to every language—the word *humanity.* Every nation hitherto had been too narrow for such a noble idea—humanity. Something wider than Greek, wider than Roman, broader than Israel—*humanity.* And "this mind which was in Christ Jesus" enhances humanity in its goodwill and sympathy.

I am not aware of a single religion that battles fairly and successfully with the selfishness of the human heart except the religion of Christ. I know of other religions that take advantage of this self-seeking spirit in the hearts of men to win disciples and to gain power, but there is one religion, and only one, that has proclaimed a war to the death against human selfishness, and before we can get this world to be anything like Heaven, before the much-expected golden age can ever dawn upon us, selfishness must be subdued and conquered to a far greater extent than it is at present. The religion for the world is the one that attempts to do this, and does it in every heart, in every home, in every country. Whatever may be said against our religion it is an undeniable fact that those countries that are influenced by its spirit, those countries leavened with "this mind," are the first to help the sufferers and to feel for suffering everywhere.

When that awful plague, the yellow fever, broke out at Buenos Ayres, when poverty and want followed in the track of pestilence, who were the first to help them? Mahometans? Idolaters? No—thousands of pounds were collected in England, and sent out to total strangers in the spirit of "this mind". When the war broke out between France and Germany, and when we heard of the small farmers of Alsace and Lorraine suffering want; when we heard that their valleys and meadows could not be ploughed or sown that spring, because already sown with more precious seed; England's heart was at once touched, and help poured forth in such abundance that the distributors were compelled to cry out, "Enough," "Enough." What was it that fed such a stream of generosity?—" *This mind.*" Was it not the same with regard to Chicago, when mothers and children by thousands were turned adrift on that awful Saturday night, their homes being burnt to the ground, and they sent forth shelterless to the night and the storm? When the news reached here the telegraph wires were fully employed for days transmitting the happy tidings of the help England was sending forth, as the fruit of *"this mind"*—help that attached one dear country to another too warmly, I trust, for all the blunders of diplomacy to provoke a quarrel between them again. What are all the charitable institutions that fill our land but the fruit of *"this mind."* Take that Home *for Incurables* in London, helped generously by the Queen, a home where all the inmates know that they are never to get well again, where they are simply waiting for the chariot of death; but that chariot may be months in coming, then let them have a clean bed, a kind nurse, and an able physician to ease the pain. They have all in that home. What built it? What keeps it?—*"This mind."*

Now the great aim of our religion is to get this self-sacrificing spirit to rule our hearts. And the weakness of religion in a single breast, in a church, in a community, is that the spirit of self-gratification, instead of self-sacrifice, still rules. I know but little of you in this place as a church, but I feel that there are self-sacrificers here, else the cause would have been dead long since. On the other hand, I feel sure that there are pleasers of self here, men who are always anxious to *get* from religion, but never ready to *give*. Ask one of them in the Sabbath school—"Will you kindly come and teach this class of children to-day? They had no teacher last Sabbath." "What good shall I get from the children? I prefer being under my own teacher; he understands the Scriptures and expounds them well. No, I cannot come to the children." That man is always anxious to get, but never willing to sacrifice. "Will you come to the prayer meeting to-night?" "No, I get no good there, their prayers are always the same; I have heard it all." "Do you come and give us a new prayer for once; we are anxious to hear a new voice. "No." "Where are you going to-night?" "I am going to the *penny readings,*" &c. Now I wish to erect the cross in the centre of this chapel. I mean to pray myself, and oh, do unite with me, that the influence of that cross may be transmitted from heart to heart, and that we may all have in us to a greater degree than ever, *"this mind."*

I. That the possessing of *"this mind"* was the grand essential claimed by Christ *in every follower during His ministry.*

His Kingdom was really founded upon the principle of self-sacrifice. This was the test by means of which He proved His followers—this was the fan that scattered the chaff from the wheat.

"And he said to *them* all, if any man will come after me, let him deny himself and take up his cross daily and follow me." "Yes, but these words simply refer to the days when religion was proved in the light of the fires of the stake, when the chaff was scattered from the wheat by the tempests of persecution. These words have nothing to do with us in these easy religious days." So some men would have us think, but observe—"He said to them all" "... let him take up his cross *daily.*" He spoke not of a cross at the end of life, but of a daily cross. I am told that if I read my own heart that I shall read all hearts. I say then that it is taking up these daily crosses that is difficult to me. We can do some great thing for Christ once in a lifetime when the world is looking on and cheering, but to be truthful, honest, and loving in word and deed in our quiet everyday life—that is the cross which, if we would be His followers, we must all carry for His sake. You can perform a great act of self-denial on a great occasion, and there are but very few great occasions in our life, but how different on a cold winter's night to visit a poor Christian who desires to be consoled on her death bed, and to go cheerfully for His sake; to leave the cheerful fire on a frosty night and to go to the prayer meeting, when we know that it will be very cold there in every sense, that only the faithful few will be present, but to go for His sake; to sacrifice your personal feeling, perhaps to be misunderstood and misjudged, and to receive unkind words until you are tempted to throw all up; but then to remember He came to Calvary for you! He did not give up though all proved unfaithful to Him. For His sake, then, I'll take up the cross. He knows all. Have you noticed that there never was a teacher in this world so ready to part with half-hearted followers as Jesus Christ? If they loved Him, although full of failings, He clung to them as He did to Peter; but those self-pleasers, He saw them leaving in crowds after His sermons, yet He never called them back. When He had fed the thousands with loaves and fishes, when He had spoken His glorious message,—see them departing! Peter is ready to call them back and to ask the Master to offer them eternal life on some lower conditions, "Shall I call them back?" "'Will ye also go away?' Unless you possess something that they do not, unless you love me and my cause in such a way that you will cling to me life through, you may as well follow them." He would have no followers unless the love of Christ constrained them. The teaching of Jesus was that nothing can control the strong passions of our nature but a stronger passion still—*love*, rising to *enthusiasm*. And this is what we want now, and what we must get before we can be faithful to the end.

We want *"this mind"* not only as a power of self-rule, but also as a source of burning zeal for the good of men. It has been well said that *"thou shalt not"* was the old formula, and that *"thou shalt"* is the new. The Mosaic Law condemned those who had done something forbidden, but Christ condemns all *for not doing good.* He habitually denounces the one who has done nothing,—"I was an hungered, and ye gave me no meat." He condemns the priest and Levite who passed by on the other side. He condemns the servant who hid in a napkin the talent committed to him. He condemns the young ruler who had kept the whole law, who had kept carefully the "Thou shalt not," but who went away sorrowfully under His *"Thou shalt."* He would have no cold indifferent men as His followers, but men with the love of Christ filling them with love for souls. There is not a single blessing for the cold indifferent professor throughout the Bible. I find a *"Woe"* "Woe" to those who are at ease in Zion, but not a single "Blessed" for them. May the Lord bless us with more zeal for His glory, more personal efforts to bless our fellow-men in the Spirit of His mind. The day to save the world by means of ministers has passed for ever. We must go forth as a great host against the enemy; then will our efforts be felt. I endeavour to convince the church under my care that it is not only my duty to have clean hands from the blood of all men, but that every Christian is under the same awful responsibility. Those are very serious words in the ninth Psalm, "When he maketh inquisition for blood he remembereth them." When a man meets with an accidental death there is an inquest, an inquisition for blood. My dear Christian friends, I fear that there will be an inquest held over every soul lost from this land of Gospel privileges. Who lived with him in the same house? Who walked the same street with him?—Who!

II. *That this mind, this self-abnegation, was the truth exemplified in the incarnation and life of Christ Himself.*

You may write upon the glorious throne He left— *"For others."* You may write upon the manger He came to, and upon every step in His voluntary humiliation— *"For others."* The words of my text are a part of one of the richest paragraphs in the Bible on the condescension of our Saviour—"Who, being in the form of God, thought it not robbery to be equal with God, but made Himself of no reputation, and took upon Him the form of a servant"—a passage that causes immense trouble to those who deny His Divinity. "In the form of God," say they, "because He had the power of working miracles." If so, Moses was in the form of God before Him; so was Elijah; whereas the language of Paul is obviously intended to confer upon Him a distinction belonging to no other,—"He thought it not robbery to be equal with God." As Bishop Ellicott explains the passage, He did not insist on His own eternal prerogatives, but, on the contrary, humbled Himself to the conditions and suffering of mortal man. The strength of the passage is that He was with God, equal with God, that He was God; and, remembering this glory, who can measure His condescension? I know not the distance from the form of God to the form of a servant, from the glory of Heaven, and the praise of angels, to the degradation of being spat upon and ridiculed by the lowest of humankind; but this I know, that it is not an easy matter to take the part of one who has lost his character, to stand by one who has disgraced himself before a whole country, and to own him as a brother. Jesus, when we had disgraced ourselves before God's universe, when we stood in the dock condemned to eternal death, took our nature, stood by our side, and owned us as His brethren. He was the first of our race of whom it could be said that He condescended to become a man. It was no condescension for Abraham and Moses to become men; they, as well as we, were obliged to put on the nature God gave us; but it is said of Him, "He took not on Him the nature of angels," showing that He had the power and right to select His own nature, and that, having that right, He became a man, and not only so, but "He took upon Him the form of a servant". I have often asked myself, what necessity there was for His becoming a *poor* man. I have not hitherto satisfied myself with a reply, but this I know, that there are hundreds of poor people who have sought His sympathy with true confidence because He "had not where to lay His head" Himself. Had He been born and bred in a mansion they never could muster courage enough to ask Him to their poor dwellings. He came low enough to touch the hearts of the poorest and the humblest. That is the prominent feature in His condescension—greatness making itself of no reputation, greatness coming down to save. That was the sign by which He was to be known at His birth—"Ye shall find the babe wrapped in swaddling clothes, and lying in a manger." "Wrapped in swaddling clothes," but angels announcing His birth—greatness coming down. The gifts brought to Him were those for a king, "gold, frankincense, and myrrh," but a King "lying in a manger!"

It was the same during His lifetime. If you had seen Him on His journey, He was dressed as an ordinary Galilean; but when He spoke on any subject He said the best and the highest that ever could be said on that point. He drew a higher law from the bird, and the flower, than any naturalist ever drew before Him; He drew higher lessons from the fall of the Tower of Siloam, and the passing news of the day, than any historian of the period. He gave us not knowledge of facts, but the wisdom of principle, the truth of God and eternity. He never opened His lips without saying something important for all time, and while the world has been outgrowing the words of the old philosophers, and casting them aside as too confined for the growth of the ages, instead of growing out of the words of Jesus the world has been growing up towards them in every age.

We have been told that it was a remarkable fact that the wise and the peasant met at His birth. He drew the wise men from the east, and the shepherds from the mountains, to His crib. It is ever the same with His Gospel, the two classes meet at His table and in His Church. His Gospel is a problem to the wise, and also sweeter than honeycomb to the poor. Had He been born in a mansion the shepherds could not have ventured in to worship Him, but He came low enough to welcome the lowest, and He was the only person ever born in this world who could have selected the position to be born into. He could have been born in the Emperor's palace if He chose; He could have had a king's daughter as a mother if He chose; He could have been wrapped in silks and laid in a cradle of ivory if He chose; He might have had sceptres of gold to play with as a child, and a throne to sit upon as a man if He chose; but He came not to seek such earthly honours as these. What were thrones, and sceptres, and mansions to Him? He had left a higher throne and a grander sceptre; He cared not for these, but for the lost, the suffering, and the dead. But let us follow Him another step in His humiliation— He *became obedient to suffer* that He might touch the hearts of sufferers in every age. When in trouble is it not a comfort that we have a Saviour who has suffered in all things as we have? He might have gone through this world without being touched by its suffering, were it not that *He suffered for others*. Watch Him when in His greatest agony, look upon Him when the bloody sweat is oozing from His body in Gethsemane. There is not a single enemy in sight; He is evidently suffering not for Himself, but for others. The night and the garden are so quiet that the disciples cannot help falling thrice asleep. Everything is so quiet. The little birds have long since nestled in the branches of the surrounding olive trees. The flocks have quietly laid themselves down to rest on the slopes of yonder valley. There is nothing to be heard except the rippling waters of Kedron murmuring on its way to the sea. Yes, there is another sound breaking on the stillness of the night; I hear the anxious tread of the Man of Sorrows, nearly sinking, yes, sinking thrice, under the burden of the world's guilt, witnessing His disciples asleep, and He obliged to tread the winepress alone. Left by all, to drink the cup brimful of woe, handed to Him by some unseen hand, who can measure His agony? And all for others! There were not nails enough in Jerusalem to fasten Him to the tree, there were not ropes enough in Palestine to tie Him to the cross, were it not that He went there freely from pure love to us all. *Yes freely.* He ascended Calvary for you and for me willingly— *"Obedient unto death."* I see no one but Christ obedient to die. We all die because we cannot live. "Take me not away in the midst of my days," says the Psalmist. Let me get better this time. Moses, when asked to ascend the mount to die wished, above all things, that he might see Canaan first. Yes, we all have our Canaan to see before we are ready to go.

We are simply passive in death, but Jesus Christ, He is active when dying, dying when He might have lived. He bowed His head and gave up the ghost, the only willing sacrifice the world ever saw. Every dove, every lamb, every creature, struggled unwillingly under the knife of the sacrificer. He willingly died that we might live; He came down from Heaven that we may ascend to Heaven; He left all that we might get all.

III. That the power of producing *"this mind"* in all His true followers *is the grand secret of Christ's success, and the certainty of His triumph.*

He lives for ever as a never-failing source of power to produce this self-sacrifice in His true followers in every age; hence it is that His religion is always young, and always full of renewed energy and power. There are other religions boasting that they are far older than Christianity, proud of their "long descent", but if they are older the marks of age are evidently weakening their power—they are too weak to leave the land of their birth. The religion of Buddha is old; it was born in the East, in the East it has remained, and in the East it will die; like an old tree it can only live and grow in its own native soil. But the religion of Christ, although born in Judæa, has spread its influence to every country, it is gradually but surely taking possession of the whole earth, and it will never die.

The religion of Confucius is old, and reckons its followers in China by the million; but when I hear of the Chinese emigrating in great hosts to America I hear very little of the success of Confucianism in the new country. No, it will hardly bear transplanting. Like an old article of household furniture it will keep together while left standing in its usual corner in the old house, but try to remove it to a new one, and its rottenness will at once appear, it will fall to pieces on the way. When the first Christians, however, sailed for the Free States of the West they felt no necessity to leave their old religion behind them in the old country. No, it was taken out as a small insignificant acorn in the Mayflower, it was planted in the free soil amid the free air and free institutions of America, and look at it to-day, how it has flourished and thrived, spreading its branches and embracing that vast continent from shore to shore! Jesus Christ was the first, as well as the last, leader of men who sent out His followers under a flag, with a world-wide motto— "Salvation to the uttermost parts of the earth"—not to one nation, not to one continent, but to the uttermost parts of the earth. When the treasures of the Gospel were first opened this was the address upon them—"To all nations, to every country, to the whole world!" And what certainty have we that they will ever reach the address upon them? The power it has shown, for eighteen centuries, to give to the world an unbroken line of men and women ready to sacrifice their best and dearest for His sake, who died for them on Calvary. Jesus once upon the cross for us and now upon the throne for us; the love that once laid in the grave for us and now reigns in Heaven for us, is the never-failing source of that self-sacrificing spirit that has made men ready in every age for His and His kingdom's sake. And let me remind you that this world was never cleansed from any of its abominations, it has never been purified from any of its foulnesses, but by means of the sacrifice and the suffering of the true and the good. If you want to cleanse Europe from idolatry, with its horrid rites and ceremonies, some must suffer to be mangled and torn by hungry lions in the Coliseum before you can do so. If you wish to purify the mercantile habits of a country some must follow honesty at the expense of poverty before you can do so. If you wish to elevate the political customs of a people, some must bear and suffer to be evicted from their holdings* before you can do so. If you want to put an end to idolatry in Madagascar, and to make a bonfire of

---

* There were many such evictions in Wales at this time.—D. D.

their idol gods, men and women must sacrifice their lives and be thrown over the horrid death-rock ere you can do so. And it is the religion of Christ that I see furnishing the sufferers; it is love to Christ that I see strengthening the sacrificers, who are ready to suffer and die in every age to cleanse the world from its sin and misery. It is the lovers of Christ that I see in the furnaces and dungeons, suffering poverty, persecution and death, in order to hand this world as a cleaner inheritance to their successors, and to make its face shine like the face of heaven.

IV. That it is by service in the spirit of *"this mind"* we are to secure *the truest and highest joy of religion.*

God has so arranged matters that the altar of sacrifice and the well of joy are always together, and, if we pull down the altar to save the sacrifice, it will fall to close the well. If you forget all my sermon, remember this—the altar and the well always go together; sacrifice and joy, no service no joy, is the unchangeable law. Is it not a fact that God has also arranged it to be so in our everyday life? Is it not from those relationships that cost us the greatest trouble and anxiety, that we drink our purest pleasures in the end? Oh, there is many a father and mother in the country yonder, could you but get them in the humour some evening, who could relate the anxieties and troubles of bringing up their one boy. They have sacrificed for years for his sake. "Oh," says the mother, "many a week's rest I lost to wait upon him as he passed from one infant sickness to another." Aye, and his father, how he has toiled, and all for that boy; he wishes him to get a better education and a better start in life than he had. He is at last fifteen years of age, and is starting for London to-morrow. The anxiety is now over. Over, no! Listen to the mother as she packs his box in that old back parlour the night before he leaves; she baptises every article with the tears of an anxious heart, and at last hides a Bible in the clothes, with her name and her wish writ upon it—"Read it every day for your mother's sake." Listen to her as she prays—"The God who accompanied Joseph to Egypt go with my boy." He is now in the City. Is the anxiety over? No, there has not been a fever or a great sickness in London since he has left that did not drive away her sleep, fearing that her child would be taken ill so far from home, and his mother not there to watch over him. "What a trouble he is to them," says some inexperienced heart, "it would be far better for them to be without him." You know nothing about it. That boy is the comfort of their old age. A letter from him, that's the brightest day in the week;

and the summer when he comes home—that year is all summer from January to December. Our boy is coming home this year. On the day when he is coming—how tedious the time *passes!* They are all quite foolish. The mother looks and looks at the clock, and honestly believes that it has stopped, and has a mind to put it on several times during the day. It will never be eight o'clock at this rate. The old man laughs at her at dinner time; the fact is, he is quite as foolish as she is; he has looked up several times during the morning, fearing that the sun had stopped for some other Joshua to accomplish his work. And as for the young man from London he is not a bit wiser than the old people. "What can be the matter with this old engine to-day; it stops in every station and drinks from every tank; and goes slower than the London omnibuses. What makes the day seem so long?" Oh, he is anxious to see his home, and they to see the boy that cost them so much anxiety. Is it a mansion? No, but a very ordinary cottage. Is there a banquet spread out? No, a very simple fare; rather better than usual that night. What is the hurry then? Oh, he is to see the mother who watched over him, and spoke to him first of Jesus; he is to see the father who worked for him and prayed for him, and the old hearth-stone baptised thousands of times with tears on his behalf. And when he comes what a night of happiness it is! The father, not sure whether he is a member of a Christian church, now wishes to ask him, but the tenderer mother tells him, "No; not to-night." At last it comes unasked. "Mother, we have a good man as minister, and a splendid chapel, and I have been the secretary of the Sabbath School for the last six months." There's the well filling their hearts with joy. "Here is my paper of church membership." Oh, how happy they are! What care they now for all the anxiety; it is all joy now!

But there is a way of closing up that well. A man told me the other day that he had never seen his mother but twice in his life, although she lived within ten miles of him. She gave him out to be nursed. She avoided the altar of anxiety and trouble; she never was allowed to drink joy from the well. You may obtain a cheap religion, a religion that costs nothing to your time, to your pocket, to your head, but it will be a religion without joy, without the well of happiness.

If the pendulum of experience swings to the altar on this side it will swing back by the same power to the well of joy on the other side, but if it rests like a plummet in the centre, fearing the sacrifice, God will see that it shall never reach the well. It was the same law for Christ as for us. Jesus "who for the joy that was set before Him endured the Cross," endured the cross that He might have the joy to save, endured their "Crucify Him," "Crucify Him," for the joy of being able to rescue them by thousands from eternal perdition on the day of Pentecost. And that is the joy He seeks here to-day, the joy of forgiving, of receiving not the good son merely, but the returning prodigal. How the old Home would ring with rejoicings were you but to return this day!

Man's Days and God's Mercy

By the Rev. B. Thomas, of Narberth.

"*As for* man his days are as grass; as a flower of the field so he flourisheth for the wind passeth over it, and it is gone; and the place thereof shall know it no more. But the mercy of the Lord *is* from everlasting to everlasting upon them that fear Him, and His righteousness unto children's children."—*Psalm* ciii. 15-17.

THERE are two very important things, closely connected with us all, presented to us in these words, namely, *Man's life*, and *God's mercy*. The one serves as a background to the other, and the contrast between them is most striking and soothing. "The days of man are as grass." Nothing can be more natural than that man's present life should be like growth of the present world. Should the inspired writer speak of the life of God, or that of an angel, he would doubtless compare it to the growth of a sunnier clime, "but as for man his days are as grass."

I. Man's life *as grass*, and as the *flower of the field*.

1. In its *connection* with the earth.

The grass and the flowers come from the earth, are sustained by the earth, and return again to the earth. So man's life, the life which adapts him specially for this world, comes from the earth, is sustained by the earth, and returns to the earth. It is only borrowed from the earth, and the earth must have it back in due time. It is only fair and necessary that it should be so. Nature cannot afford to lose any of its substance at present, and the earthly house is of no use to the spirit-tenant in another sphere.

2. As grass and flowers; for *some special purpose.*

Of all the blades of grass which, in spring and summer, carpet the meadows and mantle the hills in beautiful green, there is not as much as *one* without answering a special purpose in the great vegetable kingdom, and that purpose is set forth by the Psalmist in the following Psalm, in a way more satisfactory to *common sense* than many volumes written by some authors. "He"—by the laws of nature, or any other process if you like—"*He*, nevertheless, *causeth* the grass to grow for the cattle and herbs for the service of man, that He may bring forth food out of the earth."

I remember at the dawn of thought and reflection wondering how the tiny blades of grass in early spring could cut through the earth's hard and tough crust, and grow up in spite of apparent disadvantages, but I saw all as I read in the good old Book of my fathers and my country that *He*—the life of every life, the mover of every motion, the invisible cause of every visible effect—*causes* it to grow, and to grow for a special purpose, "for the cattle." He made the cattle; they want food; and He causes the grass to grow for them. It were a terrible thing if He had made cattle and could not satisfy their wants, but His creative power and arrangements are complete. He causes—*makes, compels*—the grass to grow for them.

And if there is a special purpose for the existence of every blade of grass in the vegetable economy, is there not, think you, a more special purpose for the existence of man, the lord of creation, the climax of God's works in this world, His tenant-in-chief on this stupendous farm, the only being with whom He can reason and speak on this planet? And what can that purpose be but to farm well, improve the soil, cultivate the fields of the mind and the land of the soul, cause some grass to grow and flowers to bloom, and pay rent to His great landlord and taxes to His vast Government.

3. As grass and the flower of the field; *very beautiful.*

How beautiful the springing grass and the blooming flowers! But of every flower life is the most beautiful, and of every life that of man is the most charming. It is the prettiest rose in this world's Eden. Look at it in the little infant; neighbours are attracted to it; they feed and revel on its new-born loveliness; angels fall in love with it and often take it away to their own land; the mother dotes on it, looks and smiles on it, and soon the smile is returned with special sweetness from that little face; it thrives, and grows, and lisps, and moves about, and soon bursts into speech and blossoms into intelligence—into a living soul!

Look at it again in the youth—the lad, happy with flowing health and mad with growing life, skipping in the playground, drinking of the founts of knowledge, bathing in the merry stream, standing on the threshold of the world, and gazing with delight on its dawning and hopeful realities!

Look at it again in the full-grown man, revelling in strength, rich in ripeness and glorious on the throne, and under the crown, of manhood. In all these stages life is exceedingly beautiful. As grass, as flowers—even the beautiful symbols vanish into insignificance before the more beautiful substance!

4. As grass and flowers; *subject to adverse circumstances.*

No sooner does the grass appear, and the flowers bloom, than they are exposed to adverse elements, which endanger their verdure and beauty. They are open to be cut down by the mower's scythe, scorched by the burning sun, or withered by the easterly blast. Thus the very elements which give them life, in other forms, and under other circumstances take that life away. So man's life is in beauty like the "flowers", but, in exposure to adverse circumstances and sudden death, is like the "flowers of the field". Man's life from the cradle to the grave is exposed to attacks from diseases, epidemics, fevers, accidents, and, at last, death in some shape or other—"The wind passeth over it and it is gone."

5. As the grass and flowers; *very short-lived.*

The grass's day is very short, it has *not a day*, in fact, only a *morning.* "In the morning it flourisheth and groweth up; in the evening it is cut down and withereth." How short is man's life? It is scarcely a journey or even a walk; only a step—"There is but a step between me and death." We often go for a walk, walk by the merry and entertaining stream, and up the mountain slopes, to enjoy the health-giving breezes, and the beautiful landscape, all around, but remember, my friend, however young you are, that it is only a walk in a "step", you have only one foot down, and who knows where the other may alight? Perhaps on the other side!

"The days of man"—The *eternity* of God, but the *days* of man. Seldom the inspired writers speak of the years of man, and, should his years be referred to, it is the "*days* of his years". It is by the year that servants are agreed with in this part of the country, but, somehow, by the day God agrees with man in this world. Thus it was in the time of Job. "Are not my days," he asks, "like the days of an hireling?"

Thus it appeared to the sweet singer of Wales—the sacred bard of Pantycelyn—when he sang

> "Great Eternity—how glorious!
> Toward thee I quickly roam,
> Only for a day I'm hired,
> Soon I shall arrive at home;
> My short day will soon be over,
> Set my sun shall quickly be,
> I am nearing every moment,
> Great Eternity, to thee."

6. As grass and the flowers; *very frail and uncertain.*

How frail is the beauty of the flower! How uncertain the verdure of the grass! How suddenly the flower's glory is gone! A few hours ago it opened beautifully, and sent forth delightful perfume. One would think that no blast could be so cruel as to fade its unassuming beauty, but look there, it withers and drops its pretty head on the lap of death! So is the life of man; very brittle and uncertain. It hangs upon a silken thread. It is anchored to time by a very fine silver cord; let a sharp breeze blow over the bay, and the cord is snapped, and the bark sails for other shores. A very little insult will often cause the soul, like a hireling, to break her engagement and leave her former sphere. Often, when no one thinks, she steals away like a thief, in the night, or early in the morning, unknown, perhaps, to any unless someone is awakened by the creakings of death's door, or by the flutterings of the spirit's wings as she takes her flight for other regions.

7. As grass and flowers; its loss *is scarcely felt when gone.*

The grass withers, and the flowers fade, but the fields and gardens in the long run appear just the same as usual, for grass as green and flowers as beautiful bloom in their stead. And let the mower cut down the grass of the meadow so close that you might think that not a blade would ever appear again, in a few weeks it begins to spring, and let the earth give one turn on its axis many of the old inhabitants will say, "We never saw such hay in that meadow before."

Thus, upon the whole, little loss is felt when we are gone, for our equals and our superiors come to supply our places. And although death like a mighty mower cuts down the human race about three times every century, and the earth empties its huge contents to the other side, yet the world goes on as well and even better. The world mentally and morally, as well as physically, is reproductive, and progressively reproductive. There are better crops now waving on Emmanuel's land than were ever seen before, and the golden future promises better still. We have better men, better neighbours and citizens, better members and deacons, and even preachers, than at any former period. I can hear many a white-headed brother whisper, "That is a mistake with regard to the preachers; I don't hear them anything like those of old." Perhaps not, my friend, neither do I. But is it the fault of the harp, or of the harpist? I remember many years ago that a harpist played a few notes on my harp, the like of which I have not heard since. I have heard the same harpist play the same harp, and with greater skill, but with far less effect, and I conclude that it is not the harpist's fault but the harp's. It is of so delicate a texture that it will only produce a comparatively few memorable notes; they are lost, and will not be heard again until it be repaired and re-tuned in heaven.

My friends, we are now on the stage of life, and probably think something of ourselves, and others may think something of us, and we may exercise some influence for good upon the age in which we live; but let us not think too much of ourselves, for soon we shall be gone, and wisdom and progress will not die with us. Our exit will not cause any revolution in the great economy of things, nor will the world come to a standstill on account of our departure. Oh, no! We shall pass away as unnoticed and quietly as the withering grass and the fading flowers. "Thou tiny blade of grass, thou art my brother; my life and thine are very much alike; when my feet tread on thee I ought to reflect that so, by-and-bye, I shall be trodden by the iron feet of the King of Terrors. When I see thee wither before the easterly blast I should think that so I shall soon fade away before the withering blast of death. O thou beautiful flower of the field, thou art my humble teacher; thou livest to show me how to live; thou diest to show how I must also die; thou openest thy pretty petals to the skies to show how I should also open my soul and heart to the refreshing dew of Hermon, and the reviving beams of the Sun of Righteousness. Thou teachest me, and all, to hasten to flourish, for short and uncertain is life—'The wind passeth over it, and it is gone, and the place thereof shall know it no more.'"

II. God's mercy.

"But"—I am glad to meet this "but" here; I have met with many a "but" which has served only as an introduction to much that was annoying and unpleasant; a man's virtues are enumerated one after another, then comes a "but," and behind it are his faults and shortcomings. The first part was traversed in order to come to this "but", which means a turning round in another direction. Here is a "but" in these words which introduces us to the mercy of God; it stands in the middle between man's short life and God's everlasting mercy, and it is most refreshing after being detained by that which is so transient and uncertain to arrive at that which is so permanent and sublime:—"But the mercy of the Lord is from everlasting to everlasting."

1. Different from man's life God's mercy is *without a beginning*.

The grass and the flowers have a beginning, and so has man's life; "we are of yesterday," but the mercy of the Lord, like the Lord Himself, is "from everlasting". Very enchanting to us is a distant sound—the sound of a distant stream or cataract. The mercy of the Lord is much more fascinating, because it comes from His eternity—from "everlasting". Why, but that the soul, being immortal, naturally responds to everything coming from the regions of its own destiny; the soul is everlasting, and God's everlasting mercy touches every chord into music and delight.

Much search was made for the source of the river Nile. It was evident that it sprang somewhere; Livingstone found it at last. But the source of the river of God's mercy as to its beginning will never be found—it is "from *everlasting*". You may trace it back for ages and centuries, back through deserts and plains, through hills and vales, through rocks and mountains; you can trace it back to Calvary and Bethlehem, to Canaan and the wilderness, to Egypt and Eden; and if you look behind the confines of creation, before the mountains were settled, before the hills were brought forth, before the foundations of the earth were laid, you can find traces of the river of God's mercy shaping its course in the direction of the habitable part of this earth.

If Livingstone and others made repeated researches for the source of the river Nile, John, the beloved disciple, in Patmos made researches for the source of the river of God's mercy, and I doubt not that Livingstone and John by this time make gigantic explorations together on the other side. John had learnt much concerning this river, had heard its enchanting murmuring in the prophecies, and its sweet music in the promises of the old Dispensation; had read in the Psalms that "there is a river, the streams whereof shall make glad the city of God".

And now in Patmos, inspired with a holy curiosity, and encouraged by intelligent and experienced guides, he ascended to a dizzy height and stood on the summit of one of the everlasting hills; gazing steadfastly in the direction of the flowing sound, he saw the river proceeding out of the throne of God and of the Lamb, but *its beginning* was not there after all, it only *came out* from thence. Beyond that he could not see, all was lost in the awful mysteries and the unapproachable continents of the spiritual world. It is "from everlasting."

2. Different from man's life, God's mercy is *"without end"*—"from everlasting to everlasting." And this is most natural; being *from* everlasting it should be *to* everlasting. The grass has an end and so has man's life; everything here will have an end. The days of the world will be numbered; the earth will give its last revolution on its axis, and take its last pilgrimage around the sun. The clock will strike the world's last hour, and indicate its last minute; and the earth's Saturday night will come when the good will prepare themselves for a Sabbath after which a Monday shall never dawn. But God's mercy is endless— "from everlasting to everlasting"—flowing on like a mighty river, branching in different directions, but still flowing on, for ever and for ever, without an ebb, quenching the thirst of the inhabitants of the eternal regions, and filling them with happiness and joy.

3. Different from man's life, God's mercy is *above adverse circumstances*. Man's life, as grass and the flowers of the field, is exposed to change, decay, and death—"The wind passeth over it and it is gone"—but God's mercy is above all adverse circumstances; storms cannot quench it, water cannot drown it, fire cannot consume it, chains cannot bind it, mountains cannot stop it; even death cannot prevent its eternal flowings, it is so strong and omnipotent, and moves in such a region, that these forces cannot interfere with its operations.

Man's life is like a "shadow *that fleeth.*" This is the characteristic of a shadow. I remember having a strange experience of my shadow, when at Haverfordwest College. I walked home all the way to see my parents, the sun set and left me on the mountains in the custody of the moon and my shadow. I thought of thieves and robbers. My imagination was rather wild before I could imagine a thief in good Pembrokeshire, and wilder still before I could think that he would attack a poor student, but such thoughts came upon me; I was consoled for a few minutes by the huge companion that walked a little ahead of me. What robber, thought I, would venture to touch me, and, if he would, one blow from the ponderous staff of that giant companion would bring him to the ground. But how childish the thought! My huge companion was only my shadow, and it fled. Try to speak to it, not a word; try to overtake it, it fleeth; go quicker, it fleeth still, and soon vanisheth away, and leaves you alone in the dark.

Such is man's life, and all below, but not such is God's mercy— "My kindness shall not depart from thee, neither shall the covenant of my peace be removed." It is not in the nature of mercy to flee from you in trouble. And in this I see the divinity of mercy that it comes to me when left by all besides.

Job had friends and relations innumerable in the palace, he was a friend, a cousin, an uncle, or some distant relation to all around; but on the dunghill he was friendless, and had no relation anywhere; those who had called him cousin or uncle Job were now silent as the grave. But when there alone, and afflicted, Divine mercy came to him and directed his thoughts beyond the visible and the present, and introduced him to more valuable treasures than those he had lost, and better friends than those who had left him, to realize the root of the matter, and God as his living Redeemer. Affliction repels man, but attracts Divine mercy.

4. Different from man's life, God's continual mercy is *to certain characters*. "The mercy of the Lord is from everlasting to everlasting *upon them that fear Him.*"

"The days of *man* are as grass." Not the days of the poor more than the rich; not the days of the ungodly more than the godly. The ungodly often lives as long, and dies as old, as the most godly in the land, and often more so. You have often seen a soul rushing headlong to misery and woe in as good a body as ever came from under the Creator's hand, while you have seen another soul radiant with purity, aspiring to the dignities of heaven, and ambitious for immortal titles, in a weak, consumptive body, trembling like an aspen leaf on "Jordan's stormy banks".

The days of *man*, irrespective of character, are as grass, but the mercy of the Lord is everlastingly "upon *them that fear Him*".

It is said that man may sin mercy from him in this world. This, doubtless, is a terrible possibility, and must be an extreme case; for it is the genius of mercy to help the most miserable, and this is specially the dispensation of mercy. When mercy is obliged to leave the sinner, it is all over; there is nothing there for even mercy to lay hold of, not even a soft emotion nor a penitent cry, and she cannot leave even then without a deep sigh, and dropping a hot tear on the reprobate, in bidding him adieu. Even at the death-bed of the vilest sinner mercy is the last to retire. The Sunday school teacher is gone; the minister is gone; the pious wife turns away in tears of despairing love; but mercy like an angel is there, and sits there to the last, watching if perchance a penitent tear is dropped on this side of the separating gulf.

Nothing can be more disheartening than to be left by a companion in the hour of need. I remember being on a tour in Breconshire. I had to cross the "Black Mountain," and being a stranger I had some horror of the journey, and a dislike for even the mountain's name. A man accidentally joined me at the commencement, and his society and conversation smoothed and shortened the way, but great was my disappointment when, at the foot of the mountain, he bade me good afternoon, and turned another way, and left me to go across alone. We all have blacker mountains than the black mountain in Breconshire to go over; God grant that when our "feet stumble on the dark mountains, and while" we "look for light, he" may not "turn it into the shadow of death, and make it gross darkness," but may He who has led us all our life long, and redeemed us from all evil, lead us then through all the darkness into the ineffable light.

Human life at times seems quite isolated, is like a small island in mid-ocean, but if so it is a small island in the "Pacific Ocean" of God's mercy. There are many countries in many respects superior to our little island of Great Britain, vaster in territories, richer in mines, more fertile in soil, more abundant in fruits, more celebrated in mountains, rivers, and cataracts, and beautiful scenery; but there is no country under the sun more favourably situated for protection, and defence, and commercial purposes. There are many worlds superior to our little planet, larger in bulk, richer in treasure, more luxuriant in growth, milder in climate, with mellower moons and brighter skies, but I am tempted to say that there is not one, with the exception of heaven itself, more favourably situated in relation to the spiritual commerce of the universe. It stands in the line of God's mercy, and in the longitude and latitude of the eternal course of redeeming love.

Thus you will see that God's inferior things are temporal, but His best things are eternal. When He gives troubles and afflictions he metes them out in days, but when He bestows His mercy He measures it in eternities. Hence, with all our physical and moral disadvantages, the brevity, uncertainty, and vanity of life, and the ills and woes of our mortal existence, there is an infinite compensation for, and a redeeming feature to, all this, that "the mercy of the Lord is from everlasting to everlasting". Our darkness is lost in the light, and our short and mortal life answers a glorious purpose as the background to the grand picture of Divine mercy.

The Transfiguration

By the Rev. R. Hughes, of Maesteg.

"And it came to pass about an eight days after these sayings, he took Peter and John and James, and went up into a mountain to pray," &c.—*Luke* ix. 28-36.

Read also *Matt.* xvii. 1-8, and *Mark* ix. 2-8.

 E do not know with certainty what mountain is referred to in the text. While some are of opinion that this mountain was Mount Tabor, others, apparently with more correctness, maintain that it was Hermon. This mountain, unlike Tabor, is in the neighbourhood of Cæsarea Philippi, the scene of the interview immediately preceding the Transfiguration, and is the only mountain in that district which may be described as "*high*". Our Lord's visits to the mountains of Palestine have imparted to them a greatness and importance which they had not originally. When all other mountains will be forgotten, the tender recollections of some of the mountains of Palestine, and of the thrilling events associated with them, will not fail to inspire the praise of the redeemed throng in heaven for ever. Above all, the Man Christ Jesus, the centre of all praise, will never be dissociated from the land which gave Him birth, and the mountains which witnessed His agony and tears, as well as the glory, surpassing the sun in brightness, which on this occasion streamed upon Him from the skies.

Let us consider—

I. Our Lord's withdrawal to the mountain.

II. His glorification there.

III. The conduct of the disciples in the presence of this glorification.

I. Our Lord's withdrawal to the mountain.

1. In this withdrawal we trace a *sacred purpose*—"Went up into a mountain *to pray.*"

(*a*). Jesus was *much given to prayer.* From His example we learn that offering prayer is congenial to a perfect man, as congenial as *hearing* prayer is to a perfect God. A God, who is not a "hearer" of prayer, would be to man a very imperfect God, and a prayerless man is the saddest instance of human imperfection in the sight of God. How wondrously did the Lord Jesus surpass all others in prayer, as in all else! The disciples, after hearing Him pray, exclaimed, "Lord, teach us to pray" (*Luke* xi. 1). They felt in hearing Him as if they had never heard a prayer before, and certainly as if they themselves had never prayed in their lives. It is when near the perfect One that we too shall feel our imperfection most, and learn best *how to pray.*

(*b*). His prayer on this occasion was *associated with circumstances of special significance.* The shadow of the cross had already been cast across His path, and His soul was filled with sadness in prospect of His approaching death. In the context we find Him tell His disciples that "The Son of Man must suffer many things, and be rejected of the elders, and chief priests, and scribes, and be slain, and be raised the third day." These considerations, like mighty winds, raised waves of strong emotion upon the great ocean of feeling within Him. Communion with His Father could best make still the troubled waters, as still as when He Himself spoke to the boisterous wind, and the sweeping waves, on the Sea of Galilee—and "there was a calm". Prayer is also our best antidote to sorrow. It is that which best of all qualifies us to meet and to pass through the afflictions of life. And, remember, there is more of *passing through* trials than there is of exemption from them. Every temptation through which the believer passes leaves its mark upon him, as the flail does upon the wheat, and the fire upon the true gold. The only successful way to overcome the dread of death, the last trial of all, is to approach it in the path of prayer.

2. We trace in His withdrawal *special force of devotion*—He goes to the mountain to pray—or, according to Matthew, to a place "apart"— where there was most quietness, and least distraction. Jesus doubtless prayed at times publicly in the temple, the synagogue, and in the open field amidst the people—but on special occasions He withdrew to solitary spots, and to places "apart". Indeed, places "apart" are those in which prayers have oftenest been offered and heard, and where the

greatest revelations have been given. Bethlehem, and the manger, where the Prince of Life was born, Golgotha, where He died, were places "apart", and in such places even to-day the cause of Christ is to be found in many towns and cities. Unworthy objects are those which have been pushed most to the world's front until comparatively recent times. To the extent that the world is brought to understand the value of true religion, will those things be pushed aside, and prayer, which has had to go "apart" to breathe freely, will have its due place and pre-eminence among the most valuable things of life. Alas! that the holiest and best of the past have had to withdraw into caves, and dens, and wildernesses of the earth for the most sacred exercises, while the world has made room for its evil-doers, and offered every facility for deeds of darkness. Blessed are they who, like the Master, withdraw into places apart rather than that the world should dissipate their devotion, or silence their prayers.

3. We trace in His withdrawal the *sociable aspect* of His religion. He was sociable even in His *most prayerful moments*. His intense devotion did not make Him unsociable, or less human, in His sympathies. Some people, by trying to be more than devout, become less than human. Jesus, the most spiritual of all, even in the most exceptional seasons, manifested His friendliness, and gave proof to His disciples that His "delight is with the sons of men". He might have had angels as His constant attendants during His earthly sojourn, and they would have accepted this as the highest honour, but He chose men, with all their infirmities and failings, to be His companions, and called them "not servants, but friends".

II. Christ's glorification on the mountain.

1. He was *glorified more than ordinarily*.

(*a*). He was *transfigured* ("changed in form" or aspect. Welsh). There is no account of anything special in the *form* He assumed until now, though the glory ever beamed forth in His life, His utterances, and mighty deeds. It was in the wedding feast in Cana of Galilee that He began "to manifest forth His glory", but here on the Mount the glory revealed itself in His *appearance*, for He was transfigured.

The change of "form" is the only change we hear of in the history of the Saviour. In His love, His faithfulness, His truth, His gracious purposes, He is "the same yesterday, to-day, and for ever". His incarnation in Bethlehem was a change of "form"—the divine wearing the human; "He took upon Himself the *form* of a servant, and was made in the likeness of men;" but on this Mount the human wears the aspect, the likeness, of the Divine. He was transfigured before them, and His face did shine as the sun, and His raiment was "white as the light," or, according to Mark, "exceeding white as snow." In these comparisons we find the highest conception of the brightness of the sun, and of the whiteness of the snow. Apart from these we might not have thought that the sun is so bright, and the snow so white, as they are. It is in the light of the spiritual that we can best see the glory of the earthly, and those who know most of eternal realities are those who are best adapted to appreciate the temporal. "His face did shine as the sun, and his raiment became shining, exceeding white as snow." What a compliment to the sun and the snow! I sometimes fancy—when I give a little rein to the imagination—if the sun could but know that it is bright enough to illustrate, to some degree at least, the brightness of the Saviour's face, that it would be more in sight, even in this humid climate, than it is, that it would show its face earlier in the morning, and that it would delay hiding it a little longer in the evening. I fancy, too, at such moments, that if the snow could but know that it is white enough to be used by the inspired writer to illustrate the whiteness of the Saviour's raiment when transfigured on the Mount, that while it would maintain unsullied its pure whiteness, it would never be quite so cold as it now is.

(*b*). In the light of the Transfiguration *some of the heavenly beings came to sight.* "And behold there appeared unto them Moses and Elias talking with Him," writes Matthew, "who appeared in glory," adds Luke. We know not who, besides Moses and Elias, may have been on the Mount, but these two *appeared*, the one the representative of the Law, the other of Prophecy. It is possible—I think probable—that if the disciples could have borne the brightness to look but a little longer they would have seen in the heavenly light a vast host from the spiritual world. It is not likely that the disciples would have known Moses and Elias in any other light than that of the Transfiguration. We do not know who we should see in our religious services, how many angelic spirits and heroes of faith would appear as a cloud of witnesses, did the light of the Mount stream in upon us.

In close proximity to the glory of the Saviour, they, too, "appeared in glory." Apart from Christ, Moses and Elias would have been devoid of all glory; but near Him all is glorious. Moses and Elias, the representatives of the Law and of Prophecy, had their faces turned toward His decease, just as the cherubim had their faces toward the mercy-seat in the holiest place, and the light of the Shechinah lit up their countenances with an unearthly glory. It was about "His decease which He should accomplish at Jerusalem" that they spoke when they "appeared in glory". They were not afraid to disturb the banquet on the Mount by mentioning the Saviour's death. It would not have been appropriate to refer to any other death at such a festive season, but the messengers of peace need not fear to disturb the best feasts of earth by proclaiming the death of the great Redeemer.

(c). In the presence of Moses and Elias, Jesus *was acknowledged openly by the Father.* "And there came a voice out of the cloud, saying, 'This is my beloved Son: hear him.'" The Father had spoken thus before in the hearing of John when His Son was baptized; but now on the Mount He added the words "Hear him". When the Father spoke the first time Jesus was beginning His public ministry, but, when He spoke on the Mount, Jesus was drawing near to the close of life. The approval of the Father on this occasion is in some respects more important than on the former, since many a father who has said over his child at the commencement of life's journey, "This is my beloved son, in whom I am well pleased," has been struck dumb with sorrow and disappointment ere that journey has been brought to a close, or, if not struck dumb, has uttered words very different from these. The first Adam commenced the journey of life in a promising way, yet it turned out sadly before its close; but the second Adam is as worthy at the close of life as at its commencement, and the precedence is given Him over all others, "Hear him." Henceforth Jesus is the Teacher of man, and all that the Father has to say He has committed to His Son to make known. Do we seek guidance in the path of life, and comfort in our sorrowing hours still? The Father's voice speaks to us, as of old upon the Mount, "Hear him."

2. He was glorified *while He prayed.*

(a). As a token of the *efficacy of His prayer.* Through His wondrous prayer the cloud of glory was rent above the mountain, and descended in cataracts of light upon its summit. It would seem as if both worlds had become one in the Saviour's prayer, and that they would never be separated again. There can be no doubt that this proof of the efficacy of prayer would strengthen Jesus for the trials which awaited Him in Jerusalem; and it should be an assurance to us that it is by prayer that we can draw most of heaven down to earth.

(*b*). As a token of the *value of prayer* independent of the answer to it:—"*As he prayed* the fashion of His countenance was altered." Prayer exerts a hallowing influence over the one who prays, even when engaged in the very act of praying. He who prays most earnestly has sometimes to wait long before he receives an answer to his prayer, but though he receive no answer at all he cannot rise from his knees without being better for having prayed, because while he prays, whether we have the eyes to see it or not, the fashion of his countenance is being changed. True prayer alters the countenances of people, and though those who pray are not therefore exempt from the trying circumstances in which others are placed, yet they excel all others in the serene aspect they wear. There are many who, like Moses of old, have come down from the Mount with far brighter countenances, and a heavenlier aspect, than when they ascended it, though they knew it not. Ah, when the world believes in prayer, and acts up to that belief, its whole aspect will be changed—as it prays the fashion of its countenance shall be altered.

3. He was glorified in the presence of three of His disciples. "He was transfigured before them."

(*a*). *To strengthen their belief in Him as their Messiah.* They had previously given proof of their belief in Him, but should the prediction of His suffering and death shake their faith, the sight of His glory in the Transfiguration would re-establish it more firmly than ever. When the Apostle Peter, in his second Epistle, refers to the honour and glory which Jesus had received from the Father, he refers directly to the Transfiguration as being the most striking proof of this:—"For we have not followed cunningly devised fables, when we made known unto you the power and coming of our Lord Jesus Christ, but were eye witnesses of his majesty. For he received from God the Father honour and glory, when there came such a voice to him from the excellent glory, This is my beloved Son, in whom I am well pleased. And this voice which came from heaven we heard, when we were with him in the holy mount."

(*b*). *To qualify them to follow Him in His trials* after the descent from the Mount. That was a hard path which they had to walk as they sought to follow Jesus through the scenes of His sufferings, but the glory of the Mount gave light and joy to them in the greatest gloom. They took the healthy atmosphere of the mountain down with them to the lowlands, where the cold mists of misgiving and fear hanged heavily, and they passed through all in the strength it had imparted to them. We, too, in spending the Lord's day, one day out of seven, on the Mount ought to remember to take the atmosphere of that holy day with us into the other six days of the week. Let us carry the atmosphere of the mountain with us into the mart, the office, the works, and the home; and thus as the plains are the more fertile for the mountains which begird them, so all the other days of the week and of the year shall be better for the Sabbaths, and special religious seasons, which tower above the ordinary level of our busy lives, and which are intended to enrich the whole.

III. The conduct of the disciples in the presence of this glorification.

1. It is said that they feared. Matthew writes, "They fell on their face, and were sore afraid;" Luke, "They feared as they entered into the cloud." The voice of God in the Garden after man had first sinned made him fear, and the dread of the spiritual and the divine has never left him since. Moses feared greatly on the Mount in the presence of the Divine glory. The prophet Isaiah was filled with fear when he saw the Lord sitting upon a throne, high and lifted up, his train filling the temple. Peter became fearful when he saw so much of the Divine brought to light in the miraculous draught of fishes, and said, "Depart from me, for I am a sinful man, O Lord."—Yes, it is sin in us that produces fear when we are so near to the Divine purity.

It would seem as if the Divine glory in the intensity of its purity had invaded the earth and taken possession of this Mount by a grand surprise, and that the disciples, in the presence of this purity were overcome with a sense of their own sinfulness. They feared as they entered the cloud. There was no possibility of hiding from God's presence in entering this cloud; they went only the more into it, for the voice of God was heard in that cloud. While we are sinful we cannot but fear in the presence of God even upon mounts of transfiguration until we realize the full import of that decease, which was the theme of this hour, and through which the great God is revealed as pardoning to the uttermost those who come unto Him.

2. It is said of one of them—Peter—that he did not know what he said. Peter had begun to feel at home in converse with the spiritual, and desired that the two worlds should not separate again, but dwell together on the Mount. Though Peter's utterance at the time was a very erroneous one, yet the inspired writer does not deal hardly with him, but speaks tenderly—"not knowing what he said." Love requires

very little to excuse a fault it makes the best use of the least plea—Peter's *ignorance*. This was the Lord's plea for His crucifiers—"They know not what they do." My friends, if you think Peter was unwise and uttered on the mountain words he should not, do not be unkind to him, speak as tenderly of him as the evangelist did.

Many a Christian to-day, like Peter of old, is often in ecstasy in meetings on the Mount, and speaks sometimes very enthusiastically without knowing what he says.—Peter knows to-day what he says. All uncertainty of thought and utterance has given way to a blessed certainty.

3. It is said that they were heavy with sleep. Sleep is one of the necessities of our earthly life, and we are often made to realize this here—sometimes in religious seasons. This was not a very long meeting, only until the "next" day, yet the disciples were heavy with sleep. Brethren, if we were allowed to enter heaven in possession of these bodies we should sometimes sleep amid the harmonies of the song of the redeemed, and the very harps would drop from our hands; but before we go there we must enter the grave and remain there sufficiently long to take the sleep out of us. When we shall awake from the sleep of the grave our eyes will never suffer again from heaviness. Let us try for a time to pass through the meetings of the Mount even when we are wearied and worn; we shall have refreshing slumber by-and-by; and if we "fell on sleep" during one of these meetings we shall rejoice on the morning of the awakening that we fell asleep in such favourable circumstances and in so happy a place.

The Women at the Cross

By the late Rev. W. AMBROSE,*
Congregational minister, Portmadoc.

AN OUTLINE.

"Now there stood by the cross of Jesus his mother and his mother's sister, Mary the wife of Cleophas, and Mary Magdalene."—John xix. 25.

THOSE women who were the last at the cross were the first at the grave, and thus of all the disciples were those who lost sight of their Lord for the briefest period. It was upon His friends that Christ looked last in dying and upon the same friends He looked first after His resurrection. (Remark—Those whom I would have nearest me as I close my eyes in death are those whom I should love to see first when I awake again.)

❋ ❋ ❋ ❋ ❋ ❋ ❋ ❋ ❋ ❋

I. WHO WERE THESE WOMEN?

1. *Mary, the mother of our Lord.* Beautiful designation! Protestants have not done her justice, while Papists have exalted her too much. We have but little of her history. She conversed with Gabriel, the wise men from the East paid their homage at her feet, angels sang the birth of her child, and a star led to where she and her infant lay, yet she was not infallible, as other instances in the Gospels prove. I am glad it is recorded that Mary was at the Cross; this is one of the beautiful touches of the sacred record.

---

* See page 276.

2. *His mother's sister, the wife of Cleophas.* Alpheus, the mother of James and Judas. This woman was stronger than her husband. If her husband was one of the two on the way to Emmaus, he had not half his wife's courage.

3. *Mary Magdalene.* The fact that Christ had cast evil spirits out of her was a sufficient reason to her why she should be among those who stood nearest to His cross, and among the last to remain there. Others might forsake Him, she *could* not.

II. The position of the women—"By the cross." The other evangelists refer to women and acquaintances beholding "afar off," but no mention is made of our Lord's mother and John. I imagine seeing them afar off, while the large crowd, the Jewish priests and elders, and the Roman soldiers stand near. But hush! earthquake! darkness! rocks rent! graves open! Hundreds of the guilty throng flee, but His friends draw nearer. This is a picture of the effects of terrible things in the Almighty— guilty foes fleeing, trustful disciples drawing nearer. Why were they there?

1. Could they minister any comfort to Him? They would have gladly moistened His parched lips, but they were not permitted.

2. Could their presence be of some comfort to Him? That is doubtful. We have heard of some submitting to be condemned, but, on seeing their relatives, losing all nerve, and failing to summon sufficient courage to put on the martyr's crown.

3. Was their conduct becoming? What is the law of propriety? Ah, if the heart burn with love to Christ, what are the world's social laws? Should anyone say to the Women, "It is not fashionable for ladies to witness execution or to stand so near to a malefactor's cross," the love which they cherished toward the great sufferer would kindle into a flame, set "fashion" on fire, and reduce it to ashes. Mary, the mother of our Lord, stood there. She looked upon Him, and He upon her. What painter could represent on canvas that interchange of looks? I do not remember that the *eyes* of Mary have been in sight in any picture I have ever seen of the Crucifixion. They are concealed, as a rule, in a swoon or under cover. She stood there listening to His latest words. They were far too precious to be lost. She caught the words of Christ at this time with the eagerness of snatching a life from a wreck.

III. The contrast which the conduct of these women presented to that of others added greatly to its beauty.

1. The absence of others—even the disciples. Nothing is a greater

discouragement to the faithful than want of faithfulness in others. Little did the disciples realize when in Bethany that the storm was so near. The utmost test was made of their fidelity, and they all, save John, forsook Him and fled, but *these women* followed Him to the cross. The weaker vessels survived the storm better than the stronger.

2. The nature of the sight—especially to Mary. No mother ever suffered more than Mary on this occasion. How sensitive she must have been at this hour to every touch of sorrow and of suffering! The prophecy of Simeon was now fulfilled—a sword pierced her very soul.

3. The painful mystery of the event. We can read the story of the Crucifixion in the light of the Resurrection. Not so they. The faith of Abraham on Moriah, when the command seemed to contradict the promise, but when, nevertheless, he obeyed because "he believed God", is highly spoken of in the Scriptures. That faith in God that sustained Abraham on Moriah was that which sustained Mary at the cross.

IV. THE POSITION OF THESE WOMEN NEAR THE CROSS IS ILLUSTRATIVE OF THAT WHICH WE SHOULD OCCUPY IN RELATION TO IT. Our most earnest thoughts and strongest emotions should centre there. No fear of opposition or dread of danger should keep us at a distance from the cross of Christ.

Satan walking in dry places

By the Rev. CHRISTMAS EVANS.*

HE following is an extract from Mr. Evans's sermon, in which he described Satan as going about seeking whom he might devour. He at length pictures him as seeing a young man in the strength of life sitting on the box of his cart and singing merrily on his way for lime:—"'There is a young man,' said the old Tempter, 'the blood courses wildly in his veins, and his bones are full of marrow. I will fan my sparks within his bosom and set all his passions on fire; I will draw him on from bad to worse, until at last his soul will sink in the lake of fire never to rise again.' Just then, as he was about to dart a fiery temptation into his youthful heart, he heard him sing,

'Guide me, O Thou great Jehovah,
Pilgrim through this barren land.'

'Ah, this is a dry place,' said the fiery dragon, as he expanded his wings and flew away.

"Then I saw him speed along," continued the preacher, "occasionally hovering like a vulture in the air. At length he came to a lovely valley, where, beneath the eaves of a little cottage, he saw a maid about eighteen years of age sewing at the cottage door, a lovely flower among the surrounding flowers. 'There is one,' exclaimed the devil, 'I will whisper an evil suggestion into her heart and repeat it over and over again until it shall become an evil deed, then she will be obliged to leave her home and wander far into sin and shame.' With this he hastened to hurl his fiery dart into her mind, but as he approached

---

* See page 266.

the hills reverberated with the echoes of her sweet voice as she sang,

'N mhen oesoedd rif y tywod man,
Ni fydd y gân ond dechreu, &c.'

[In ages numerous as the sand
The song will be commencing.]

'Ah, this is another dry place,' exclaimed the Tempter, as he again took flight.

"Filled with fury, he rushed madly on and exclaimed, 'I will have a place to dwell in, I will now try the old.' Then seeing an aged woman sitting at the door of her cot and spinning with her little wheel. 'Ah,' said he, 'I will try to bring her grey hairs with sorrow to the grave, and allure her soul to destruction. He descended toward the little cot, but as he drew near he heard the tremulous yet exultant voice of the aged saint repeating the promise of her gracious Lord—'For the mountains shall depart and the hills be removed, but my kindness shall not depart from thee, neither shall the covenant of my peace be removed, saith the Lord that hath mercy on thee.' He flew away as if pierced to the heart, exclaiming—'Another dry place—*another dry place!'*

"Ah, the old Destroyer of souls received poor welcome now. At length the night drew on, and he, like a bird of prey poured forth shrill cries into the air. Anon he passed through a little Welsh village under a hill. He saw a faint light in an upper room, and said to himself, 'There old William is slowly pining away. He is over eighty years of age, and hasn't much mind left. Thanks to me, he has had a hard time of it often, and hasn't found serving God altogether a pleasant thing. It will be a grand thing if I get the best of him after all, and make him doubt his heavenly Father.' Thereupon he entered the room where the aged man lay on a hard bed, with his eyes closed, and his silvery hair falling in sweet confusion upon the pillow. The devil had no sooner drawn near to accomplish his wicked design than the aged saint sat up in his bed, and with a smile like the light of heaven upon his countenance he stretched forth his hands and exclaimed, 'The Lord is my shepherd, I shall not want... Yea, though I walk through the valley of the shadow of death I will fear no evil, for Thou art with me, Thy rod and Thy staff they comfort me. Thou preparest a table before me *in the presence of mine enemies*.' The aged man fell gently back upon his pillow. Those were his last words on earth before he passed into his Master's joy. 'Ah,' exclaimed Satan, 'this is a fearfully dry place,' and glad to escape from such confusion and shame he added, 'I will return to my place; I had rather be there than here.'"

Standing at the Door

By the Rev. Christmas Evans.*

"Behold I stand at the door and knock."—*Rev.* iii. 20.

PREACHING from the above text, he said in closing the sermon:—"Oh, my dear brethren, why will you pay no heed to your best Friend? Why will you let Him stand knocking, night and day, in all weathers, and never open the door to Him? If the horse dealer or cattle-drover came you would run to open the door to him, and set meat and drink before him, because you would expect to make some money by his visit. But when the Lord Jesus stands knocking at the door of your heart, bringing to you the everlasting wealth, which He gives without money and without price, you are deaf and blind; you are so busy that you cannot attend. Markets, and fairs, pleasures, and profits occupy you; you have neither time nor inclination for such as He. Let Him knock! Let Him stand without, with the door shut in His face, what matters it to you? But it does matter to you.

"Oh, my brethren! I will relate to you a parable or truth. In a familiar parable I will tell you how it is with some of you, and, alas! how it will be in the end. I will tell you what happened in a Welsh village, I need not say where. I was passing through that village in early spring, and saw before me a beautiful house. The farmer had just brought his load of lime into the yard; his horses were fat and all were well to do about him. He went in and sat down to his dinner, and as I came up a man stood knocking at the door. There was a friendly look in his face that made me say as I passed, 'The master's at home; they won't keep you waiting.'

---

* See page 266.

"Not long after I was again on that road, and as soon as I came in sight of the house I saw the same man knocking. At this I wondered, and as I came near I saw that he stood as one who had knocked long. As he knocked he listened. Said I, 'The farmer is busy making up his books, or counting his money, or eating and drinking. Knock louder, Sir, and he will hear you. But,' I added, 'you have great patience, Sir, for you have been knocking a long time. If I were you I would leave him to-night and come back to-morrow.

"'He is in danger, and I must warn him,' replied he; and knocked louder than ever.

"Some time afterwards I went that way again; there the man still stood, knocking, knocking, knocking. 'Well, Sir,' said I, 'your perseverance is the most remarkable I ever saw! How long do you mean to stop?'

"'Till I can make him hear,' was his answer; and he knocked again.

"Said I, 'He wants for no good thing. He has a fine farm, flocks and herds, stack-yards, and barns.'

"'Yes,' he replied, 'for the Lord is kind to the unthankful and to the evil.'

"Then he knocked again, and I went on my way, wondering at the goodness and patience of this man.

"Again I visited that district. It was very cold weather. There was an east wind blowing, and the snow fell thickly. It was getting dark, too, and the pleasantest place, as you all know, at such a time, is the fireside. As I passed by the farm-house I saw the candle-light shining through the windows, and the smoke of a good fire coming out of the chimney. But there was the man still outside—knocking, knocking! And as I looked at him I saw that his hands and feet were bare and bleeding, and his visage as that of one marred with sorrow. My heart was very sad for him, and I said, 'Sir, you had better not stand any longer at that hard man's door. Let me advise you to go over the way to that poor widow. She has many children, and she works for her daily bread; but she will make you welcome.'

"'I know her,' he said. 'I often converse with her; her door is ever open to me, for the Lord is the husband of the widow, and the father of the fatherless.'

"'Then go,' I replied, 'to the blacksmith's yonder. I see the cheerful blaze of his smithy; he works early, and late. His wife is a kind-hearted woman. They will treat you like a prince.'

"He answered solemnly, '*I am not come to call the righteous, but sinners to repentance.*'

"At that moment the door opened, the farmer came out cursing and swearing, carrying a cudgel in his hand, with which he smote him, and then angrily shut the door in his face. This excited a fierce anger in me. I was full of indignation to think that a Welshman should treat a stranger in that fashion. I was ready to burst into the house and maltreat him in return. But the patient stranger laid his hand upon my arm, and said, 'Blessed are the meek: for they shall inherit the earth.'

"'Sir;' I exclaimed, 'your patience and your long-suffering are wonderful; they are beyond my comprehension.'

"'The Lord is long-suffering, full of compassion, slow to anger, not willing that any should perish, but that all should come to repentance.' And again he knocked as he spoke to me.

"It was dark; the smithy was shut, and they were closing the inn; I made haste to get shelter for the night, wondering more and more at the patience and pity of the man. In the village inn I learned from the landlord the character of the farmer, and, late as it was, I went back to the patient stranger and said, 'Sir, come away; he is not worth all this trouble. He is a hard, cruel, wicked man. He has robbed the fatherless, he has defamed his friend, he has built his house in iniquity. Come away, Sir. Make yourself comfortable with us by the warm fireside. This man is not worth saving.' With that he spread his bleeding palms before me, and showed me his bleeding feet and his side which they had pierced; and I beheld it was the Lord Jesus.

"'Smite him, Lord!' I cried in my indignation; then perhaps he will hear thee.'

"'Of a truth he *shall* hear me. In the day of judgment he shall hear me when I say, Depart from me, thou worker of iniquity into everlasting darkness, prepared for the devil and his angels.' After these words I saw Him no more. The wind blew, the snow and sleet fell, and I went back to the inn.

"There has been much knocking in the night at my chamber door, 'Christmas,' cried my landlord, 'get up! get up! You are wanted by a neighbour who is at the point of death!'

"Away I hurried along the street to the end of the village, to the very farm-house where the stranger had been knocking. But as I got near I heard the voice of his agony: 'Oh, Lord Jesus, save me! Oh, Lord Jesus, have mercy upon me! Yet a day—yet an hour for repentance! Oh, Lord, save me!'

"His wife was wringing her hands, his children were frightened out of their senses. 'Pray! pray for me!' he cried. 'Oh, Christmas, cry to God for *me!* He will hear *you; me* He will not hear!' I knelt to pray; but it was too late—He was gone."

"Away with Him"

By the Rev. J. R. Kilsby Jones,* Llanwrtyd Wells.

An Outline.

AWAY with him! Away with him!' (John xix. 15). Away with *whom? Who* is He? Away with Him whom no one could 'convince of *sin*,' and who went about doing *good?* Away with Him whose *character* was the realization of the highest ideal of excellence? It was an awful manifestation of the state of men's minds when they could say, 'Away with *him*,' even when here in the form of a servant. What is He now? What saith his Father of Him? What think and say the angels of Him? What think the ransomed of Him, at whose girdle hang the keys of the future world?

"(2). '*Away* with him.' *Why? What* has He *done* that you should say '*away* with him?' There are certain characters of whom you *ought* to say, '*Away* with *them. Away* with the tyrant and oppressor—away with the drunkard and glutton—the fornicator—the miser, and the extortioner. Their deeds condemn all these. But He? What has *He* done? He had compassion on man and died for him. That is what *He* has done. Away with *Him!*

"(3). '*Away* with Him.' Can you do *without* Him? You may till you are convinced of sin, till the Law thunders in your ears, till the weight of guilt presses on the conscience. When the heart is faint and the spirit fails can you do without Him? When the hour arrives when man can do *nothing* for you—*what* and how *then?* 'Away with H*im!*' Let the thirsty man with his lips parched and his tongue cleaving to the

---

* See page 260.

349

roof of his mouth say to the sparkling stream, 'Away with *it.*' The hungry man to bread, 'Away with *it.*' The naked to clothing, 'Away with *it.*' The lost wanderer to the guide, 'Away with *him.*' The helpless infant to his mother, 'Away with *her.*' The parched and thirsty earth to the cloud bearing refreshing rain, 'Away with *it.*' The dead and dreary winter to the reviving spring, 'Away with *it.*'

"(4). 'Away with *Him.*' Very well; if you are prepared to brave the consequences. Do not turn cowards; quit you like men; stand your ground without flinching. The Jews *invited* God's judgments. Suppose He were to take some of you at your *word.* I see another day. A white throne is set up in the heavens. Ten thousand angels herald the coming of the Judge. The trumpet sends forth a loud, long blast, and earth and sea give up their myriad dead. 'Open unto us, open unto us' is the cry, but the ear, once the quickest to hear, and so quick that the sigh of penitence does not escape it, is *now* deaf. 'Away with *you*—depart from me!' The multitudinous throng begins reluctantly to move. Ah! it is gone for ever! Its wail fills the air. My erring brethren, recall the words. It is not too late. God be thanked for that. Shall *we* do it for you?"

The Lord Jesus

By the Rev. Evan Thomas,* Baptist Minister, Newport, Mon.

"He was in the world and the world was made by him, and the world knew him not."—John i. 10-12.

EVERYTHING connected with the Lord Jesus is worth telling. This chapter assures us that (1) He has touched the farthest extremes of intelligent existence—v.1 "with God," v.14. "among us;" (2), that He is the same in all circumstances and in connection with every change and as such can be known everywhere, and (3), that He is at home alike with God and with us. Our text teaches us—

I. That our Lord's presence in the world was of importance to the world.

Three things prove this—

1. The record of His life in the world. He ennobled everything He touched. He sanctified everything—poverty—suffering—yea, even the cross, taking from it the shame—and the grave, robbing it of its gloom and terror. When He was present at a funeral it was no longer like any other funeral. Funerals in other circumstances did not stop until the grave was reached, but when He only met a funeral it turned back. When He was present at a wedding, too, the water was converted into wine. Everything He touches derives a glory from the touch—Baptism—The Lord's Supper. If He is in the service His presence makes it very precious.

2. The work attributed to Him—"All things were made by him." No one, save Himself, *makes* anything. Men but modify and reproduce.

---

* See page 260.

Only He has the *creative* power. This power is irresistible—He who can make a blade of grass can make an Apostle when He needs one.

3. His position in comparison with all things. He was before all things. It is a great disadvantage to be *before* things, as in the case of those who lived *before* religious liberty was extended, *before* the days of railways, telegraphy, &c. It is a great advantage to come into the world in the train of grand discoveries and glorious reformations; but He was before all things. There was nothing with which to begin, He had only Himself, He made everything else.

II. Yet He came into the world and passed out of it without being known by many.

1. Many of the best and noblest of men have passed through the world without being known. But this is the greatest oversight in all history, an oversight which involved the greatest loss—"He came unto *his own*, and *his own* received him not."

2.—The reason why He was not received was that the world did not know Him. It is impossible to *know* Him and not receive Him.

3. The world judged Him by the wrong standard—hence they mistook Him for a prophet, *v.* 21. He was not like anyone else, and belonged to no class of men, but stood by Himself. There was no use in going in search for Him among others, not even among the prophets.

4.—If He must be compared with anyone let Him be compared with Moses. The Jews compared Jesus to Moses on one occasion. Jesus gave one meal to five thousand, but Moses had fed hundreds of thousands for forty years, hence Moses, they thought, was far in advance of Him. Jesus asked what had become of the people who partook of that manna? They were dead, but, said He "I am the living bread which came down from heaven; if any man eat of this bread he shall live for ever."

III. Though He was rejected by many, those who received Him did not therefore suffer. "As many as received him to them gave he power to become the sons of God, even to them that believe on his name." They could not have had more if all had received Him. We should have expected that after all the treatment He received He would have turned His back upon the world; nay, He did not reward those who received Him any the less because so many rejected Him. Nor did He appear any the less in their estimation because others turned their backs upon Him. Not even His poverty and homelessness kept them away from Him.

"To them gave he power to become the sons of God." "What the law could not do in that it was weak through the flesh"—the Law was not weak in itself. It was the strongest thing in the world next to the Gospel. Yet the Law could not give the Spirit of sonship, only the Gospel could do that.—"Ye have not received the spirit of bondage again to fear; but ye have received the Spirit of adoption, whereby we cry, "Abba, Father."

The Angels of God

By the Rev. W. REES, D.D.,*
Congregational Minister, Chester.

"Bless the Lord, ye his angels, that excel in strength, that do his commandments, hearkening unto the voice of his word."—*Ps.* ciii. 20.

FOR all that we know of the angels and their history we are indebted to this Book only. The invisible things of The Invisible, Almighty, and Eternal One are clearly seen, being understood by the things that are made independently of the supernatural revelation of Him in His Word; but we should not know about the existence and attributes of these created invisible beings, apart from the testimony we have in the Word concerning them.

❋　❋　❋　❋　❋　❋　❋　❋　❋　❋

It is to the good, holy angels who have kept their beginning that the text calls our attention. It is not of them but to them that the Psalmist speaks here. We find him at the close of this glorious Psalm like the tax-gatherer of the universe collecting the taxes of the great King. Having borne testimony to the greatness and glory of the King as the God of providence and grace, he calls upon all His subjects to pay the tribute due to Him—that of praise and thanksgiving. His subjects have nothing of their own that they can offer Him except obedience and praise, and nought else is asked of them—"Offer unto God thanksgiving, and pay thy vows unto the most High." This collector of tribute pays his own before he calls upon anyone else to do so. "Bless the Lord, O my

---

* See page 260.

soul, and all that is in me, bless his holy name," exclaims he in the first verse. He proceeds to call again upon his soul, and brings forward the many great obligations which rest upon him to pay this tribute of praise—"Who forgiveth all thine iniquities, who healeth all thy diseases, who redeemeth thy life from destruction, who crowneth thee with loving-kindness and tender mercies." These are sufficient reasons for calling over and over again upon his soul and all that is within him to the task. Then he calls upon others to pay their debt of gratitude... He summons all beings and things within the limits of the Divine government in heaven and earth to join in the offering; and then closes as he began, with his own soul.

In our text he calls upon the angels; they have always been ready and willing to pay tribute to their King. Many of their brethren proves disloyal... but those addressed here are the pure and loyal, those who pay their way; there are no arrears on the books of the government against them; the King has never lost aught of His revenue through them. It is to them that the Psalmist now speaks. May a poor preacher thus follow up his subject for once, and that without presumption, in addressing so august an audience? Poor child of the dust though he be, he is permitted to address the Creator of angels, who Himself calls upon him and teaches him how to approach. We believe, therefore, that the angels will not consider us presumptive, and that they will not be offended if we address them in these words. "Permit us, ye glorious angels, as your 'fellow-servants' to tell you that we hold you in high esteem; though none of us have ever seen one of your number, yet we know a little of your history. Our fathers who had that high privilege have told us how tender, kind, and obliging you were in your visits to them. As messengers sent from the throne, you made known some of the mysteries of life, in order to reveal them to us by the prophets who spoke in the 'name of the Lord'. It was one of your number that first announced to us, the children of men, the 'good tidings of great joy' concerning the birth of our great Saviour, and you all came down from heaven that morning to worship Him—a babe in our nature—in the poor manger; you also sang the joyous anthem of His birth, whose sweet echoes have lived ever since in every breeze that visits the earth. Yea, you ministered tenderly to our Saviour in the wilderness and in the garden. It was one of you that rolled back the stone from the grave the morning of the third day. How kind some of you were to those dear women who 'followed Him from Galilee', who came with fear and sorrow to the grave that morning 'while it was yet dark', in telling them that He had risen! In a word, all the history we have of you clothes you with a charming beauty and loveliness in our sight.

"Our text tells us that you 'excel in strength', and we have abundant proofs of that in the record given of your deeds, such as your great achievements at Sinai on the 'day of the Association' when you brought out the clouds and darkness, the storm and fire, the thunder and lightning, and all the terrible elements of nature in their full force and wild play, so that 'the mountains leaped like rams and the hills like lambs'. One of your number slew at the command of your King nearly two hundred thousand armed men at a single blow. Another touched proud Herod the Great, the foe and persecutor of the first church, so that rottenness took hold of him and 'he was eaten of worms and died'. The bars and doors of the prison where Peter was bound opened at your nod as if of their own accord... We know that one of you could extinguish the life of this vast throng in an instant, leaving us dead in heaps. If one of you but withdrew the veil that hides His countenance, and reveal His face to us for a moment we should all faint with fear, as did the Roman soldiers who watched the grave of our Redeemer on that morning in the garden of Joseph. Holy angels, still conceal yourselves in the invisible for a while we will come to you ere long when we hope we shall be strong enough to stand and look at you face to face, and commune with you as brethren without dread or fear.

❋   ❋   ❋   ❋   ❋   ❋   ❋   ❋   ❋   ❋

"But our text tells us one thing more of you, that you 'do his commandments'—this is the highest praise of an angel... Happy are ye; the sting of a guilty conscience never pierced your bosom; repentance cannot be preached to you, for none of you have ever done aught for which to grieve. There is no use preaching the forgiveness of sins to you, you have no sins to be forgiven; you cannot apply to yourselves the great doctrine of justification by faith; you are righteous and faultless before the eternal throne—righteous in the righteousness in which you were created. Yet we guilty, sinful men will take repentance, forgiveness, and justification by faith; and we shall see some day whose robe will be the most beautiful, when the sinner clad in his new robe will appear before the throne and sing,

"Jesus, Thy robe of righteousness,
My beauty is my glorious dress
Midst flaming worlds in this arrayed
With joy shall I lift up my head."

"Again, our text tells us that you hearken 'unto the voice of his word'... Oh, ye angels, there are men in this congregation who have lived within the sound of His voice for the last forty years without having yet hearkened and obeyed—yea, for forty years has He been grieved with this generation, and it is a numerous generation in Wales. It has withstood all the power of the ministry of His word in its unbelief and disobedience until now!... Ye angels, what think ye of these men?

"Again, the Psalmist calls you to this important duty, not because he thinks you have ever neglected it, but in order that you may induce us to join in loyal adoration and praise... Adieu, ye holy angels, we are sometimes prompted to thank God for you, though not as often as we should. We are accustomed to thank Him for rain and heat, for fruitful seasons and ripe harvests, for our daily bread, and all the blessings of this life, and surely we should thank Him for you, since men in all ages have been the recipients of kindnesses from your hands. Adieu, ye angelic hosts, still continue to praise your King; we will join you by-and-by; meanwhile may His favour rest upon you—Amen."

❊　❊　❊　❊　❊　❊　❊　❊　❊　❊

We find the Psalmist after having journeyed through all creation collecting tribute to the great King who had "prepared his throne in the heavens," and whose "kingdom ruleth over all," returning home. He began with his own soul, he also ends with himself. "Bless the Lord O my soul." This is the third time in this Psalm in which he calls upon his own soul to pay its tribute, mindful as he is of the exceptional obligation which rests upon him... "My soul, though all in heaven be silent, bless thou the Lord. See, consider, think of 'all his benefits'—the blessings of His grace and salvation, His best, highest, and most precious gifts. It was not for angels that He prepared them, but for thee, O my soul. He hath saved thee from perdition, though thou hast sinned and rebelled against Him. He 'spared not the angels that sinned, but cast them down to hell' (II. Peter ii. 4), but He spared thee, though thou hast sinned like them, and that a thousand times. 'Bless the Lord, O my soul.' If thou art silent, angels and devils will wonder at thee. Consider again, for He hath not spared thee, but He also 'crowneth thee with loving-kindness and tender mercies,' and 'satisfieth thy mouth with good things'. Tell me, if thou knowest, where else in all His dominion is there another sinful creature toward whom He has so acted. He came Himself after thee to seek and to save thee, when thou didst go astray like a wandering sheep. He took thy nature in becoming partaker of flesh and blood, for 'verily He took not on Him the nature of angels, but the seed of Abraham. Wherefore in all things it behoved him to be made like unto his brethren that he might be a merciful and faithful high priest in things pertaining to God, to make reconciliation for the sins of the people.' Yes, He gave Himself for thee a blameless sacrifice and offering to God! Stand, therefore, before the cross and ask, 'How much dost thou owe thy Lord, more than every other creature in His vast empire?'"

"Beginning at Jerusalem"

By the late Rev. W WILLIAMS,* of Wern.

(*An Illustration.*)

A T the village of Bersham, near which I live, there is a foundry for casting-cannons. After they are cast they are tested by the founders, who first of all put in a single charge, and if they carry that then a double charge, and if they carry that without bursting they are pronounced fit for the deck of a man-of-war or the battlefield. The Gospel was a *new* and an *untried* instrument. It had first to be tested; and where, on the face of the whole earth, was there a more fitting place than Jerusalem for making the first experiment? If the Gospel proved itself *instrumentally* equal to the conversion of sinners at Jerusalem, no misgiving could ever afterwards be entertained respecting it. Peter was the man appointed to test this new gun. He charged and fired it. *Three thousand were converted in one day!* After this successful trial the fishermen of Galilee went forth everywhere boldly to 'preach the word', fully assured that in no quarter of the globe were there to be found more hardened sinners than those who had stoned and killed the prophets, and who had reached the climacteric of guilt by putting to death the Heir of Heaven Himself. Well might the great Apostle of the Gentiles declare his readiness to preach the Gospel in Rome *also*, knowing it was the '*power* of God unto salvation to everyone that believeth'.

---

* See page 268.

Noah's Ark

Extract from a Sermon by the late Rev. DAVID EVANS,* of Ffynonhenry.

OAH began the ark, and did all according to the plan "What size is the door to be, father?" asked Shem "Look at the plan, my boy," replied Noah. "I have looked at it," said Shem, "but the measure isn't given there." "Not down?" asked Noah with surprise. "No, really, you look." "Nor is it; what shall we do?" asked Noah. "But," he added, after a little consideration, "I will tell you what we will do. Go down to the wilderness and look out for an elephant, watch him passing between two trees, and mark well his height and width, and if we have a door big enough for him every other creature will pass through easily." "That's a capital idea, father," answered Shem. "Japhet, come with me," and off they went. In a short time they returned. "Have you seen the elephant?" asked Noah. "Yes," replied they, "but we saw a queer creature much higher than the elephant." "O well, that gentleman will have to stoop, then," said Noah. It is probable that it was the camelopard *(sic.)* or giraffe that the boys had seen. Now the ark was "the like figure whereunto Baptism doth also save us... by the resurrection of Jesus Christ" (I. Peter iii. 21)—"so great salvation;" great enough for the greatest sinner. The door is sufficiently high and wide in the Gospel ark. The greatest sinners have passed through. But what of the Pharisaic "giraffes" who hold up their heads so high? Will they ever go in? Ah, they must bend their necks or remain outside. The door isn't made for them to pass through with their heads lifted up like that; an "elephant" of a sinner may enter, but not a single

---

* See page 276.

Pharisaic "giraffe" unless he stoops... The creatures came into the ark after their kind, but all were at peace with each other. See there, two large serpents come trundling like two cart-wheels. "Father, father," exclaimed Shem, "here are the snakes coming; they'll be sure to sting us." "No, my boys," replied Noah, "you can play with them now; this is a race for life, they only want to come in." "There are two snails coming with their castles on their backs they began their journey early. Just look, there's the lion and his mistress coming, and after them the old fox and his mate, trot-trot, and after them the goose and her lord. God help the goose," said the boys to Noah. "Ah, she'll receive no harm, boys," replied the old patriarch. When all the creatures had entered Noah shut the door, but just as he was shutting it he heard the sound of tiny wings beating against it from one end to the other. "Halloo!" asked Noah, "who's there?" " I," said the wren. "Where hast thou been so long?" asked Noah. "O," replied the wren, " I was on the banks of Jordan the same time as the hawk, but I slackened speed a little that he might come first." "Ah, there was no need for thee to fear him," said Noah, "Come in; stand by the side of the old fellow there." There they were in the ark, one large, peaceful family; the lion and the lamb, the fox and the goose, the little wren and the hawk side by side. So those who come to the Gospel ark—"They shall not hurt nor destroy... saith the Lord."

By the same author:

John Vaughan and his Friends

OR

More Echoes from the Welsh Hills

by the
Rev. David Davies
Brighton

First published in 1897
Available in 2000 from Tentmaker Publications

From reviews of "Echoes from the Welsh Hills"

"A charming and instructive book… There is scarcely a page that does not contain something worth quoting and learning. Mr. Davies tells us that he has gathered materials sufficient for a companion volume. We are glad of that. They are sure to be wanted, and we would recommend the author quickly to get them into shape." — Rev. Agar Beet in *The Methodist.*

"Mr. Davies, whose sermons we well remember, has produced a remarkable book, full of fine specimens of Welsh oratory.

"One is made by these 'Echoes' to fall in love with Welsh piety and to long for its like in our English villages… We shall not be surprised to hear that Mr. David Davies's books obtains a high meed of praise from his own countrymen, and that it interests many readers in other lands. We know of no volume which gives so good an idea of the power of the living ministry of Wales." —The Rev. C H. Spurgeon, in the *Sword and Trowel*

ISBN 1 899003 40 1

Tentmaker Publications

121 Hartshill Road, Stoke-on-Trent, Staffs, ST4 7LU

LIFE OF
HOWELL HARRIS

THE WELSH REFORMER

BY

HUGH J. HUGHES

The great awakening of the 18th century is surely one of the most exciting periods in the annals of the Christian church in England and Wales, and Howel Harris, with Daniel Rowland, were two of its pioneer preachers, who laid the foundations of the Calvinistic Methodist movement in Wales. Whereas Daniel Rowland ministered mainly in one place, at Llangeitho, Howel Harris, who was never ordained, itinerated all over Wales as a lay 'exhorter' from his home in Trevecca. During his varied activities he established the controversial Christian community at Trevecca. He co-operated with the Countess of Huntingdon in establishing a college to train students for the Christian ministry and set up societies all over the principality. His life was not without controversy however, and a rift developed between him and Daniel Rowland, which had an adverse effect upon the revival for some years; but Harris, without a doubt, was a man greatly used by God in the furtherance of the gospel during the 18th century revival in Wales. He died in 1773 and, according to the Countess of Huntingdon, his funeral was attended by 20,000 people, revealing surely a nation's esteem of this great man.

   The author of this volume, Rev. Hugh Joshua Hughes, was born in Swansea in 1846, and lived a long and busy life, dying at the age of 91 in 1937. He appears to have been one of the denomination's early historians, and was deeply interested in Howel Harris.

ISBN 1 899003 18 5

Tentmaker Publications

121 Hartshill Road, Stoke-on-Trent, Staffs, ST4 7LU

Some of the
Great Preachers
of Wales

BY

Owen Jones, M.A. (Lond.),

Newtown

Originally published in 1885, this previously scarce work has long been treasured by those who possessed a copy. Introducing some of the most famous of the great Welsh preachers, it does so in a way that both inspires and informs. This is not merely a series of biographies, but rather an examination of the most significant elements of Welsh preaching as seen in its greatest exponents. It is thus a book of interest to all preachers, whether Welsh or not. Examples of differing technique are given together with samples of the sermon material preached.

CONTENTS

Introductory Essay on Welsh Preaching
Daniel Rowlands
Robert Roberts
Christmas Evans
John Elias
William Williams
Henry Rees
John Jones

540 pages, completely re-typeset and now available in a quality binding.

ISBN 1 899003 15 0

Tentmaker Publications

121 Hartshill Road, Stoke-on-Trent, Staffs, ST4 7LU

THE LIFE AND TIMES OF
SELINA,
COUNTESS OF HUNTINGDON

By
A MEMBER OF THE HOUSES OF SHIRLEY AND HASTINGS
(AARON CROSSLEY HOBART SEYMOUR)

"The object of the present work has been to afford a view of the Life and Times of this distinguished woman so clear and ample as to render superfluous all future or collateral efforts at illustration. Every fact and incident of her long life is here recorded; every triumph of the cross under her vigourous and well-directed leading; every place of worship opened under her auspices, and every mark of divine favour and encouraging grace bestowed upon her labours.

"The author has drawn from all accessible sources, the illustrative matter of his memoir. The biographies of WHITEFIELD, WESLEY, VENN, and the works and letters of FLETCHER, BERRIDGE, ROMAINE, WATTS, HILL, and other eminently pius individuals, have supplied invaluable contributions to the work now before the reader. But its more valuable portion consists in the original letters and anecdotes with which it teems, and in the straightforward integrity of purpose in its author." *Extract from the preface.*

"The personal character of the Countess of Huntingdon will be seen in the general history of her *Life and Times*: she stands, indeed, so connected with almost all which was good in the eighteenth century, that the character of the age, so far as religion is concerned, was in some measure her own. It is not insinuated, that she alone impressed that character on the Church, but that she entirely sympathised with it, and was not one whit behind the foremost in affection for souls and zeal for God." *Extract from the Introduction*

"This memoir is not only absorbingly interesting as a Narrative, but is indispensable to the historian, developing, as it does, the origin and progress of the most important and influential denominations of Dissenters at the present day; as well as the effects produced by her Ladyship's indefatigable zeal in behalf of the Church.

"Notwithstanding the utmost care in condensing the immense mass of materials, it has been found impossible, without injury to their effect, to reduce them within the compass of a single volume. The conductors are therefore compelled to revert to their original plan of publishing THE LIFE AND TIMES OF LADY HUNTINGDON in two handsome volumes, ... containing upwards of 1100 closely printed pages, with copious notes." *Extract from the original prospectus of 1839*

The Life and Times of Selina, Countess of Huntingdon is now republished in two volumes, completely retypeset from the third edition of 1840, published originally by William Edward Painter, The Strand, London. The original edition did not have an index until the sixth edition was produced in 1844. This new edition benefits from the index to the two volumes published by Francis M Jackson which he produced for The Wesley Historical Society in 1907.

Two volumes (each with over 650pp) hardback.

ISBN 1 899003 36 3

LIFE OF GRIFFITH JONES OF LLANDDOWROR
by DAVID JONES

Griggith Jones was known primarily as the founder of the circulating school movement which did so much to prepare a whole generation for the gospel, but he was also an outstanding preacher in his own right. It was under his preaching that Daniel Rowlands was so deeply affected and Jones was to play an important part in the lives of Howell Harris and George Whitefield.

200pp paperback.

ISBN 1 899003 13 4

Tentmaker Publications

121 Hartshill Road, Stoke-on-Trent, Staffs, ST4 7LU

TENTMAKER PUBLICATIONS was set up in 1993 with the aim of supporting missionaries and Irish believers working in the Republic of Ireland as pastors and evangelists. Many evangelical churches in the Republic are small and unable to fully support their own pastors. With this in mind we have followed the pattern of the Apostle Paul and hence the name Tentmaker, from Paul's practice of supporting himself on the mission field by making tents.

Our books are reproduced using modern technology and are printed in small runs thus allowing us to publish works which otherwise might not be reprinted.

The costs of production are higher as a proportion of selling price and we rely substantially on direct sales to the customer. With this in mind we send out a free newsletter giving details of new publications and discount offers. In the future a number of our publications will only be available direct and not through shops. To ensure that you are kept informed, please write to us at:

Tentmaker Publications

121 Hartshill Road, Stoke-on-Trent, Staffs, ST4 7LU